Where the Wings Grow

Conversations with Pioneering Women Pilots

BY IRV BROUGHTON

Books

Where the Wings Grow:
Conversations with Pioneering Women Pilots

The Gracious Afterward: Delta Stories

Walking Around Lucky: *The Story of Sportswriter Red Smith*

The Levees that Break in the Heart: *A novel*

Gotcha! Watcha! Drugs are a Trap:
Poems about Drugs and All Kinds of Other Things

Wondrous Peninsula:
Tales of Fishing, NASCAR, Gators, Water Skiing,
Baseball in the Sunshine State by Those Who Lived Them

The Long Net:
Poems about the Great Game of Basketball

ESPN: *The Untold Story (with Stuart Evey)*

Forever Remembered: *The Fliers of World War II*

Hangar Talk: *Conversations with American Fliers*

A Good Man: *Fathers and Sons in Poetry and Prose*

The Writer's Mind: *Interviews with American Authors Vol. III*

The Writer's Mind: *Interviews with American Authors Vol. II*

The Writer's Mind: *Interviews with American Authors Vol. I*

Producers on Producing: *The Making of Film and Television*

The Art of the Interview in Television, Radio and Film

Surveying: *Poems*

The Blessing of the Fleet: *Poems*

Plays

Love Seek Fools: *The Musical*

Three to the Heart: *A Life with Frank Stanford*

*Stand up! Keep your
backs straight!
Remember that this is
where the wings grow.*

Martha Graham

Contents

For our daughters

INTRODUCTION
BY AUTHOR

I have always been fascinated by flight. Even though my eyesight may have deterred me from pursuing it as a career, I loved being around flight, reading and learning. As a kid, I engaged busily in building models and holding them up for rides across the sky.

In 1970, at Hollins College, I met a wonderful woman named Ann Darr. Ann was there as a poet—and I found her to be fascinating, vital and alive, animated in gesture, broad in generosity, and a grand and expansive storyteller. But she had another side. At the campus coffee shop, between readings, we kibitzed about poetry and other interests, and I learned of perhaps her proudest accomplishment: Ann had flown for the Women's Air Service Pilots (WASPs) during WWII. Over the years, Ann and I developed an enduring friendship, and I often visited her and husband and family in Chevy Chase. Ann would become the first in a long chain of interviews leading to the book, *Where the Wings Grow.*

Represented in these pages are a wide variety of pioneering

women fliers—not just military—a formation powering through the clouds, for they succeeded in establishing the remarkable ability of women to achieve, often against the highest odds and obstacles. It was Amelia Earhart, who said of Dorothy Hester Stenzel of Portland, "That girl could fly." Indeed, so could they all.

This collection is a labor of love, a tribute to the openness and warmth of its participants, and represents a long haul, to say the least. The interviews took place over more than 40 years, and sadly a great many of its subjects by this time have passed. Sequestered in corners at airshows, in my living room, in airport cafeterias, or in the fliers' homes, we leaned into old-fashioned cassette machines and recorded the interviews, several of which, due to logistical considerations, were done over the phone.

Writer George Eliot said, "Our deeds still travel with us from afar, and what we have been makes us what we are." The women in the book—and others who aspire to meet their dreams in the air or elsewhere—know this all-too-well. These interviews are pieces in time and they represent a rare talent and determination, a time and place, a telling.

Now and then, I ruminate at the pleasure of our meeting, thinking, for example, of five-foot-small, Violet Cowden, more powerful in maneuvering the big planes than any delicate frame could possibly do (Violet could still fit into her uniform when she visited me in Spokane from her Huntington Beach home.) Or I can imagine my friend Ann, rollicking out a story for her fellow WASPs after a scary flight on a rickety plane, or of Dorothy Hester Stenzel, gasping for breath and cursing cigarettes she had smoked all those years and insisting we go on, despite my protestations and concerns; or of dear Teresa James in her flower shop in Virginia, awaiting belatedly the return of her flier husband from France, something that would never come.

Neta Snook, who taught Amelia Earhart to fly, said, "Women

are more adventurous in their hearts than men are." Certainly, there is plenty of adventure here. I would hope that these adventures are not forgotten and serve to remind us of a great achievment. Certainly the goal of any documentarian or oral historian is to help us all remember. And, personally, how I do remember! I will always cherish the wonderful women I was fortunate enough to interview and know if only briefly: their brilliance, their grace, their courage, their modesty and stunning equanimity.

Irv Broughton
Spokane

Dorothy Hester Stenzel

Dorothy Hester Stenzel
"Pioneer Barnstormer"

Many people "invented" it, but one name contributed more than her share to the acceptance and development of early flight: Dorothy Hester, now Dorothy Hester Stenzel. She was a record holder in aerobatic flying, holding early world records in loops and several other categories. She was sought after and honored in her time, offered free airplanes and large sums of money to perform her flights of daring. But despite a somewhat meteoric rise, it was not easy getting there, as she explains in the interview.

Dorothy Hester Stenzel was born in Milwaukie, Oregon, in 1910. Her family later built a home in Ardenwald, Oregon, where she grew up. Dorothy Stenzel began flying in 1927 at the age of seventeen and shortly thereafter began to fly in exhibitions with Tex Rankin for four years from 1928 to 1932. They performed at air shows and Rankin, the master showman, was her mentor. In the interview, Dorothy tells how she finally came to be treated as a peer by the flight pioneer, of the joys and obstacles of early flight.

At the end of the interview, I asked the long-retired, eighty-year-old flier if she could remember her last flight. She said, "That's what's worrying me now. Is this my last 'flight'? I can't breathe." Throughout the interview the courageous old flier gasped and gasped, but gamely pushed her way along, at times decrying the cigarettes she had smoked which had brought her health to this.

Amelia Earhart said you were the "one girl who has made good almost from the start." Did flying come naturally to you?

Yes, very naturally.

So she knew about you?

Well, I think she was looking at my records or probably saw me fly.

Did you meet her anywhere?

Yes, at different air shows.

Do you remember the first time you were ever in an airplane?

Yes, that was my downfall. It was just about a week before my seventeenth birthday. I hadn't known anywhere that anyone could get near an airplane, and someone told me there was a place that you could go and pay for a ride—which I did. I went on a street car and when I got off, I could see the airplanes flying and I started running. I was afraid they were either going to run out of gas or crack up before I could get my ride.

I liked it and I told them so. I said, "If I was a boy, I'd certainly learn to fly." And they said, "You don't have to be a boy to learn to fly. Come in the shack and we'll talk about it." So we went in, and I found out how much it was, and then I went home and started working for it.

What did you do, save money?

Save money—I had to earn money.

How'd you do that?

There were a lot of different ways of making it and things were different then. I did it by doing parachute jumps at one-hundred-dollars a jump. That was before there were any regulations where you had to have a spare chute. People would say "My God, that's dangerous!" I knew it was, but I'd tell them, "Well, if I can't learn to fly, life isn't worth living anyway." That was my thought on that one.

Remember the first time you soloed?

Yes I do, I couldn't forget it. I'd tried to get that fellow out of the cockpit for so long.

What was it like?

Well, that fellow didn't think women were here to stay, but he finally figured out it wasn't his airplane anyway. So he got out. He told me to go around once and then land. It was late in the afternoon, almost dark. So I did that. Then I saw him coming towards the airplane and I thought, "The heck with you," so I took off again. I hadn't been up when it was that dark. Fire was coming out of the exhaust stack. I didn't know it would do that. So I thought, "Dorothy, you're not as smart as you thought you were." So I came down and landed.

You were scared by the fire?

No, I was just unhappy that I had pulled a boner.

But it wasn't really a boner, was it?

7

Nothing is if you get away with it. I didn't want that fellow back in that front cockpit again. That was it.

You traveled with flier Tex Rankin.

They were all interesting times. We went through this more or less together, experimenting and seeing how we could perfect our flying and our aerobatics, and what an airplane would do.

What were you trying to push an airplane to do?

We were trying to prove flying was safe. I performed everything, all the aerobatics that any man would do, ordinarily right-side up, but I would do it inverted, and it was trial and error.

I know the poor old airplane cried, but we took really good care of the airplane. We had to—it was our life. We just went step by step and rebuilt the airplane. The struts, for example, were supposed to be straight, but would be bent when we'd come down. Our propellers would break! You know those kinds of things happen. And, if a nineteen or twenty-year-old girl could do those things, that said something. I'm sure that's the reason Mr. Rankin taught me those things. And we learned things together. He had the flying school and sold airplanes.

What kind of teacher was Tex Rankin? Was he tough?

Oh, he really was, yes. There was no sloppy flying because it would show on his record the way I flew.

How long did it take Tex Rankin to accept you as an equal?

I tell you, a long time. Before I could even get near one of their airplanes, I had to pay $250 for a ground course. I had to pass these tests, written and oral, before I could start my own instruction. It was a night school. His school was a large school. There were probably forty or fifty boys in the night part. After you passed your tests, you'd fly with Mr. Rankin. He did not instruct—he went out making records, handshaking, and selling airplanes. The night we graduated, he came down and gave us a pep talk. He was saying, "You fellows can go to Alaska"—which was just opening up. "And you can teach flying or start an airline." Do this or that. You see, mail was all there was—there were no passengers on the airlines then. Just mail. So he told them all what they could do, and then he saw me, and looked down and said, "And the girls can work in the office." Well, you can see how that went over. It was like a flat balloon. I can tell you I didn't care too much for that man. But I never worked in his office.

How did you manage to avoid working in the office?

Well, that isn't why I risked my life making parachute jumps, to get money to work in his office. Unh, uh, no!

So when'd you start flying with him?

He would come to the airport about once a month, on Sunday, and go up with a boy after he had about ten hours total flying time. And he'd fly with him and give him another pep talk. But you'd have to put your name on a chalk board, and he only took about five or six.

I finally got the nerve to put my name up there, and so he had to, and so he did. And I only had a fifteen-minute ticket, and he kept me up there for forty-five minutes. He said, "Hester, you fly like a boy." I liked that.

Anyway, so he started thinking about getting more students. And if he could have a female show that she could fly, why any old fool could fly, see? That's how we got going.

How much money did you make when you were together doing these air shows?

Well, we'd fly to the shows with a contract, and maybe we'd fly for two or three different afternoons. I made $4,200 for three days.

That was a lot of money then, wasn't it?

Yes, it was, because I know we'd go into a hotel, and they'd show you about six different beds that you could sit on to see if you liked them. They'd show you four or five rooms, and you'd chose which one you wanted for the night. Then you'd get a filet mignon, a baked potato, apple pie, and everything probably for a dollar.

How much did your first plane cost?

My first plane didn't cost me anything. The Great Lakes people built me one because I had been flying their airplane, and consequently they were selling more airplanes because of me. And they felt that more people were learning to fly—that people felt it was safer and women wouldn't be as worried about their husbands learning to fly, straight and level, if a nineteen or twenty-year-old girl could do the kind of flying I was doing. It sold airplanes for them. It sold gas, it sold oil—things like that. But people were awfully nice to me.

What kind of plane did they give you?

It was a biplane. And I used that all the time.

Was that your favorite plane?

Yes. I liked it because she hung by me. She was really a tender plane—her maneuvers were quick; she would react beautifully—she was just a nice little airplane.

You make it sound like you and she were partners.

We had to be. I took care of her and she took care of me.

What was your record for loops—you held the record?

Sixty-two perfect outside loops—May 17, 1931, at Omaha Air Races, Nebraska; fifty-six inverted snap rolls—a record which stood a long time for both men and women. It was set May 15, 1931, at Omaha Air Races.

Tell me how you broke the record.

Any record I broke was my own record. See, no woman did the kind of flying I was doing, so I had no competition. The first outside loop record that I made I was three out of five tries in Portland June 30, 1930. They had to be perfectly round. No U's, no ovals—they marked you down on that.

Then I went through and did twenty-three at Burbank, California. I broke a record, but it was my record. I just kept building up records until I got to Omaha, Nebraska, an air show on May 17, 1931, and I did sixty-nine there, of which sixty-two were certified perfect by three observers from the National Aeronautical Association.

Did you think you were going to set the record in Omaha?

Yes. Tex told me how many to make, and that's what I did, and came down. I came close to breaking his record—the man's record, but he was my instructor. I couldn't break his record.

Sounds like he told you to come down so you wouldn't break his record?

That's right. And later he went up and raised his record. But that's the way the ball bounces. Anyway, that day it was pretty rough flying. I used to sleep a lot. Those Gs are hard on the body—I'm referring to pulling Gs. I could never go out at night, no, no, no. I was on a strict schedule, going to bed and getting up. Anyway, I was in the administration building, lying down afterwards, and I heard the sirens sound. But I went on and slept. They woke me up when it was my turn to fly. They always held me until the last. And so, when I came out to fly, people acted kind of funny to me. I said, "What happened?" And they wouldn't tell me. I went on and performed.

At the show there was this gold Laird airplane that belonged to Charles W. ("Speed") Holman from Minneapolis. Oh, it was a three-place open biplane, and he used to do aerobatics with it. Oh, it had more power, and it made more noise. It was beautiful. It was an expensive plane. He had flown earlier in it.

Well, what had happened, he was a big man and during his performance, he came down low, right in front of the grandstand, inverted. He pushed the stick forward to go up and when he tried to pull it up, the whole seat fell off, right in front of all

12

these people, and he was killed. So, you can see how we reacted, hurriedly scratching around to see how our seat was put in.

Did you ever have any death-defying close calls?

I suppose so. But you always learn.

Anytime the weather was bad?

Oh, the weather's bad—I loved that one! That's the only time in the world I've been frightened. And that's the truth. I was delivering this plane up to Great Falls, Montana, and it was in the fall in the smoky season. The airplane didn't have a compass on it, but that's all right. I figured I'd do pretty well with dead reckoning, but I hadn't reckoned with so much smoke that you can't see the sun. Anyway, I got myself mixed up on what speed I should be making and where I should be. And the Continental Divide, that's rough stuff up there. I actually got lost. I couldn't see anything. I didn't know where I was. That's what I mean about learning. I learned it! Little Dorothy wasn't as smart as she thought she was. It was so smoky that when I landed in Great Falls, there were ashes on top of the wings. Some people can't understand how there could be ashes on the top of the wing. But there was. You know how the air works around a wing. Ashes up there. So you see, I learned.

So how'd you manage to get there?

I just kept going straight. I thought something would show up sometime. I was just ahead of where I should have been in my flying.

You've said several times that, "Dorothy wasn't as smart as she thought she was." Are you saying you were a little cocky or overconfident as a young woman?

No, I wasn't. But what I did I thought I did right. Well, I wouldn't have been doing the things I was doing unless I thought I could do them. And, if I thought I couldn't do them good enough, I'd find out why.

You know the Belanca people. Belanca was the airplane Lindbergh wanted to fly to Paris with. And he wrote them a letter—you've read his books. He got all dressed up and went to see them. But Belanca wanted one more man in there, and it wasn't going to be Lindbergh. Well, anyway, after the National Air Races in Cleveland, Belanca came to me and said, "Dorothy, we'd like you to fly our airplane to Paris. We'll build it to your specifications, and after you get there, we'll give you $125,000 and the airplane."

But you see, I knew I couldn't stay awake that long. I was good at what I was doing, these short flights, but I wasn't good on the long ones. You know they never offered that to any other woman.

What did they say when you turned them down?

They said if I changed my mind, let them know. And I said, "I don't think so." But I did appreciate it. That was quite a thing. When they wouldn't give it to Lindbergh, they offered it to me.

Did you ever get dizzy doing loops?

No, but I was the first woman to take the G-test at Pensacola, Florida. I did that for the United States Navy.

Did you ever completely trash an airplane after one of your aerobatics performances?

No, I only scratched one airplane. My first time away from the Rankin School of Flying, when I went to perform and compete with men, I ground-looped. Well, I still say that that's one world's record that I hold, but it's not official—"Least Damage to Planes."

Dorothy Hester Stenzel in front of her Great Lakes Model 2T-IA Special. Undated.

That Great Lakes airplane they built for me was one of the first that they built; it had a small tail, hard tires, and no brakes, and it was a ground-loopin' baby. If you got a side wind or something, she'd go right into it. Anyway, Mr. Rankin and I went up to Kelso, Washington. It had two runways, and the wind was coming from the south, and people were lined up along that runway. And so Mr. Rankin said, "No, I don't want you landing into the wind there. You go down and land on the east-west one. And you're going to ground-loop, but that's all right. I'll just tell people that's just one more little trick that you do." Well, I did that. I went down there and naturally I felt it, and it went around. The wing hit a fence post. And, oh God, my first time showing off, and look what I did. I was bawling my eyes out and the inspector—Captain Pettis was his name—came down in his car. Oh, God, he got out and came over and put his arm around me and he said, "Honey, you just stop crying." He said, "If you knew how many airplanes I have cracked up for Uncle Sam! But I tell you what I'm going to do. I'm going to tell Mr. Rankin that if I catch you up there doing aerobatics until you've had more landings, I'm taking *his* license away." But that was the only time I hurt any airplane."

What did Mr. Rankin say when he heard that?

Well, I don't know what he said, but he didn't lose his license. Most people have ground-looped with that side wind.

What year was that?

1929.

Any misconceptions about early female fliers?

Yeah. I had to get a physical every six months, and there

were some able men and some women who were cracking up quite a few airplanes. They would say, "Oh, I got a bug in my eye" or "This happened and that happened." And if the women couldn't come up with something new once in awhile, they'd say they were menstruating. So, when I went to get my physical, they'd tell me that I couldn't fly when I'm menstruating. I'd say, "Hummm! You haven't heard the last of this old boy, because I'm going to go straight to the president, because this is not right." I said, "I absolutely do not know—and I cannot say—whether on the days that I made my records, whether I was menstruating or not. Well, if that isn't proof enough. Maybe some people can't, but don't you say I can't." I didn't hear any more about it.

Were woman fliers treated differently in other ways, too?

I don't know. They always treated me well. I wasn't really competing with men. There was only one man that ever wasn't very nice to me. I can't tell you his name. He's still hanging on.

Did you have fierce arguments with your parents? How'd your parents take to this idea of flying?

Well, my mother died when I was nine. I had three older sisters and one younger. And we wouldn't let a lady in the house for anything. My father couldn't find a lady who'd want to be in there with us. We were very possessive.

What sort of things did you do? Ever try to break up friend-ships your father had?

Well, he'd bring them home, and we would just act horribly. "That finished that one."

17

What was the strangest comment you got from someone regarding your being a woman flier?

As I said, they'd hold me until the last at the air shows. In between acts, they would take people up for rides—the operator of the airfield would. Once in California, this fellow, his name was Hal Sweet, who had a Tri-motor and would haul passengers, asked me one day, "Would you like to copilot with me?" And I said, "Oh, my God, would I like that?" So I did it and on the second day I think it was, when they came out and yelled up at me that it was my turn to fly, I came out of the front cockpit. The passengers were just leaving, and this man turned around and he saw me. He started screaming. I was nineteen at the time, and that man just kept it up all the way out to the fence, telling everyone how fortunate they were to be down. "You could have killed us."

Anyway, I used to stutter badly, and they always said I wouldn't stutter. "Ah, come on, get up here and say something," things like that. So this policeman kept coming up to me and saying, "There's this fellow out on the fence. He wants to see you." Finally, I went over there, and there's this hand sticking through the fence. He had a card or something in his hand, and he said, "Please Miss Hester would sign my ticket? I was one of your passengers today. I live in Omaha and I'm sorry I hadn't realized who you were." He said, "I want to go home and show this to the people." He had flown with me, and he was proud of the fact. I thought that was kind of nice. He did come back and apologize. But, of course, Old Hal Sweet, his flying was over for the day with this feller yelling around because no one knew who I was there at that air show.

In other words, this guy found out you were this famous flier?

Yes, and he was going home to brag. But anyway, I did feel

quite a bit sorry at the time for Hal.

Here's a word association game: sideslips.

Fun. God, I wish I had some pictures of how I used to sideslip with this little airplane. Whew, whew, whew. I'd bring her on until the wing was a foot and half from the ground then kick her around, and she wouldn't roll at all, because I flew that airplane so much. She and I were pieces of one another, you know. Sideslips were fun.

Dorothy Hester Stenzel with German WWI Ace Ernst Udet at National Air Races in Cleveland, 1931.

In Cleveland at the National Air Races, they had to be very strict because everyone had a time to fly. So you flew, and boy you were out of the way so the next fellow could go. And this man—one of the earlier fliers, who was pulling four gliders in a V behind him—did his act and went out and flew over the lake, I gathered. Anyway, he left so I flew. Normally when I was through, I would roll her over and lose altitude in an inverted spin, come down into that. So that's what I did. Then I thought, "My God, what just went by me?"

What had happened was this fool went out over the lake and came back and flew over the crowd. I didn't see him, and I came down in an inverted spin right through those four gliders.

Did he see you?

The gliders saw me coming, but they couldn't do anything about it. God, I came down right through the V. Anyway, Mr. Rankin was on the loudspeaker down there and he said everyone could imagine all this kindling coming right down on their heads.

Stalls?

Well, you've got to really stall it if you want to spin it. That's the only time I kind of fell down on Mr. Rankin. See, he would go with me—we would go together—and he would teach me these things.

So the first time I was to go up alone and do this inverted spin in front of all these people at an air show in Portland, I went up and she wouldn't stall. This was at his school. On Sundays I would perform for him—that's how I got my flying time—for nothing.

Anyway, she wouldn't stall, she wouldn't spin. So I came down and he said, "You just didn't hold it long enough. Just a minute." So he got out a wrench and lifted the cowling and tapped around. He told me that the problem was I had been doing it with him, and if the plane was heavier, it would stall easier. At that time I was just learning. I didn't have the feel of the airplane. So he told people that there was something the matter with the airplane, but that he had fixed it. And now she was going up and doing it—which I did. But that's the only time I didn't do what I was supposed to do for him.

Barrel rolls?

That's fun. All these things are fun. A smooth flier, that's what I wanted to be. You can do anything with an airplane if you do it smoothly. But just like this Holman fellow up at Omaha, I didn't see it happen. You can pull the wings off of anything by being rough. That's why you slow down in rough air, drop your gear and stuff, you know. I always did barrel rolls and everything was inverted.

Loops?

Ground loops? Loopity-loops. Well, that's the only time I'd black out. You see, when you're doing outside maneuvers, you're pulling the blood to your head, and inside, you're pushing it down. Well, I would do a vertical-eight—an outside loop where all the blood would come to my head—and when I came out of that, I'd go into an inside loop, which would push all the blood away from my head into my feet—and that's when I would black out.

What would happen?

Well, you just couldn't see. You were aware, but just couldn't see.

How long would it take you to recover?

Thirty-five degrees of a circle.

You need speed on the snap roll.

The inverted snap roll, yes. It's awfully hard on the airplane. A slow roll is practically nothing. You just roll slowly around. When I was learning to do outside loops, I would know when I had enough speed to go around. In the open cockpits, I could tell from the windshield. When the windshield flattened out completely, I had enough speed. I could do most things beautifully, let me say, with my eyes closed.

Who were your flying heroes?

Oh, there were so many. And now most of them are gone.

Name a few.

There you go again. When I mention one, I leave someone else out.

What about Lindbergh?

Oh, yes. He was really a determined gentleman, wasn't he? He was the one that really started it off.

You named one. You better name another so you don't leave that person out.

Tex Rankin was one. Phoebe Omlie was one. She was really

a good flier. She flew because she wanted to fly. She flew not for the publicity but because she enjoyed it. She was very good. She was such a nice person. She had one airplane accident, where she'd hurt her knee and she limped.

So you looked up to her?

Oh, sure. When I was trying to climb the ladder, I told her lots of times that she's been "my star in the sky."

Do you remember what you were doing when you heard about Lindbergh landing in Paris?

Yes, I remember. I was alone. I was sixteen when he did that. But I hadn't known anything about flying at all. Most people hadn't.

Did you ever fly low to read the signs?

There weren't airports around, so you'd land in ball parks, you'd land in fields. But when you needed gas or something, you get down by the railroad, to a Standard station, spiral on down and yell, "Five or ten." See, they'd be out looking because everyone ran out to see when an airplane came. And you would have a place picked out that you were going to land, and you'd yell down to them, "Five or ten (gallons)—to the ball park." Or they'd see which direction you were going and, after you'd landed, they'd come chugging out with gas.

So you had some strange landing places?

I remember I'd go up to Hood River—they wanted me up for

one of their luncheons—and I'd just go there and land out there on the sand island, and they'd come over in a boat and get me.

I had a flying service and school on Swan Island in Portland, and I remember this fellow was a lawyer and he needed a quick trip to Byrne, Oregon. His wife was having a baby anytime so he had to get right back. There was a lawsuit up in Byrne, and he wanted to come back that night. So I took him up there.

There was this man named Hanley, a big rancher up there, and he kept a place mowed. I don't know how many sections he had up there for airplanes. Well, I thought I'd land there. But he died in the meantime. I got up there, and there wasn't any place to land.

I looked around and I saw this place, and it looked pretty good. It was summer and it was hot. I came in and I got right down to the place of no return, and I realized what I saw: I was landing in a wheat field, and it was deep. But it was too late, so I just finished my landing as slow as I could and everything was fine. Wheat all around us. He was in a hurry to get to town and, of course, everybody used to come out to see the airplane. The man who owned the field was there, too. He was nice even though I had ruined his wheat. He said to me, "I'll tell you what I'll do." He said, "You tell me how much of a strip you'll need and I'll mow it for you." I said, "Oh God, that's fine." But he said, "I want to tell you, there's a irrigation ditch down there." That wouldn't work because I might hit the ditch.

The police came and the plane was alongside a simple, gravel road. You know what people did? They just took down the fence, picked up my airplane, and set it alongside the road. And they took the lawyer to town. That left me out there, and it was hot. When it was time to go, the police came and stopped traffic up the road. That lawyer was brave; he got in. We got home a little bit after dark, and his wife had her baby just fine.

A lot of fliers lost their lives in the Cleveland Air Races.

Well, it was to be expected. I had a fellow down in New Orleans who wanted me to take him up to make a parachute jump. He was so nervous anyway; I didn't want to take him up. So he asked other people. Wiley Post was there, and he and I were sitting on the ground when someone took this fellow up and, my God, his parachute didn't open and he just missed us. Thank goodness. Poor guy, I don't know whether he packed his own chute or not.

Did you have a feeling of anxiety or fatalism from what happened to Wiley Post and others?

No, I didn't think it was going to happen to me but, if it did, it was going to happen—and at least I'd lived. As the old quote goes: "If you're alive, start living."

If you could be remembered for one thing, what thing would that be?

I think, I hope it would be that I simplified flying for a lot of people. It made it possible for them or it made them start thinking along those lines.

Fay Gillis Wells
"The Founding of the The Ninety-Nines"

Fay Gillis Wells was born in Minneapolis on October 15, 1908. At the age of two the family moved to Great Falls, Montana, where her father Julius H. Gillis, a metallurgist, was the supervisor of a smelter at the Anaconda Copper Company. During the early years, the family moved a lot. In Toronto, Ontario, Fay and her sister Beth started school, and later, north in Sudbury, Ontario, Julius became superintendent of the smelter for the British-America Nickel Company.

By now, the girls were in high school, but the family moved again – this time to Elizabeth, New Jersey, where their dad became an executive with the Raitan Copper Works. The sisters graduated from Battin High School in 1925 and then attended Michigan State College (now University). They planned to go to Alaska, grow wheat in the spring and summer, and run a hunting lodge during the winter. "We didn't know anything about agriculture, so we picked the oldest agricultural college in America," Fay says. "The dean looked at us in amazement when we said we wanted to study agriculture, because he couldn't find a hayseed on us anywhere." Instead, the dean suggested they sign up for science, which the girls did. That ended their Alaska dream.

Fay had her first flying lesson at the Curtiss Field, Valley Stream, Long Island, August 9, 1929; soloed August 31; and joined the Caterpillar Club on September 1. On September 15, Curtiss-Wright hired Fay to demonstrate and lecture on the safety of aviation. Fay got her flying license (#9497) October 5, and by November 2, attended the first meeting of the women pilots who formed The Ninety-Nines, International Organization of Women Pilots, which was named after the number of their charter members. (Today there are nearly 7,000 members around the world.) Amelia Earhart was its first president.

Fay is one of America's most extraordinary adventurers. During the four years she was in Russia—September 1930 to October 1934—she was the aviation reporter for *The New York Herald Tribune* and became the first American woman to fly a Soviet civil aircraft, and was the first foreigner to own a glider in the Soviet Union. In 1932, she flew as a guest aboard the first plane to Tashkent to open the Asiatic Airline to Kabul. In the spring of 1933, Wiley Post sent Fay a telegram asking for her help to arrange his fuel dumps and to get the necessary official papers to fly over Siberia. He also requested that she meet him in Novosibirsk early in July, and then fly with him to Khabarovsk to help him in eastern Siberia. There was no airline to Novosibirsk, so the Soviets invited her to fly on the mail plane.

Wiley arrived in Siberia in the middle of July and received the bad news that Fay couldn't fly with him because two pilots in the plane would negate his solo record. He also told Fay he had a contract with *The New York Times* to write an exclusive article at every stop. Behind schedule, Wiley didn't have time to write anything, so he dictated a piece to Fay and made her promise she would send his piece to the *Times* before she filed her story. So Fay not only was left behind in Siberia, but was scooped on her own story. However, she was delighted that Wiley set the round-the-world solo record.

In January 1934, Fay was again on the Trans Siberian Railroad, this time to investigate the rumors of Soviet troop build-ups along the Far Eastern borders, then to continue on to Manchuria to cover the enthronement of Henry Pu Ye, the Puppet Emperor of Manchukuo. After the coronation, Fay went to Tokyo, bought a ticket on a freighter, and returned to Russia by boat via Hong Kong, Singapore, and Athens where she changed to trains through Europe back to Moscow. Fay returned to America in the fall of 1934 and continued her flying career.

She died December 2, 2002 at the age of 94.

Did you have any forced landings?

Only that one time when my instructor was teaching me aerobatics on September 1, 1929. We were flying upside down in an experimental airplane that several instructors had been testing for its ability to take stress. It was Sunday, and in those days, the airport had special attractions to show the people the many facets of aviation. This Sunday the spectators got more than they expected. My instructor said, "If you would like to fly with me, I will show you some aerobatics." I was thrilled. At the time, all students were told that if anything happened to a plane, they should put their hand on the ripcord and step out, then count to ten and pull the ripcord to open the parachute. Before landing, they instructed us to grab the shroud lines and bend our knees so we wouldn't break a leg when we hit the ground.

Anyway, we were flying upside down when the wings started to flutter. The vibration knocked the motor out of its mount, and the plane disintegrated. I didn't have to undo my safety belt— because it broke. But I didn't have my hand on the ripcord. At about 400 feet, the people at the airport said they saw a chute open. My dad and my sister were watching, and they assumed that the chute belonged to Sunny Trunk, my instructor. But it didn't. A part of the plane had struck Sunny on the way down. He managed to pull his ripcord enough so the chute streamed out and caught in the trees and kept him from crashing into the ground. Fortunately for me, my chute canopied over two trees, so I was left hanging sixty feet in the air, but completely unhurt. I had to wait for a fire engine ladder to come and pick me out of the trees. As soon as the firemen got me down, I was taken back to the airport, and they put me in another plane and took me up again. They did not want to lose a paying customer. On the other hand, when Sunny was taken to the hospital, a car struck the ambulance he was riding in, so they had to get a second ambulance. Sunny was in the hospital for three weeks.

Did you have any misgivings about flying after that?

I had only been flying for three weeks. I hardly knew the rudder from the ailerons. But I thought that becoming a Caterpillar was just a facet of flying. We were called Caterpillars because when a caterpillar is in danger, it lets itself down with a strand of silk. Back in those days all parachutes were made of pure silk.

You didn't protest at going up again like that?

No, it didn't bother me at all. When the newspapers came out with the story about us joining the Caterpillar Club, Curtiss-Wright figured if I could do that, they should hire me to go around to airports and air shows and tell people how safe aviation is—which they did. I literally fell into my first job.

I bet you were an outspoken advocate for airplane safety after that.

(laughs) Yes. I figured after that happened it couldn't possibly happen again. After all, I'd flown for three weeks and had only one accident. In my travels to aviation events I met so many wonderful pilots—some of whom would become famous. Little did we know that someday Jimmy Doolittle would be *Thirty Seconds Over Tokyo.*

The Depression was beginning in America, and Joseph Stalin was working on his first Five-year Plan. Stalin had decided his agrarian nation could not survive in an industrial world without changing, so he hired American technicians and businessmen to help industrialize the Soviet Union. My dad was hired to build two electrolytic zinc plants. Dad wanted Beth and me to go with him, but we didn't want to go. Beth was working on her master's degree at Columbia University, and I was having a great time in the world of aviation. We couldn't see going to Russia. Soon Dad had headed off to Russia—after marrying a high school classmate of ours, who went with him.

The story of the marriage is something. When I joined the Caterpillar Club, the paper in Sudbury, Ontario, where we had lived and gone to school, picked up the news. One of our class-mates, Berthilda Hawthorne, in Sudbury, saw the article. She contacted us and said she was coming down to New York to get her master's degree in journalism at Columbia and asked if we knew where she could stay. We told her she could stay with us until she found a place, so she came down to New York City. Beth went off to get her MA, and I went off to do my flying. One day I got a phone call. The caller said, "Is your father Julius H. Gillis?" I said, "Yes." He said, "Do you know he got married this afternoon?" I said, "No." We were completely amazed. But it turned out to be absolutely wonderful for Dad, because Berte was so great. She never complained. They spent several years down in the Caucuses—no heat, no refrigeration, no anything. And when the plant was finished in Ordzhonikidze, they moved to Chelyabinsk near the Urals to build the second electrolytic zinc plant. Our half brother, Ken, was born in Moscow, in 1939.

Your mom was deceased?

Yes. She died when we were juniors in high school. She had diabetes and was used as a guinea pig for penicillin, but it wasn't right for her. Anyway, Dad had a five-room apartment with three maids in Moscow, but he and his bride were down in Ordzhonikidze. So when Beth got her degree and the Russians said I could do some flying if I went to Moscow, we headed for certain adventure in the Soviet Union. There were only seven foreign correspondents in Moscow at the time, so work was waiting there. Beth became the assistant to Walter Durante of *The New York Times*. I became "aviation expert" for the *New York Herald-Tribune* (laughs). We had a fascinating life. We had to go to the Bolshoi theater about four nights a week to entertain the likes of George Bernard Shaw, Lady Astor, ee cummings, Alfred Lunt and Lynn Fontanne, Harpo Marx, and so forth. Moscow was the ultra-tourist attraction during Stalin's first Five-Year Plan, and the foreign correspondents were the tourist guides until the American Embassy was established, with Ambassador Bullitt, in 1933.

Did Harpo play the harp?

In spite of his antics, Harpo was a professional harpist and a wonderful addition to the farewell dinner the Foreign Correspondents gave for Ambassador Troyanovsky, the first Ambassador from the Soviet Union to the United States. Jody Richardson, the wife of the Associated Press correspondent, and I were appointed to travel to Berlin to get the food for a real American Thanksgiving dinner, including turkey, cranberry sauce, ham and all the trimmings. As another added "first," we had the Soviet and American flags printed on the dinner menus.

It was an incredible coincidence that Harpo was on our train returning to Moscow. We had to go through customs at the border between Poland and the Soviet Union. Poor Harpo had a terrible time. When he opened his harp for inspection, a shower of silverware scattered all over the floor. We tried to explain that the silverware was part of his professional act, but the customs officers were sure he intended to open up a restaurant in Moscow. (laughs) The train was delayed while the officials decided what to do. Finally, Harpo, in desperation, put on his costume and went through his act for the officials. It ended when he dropped his arms, and he stood knee deep in the silverware he had up his sleeves.

What flying did you do there?

I was invited to fly on the first plane to be delivered for the new Asiatic Airlines between Tashkent and Kabul. I gleefully accepted, anticipating another adventure. Unfortunately, the plane had water-cooled engines, and the radiators leaked like sieves. In flight, the engineer would sit at the window—just aft of the motor on one side—and I would sit by the window just aft of the motor on the other side, and at the second the radiator stopped leaking, we would yell "cut," and the pilot would shut off the engines and look for a place to land.

How many times did you have to land like that?

It was supposed to be a thirty-seven-hour trip, but it took us nine days. We had fourteen forced landings. I didn't mention them in the answer I gave you earlier about forced landings because I only had one where I actually was involved in flying the plane.

What was the worst of the forced landings?

We really had no real trouble. Fortunately, we were flying down over the Steppes and not up in the mountains, so it was easier to spot a flat area. The pilot was superb. He and his efficient co-pilot cheerfully repaired the radiators as best they could with the materials they had. At most landings, curious peasants, who had guessed something was wrong, came out of nowhere with great caldrons of hot cabbage soup and their inevitable and soulful balilaikas. We were most grateful, for they turned what might have been a tragedy into another memorable experience, as we watched the sun slowly disappear below the horizon. Depending on the weather—on those forced landings—we either curled up in a seat in the plane or slept outside under the wing of the plane.

The people in the Soviet Union didn't have much opportunity to fly. Though they had plenty of airplanes, they had few airplane engines. As a result, gliding was the "in" way to get up in the air. An enthusiast would climb up to the top of the hill, climb aboard the glider, get strapped in, and then be shot off the ramp for about a five-minute glide, riding the currents down to the bottom of the hill. Then it would take almost two hours to pull the glider back up the steep hill for another take-off. It was strenuous, but it cost nothing but your energy and ingenuity, and it was such healthy exercise. Just before I returned to America, I gave my glider to the Soviet Women's Gliding Club. I hope they enjoyed it as much as I did.

The Russians loved parachute jumping. I thought it was strange how they would simply jam their chutes back into their cases and take off and jump again. It was a great sport for them. I never saw anyone get killed jumping with a casually packed chute. We were always so meticulous about how we packed our chutes, to be sure nothing would hamper the unfolding of the parachute when the ripcord was pulled. At the Curtiss Flying Service, professionals packed our chutes.

I lectured about parachutes when I first went to Moscow. When I informed the Civil Aviation Board that Amtorg, the buying arm of the Soviet Union in New York, had told me I would have permission to fly in the Soviet Union, the official suggested that I begin with a lecture about parachuting. So I lectured in the Civil Aviation Auditorium—just one time. I had my whole speech written out in great detail for my translator. In the beginning, I followed the script exactly, but I soon was overwhelmed by the whole concept of the event, and I completely ignored the script. The poor translator was completely bewildered, and though I tried to apologize in my broken Russian, he didn't understand that either.

When I came back to America at the end of 1934, Wiley Post had decided he was going to fly to Siberia by way of Alaska. He flew to see me in New York and asked me if I would go with him. Again, I was flattered and told Wiley I would love to fly with him. I agreed to get all the necessary visas, and all from the Soviet Embassy. But once again, Fate intervened. On April first, 1935, Beth and I had dinner with Linton Wells, one of the foreign correspondents we knew in Moscow. During dinner, Beth said, "Why don't you two get married?" Linton replied, "I've asked her for the last time." I said, "Ask me just one more time." He did, and I said, "Yes!" Then Lint announced, "We'll have to get married tonight. It's my birthday. It's also April Fool's day." Undeterred by the late hour (it was 9 p.m.), Lint hired a car and got our friend Clyde Pangborne out of the Quiet Birdmen (QB) meeting, and we drove up to Harrison, New York. At the time, Harrison officials did not require a two-week waiting period. We woke up a judge at 11:45 p.m. and said we had to get married on the first of April. The judge was a little upset by the abruptness of the request, but he married us before midnight, with my sister's borrowed wedding ring.

Even though I was married, Lint, who was a pilot, said I had to keep my commitment with Wiley. "You go with Wiley, and we will have our honeymoon later," he said. I was in Detroit at an air show, on my way to team up with Wiley, when Lint called to say he had just been hired by *The New York Herald-Tribune* to cover the Italian-Ethiopian War from the Abyssinian side. He asked if I still wanted to go with Wiley or if I wanted to have our honeymoon covering the war in Ethiopia. It took me about thirty seconds to find an answer. I called Wiley and told him I was going to the Italian-Ethiopian war with my husband. Wiley was very understanding and sweet about the change of plans. I knew he could get practically anybody to go with him. Of course, he picked Will Rogers, his Oklahoma buddy, and, as you know, they were killed in a crash in Alaska.

Reconstruct where you were and what you were doing when you heard the news of the crash.

We were sailing for Ethiopia when our ship docked in the port of Marseilles, France. The headline on the morning paper read, "Post and Rogers killed in Alaska." I thought, "How horrible—the loss of two very great people!" But I realized that if I had gone with Wiley, we would have followed his course via Anchorage, Alaska, and across the Bering Strait. Instead, Will Rogers wanted to go up near the Artic Circle to see his Eskimo friend. Wiley couldn't complain because Will was contributing to the expedition.

Did you do a lot of flying when you got back?

I did not go into professional flying after I returned from Ethiopia. I just flew for pleasure with my friends. I never had an airplane myself, but I did have my glider that I left in Moscow.

You were a founding member of The Ninety-Nines?

When the girls, who flew in the first woman's air race, decided they wanted an organization to help keep in touch with each other, they asked Amelia Earhart if she would help found an organization. Amelia came back to New York and went to Mr. Lawrence, head of PR for Curtiss-Wright, and asked him if he would help organize the group. Lawrence said he would be delighted. He had his secretary, Clara Studer, write a letter, and the four girls, who were working for Curtiss-Wright at the time, signed it. They sent the letter to the 117 licensed women pilots, inviting them to a meeting on Long Island on November 2, 1929. Twenty-six girls showed up, and everyone agreed that we should have an organization. Some of the girls wanted to call it the "American Association of Women Pilots" and some the "Lady Birds," or "High Flyers." We chatted back and forth. I remember that we were served tea in a porcelain teapot with a broken spout. It was all very congenial until we tried to name the organization. Finally, this quiet voice in the back of the room said, "Why not name our group after the number of charter members?" That voice was Amelia Earhart.

You were there then?

The others were dressed in high fashion. I was that crazy kid in the front row—the only one dressed like a pilot! This marked the first time I had met a group of woman pilots, so I did not know what to expect. I had just flown in from the Long Island Country Club and did not have a chance to change. In fact, I hadn't even thought to change, because this was just a bunch of women pilots (laughs). I never lived down that crazy picture of me in my coveralls. We sent out our second letter and received 99 responses, so the group became The Ninety-Nines, the International Organization of Women Pilots.

Did the members of The Ninety-Nines *establish close relationships?*

Yes, we were all very close. So few of us flew at the time that, if one girl had twelve sparkplugs, and she only needed six, she would give the other six to one of the other girls in need.

After we got started, Curtiss-Wright had to cut back the public relations department, but Amelia Earhart paid Clara Studer's salary for a year to keep The Ninety-Nines going. For the second year, Annette Gibson, our second president, paid Clara's salary for The Ninety-Nines.

Do you have an Amelia Earhart story?

Yes. Amelia was always very compassionate toward people. At one point, Clara, her secretary, married a young man from Italy. He had come to America on a six-month green pass. The pass was about to expire, and he would have to go back to Italy. Clara discussed the situation with Amelia, who found a job for Alfredo so he could stay in America. During Clara's whole life, she was dedicated to Amelia. When Amelia was lost, the first thing Clara did was to drum up support for a commemorative stamp for Amelia. Clara got us all to write letters, but the post office said that nobody could have a commemorative stamp until they had been dead for 25 years. That was in 1937. Clara wrote down the year 1958 on her calendar as a target for advanced planning. When 1958 came around, she began again to organize the teenagers for Amelia on the East and West coasts. Finally, in December of 1962, 25 years later, we unveiled the Amelia Earhart commemorative stamp at the Washington Hotel in Washington, D.C. On July 24, 1963, we unveiled the stamp in Atchison, Kansas, where Amelia was born—all thanks to the work and dedication of Clara Studer.

Talk more about flying in the early days.

I used to stand wistfully by my plane pretending I was cleaning it. I really was hoping someone would ask if I needed any help. When that happened, I would say, "Would you mind spinning my prop?" I could do it myself by tying the throttle down and running around and spinning the prop, but this was more fun.

Any men that helped you, or men that fought you?

No, the men were always very helpful. But remember I was not competing for anything. I was just showing how safe flying was. I was simply flying and having fun.

Did you want to be a member of the WASPs?

No, I was in Angola all during the war. My husband had just finished a private survey for President Roosevelt regarding a second home for the Jews. Then the war broke out. After the Japanese bombed the Philippines, we lost our supply of hemp, which was important for lines for the Navy. So the United States needed to find a substitute fiber, which they did with sisal, considered the next best thing. It was grown in Portuguese East Africa, Mozambique and Portuguese West Africa, Angola. During the war, Lint and I went to Angola for four years, as a member of the U.S. Commercial Company for the War Production Board. We got involved with sisal. Ironically, the Germans in Angola were the biggest producers of sisal, and our job was to convince the Germans to increase the production of sisal to help America. We were able to do that because the United States controlled the export licenses, and if the Germans wanted gasoline or tires or cars, they had to go through us. We would not give them the licenses unless they sold us their sisal.

Was that a scary job?

We occasionally camped in the compounds of these German growers. People said that the Germans were going to cut our throats. Sometimes in the evenings, the Germans would invite us into their living rooms to listen to the radio broadcasts and to hear who was winning the war that day. Overall, though, the Germans in Angola were very polite. They were astute businessmen, who understood who had the upper hand. No sisal, no export licenses for their other products.

Whenever a ship came in, my husband or I had to fly from Luanda to Lobito, the main cargo port about 300 miles to the south. Our job was to see that all the cargo got aboard. The Norwegian captains preferred to carry coffee instead of sisal, because a ton of coffee took up less space than a ton of bulky sisal. The rule was that the captains had to carry so many tons of sisal to so many tons of coffee. Otherwise, the captains would not get any cargo at all—again relating to export licenses.

There was no official American representation in Angola

when we arrived, so we had to keep the State Department codes for transmission of U.S. messages under our bed, in the hotel. When the embassy in South Africa heard about it, they rushed a consul general to Luanda to set up an official consulate and keep the codes in a safe. We were relieved to turn over the responsibility for the codes to the responsible officials.

What was the crowning day of your life?

I could name a few days. One day was when I literally fell into my job at Curtiss-Wright Aviation. Also, the day I received the telegram, in Moscow, from Wiley Post asking me to help him with the Siberian section of his solo flight around the world. I couldn't believe he would trust me with such a responsibility when he had no way of checking on my progress. He needed gasoline, oil, maps, and permission to fly across Siberia. I needed also to find out if the airport was ready for him when he landed at Novosibirsk in Siberia.

Another day would be the anticipation and excitement of almost flying with Wiley Post, via Alaska across Siberia back to Moscow. Of course, my elopement would be one. Also, the time in Russia when they invited me to fly to Tashkent in the first airplane delivered for the Asiatic Airline was another crowning day. Finally, when I came back to New York in April 1939, I was involved in the forming of the Overseas Press Club. The membership was made up of foreign correspondents from around the world. There were only two of the original thirteen members at the organizational meeting still living.

Amelia Reid

"Amelia's Way"

Amelia Reid's first ride took place when she was in high school, in the summer between her sophomore and junior years. Her hometown of Ord, Nebraska, did not even have an airport at the time. But it did have one of the youngest female pilots who had ever earned a commercial license, at the tender age of 18. Her name was Evelyn Sharp.

Born November 13, 1924 in Ord, Reid soloed in the fall of 1945. She earned her license in May of 1946 in Washington, D.C., and later flew for Ames Research. A consummate flight instructor, Amelia has taught more than 2,000 students to fly and has logged 56,000 hours herself. Until recently, her hobbies included roller-skating. "I was really good," she said. "I was doing turns and skating backwards when I took a really bad fall and hurt my back. I said, I don't think I'm going to do this anymore." She said she is smaller than she used to be. She claimed she had gone from 5'4" to 5'3"—but still stands tall as a pioneer in aviation.

Amelia died March 3, 2000, at the age of 76. After her death, one friend wanted to honor this remarkable woman and change the name of the street in front of her place to "Amelia's Way."

What in particular do you remember about that ride with Evelyn Sharp?

I remember going up for the ride and looking down.

41

Everything looked so small. It impressed me. My parents knew her parents, and they gave me this ride. She landed in a grain field northwest of town. I was so impressed with it that all I could think about the was that ride. I started buying any books I could find on airplanes. At that time, there were a lot of books on the military planes, so I bought a lot of them and started reading up and studying the different planes. I was so interested in flying that I went to college where there was an air base.

What was the name of the college?

Kearney State, and I stayed in a dormitory and would go upstairs to get a suntan. While I did that, I could be watching the military airplanes fly over the dormitory. I got pretty good at identifying them because of all the books I had read.

What did your classmates say? Did they think you were kind of "kooky"?

They didn't say anything really. In college, I did a four-year program in three years and two summers. I didn't have a car at the time, but I did have a bicycle. So I used to bicycle out to a private strip that was really a grass field south of the college, about three miles away. There I would take the spending money I saved and spent it on lessons. My whole goal was to get a pilot's license. I took my flying lessons in a J-3 Cub.

What do you remember about Ms. Sharp?

She was five years ahead of me in high school and had taken flying lessons in a neighboring town, which was 70 miles west of our hometown. When she got her commercial license at age 18, she was doing some barnstorming to pay off loans. But I didn't know her when she was taking lessons. She soloed when she was 16, got her private license when she was 17, and then a commercial license at 18. She went on to become a WASP in World War II.

Did she give you any advice or tips?

No, I didn't talk with her. The only thing I did was ride with her. But I never forgot it.

What did you think of a female doing this? What were your feelings?

I don't think I had any thoughts about this. My dad had a hardware store, so I was raised with tools and hardware, and I just thought nothing of it. The thing that always got me was that my mother used to say, "You're a girl, you can't do this." But I really wanted to do it, and she knew that she could never stop me.

You were pretty strong-willed?

Oh yes, I was very strong-willed. I still am! I just wanted to do something, and I did it. After I graduated from college with a teaching degree, I realized I would not take a job in the home state teaching school in my hometown. I didn't want to do that. When I graduated from college, my goal was to go some place where I could learn to fly. I wanted to finish up my lessons and get my pilot's license.

Tell me about your first solo.

I remember my first solo took place on a field in Washington,

D.C., that doesn't exist anymore. I used to hitchhike out to the place, which was called Congressional Field. It was a square grassy meadow. I soloed in a J-3 Cub, and I still remember bouncing the airplane around, landing and taking off.

What was the best and worst advice you ever had in your early days of flying?

I don't recall anyone giving me advice—or if I paid any attention to it, I don't know. I went through classes that taught us how to navigate, and since we had a woman instructor in the school, I never thought anything of it. The East Coast was very liberal at the time. If a girl wanted to do this, it didn't make any difference. When I moved out to California, I noticed things were a lot different – they thought I was crazy to be flying. Back on the East Coast, there were other girls learning to fly, and there was actually a woman instructor.

Do you remember any of these other girls?

I didn't really have time to associate. There was one girl— though I don't remember her name—who was working at the airport doing fabric work, and I really thought that was neat. I got a job at the airport taping joints, and nobody thought anything of it.

Is there anything that shows just how obsessed you were with flying?

I was so determined. I didn't have any transportation when I went out to Washington, D.C., so I had to get a job. I worked during the week, and my whole goal was to get a job and earn money to fly. That was the goal: to fly. I was renting a room in a house, and there were streetcars running out in front. I could take the streetcars out to the edge of the city, and then I would hitchhike. That's something you wouldn't think of doing now, but I did it then and didn't think anything of it. So I could look like a pilot, I bought myself a pair of khaki pants and a khaki shirt (like the guys wore in the military) as well as a leather jacket. I was that determined. Traveling salesmen would pick me up, and they'd say, "Hey, young man, where do you want to go?" and then they'd recognize me and say, "Oh, you're a girl!" I'd be out there at the airport every day.

I worked at two places in Washington. The first was in the Navy Department. I was only there about six months. I also spent six months with the Bureau of Standards. We did research and testing on ballistics, and we had a course where we fired a gun. The work I did there was really interesting.

Then you were contributing to the war effort in a way, weren't you?

Yeah, in a way. My whole goal was to get my pilot's license and then fly with the women in the service. But I got my pilot's license about six months after they closed down the WASP program.

You must have been broken-hearted?

Yes, because I wanted to fly in the war. I really wanted to be a fighter pilot!

Did you really? Did you have dreams of that?

Yes! I wanted to fly P-51s. Of course, I never got to join the

45

Women Airforce Service Pilots (WASPs).

I was working for the Bureau of Standards at the time, and I wanted to transfer to NACA (National Advisory Committee for Aeronautics). They did research on World War II airplanes, and I thought that would be really interesting. So I had a choice between transferring to the NACA on the East Coast or the one on the West Coast. Since my parents had moved from Nebraska to California, I thought I would transfer to California. I had gotten a degree in college in mathematics, so I got a job working at NACA working as a "computer"—as they called it in those days.

You were a computer?

Yes. They had desk calculators that I did equations on. I don't remember too much about the course there. The gun trajectory didn't really interest me. I was more interested in the flight characteristics of the military planes. I can remember what really intrigued me was when they would change the angle of attack of the wing. The plane would stall. They would change the design of the wing— the angle, thickness, curve, —and it really interested me.

When I moved out to California, I continued to fly. Then I quit flying for about five years when I put my first husband through college because we didn't have any money. After the divorce, I went back to flying again. That was when I got interested in becoming a crop-duster pilot. My second husband was a crop-duster pilot, and that's what I really wanted to do. So I flew his crop-dusters for awhile, but never dusted any crops.

When I got pregnant, I lost my job at NACA because, in those days, there was no pregnancy leave. You had to quit and they wouldn't save your job for you. I loved flying, so I joined a flying club flying as a private pilot and just had fun.

After the baby was about eight months old, I decided I had to do something with myself. So I became a flight instructor. I earned my teacher's credential when I got my bachelor's degree, so I thought why not go ahead and get my instructor's rating. I had been flying all along and had compiled about 525 hours by then. I worked part-time teaching and would still bring my baby boy out to the airport. So, I ended up raising my son out here.

Where is he now? Does he fly?

He flies for Northwest Airlines as a copilot on 747 jets.

Any memories about when you learned of your son's earliest flying?

My son was born in May 1959, so it was a year later, in December 1960, that I got my instructor's rating and started teaching. I used to take him with me when I'd go out and fly cross county with students. I'd put him in the back seat.

My son was with me all the time while I was out there teaching. He was just raised in the airport atmosphere. When kids were about three or four, parents would start teaching them the numbers and the alphabet, but he just wasn't interested in that. He just liked being around the airport. I knew he had to learn to read and learn his numbers so I bought him a model airplane kit. He was about three years old at the time, and the book was a very simple one with simple instructions, but I decided I wouldn't read them to him. He had to learn to read those himself. That's how he learned to read—by building model airplanes. After that, he could read instructions and started building all kinds of model airplane kits.

All the time, he was learning all this at the airport, and when he was 15, he said, "Mom, I'm going to be 16. I'd like to solo." He had decided on his own that he wanted to solo.

That was kind of a proud moment for you, wasn't it?

Very proud, yes.

What did you do?

I soloed him in five, tail dragger airplanes.

You still teach in tail draggers?

Most people come to me because that's what they want to fly in. They know that's the best way to learn to fly because they learn more about the fundamentals of flying in those airplanes than they do in anything else. They learn to use more than three controls.

What's your favorite tail dragger?

When anybody asks me that question, I always say, "The one I'm flying right now, the one I'm in."

Did you ever get any grief when you had your little boy with you? Did anybody ever say to you: "Mothers shouldn't do that"?

One time, my son and I were flying a tail dragger—a Taylorcraft L-2 from Evansville, Indiana, back to California. I usually would follow the highway on the leg from Midland, to El Paso, Texas, because you've always got a place to land when you're on the highway. It was overcast that day, and my son was sitting in the back seat. The ceiling started coming down, and I made one attempt to turn around over the highway. I said, "Well, let's go back to the airport." We did and landed back at Pecos, Texas, and waited a couple hours, then we tried again. There was just no way to get through over the ridge because the clouds went right down to the highway. When I made the second turn-around, I was pretty low, and the cars that were driving down the highway started scattering when they saw the airplane. At that point, a Texas Ranger called the airport and complained that there was a low-flying, blue and white airplane. The airport manager told the ranger, "I have two airplanes there—a red and black Cessna and a lady with her little boy."

Did anybody say anything like, "What are you doing taking that boy out; it's dangerous"?

My son was 16, on May 13th and about three months after he had soloed, there was a fly-in for an air show. He said, "Mom, I'd like to go to the fly-in in Vancouver, Washington." I didn't think that sounded like a bad idea. I had already given him cross-country training, so he knew how to do all of that. He had had 150 hours of flying cross-country, but he didn't have his license yet. Here he was, 16 years old, student pilot, had just soloed, and I let him take my Cub and go with a bunch of guys to this fly-in. The ladies at the airport were shocked. They said, "How come you're letting your son go all by himself clear to Vancouver?" They couldn't believe it. I said, "Well, I wouldn't let him drive a car that far." I wouldn't even let him drive the car to Santa Cruz when he was that age! But, I'll let him take the airplane and go clear to Vancouver.

What makes you a great teacher of flying?

When I teach, I try to break down everything so simply that absolutely nothing can keep somebody from handling the controls. I tell my students to make it fun.

What's the strangest thing you've had happen when you were teaching a student? You've had some unusual students I'm sure.

I think one of the strangest things I've had was when a student who wanted to learn to fly in one of the Taylorcrafts said to me, after his third lesson, "I want to rent it now, and go to Los Angeles with it." I thought, "There's no way!" He was dead serious he wanted to do that. But I refused and never saw him again after that.

Have you ever run in to anybody that was just indefatigable, "I want to do it my way," maybe too strong-willed?

Oh yes. I finally tell them, "All right, go ahead and do it your way." But when the student loses control of the plane and I have to straighten it out, they get very subdued.

One fellow right now taking lessons from me is an example. He is so strong-willed that I just sit there in the back seat and let him goof around and do what he wants with the airplane. I'll retrieve once in awhile, when he does something wrong. I figure he'll be out there messing around with the plane, and I don't like that. So sometimes I'll pull a little reversal where I just will not rent the airplane to the student.

So you have to be strong-willed, too, don't you?

Yes, very strong-willed. I had one student who wanted to

teach himself to fly. He didn't want to listen to me, so I said okay, and I let him go as far as he could. When it came to the landing work, there was no way he could do that, or even perform the takeoffs, so I would retrieve the controls and finally he'd give in. After they scare themselves a little, they'll finally give in.

Did you ever have any forced landings with students?

I had an emergency landing one time with a student in a Taylorcraft. We had a hole in a piston, and we lost all the oil. That was in the day where there were a lot of fields, and so when I noticed our oil pressure had dropped down and temperature had gone up, I knew we had to make an emergency landing. We landed just fine in the field about five miles from the airport. We found a house and called the airport and they came out with some oil. We put the oil in the airplane, but I had the student drive back in the truck to the airport and I took off. I took it at 1,800 rpm's. I thought that was enough to get me airborne in this craft. I flew it and landed on the taxiway at Napa airport. I had to fly under power-lines in order to make it, since I couldn't get any altitude. That student went on to become an airline pilot. He checked out on the 747.

You must've come awful close to power-lines.

Yes, I did. I had to go underneath them.

Were you frightened afterwards?

No, it didn't bother me. I just went ahead and did it. I had another exciting experience when I was by myself one time. I was up practicing spins, and the engine was idling a little slow, so I pulled the nose up and I closed the throttle all the way back, and all of a sudden, the prop just stopped rotating. It came to a dead stop. I was at 3,500 feet. Without any training, just from things that I had done hand-propping airplanes, I thought, if I dive this Taylorcraft straight down, the red line is 130 mph. I figured with air pushing on that prop, maybe it will start. By golly it did! It started and I got back to the airport!

Back in the seventies. I was trying to teach myself aerobatics. At the time I was having trouble doing hammerhead turns, so I talked to some guys about how to do them. They told me to put the plane in a very flat spin. There was a funny sensation. There you were, hanging on the belt rotating upside down. I'd never experienced that before. I'd gone to seminars, and they said, "If you ever get a flat spin, don't fight it – just relax and cut the power off." I had full power and was rotating like crazy, so I cut the power, let go of the control, and then I came right out of it into a regular spin.

You sound like a kind of cool customer. Have you ever been frightened?

I don't think so. I don't ever recall that. I just do the job.

A lot of times people talk about coming back from something scary and sitting there with their knees shaking.

I've never had that happen.

Do you have a personal idol?

Evelyn Sharp is the one I always admired. Otherwise, I don't think I think of anybody as a hero.

You didn't think much of Amelia Earhart?

I didn't think much of her flying. She had the money and didn't do it the hard way. I think I would be more interested in somebody who struggled.

How do you account for that kind of admiration?

I think it's from my family. My parents are both from Czechoslovakia, and they have struggled very hard to get anywhere. They worked hard all their lives. I think that's where it all comes from.

Were they as unrelenting as you are?

Probably. My mother didn't go along with my flying, and my father really didn't care.

When did they give you some sign that they were proud of you?

My dad didn't live to see all these things that I'm doing now. He just didn't live that long, but I think he would have been proud. I think they both were. They rode with me a few times in an airplane. They didn't stop me from doing anything. If I wanted to do it, it was okay. That was kind of their attitude: "If it's what she wants to do, let her do it."

What traits do you get from your father and what traits do you get from your mother?

That's a good question. I don't know. They both worked

hard. My father ran a hardware store, so I think I might get my business sense from him. But they were both proud of their kids whatever they did. They just accepted whatever the three of us did.

Do you recall a student that you are most proud of?

Yes, Sean Tucker. When he came to me, he was just frightened of airplanes. He had been a parachute jumper, but for some reason he decided to learn to fly. He was dead serious, even though he was scared. He thought maybe he could learn aerobatics. I took him up, and I started teaching him aerobatics. He became so intrigued with it—especially when he found out that the airplane wouldn't come apart! He got so excited and exuberant! He loved it. The funny thing was that he got so interested he wanted to learn more stuff. So behind my back, he decided to go out and practice slow-rolls, and he broke the door in half. I grounded him! He still talks about how I grounded him.

You say he broke the door in half?

He was trying to do a slow-roll, and the door started vibrating, and the vibration broke it in half!

Who else are you especially proud of as a student?

I was proud of my son—very proud of him. He flies so many different types of airplanes that I have never flown. I keep flying the school planes, but he gets into everything.

Once I had a lady who came to me, and she wanted to travel around the world, but she was absolutely frightened of airplanes. She would sit there and chew her fingernails off. Her roommates suggested that maybe she ought to learn to fly to get over her fear. She was absolutely scared to death. I remember giving her lessons, and she would come back after a flight looking so frightened she was just white.

Well, I like to analyze my students and then give them the kind of attention they need. Some of them you can yell and scream at, and some of them you can't—you have to be very gentle. I remember making some remark about flying: "Well, maybe girls shouldn't be hand-propping airplanes. Maybe we should just let the guys prop the airplanes." That really upset her because she wanted to be independent and do it herself, just like I did. She was bound and determined that she was going to learn to fly, and she got over her fear. Later on, she got all her ratings, and became a flight instructor. I was very proud of that.

What's the wildest stereotype you believe someone's had about women flying? Some statement or something you've heard?

Generally, most of the men say that the women have a lighter touch on the controls, but that's not always true.

So you've got the gentle touch, huh?

Yeah, that's what people say about my aerobatics. When I take someone up and perform aerobatic rides for someone, they say, "I can't believe it. We didn't feel anything," because I can do it so gently for them. That's what I try to do, and that's how I try to teach aerobatics.

One day when I was flying aerobatics, I was trying to do a multiple-turn spin. I went in to the first turn, the second turn, the third turn, the fourth turn. During the flight I had a student in the plane. All of a sudden, I started a spin recovery—like they teach it— and the airplane wouldn't stop spinning. I cut the power all the way back, and it just kept rotating. Finally, it slowed down after we lost some altitude, and we came out of the spin. I got to thinking about this: "Why did this airplane do this?" It was a few weeks later that one of my competitors here at the airport had an aerobatic pilot out doing the multiple-turn spins. When he went into the last turn, he didn't recover in time and flew right into the mountain and killed himself and his pilot. There was a lot of discussion about what caused this. Word of this got back to the factory, and they did some spin testing.

Some FAA certified airplanes are spinnable and are able to recover in one turn by letting up control, but they didn't do any tests for multiple-turn spins. So the factory tested the airplane and found out that, sure enough, this particular airplane would not recover. To this day, when I teach students, I restrict pilots to only two turns. You don't need to do any more than two, and we won't have any problem with recovery.

What's your favorite aerobatic move?

I like the rolls in an Aerobat. It's just beautiful. I do one that's called an avalanche. I really like that one, where I do a snap roll on top of a loop. But, then again, I like them all.

Why do you like that avalanche?

Because it's fun and you tumble in it.

Was there ever a show where everything clicked so perfectly that it was an absolute dream?

I would say that this last show that I flew probably fits that. I had had so much practice that everything just clicked. I did four routines in Santa Rosa, and every single one of them was identical. I think the reason I felt my performance must have clicked really well is because after I landed and got out of the airplane, lots of people came up to me and seemed to be in awe. In fact, I couldn't walk three steps before somebody would come up to me. But, when I think about it, I realize it was just a lot of hard practice. I practiced very hard for that routine. There were just two of us flying in that show, and I wanted to be perfect. On the other hand, I don't like to think that I'm doing something perfect, because then I think I can't get any better.

What were some of the maneuvers you did?

I did a three-turn spin, I did loops, and I did a Humpty Dumpty.

Do you do Immelmans?

I do. I also do hammerhead turns, snap-rolls. Aerobats do nice snap-rolls.

Is there an aerobatic move that best matches your personality?

Yes, it's the one that everybody likes: the Butterfly. It's not an aerobatic maneuver, but it's my low-altitude, 40 degrees of flat turnarounds.

How does that match your personality?

Because I'm down low on the ground and my wingtip is almost scraping the ground on the runway. Then I make a turn and I peel on up at 40 degrees so the airplane is just about hanging on the prop, and then I dive back down toward the runway.

I call the maneuver a Butterfly. The people are very impressed with that routine. I think I enjoy that one the best.

So that matches your personality?

I don't know why exactly, probably because I'm up and down all the time!

How many students do you generally have in a day?

I run between five and six flights a day. That's five or six hours.

Where do you get your energy?

I'm very careful what I eat.

Is that right? Tell me what a little about your diet.

I eat oatmeal for breakfast, grapefruit, orange juice, and milk. I have a banana snack, broccoli snack, carrot snack, apple snack. A Swiss cheese sandwich on rye bread. I love Turkish dried apricots. They're really good. That's the kind of stuff I eat. I try to avoid anything greasy – hamburgers and such. I'm not too heavy on meat.

What are you proudest of generally, in terms of what you've achieved?

I'm proudest of doing aerobatics, which I've always loved. I'm proud of being able to do that. I think I'm proudest of being able to teach people to fly, of taking folks who just knows nothing, and making pilots out of them. I think that gives me a really big thrill.

Have you ever taken any grief for being named Amelia?

Oh, everybody thinks I was named after Amelia Earhardt. When my mom and dad were courting, they were in a play in which my mom's character's name was Amelia.Of course, it was a Czechoslovakian play, because they were from Czechoslovakia. The Czechoslovakian translation for Amelia is Amarka. So my birth certificate says Amelia on it. I was named after a part that my mother had in the play! What embarrasses me is the actual part she had in the play. She was a maid! She wore a little apron and dusted furniture.

You decided against being "Amelia the Maid"?

I didn't want to be "Amelia the Maid." That's probably why I never do housekeeping!

How helpful were men to you early on?

Back on the East Coast, my instructor was a man, and he was a good instructor. Teaching a woman was no different than teaching a guy to fly. The men gave me jobs, and they worked with me at the airports. I worked at the airport. I hitchhiked out there, and I'd work all day Saturday and all day Sunday for one hour of flying time. Can you believe it? There was a guy out at the airport that let me drive his car back. He had a brand new Taylorcraft that he'd bought, and he had to go to Cleveland, to drive his car back, and he let me drive his car back so he could fly the airplane. I was driving in unfamiliar country that I'd never driven through before—and he let me drive his car. It worked out fine.

Do you consider yourself a brave person?

I just consider myself doing what I want to do. But I don't necessarily think of it that way. I don't let someone stop me from doing what I want to do. They tried to stop me from building my 60 by 100 foot building back in 1967. The Reid family owned the airport, but they sold it in 1960 to the County of Santa Clara. The plan was that I could operate there for three years and then, after the three years, the county was going to tear down all the old buildings. At the time, I was operating out of a trailer, and everybody had to get a contract and a lease with the county in order to build. The county came to me when I was in my trailer.

I'll never forget the day they came to me after hearing I wanted to build a building, saying, "Women don't do that. Women do not build buildings. Why don't you lease some space from somebody else who's building a building?" I said, "No, I want to build my own building." So I hired a lawyer. That's how determined I was.

One of my students was a contractor, and we got together. We got extensions month to month from the county to continue operating until my building was built. I took a loan, mortgaged my house, and with my retirement money that I hadn't used, I had enough money for the building with the hanger and everything. It cost $12,000 to put the hanger up. It's a four-beam building, and I got two-and-a-half acres of property that I paved and I got the whole job done for $37,000. That was back in 1967, and we used 30 years up on the lease and still have 20 years left.

Do you have 20 years left?

That's going to be a long time isn't it! I don't know!

Do you ever get tired?

When I get sick, I do. I usually go to bed about two o'clock, and get about six hours of sleep.

And then you work a full day?

Yes.

Boy, is it the genes, or the Turkish apricots? This is uncanny, though. Do you get any comments from senior citizens?

You should have heard them at the air show when they saw me fly. All the seniors come. The senior citizens just can't believe I'm still doing it. They say, "Don't you get dizzy?" They just wonder how I do it.

Is there another example of your business savvy that has really worked for you?

I think that it helped in college when I studied typing and I learned how to use an adding machine. I experienced using an adding machine while I was working at NACA. I majored in math, and I think my mathematical background has really helped me a lot.

Give me about a couple of pivotal points in your life.

I think learning to fly was a very pivotal point. That was very important to me. Raising a son was very important too, and that he's successful. The flying is what I do all the time.

How many hours do you fly in a year?

I have flown between 1,000 and 1,200 hours a year, except for the five years the first time I was in college.

You might be going for a world record one of these years!

I don't know! I don't think about world records or anything like that. There's no goal to achieve anything. It's just what I wanted to do.

What do you tell young women today who are interested in flight?

If this is what you want to do, do it!

How would you like to be remembered?

I don't know. As a crazy lady, I guess.

Talk about aging?

I'm shrinking. I was 5'4", 120 lbs. I'm 5'3" now.

Do you have any hobbies or anything?

Well I used to roller-skate, until I hurt my back. I roller-skated until about three years ago.

Were you pretty good?

I was really good. I was doing turns and skating backwards. I took a really bad fall, and when I hurt my back, I said I don't think I'm going to do this anymore.

Any other hobbies? You don't have a lot of time for more, do you?

I don't have a lot of time. I still do a lot of dancing.

What kind of dancing?

Swing, jitterbug.

What did you think this year when you saw Sean Tucker at Oshkosh? Did he confide in you?

We just visited a little bit. He was really busy.

Are there any old-timers you thought were pretty amazing?

My ex-husband was a tremendous pilot. I thought he was one of the best natural feel/field pilots that I've ever seen in my life. He could just wear an airplane. That's kind of the thing I like, is somebody who's such a natural at flying. We didn't stay married but I always admired his skills.

Dicey Miller
"Civilian Flight"

Dicey Miller started flying in 1934 in Long Beach, California. She was fourteen, and though her parents thought she was at the beach, she was at the airport. She hung around there for a couple of years and cadged rides by making herself useful—or a nuisance. Sometimes she would sweep out the hanger, wash the airplanes, and do whatever little things needed to be done. The guys around the airport were very helpful, and eventually she did learn to fly. Sooner or later, someone would say, "Hey, Squirt, you want to go for a ride?" At the time, Dicey was short— about four feet ten inches. She later grew to five feet one. She looked even younger than she was, with freckled face, red hair and pigtails. Then, one day flying, the pilot said to her, "Hey, kid, you want to fly for awhile?" And that's the way it was. In fact, she never spent a penny on her early flying. It was always voluntary instruction. Thus began a wonderful career in private aviation for Dicey.

Dicey went to work at Douglas "on the board," doing drafting and production illustration during the war, then later worked for American Aviation. Dicey told me in the conversation—before I set up my recorder— that she married a Navy pilot, but that he was killed before WWII, when a student of his, at Pensacola, froze on the controls and flew him into the ground. I led with a question about that terrible incident.

Was it hard to fly after the death of your husband?

No, you can get a fatal wreck in a car. It happens. It happened a lot in those days. It wasn't something unusual. You just had to accept it.

Did you have any problems with guys?

No, I had no problems with the guys. Those of us in the early days really didn't have that much of a problem. The guys were more helpful than the opposite. I've always said, "Hey look fellows, I'm not trying to compete with you. I'm just a gal who likes to fly airplanes, and the airplane doesn't care if I wear pants or skirt." That's my attitude and the way I feel about it.

Who was the biggest influence on you back then?

Milo "Mike" Burchman was my hero. He was Mr. Big there at Long Beach and held the world's record for upside down flying. In fact, he used to hang himself in the garage upside down in a chair to get used to being upside down. He gave me a lot of rides and taught me a lot. One of the things, he used to emphasize was not to use the term "aerobatics"—it was "precision maneuvers." Precision maneuvers were what pilots did with the airplanes, like loops and stuff. Stunts were something else. They came under the heading of what people other than pilots did, such as ribbon cutting, wing-walking, and other things. But anything a pilot did with the airplane was precision maneuvers. He made that very clear. He also emphasized one must fly with precision at all times with no sloppiness. The lesson stayed with me long after that. I hadn't done any flying for about twelve years, and I was able to pass my waiver ride with just a little brush up to get used to the Cessna 152.

Remember the first time you went up in a plane?

It was in a Ford Tri-Motor in Wichita, Kansas, at night. I was eleven years old, and my uncle gave me a flight as a birthday present. He was only six years older than I was, and more like a big brother. His money came from a paper route, and the cost of $5 was a lot for him at the time. That's how I got my first ride.

What did your parents say when they learned you were flying?

My father died never knowing that I flew, and my mother didn't learn I flew until my son was flying.

What did she say at that point?

She was just kind of stunned. The way it happened was that we were in Huntsville, and my mother was visiting my daughter who lived in New Orleans. So my son and I went down in a Cessna 172 to pick her up. He was flying at the time, but he was still a student pilot, and I had to fly the right seat as an instructor, so he could fly. Anyway, we got down there, and grandma wanted to ride in the front seat with Bill, my son. Bill says, "I'm sorry, you can't. Mom has to ride there." "Why?" "She's the instructor." (laughs)

So, your mother adjusted okay?

It was all over. There wasn't anything she could do but adjust to it. Actually, I think, she would have been supportive—but she would have told my dad—and that would have ended it.

Any forced landings?

We didn't have all the instrumentation, and we did a lot of seat-of-the-pants flying. We didn't have a lot of maps—we just used a Shell Oil road map a lot of the time. You were always ready to set down because the planes and fuel were not all that reliable then. We used to strain all our fuel through a chamois.

I've had quite a few forced landings in my day. They're off-airport landings, discretionary landings, but I've never scratched a plane. One of them involved me landing on the Interstate Highway between Huntsville and Nashville—which was caused by carburetor ice. Nowhere to go, so I just set down. It was only five minutes from the field, so I let things thaw out, then took off and landed at the field. As it turned out, nobody reported the incident, or said anything, so I never said anything about it either.

In the case of another forced landing, I was with a student, and he was getting ready for a commercial check ride where you cut the power, find a field, and simulate an emergency landing. As the student was simulating, re-starting the engine, and switching the fuel tanks, he inadvertently turned off the fuel completely. Normally, during the procedure, when we had the field made, I said, "Okay, we've got her made, let's go." I would push in the power, which I had simply pulled off to simulate the emergency, and we'd start flying again and not bother to land. This time, when I pushed in the power, nothing happened. So then, I immediately realized what had happened and flipped the tank back on.

In the meantime, the prop had stopped wind-milling, and it didn't want to start. Now we were much closer to the field, so I said, "Push the starter!" The starter was on the left where I couldn't get to it. "Charles, press the starter!" And he just said, "Heh?" I said, "Never mind." About that time, we were coming on in to the field, and we landed. On the way in, we had clipped something. It looked like a fence post, though we had cleared the fence, but a farmer had actually put in a dead tree, and we clipped the tail on it. Later, when I went over to Huntsville Airport to report, the tower said, "Cleared to land, Dicey, but check the land for fence posts."

Flying in those days was a very friendly business. There was always a lot of chitchat like that, and of course, I flew in a goldfish bowl. There weren't many women pros or instructors then, so I was "highly visible." If I had a cold, they not only knew I had a cold, but what color handkerchief I blew my nose on. It still is like that a certain extent today, especially at smaller fields. The flying world is what Ernie Gann calls a "band of brothers." I feel like I have a whole slew of brothers out there. I don't feel as if so many of the women out there now seem to feel – or do the girls coming along – that the guys resent women flying. My brothers didn't resent me. If anything, they were helping me. Today, it's a do-it-myself bunch of gals. Me, I was always looking for all the help I could get.

Worst condition you've flown in?

I hit a buried thunderstorm just as I was turning on to a back course approach. In other words, I was IFR, and I inadvertently went into thunderstorm activity, which ordinarily I would never have done, but it was buried. There was no warning. I didn't know it was there. I just flew into it, and the next thing I knew, I was fifteen miles east of where I started and 6,000 feet higher before I got straightened out.

Were you frightened?

I can't say I was truly frightened. I was damned "concerned."

No, but not frightened because I had the airplane under control, as much as you could have. And I wasn't worried about the airplane coming apart. I had a Mooney, and they're extremely sturdy birds.

Unfortunately, this happened before we had radar, so the tower and approach didn't have any idea where I was for awhile, and neither did I. I told the tower I had missed my approach, hit a thunderstorm, didn't know where I was, but I was in a rack-track pattern in-bound, on the Huntsville VOR 160 - degrees radial. Tower replied, "Roger, we're holding clear 6,000." So, they cleared everybody out at 6,000 feet till I could get my position established by cross-fixing with the VORs. So, we had Eastern, United, and Southern Airlines all holding at different levels just outside the Huntsville area, waiting till I found where I was. I felt bad about holding all these big guys up and said, "I'm sorry, fellows," over the radio. And one of the airline pilots came on and said, "That's all right, honey. I'm just damned glad it was you and not me."

What was your favorite plane?

Whichever one I could get a ride in? (laughs) Oh, I don't know. I've flown a lot of different planes, but I think, one of my favorites – as with almost everybody else – has to be the Stearman.

I fell in love with airplanes in general when I was about eight years old. I used to build them out of balsa wood and tissue paper. I had boy cousins who enjoyed building models too, so instead of playing with dolls, I played with airplanes. We used to get these paperback books, which were full of sets of plans for different model airplanes, so as to learn to build them. Then, we'd fly them with wind-up rubber bands for power.

What did other little girls think about your interest?

Well, I was kind of loner. I never played with other little girls a lot. I was too busy building airplanes. I also read a lot.

Let's talk more about old days.

Rather than old days, I'm much more interested in 1960, though 1960 is early days now. I think some of the best flying we had was in the sixties, a kind of golden age in general, of aviation. It was a time when we had a lot of encouragement. We had a situation where people could learn to fly on the Veteran's Administration. There was a lot of student instruction and lots of upgrades – a big surge in both general aviation and commercial and airline flying. That's what I liked. I started instructing in the sixties and thoroughly enjoyed it. In fact, I was still instructing up to two years ago.

When I started back to re-qualify after being off for so long, I had to retake all of the instrument training. Of course, everything had changed from instruments to radios to navigational aids. I drew a fellow, who had been a military instructor and just retired. I was his first female student. And he was rough. He used to give me a really bad time. He'd get me so mad that I'd be crying. He'd say, "Fly the damn airplane. Fly the damn airplane; don't cross-control and watch your headings," and so forth. When we got all through, and I was getting ready to take my check ride with the FAA to get my new instrument rating, he said, "I don't know how the FAA will feel about it, but you meet military standards." And he gave me a little pair of military wings, which I thought was rather nice (laughs). So, I gave him a cigarette lighter that said, "Don't cross-control and watch your goddamned headings."

Was there any misconception about early flight?

I would say the biggest misconception about it, which has crept into the literature, is that it was full of hard drinking, hard-living pilots. This was not what I knew to be true. Certainly, if you drink very much, you don't fly very well or live very long. I'll tell you that very bluntly because it really plays hell with your coordination. You don't drink and fly, or if you do, you're going to be pretty damn dead pretty quick.

There was no opposition to you as a woman in the early days?

The only time, I ever really encountered it—and it was kind of amusing – was when I was doing some flying with a small airplane down south. I was in my middle 50s at the time, and I had a nice young man for a co-pilot (or first officer) at the time.

No big deal—it was a very small airline. One of the passengers said to my nice, young co-pilot, "How does it feel to be flying second-seat to a skirt?" And the nice, young man looked him up and down and said, "She didn't get there by battin' her big, blue eyes, Buster!" Neatest putdown I ever heard – but courteous!

I think primarily that most of the resistance didn't come from the pilots, as much as it did from the general public. It seemed like the public resented us more than our fellow pilots did. Look at it this way: flying is something that you can't fake. You can't pretend. I mean, you either can do it or you can't. Furthermore, you're right out there in front of God and everybody (laughs). As I said before, fliers do what they do in a goldfish bowl, particularly the ladies, and it becomes obvious very quickly whether you're a good or a lousy pilot. All they have to do is watch you in the pattern and your landings.

I suppose, you've heard from other pilots that Amelia Earhart was not such a hot pilot. Again, that's something that people in the flying business knew, but you protect your own. We all felt very sorry for her because her husband pushed her into it. My own personal opinion was that she never truly liked to fly.

Did you ever meet her?

Upon occasion, yes. I was never a particular friend of hers; she was merely someone, I'd met. We were at the same-place-at-the-same-time sort of thing.

You didn't feel like you were carrying a banner then over the years?

Heavens, no! I was just doing a job and taking care of my own life. I wasn't carrying a banner for anybody.

Your son flew. Did he have a flying career? Does he still fly?

No. To him, it was no big deal. That was his mother's bag. The only thing, I'll say is that when he was a senior in high school, before he got his driver's license, he flew. Most kids think that driving a car is ultimate. He told one kid who was talking about doing 90 miles per hour (in a car), "So, what's the big deal? I land an airplane doing 90, steering with my feet." Which is true, of course, because you steer with the rudder and brakes when you are on the ground.

Remember your solo flight?

This sounds silly, but I don't remember nearly as much about my first solo flight as I recall about my second solo. The second solo, as I told you, took place after I hadn't been flying for twelve years. Remember, the last thing I had been flying was

P-51s. I was out at the airport, waiting for my son to make his solo flight, and a fellow came in flying the University of Alabama Commander. We got to talking and, come to find out, he'd been a squadron-mate of my first husband. He wanted to know if I was still flying. I told him no, that I had some problems with my eyes. He said, "Maybe you could get a waiver." After that, I decided to see if could get back into flight, so I went up with one of my son's instructors in a Cessna 150. You can imagine what it was like. It was a somewhat different airplane than the last plane I'd been flying.

So, we went up and flew around for about an hour and a half, I guess, did some landings and some air work and generally got acquainted with the airplane. We came back to the field, and he said, "Well, if you had your medical, I don't see any reason why I couldn't let you go. " So, I said, "Okay." You see, because I didn't have my medical, he couldn't rent the airplane to me. That meant, I couldn't go full solo. So, I went and got my medical, but I did have to get a waiver. The FAA had to approve it and say that, although I didn't meet flight standards because of my eyes, I could still fly the airplane safely. All my check rides had to be with the FAA. The waiver has to do with my right eye – I'm almost blind in it. Anyway, I came back waiving my medical. So, the guy looks at me and says, "Take it away" (laughs). That was my second solo and a lot more thrilling than my first.

Try to recall the first day after you quit. Ever feel nervous the first day or the week after, or ever?

Oh, the worst part of it was selling the airplane. Now, you've got me in tears.

Tell me about that.

(Pause) I'm sorry. I couldn't keep the plane if I couldn't fly. That was very hard. A fellow that I worked with, at McDonald Douglas Helicopter at the time, heard that I had my Grumman Tiger up for sale. We didn't even quibble about price. I told him what I wanted for it. He said, "I'll take it." That was it.

Ever want to go back up?

I have lots of opportunity to fly. In fact, the FAA told me that I could keep on teaching, but that I just can't teach primary. It had to be commercial or instrument, that is, where somebody already has a ticket. I'm on medication, but I'm in pretty good shape. As my FAA doctor put it, "Dicey, you just need a new alternator." My heart has to have some stimulation, so I take a drug for that, and I can't fly solo or pilot-in-command without another pilot present.

If you hadn't been able to fly, what could you have done?

I suppose, I would have done pretty much what I did in the twelve years when I didn't do any flying. I think I probably would have gone further with the architecture. I went back to school in my late 40s and studied architecture at the University of Washington and University of Alabama. I never did get my degree.

I liked designing houses. I didn't want to get into big buildings. In fact, I got interested in architecture when I went shopping for a house, and I got disgusted with what I saw. I got tired of being told, "What do you know about it?" I thought, "By golly, I'll find out."

What's the metaphor for flight?

I don't know. I enjoyed flying. When I had to quit, I missed it. Above all, I guess the thing that I miss most, however, about flying is the mobility of it – being able to get in the airplane and go someplace without all hassle. I hate to drive a car (laughs). I still do. It bothers me because it's such a frustrating way to get from place to place when you're used to flying (laughs). And up there, it's a different world. What is it they say? You put on the airplane and wear it. You and the airplane do things together. You can't fly without it. It can't fly without you. It's sort of like a love affair—if you cooperate together, you can do beautiful things—if not, it can be a disaster. Lindbergh said it all in his book about his flight to Paris: "We—we flew to Paris."

You asked me about my proudest achievement? I guess I would have to answer—my involvement with the development of the American Aviation—later Grumman—line of light civilian aircraft. Back in the late sixties and early seventies, my flight school was very instrumental in keeping the line alive. Back when it (the American Aviation "Yankee") was a very controversial airplane, and Beech, Cessna, and Piper were all screaming about what a "DANGEROUS" airplane it was, I was operating nine of them as primary trainers in a very successful flight school with 240 students and five instructors in the Seattle area. In three and a half years of operation, we never even "scratched" an airplane, let alone had an incident or accident. When they had a complaint, the FAA would point to the flight school and essentially say, "How come? They don't seem to be having any problems." And that's how I got to be so well known to the FAA, particularly to the instructor guys. My point is this: all of my life, I have been defending the airplane, from balsa wood and tissue paper days to the present.

The airplane can only do what it is either designed to do or do how it is flown. If there is a problem, it is with the designer, or the builder, or in the way it is being flown – the pilot. Basically, it doesn't care a darn bit whether or not you wear pants or skirt, whether you are black, white, yellow or green, or whether you are a teenager or an octogenarian – it only wants to know how you can fly it. There is no "faking"it possible, you either fly it or you don't and it is very public, both ways. Unfortunately, or maybe fortunately, I don't know. All I DO know, is that I resent the media blaming airplanes for what are essentially human deficiencies.

End of soapbox.

AIR SHOW

WILKINSBURG
AIRPORT

Graham Blvd. at Wm. Penn Highway

Two Parachute Jumps

By "Cloud Buster" Langer
World Famous Parachute Jumper

AIRPLANE STUNTING EXHIBITION
By THERESA JAMES, GIRL STUNT PILOT

(Theresa James stole the show at the Air Progress Week
Show at the City-County Airport Last Saturday and Sunday)

HARRY FOGLE, THE FLYING ICEMAN and His Travelair

(Instructor of Miss James)

LITTLE GEORGIE HELLER
Flying a Waco F.

EXTRA SPECIAL
Children Under 12 Can Fly For 50c Until 2:30 P. M.

Sunday Afternoon
October 27, 1935

IN CASE OF BAD WEATHER SHOW WILL
BE HELD THE FOLLOWING SUNDAY

Teresa James
"With the Women's Auxiliary Ferrying Squadron"

Teresa James takes an oath.

Teresa James earned her private pilot's license on October 12, 1934. After her solo, she flew air shows in Pennsylvania as a barnstormer. She performed stunts such as loops and spins and transported parachutists, including a man known as "Bat Man," who unfolded his bat wings and landed to everybody's amazement. About this time, she won the title of "Pittsburgh's Number One Woman Stunt Pilot." When at the Puxsutawney VFW Post Air Show, she performed twenty-six and a half complete flat spins, which she followed with ten loops. And then, in 1939, she received her transport license.

In 1942, Teresa was working as a flight instructor at Pittsburgh, when she received a telegram from General "Hap" Arnold, requesting she report for a flight check at New Castle Army Base in Wilmington, Delaware, for possible work ferrying army aircraft as part of the WAFS (Women's Auxiliary Ferrying Squadron). There were two main objectives of the women pilot program: 1) To see if women could serve as military pilots, and if so, to develop the nucleus of an organization that could be quickly expanded. 2) To release male pilots for combat. The WAFS proved their capabilities, which led to a school for female trainees in Houston, Texas. Then, in August 1943, the women pilot trainees merged with the WAFS to form the WASP, the Women Air Force Service Pilots. A total of 1,074 women in the WASP organization flew about 60 million miles in the service of their country.

During the 27 months Teresa flew for the military, she had to check herself out on such planes as the P-51 and P-47. The reason was that there were no piggyback seats for those aircraft.

She was deactivated in December 1944 and returned to Pittsburgh, where she managed her parents' two flower shops. In the interview, she tells a bittersweet story about a stranger who came into her shop to tell her of her husband who was missing in the war.

Teresa was commissioned a major in the Air Force Reserve in 1950. Her duties included special services officer to the 375 Troop Wing at Greater Pittsburgh Airport, and an assignment to the 5040 Air Base Group, Alaska Air Command, Anchorage, Alaska. It was in Alaska that she received two commendations for casualty assistance.

She was a member of the Ninety-Nines, International Organization of Women Pilots, OX5 Aviation Pioneers, WASP, Silver Wings, The P-47 Thunderbolt Pilots Association, Women Military Pilot's Association, and the Grasshoppers (the Florida Race Pilots).

Teresa James died July 27, 2008, at age 94. At the funeral, Lake Worth Mayor Rodney Romano declared Veteran's Day

Teresa James and WASPs Day

Tell me about your solo flight.

It was a long, long time ago. Can I tell you how scared I was? My solo flight was one frightening experience. I didn't know I was coming to solo that day. It happened after four hours of instruction in a Waco OX-5 Travelaire. It was on a Sunday morning; early in the morning, at seven o'clock, when the air is real still, and you don't have the crosswinds or up-and-down drafts that you normally have during the day. It was a sort of morning that the airplane would really fly itself. My instructor said to me, "We're only going to shoot a few landings early this morning." And I said that whatever he was going to do was okay with me. He pulled up on my second landing. I wasn't flying out of the airport. It was nothing but a field, an up-and-down grade. I think the field was 1,800 feet long and about 800 feet wide. There were trees and wires on one end, and it's sloped on the north side so it was a kind of hook. Anyway, on my second landing, Harry got out of the back of the airplane, and he said he was going to check something in the back of the plane. Then he picked the fuselage up and turned it around. We didn't have a tail wheel at that time. All we had was a tale skid. We didn't have any brakes. We had a tale skid that dug into the ground, and that's how you stopped the airplane. So, after he swung the tail around, he said to me, "Okay! Take her up. It's all yours." So before I even had second thoughts about it, I pushed on the throttle and I was in the air. Prior to this, I'd had a traffic pattern. I'd take the plane up to 200 feet and make a turn at Grand Boulevard and go 400 feet down the highway, and then 600 feet over Churchill Valley Country Club. This was in Wilkinsburg, Pennsylvania.

After Harry got out with his weight, the airplane got off

faster and climbed higher. As a result, I was 200 feet higher than I should've been at each turn. So on my final approach to the field, I had to flip the airplane. I don't know where I learned this. Perhaps this came from watching Bill, the guy who introduced me to flying. Once I landed, I taxied up to the fence and jumped out of the airplane. That was it. I said, "Never again will I ever get up in the air. Never, never, never again." When I landed, I kept hitting my right leg, going up and down on the rudder. I was so nervous. I kept hitting my leg above my knee hoping to stop it from jumping up and down. They couldn't get me back in the airplane until much later. And they said, "Do you realize that you got up and down?" That thought never occurred to me. I was terrified, really terrified. And I said, "I will never again go up." That was in 1934.

Can you explain that fear?

I told some of my students that I could almost pick up fear in them, I guess maybe due to my own fear. I could tell it when we made the plane turn, they would pull away from the turn and not want to look out. I related my experience to some of them that I taught. I told them how apprehensive I was. I'd say, "That's a normal reaction, I think." I sort of allayed their fears. It is hard to explain fear because you're the one in control of the airplane. You don't know if you're doing it right or you're doing it wrong, especially when you have had only eight hours of instruction. That's not much when you think about it. Imagine having to solo after only eight hours of flying. I soloed a lot of students. I could tell when they were ready to take the airplane up and bring it down and land it.

Who was this Bill that introduced you to flight?

That's a funny story. I have to tell you how I got into aviation. I never thought about airplanes. My brother bought into a club with two other guys, and they bought an airplane, an OX5 Trailblazer. They were flying out of an airport in Pittsburgh, Pennsylvania, known as Bettis Field. They decided they were going on a cross-country flight up to Detroit, Michigan, to see my uncle. He was in the forest business up there. They didn't have enough fuel to cross the lake in Cleveland, so they had to go around through Cleveland to get up to Detroit. I didn't know this at the time, but they encountered a head wind and then ran out of fuel. They made an emergency landing in a field. They hit electrical wires and totaled the plane. The hospital called and said my brother had been in an accident. So I went down. His leg was so bad, they thought they'd have to amputate it. He remained in the hospital for perhaps a month, then we brought him back to Pittsburgh. He asked me to drive them over to Wilkinsburg Airport. He wanted to talk to the pilots over there. I can remember telling him how crazy he was. I couldn't believe he was even thinking about flying again. He almost died. Driving him back and forth to the airport is really how I got into aviation, and I met some of his friends. One friend in particular, who arrived in an airplane, was the best looking fellow I had seen in a thousand years. Oh, man, the man-of-my-dreams kind of thing. His name was Bill Angel. At that time, the guys who owned airplanes and had girlfriends or wives, would pack a picnic basket on Sundays. They'd get up early on Sunday mornings and fly someplace. They'd land and play cards or baseball or something during the day and then fly back to the airport. On my first cross-country, I remember that I was terrified, absolutely terrified on every Sunday flight. I guess my infatuation with Bill helped me to overcome my fear. Once I landed, I was happy doing all the festivities.

Later, Bill took a job as an airline pilot in Chicago. There was a fellow there who had just come back from Park College, and he knew I was crazy about Bill. He said, "Why don't you learn to fly and surprise Bill when he comes back to Pittsburgh?" So, that's how I got into aviation. I learned to fly, but in the meantime, Bill got married out there. He wrote a letter to one of his friends at the airport and told him he got married. So I learned to fly, Bill got married, and that was last I saw of him. I still was absolutely terrified of flying. It took me a long time, almost up to my private license, to get rid of a lot of that fear.

Did the fear come from the episode your brother had?

I don't know. It wasn't only that. When I thought about it, I remembered, when I was a kid how my dad took me up in a balloon. I guess I was about six years old. All I remember was squatting in the bottom of the basket. We wind up in a balloon in Asenwall, Pennsylvania. We were at a balloon convention. Perhaps this is why I was so afraid of flying.

When I was about 12 or 13 years of age, an airplane came over our home, and was sputtering, the engine cutting in and out. It was getting lower and lower, and it just about cleared our neighbor's house. Our neighbor's house was almost at a 90-degree angle from where I was looking. My dad had a Ford truck, and I jumped in the truck and went out to where I thought the airplane was. That was only five minutes or so from when I heard the sputtering. It was an Army airplane, but I didn't know it was an Army airplane then. I got to watch it burn. It burned to a crisp. There were two guys in the plane.

Were they lost?

I don't know what happened to them. There was a write-up

in the paper about it being an Army Air Force airplane in a forced landing. It was already on fire when I got there. I don't know whether that contributed to my fear or not.

Did your family have any misgivings about your interest in flight?

Well, my dad never said anything to me about flying. My mother and dad used to go flying with James Wright. I went to air shows where I'd be gone all day on Saturday and Sunday. My mother and dad would fly with me. They would stay wherever I was. I'd have flying positions that involved flying passengers, but they never criticized me. They never asked me not to fly. I think they were alarmed at what happened to Franny, my brother. My mother said, "You know, what's going to happen is going to happen." She was that sort of person. When my mother was in her 50s, she said she'd like to learn to fly. Then she had a heart attack. It was a mild heart attack, but that was the end of her aspirations to fly. My parents were really wonderful. They supported me all the time, no matter what.

Did you ever come across any non-supporters throughout the years?

Of course, maybe I took a little heat as a female when I went up to Buffalo, New York, while I was taking my instructor's rating. There were a bunch of guys up there, and that was the only time I heard criticism. I don't remember whether it was funny or not, but I do remember there were comments made. Of course, when I went to Roosevelt Field, I went there for my instructor's rating for teaching inverted flying. There were some comments made about the instructor who gave the licenses. He supposedly had flunked a couple of guys before I went up. Max Rappaport said that I was thoroughly indoctrinated into the type of flying I was doing. In fact, there was a guy 18 or 20, Bill Piota, who taught me inverted flying. He did a tremendous job. I really never heard any criticisms until I got in the Service.

What did you hear in the Service?

I can't remember exactly, but I believe it was some sort of resentment due to the fact that women were taking their jobs. It came particularly from the ones who were coming back from combat. I can understand that. I didn't understand it at the time, but they were afraid that they'd be returned to the ground, and they wouldn't be flying anymore. This was especially true of the instructors who were teaching the CPT program. The fact that they were instructors kept them out of the Army.

I did try to get on with the airlines when I came out of the service, but they wouldn't hire me because they said that prevailing opinion wouldn't permit a woman flyer in the cockpit. Some people's opinions were opposed to that. I even tried to get in the Chinese Air Force. Barbara Poole Shoemaker and I tried to get jobs with the airlines. We were so desperate to fly that we applied to the Chinese Air Force. I still have the letter from the Chinese Embassy. It said that they didn't have the facilities to acquire women for flying at that time. I don't remember the wording, but I still have the letter. It was funny. That's how desperate we were to fly.

Tell me about being a WAFS.

I was one of the first 28 women in the Women's Auxiliary Ferrying Squadron. Nobody ever heard of the WAFS. It was just like a lost entity. This was back in 1939, when Nancy Love

86

WAFS pilot Teresa James during World War II

and her husband Robert could see that there was going to be a war. After the invasion, Nancy Love went to the CAA, which is now known as the FDA, to see how many qualified women pilots would be available to fly airplanes. This is before Jackie Cochran's work. Apparently, Jackie Cochran had talked to Mrs. Roosevelt about this, but Cochran was on to England in 1940. She took some of the American girls over there to fly. However, Nancy Love went through the CAA records and got the names of the commercial women pilots here in this country. And she was the one that started the WAFS, the Women's Auxiliary Ferrying Squadron. The WAFS, as an entity, is lost today in history.

Why is that?

We started in 1942. Of course, before 1942, the women were commanded by Nancy Love on the air base at Wilmington, Delaware. We were assigned to the Air Transport Command for ferrying duty. We were the initial group of 28, the WAFS at the time. And then later, Jackie Cochran initiated the women's military training program, with the first group of 28 being trained at Houston. What we were doing was absorbed, when, in 1943, the WAFS merged into one organization called the Women's Air Service Pilots. Jackie Cochran was named director. Nancy Love, who started the WAFS, was named the WAFS executive for the Ferrying Division of the Air Transport Command.

How do they explain the slight?

There's probably some conflict there in Washington, D.C., Irv, I can't tell you. All I know is that Jackie Cochran came back here from England, and she was hell-bent on starting this school for women pilots. Remember that the WAFs were experienced pilots. And what were we supposed to do? The WAFs were to ferry small aircraft to the men. This would release the men to fly bigger aircraft and allow them to go to combat.

Jackie Cochran had been in England with 25 or 30 women pilots, but when she found out that Nancy Love had started this group, she flew back to Washington, D.C. She asked for permission to start a school in Texas to train women pilots. Jackie's husband was Floyd Audlum. He was Mr. Charles Atlas. Her idea was to take the women, who had maybe 35 hours of flying time, and to bring them up to the specifications we possessed. Several thousand women applied for the Flight Training Command in Sweetwater, Texas. Training at Venture Field was primary, basic, and advanced. I had 1,800 hours when I went in. By the time the WASPs came along, we had flown for a year. I don't know what time the WAFs had because Cochran came back and started the school. She began taking in private pilots who had to have at least 35 hours. Then she would bring them up to training on heavier aircraft.

Did the WAFs feel anger or resentment at any stage?

No, no, no, they were welcomed. They knew they were needed. There was never any jealousy or resentment.

Tell me about the early WAFS flying experience. Did you have any forced landings? What was your toughest experience?

Thank you, Lord, I never had any forced landings. I happened to be the first WAF to ferry an airplane from one coast to the other. That was a PT-19. I did a ferry for a movie they were doing, *Ladies Courageous*, with Loretta Young. The part of Nancy Love was played by Young. I'd never flown past Chicago, but for some reason or an other, I got the job of flying this PT open-cockpit airplane. It was in March, and I left Hagerstown, Maryland. At the time, I think it was around 15 or 20 degrees. I flew out to Long Beach, California. It took five days to get there, and we had no radios at the time. All we had was maps. We drew a line and marked off every 10 miles en route. That to me was the most outstanding trip I ever had in my life. It was also when I was the most scared. I never knew where I was going to land at night. That was my most famous trip.

Where was the strangest place you landed? Was there ever a point where you just thought you never were going to find a place to land?

We were building bases everywhere. There was one place I landed, in Pyrot, Texas, and I never heard of such a place. It still makes me laugh. I landed at this field, and they had no place to put me, so they took me to the sheriff's office, and he took me to his home. He had about eight children. He was the sheriff, the druggist, the doctor, everything. There were no locks on the doors. It really was one of the highlights of my whole life. That's all I can tell you. We never knew where we were going to stay at night, never.

When I got back to Long Beach, they had camouflaged everything. When I say camouflaged, I mean the buildings, the roads—everything. Everything looked like those crazy camouflaged outfits. I was looking for a Lockheed Aircraft in Long Beach, California. I pinpointed it according to my time. I finally found Long Beach and the building for Lockheed. It looked like a landing field, but when I started to approach it, I found out that it was the roof of Lockheed Aircraft. Then I saw the runway. That's how well camouflaged it was. It was funny, but not at the time. It was one of my crazy moments. I made it down okay. It took me five days to get there, but I got there.

Did you have any other adversity along the way?

I stayed at March Field that night and had never seen an orange tree before. Now this was crazy. You're dragging stuff up out of my memory now. I will never forget the canyons, the mountains that I had never seen before. I was amazed. There was a big difference flying from East Coast to West Coast. We couldn't go over 10,000 feet because we had no oxygen. In some places, you had to go through passes. They were really hairy. I'd never seen anything like that, especially going through Colorado.

Did you get any strange reactions when you landed, being a female?

Oh, boy, did I ever. First of all, they couldn't believe a female would be flying a military airplane. I was the first WAF out on the West Coast. Paul Mantz, God rest his soul, was one of the big guns out there in aviation. He did a lot of flying for the movies, and he took me in tow because I was delivering this airplane for a movie. I never did see the movie, as a matter of fact. Paul took me to all the studios. In fact, I got a two-week leave. I had to call the base in Wilmington, Delaware, to talk to my CO. I got a pass for two weeks. I met Bob Hope and many, many movie stars out there. Oh, I tell you, the uniform made a hit, not me. It was the uniform and the fact that I flew. It had nothing to do with me. You know how that goes.

Do you have a favorite celebrity story?

I attended a lot of parties. My big thrill was going to Coconut Grove where they had, at that time, all the big bands. The girls out there were hosting the men who were going overseas. Every night was a party night at the Coconut Grove. Being from the East, I had never heard of all this stuff. Benny Goodman was playing there that night and I was a celebrity. From the air, I went on different programs. I went to all the studios. Bob Hope took me every place. I don't know how many movie stars I met. Gary Cooper was one of my favorites and Ingrid Bergman, too. I wanted to meet Bing Crosby, but I never did. I met everybody but Bing. Boy, they wined and dined me. The PR man took me to the Beverly Hills Hotel. There, the manager of the hotel took me up to his suite and said, "You must rest now, and we're going to give you, rent free, the bungalow that the wife of the owner of the Palmer House in Chicago is vacating." I don't know how familiar you are with hotels out there in Hollywood, but the prices were sky high. It was there that I met Spencer Tracy. Oh, I've got a lot of stories.

Did any of the stars take a liking to you, romantically?

Romance? Me? No. I was extremely careful. And being a Catholic, I really kept my head on my shoulders. You could easily get carried away out there if you listened to all the stuff they poured into your head. You know, how gorgeous you were, and you were a flyer, and blah, blah, blah. Air Force, airplanes— it was really something else. I met so many movie stars. Gary Cooper, God bless him. He was the shyest person I ever met in my life. He was really interested in flying. He would look down and shuffle his foot. Then he'd say, "Oh, shucks," and look up. It was just like he did in the movies. For some stars, their beauty didn't show up on the screen. Take Lena Horn. She was gorgeous in *Cabin in the Sky*. On the screen, she doesn't look as pretty as she does in person. Everyone thought I was something else! I was flying in an airplane. I was a woman flying in an airplane.

Were you sorry to leave?

Oh, was I ever! I went to see my husband, George Martin, who was in Santa Maria at that time. He couldn't get off base, so I had to go from Long Beach up to Santa Maria. They let them off base for one night. It was really disappointing after going all that distance to see him. He was a B-17 pilot, and he was getting ready to go overseas. I never got too much information from him about his flying exploits. He would say that things were getting heated up, and that he had to wear a flack suit every day. He was worried about me flying, especially when I got into P-47s. He said, "Make sure you check everything." He was extremely worried about me, and I was extremely worried about him in a B-17. I met his crew in Roswell, New Mexico, before he went over.

After I met his crew, he didn't have to go overseas. He was

an instructor pilot at Roswell, New Mexico. He volunteered to make up the thirteenth crew member or something like that. Later, an article with a photo appeared in a New York paper. It had this caption: "American airmen captured by Nazis." It looked like his crew, a side view of three members of his crew. That's the reason I thought that Dink had been captured. Later, I got word that he was missing in action. I figured that maybe he was a prisoner of war all those years. I got letters, supposedly about what happened to him. His airplane went into a spin, then came out of the spin. Then it went back into a spin and back out. He was buried in France. People thought he was in St. Louis. It was the kind of thing that never was verified. In wars, a lot of things cannot be verified after the loss of millions of people.

In 1984, I went to France. I belong to the P-47 Pilots Organization, and we were having a reunion over there. This chap from France told me that he had called one of the heads of the veteran's organizations over there because there was a plane that landed in Cheon de la Pone. The plane landed on a narrow street, and this guy had kept a plaque on the fence outside his home bearing the name of Martin, Lt. George Martin. He was honored and remembered all these years.

I met with the mayor of Cheon de la Pone. I shall relate the story as I heard it. Apparently, there was an air raid. Sirens were going off. A man and his two sons ran into their garage. The children were young at this time, and it seems that my husband George had landed the airplane on that very street. The children had pieces of the airplane that they had saved all those years, including part of the landing gear.

I met the lady that lived in the house where the wing of my husband's airplane hit. She was in her 80s. I saw the plaque on the iron fence gate that read, "In memory of Lt. George L. Martin and crew." I am not sure how long it had been there. I met the two sons who, with their father, had run into the garage prior to the crash. The sons were in their 50s, and the father had died. The father had a coin, supposedly from my husband's pocket, which he kept as a talisman. After he died, the children kept it. They presented it to me in a blue velvet box. Now I have it.

How did that make you feel?

Oh, God. Listen. That was one of the saddest moments of my life. On Mother's Day, no less, they gave up their time to meet with a woman coming from America whose husband crashed an airplane and saved them apparently from the destruction of a bridge. This I did not find out until that day. I don't know how to explain it. However, apparently, the B-17 that he was flying, alerted the people, who then sounded the alarm. Somehow or other, he diverted the bombs away from the bridge that would have cut them off from civilization. Anyway, they had this reception for me, where they presented me with the coin and the most gorgeous flowers I've ever seen in my life. During all these presentations, I stood up and couldn't say a word. I just stood there and cried. Really, that's exactly what I did. I just stood there and cried because I couldn't believe—it was almost like a movie that was happening. Then the mayor and his wife took me out for dinner. It was the most moving thing that ever happened to me.

You might wonder how, after all these years, do people remember such things? The mayor's wife explained, "In France, nobody ever moves. They all stay in the same place." You know, over here, we move around from city to city. Apparently, the French stay where they've been raised.

It sounds like you were in limbo, not knowing where your husband was.

I had no idea. I still have a letter from this friend of mine, Helen Richie, who was a WAF. She flew in England, and she was the first woman airline pilot that flew for airlines. She flew for Capitol, which later became Eastern. She and Jimmy Doolittle were real good friends. So Helen said to me, "I'll write to Jimmy," because Jimmy Doolittle, at that time, headed the Eighth Air Force. She wrote them to find out what he knew. Jimmy Doolittle said that, according to the information that was given by the pilots who were flying with Dink, he was gone.

How did you meet your husband?

It was really weird. He came to the airport, and he was the nicest guy. He invited me to his mother's house. His mother was from Hungary, but at that time, I didn't know it. They lived in a big house, and I think they had eight children. I remember this huge kitchen. They had a big long table that was full of food. I walked in the backyard and it was full of flowers. It was the most gorgeous thing I've ever seen. We walked into the house, and there was this table full of nut rolls and all kinds of bread and cheeses. I was so impressed. Everybody in the family was just sitting around chewing the fat. And that's what we did. I said, "Well isn't this nice?" I thought, this is a guy that doesn't even exist in this world today. It was that kind of thing. His family was something to behold. We don't meet families like that any more—so close knit and old-fashioned. That's all I can tell you.

When George enlisted, I was real upset. The FAA director called me and said, "You know, we can get George into the Ferry Command." Now, this is when the war broke out. He said he could probably get him into flying right away in the service command. I said, "Too late." He and his buddy had already gone down and enlisted. At that time, being enlisted meant getting away from the house. It was a big deal. First, he wound up in mechanics school in Louisiana. Then he went through photographic school. Imagine now, this guy is a commercial pilot, and he had to go through aviation cadet school out in California. Back during wartime, things got really fouled up. When he was in Colorado, he and his mom and my sister Betty and I, went out to visit him. That's where we got married, in Colorado Springs. I was a Catholic. He was not. I insisted I was going to get married in the Catholic faith. I was afraid he was going to go overseas. This was right before I went into the WAFS. That was the end of the ballgame.

Did you ever remarry?

No, I didn't. People ask me that. It's because of the picture that was in the paper. I thought he was still a prisoner of war. Plus, the fact that I'd gotten the letters from General Eisenhower and Jimmy Doolittle. What really put the plug in me was, one day after the war, I was in my mother's and dad's flower shop. We've been in the florist business for ninety-eight years in Wilkinsburg, Pennsylvania. A fellow came into the store and asked if Mrs. George Martin was there. My ears perked up because nobody had called me Mrs. George Martin for a thousand years. He told me he was a crewmember on my husband's airplane. He said he was on his way to New York with a friend, and that he'd stop on the way back. I never did hear from the guy again, ever. So that was the reason I thought "Dink" was still alive.

In a way, your loyalty and devotion worked against you.

It did. It really did. But then again, when I think about it, I've been active in a lot of things in life that I normally probably wouldn't have been active in. So, as I reflect now and look back

96

on it, who knows? The thing that is missing is the children, and that is my only regret. But when you think about it, maybe it was the best thing that ever happened. When I look and see a lot of my friends and children going awry, it is very sad. The sixties were quite a time, and parents are bitching about their children today. But what about what happened then? They weren't so easy to raise. It's been a crazy world. What can you say about it? I've lived so long and I reflect. I don't reflect too often. I'm reflecting now, talking to you. You look back and you see this world has changed so much in the past thirty years, it's unreal. It really is.

How old are you now?

Oh, please, the worst thing you can do is ask a woman how old she is, because she's going to lie anyway, right?

Well, lie to me.

I learned to fly back in the thirties. That ought to give you a clue. My favorite stunt was my twenty–six–and–half–turn spin that I used to do in the airplane. I began with only three or four turns and just kept adding them on. I finally got up to twenty-six and a half turns in a spin. I used to ice skate, and I used to dance a lot, and I used to spin. It was like a Spanish dance where you spin, spin, spin. We used to do that when we were younger to see how many turns we could make on the dance floor without getting dizzy. That's where that started, really.

So that's why you think you are better at spinning in airplanes, because of your spinning while dancing?

I really think so because I could really spin around the whole dance floor. Of course, your partner had to do it with you. I hadn't had any fear of it until different pilots told me that it looked like the airplane had flattened out. Instead of the nose being below the horizon on an angle, it would almost flatten out like it was flat, spinning flat.

At one of the air shows, Walter Beech, who made the Beechcraft, said to me, "Teresa, you ought to quit doing it. Someday, you're going to go into a flat spin." And I said, "I've heard that many, many times before." But after he told me that, I quit doing it. I quit doing the twenty-six turn. I backed off. I cut back to ten or twelve spins. It didn't seem to have been flat at all. I felt, "Well, this is crazy. I might as well go back to my twenty-six and half turns." I never got the chance because when I came down, the guy who owned the plane sold it. It was in Wilkinsburg, Pennsylvania. After he sold the airplane, the guy cracked it up and it turned out that one wing was put together with piano wire. I said, "Thank you, God!" You know me; I'm so close to the Lord, though you'd never know it. Maybe that was the reason Walter Beech said I had better quit doing the spins. I was glad then that I had quit.

Barbara Erickson London
"With Airplanes: I Loved Them All"

Barbara Erickson London was born and raised in Seattle, Washington. After high school, she attended the University of Washington and learned to fly at nearby Lake Union as part of the Civilian Pilot Training program (CPT). Half of the people in the CPT program trained at Boeing Field and the other half at Lake Union, where Barbara ended up. She made her solo flight in December of 1939 while holding down a job at Sears Roebuck in the cosmetics department over Christmas vacation.

After CPT, Barbara instructed in the years 1939 and 1940, until the war came, which necessitated a move inland, as she explains in the interview. Later, Nancy Love wrote to her to try out as part of a new group of women pilots. This lead to her becoming a part of history as a pilot for the Women's Auxiliary Ferrying Squadron (WAFS) and Squadron Commander for the 6th Ferry Command. She once flew 8,000 miles in ten days, which included four trips of 2,000 miles. Barbara left the military in December 1944. Commissioned a major in the Air Force in 1948, she stayed in 20 years and retired in 1968.

With her daughter, Artizonne, she founded Barney Frazier Aircraft in Long Beach, California, and a street commemorates her love and support for the city and Long Beach City Airport.

After almost three years in WWII and 20 years in the Air Force, the government still could not pull all her time together to give her any kind of retirement. "I donated that to the government," she says. Her husband, Jack, died at 59, so he received no pension because he did not live to be 60. She says, "Last year they passed a law called the 'Forgotten Widows.' I found out by accident. I was complaining that after 23 years in the military, I was not on active duty enough to get a commissary card." Barbara received $130 per month. Still, despite the setbacks, Barbara was strong, resilient, and philosophical about her contributions.

Barbara Erickson London died at the age of 93, July 7, 2013.

Was it hard to go back to work after you soloed?

I do remember that it was pretty exciting. By then you have shot so many landings that you figure that you know how to do it. You do get rather excited when they finally let you go the first time. I called my mother, because I did not tell her I was going to solo until after I soloed. When I finally received my license, she was the first one I took for a ride.

My mother figured I was going to fly, but I figured it would be easier on her if I did it and then told her. My folks were very, very supportive. When I signed up for the CPT program, as long as I did what I was supposed to do like go to school and do my school work, this was extracurricular, and I could do it. I really wanted to do this. They had no fear and neither did I.

I was never exposed to an airplane before CPT. I did not know anything about what it was like. When the advertisement appeared in the paper that the program was going to be given at the University of Washington, another gal friend and I thought it sounded like it would be real fun to fly.

We went down and applied and took the physical. I got in, and she didn't because she was too short. She was a tiny little thing, just barely five feet. At that point, there really was no written rule, but they turned her down because she was too short. I was very, very sad because she was so enthusiastic about it. There have been two or three other girls through that period that didn't make it, and I felt very sorry for them. They should have made it. They would have made very good pilots.

The girl that went with me to apply had flown, but when she went to take the physical, they found some problem with one of her ribs. The rib was either cross ways, backwards, or missing or something stupid. It was the equivalent of not being able to go in the Army because of flat feet. It doesn't keep you from shooting a gun but it detours you from walking.

Although she did not make it, all of my life, and to this very day, she's kept right up with me just as if she was one. She kept up with the program. She knew what we were doing. I've always corresponded with her. I'm still a good friend after 55 years. Her name is Dorothy.

It was Caruthers then, but is Fields now. She would have made a fantastic pilot. She was a pilot. It is one of those quirks that should not have happened. They ended up with four girls out of 40 boys. We were allowed one girl for every 10 boys.

What were the seaplanes like that you flew?

We were flying Taylorcraft, which were little 65 horsepower, side-by-side planes on floats, out of Lake Union. We just brought them up on to a ramp off the water and then they towed them into a hangar.

I finally got my license and came back to the same flight school and started instructing in the same program. I eventually branched out from teaching just CPT students to some civilian students. In fact, the press came out and took a picture of my first civilian student and me. We were pictured in the cockpit of this airplane. A few days later, the police came out to the flight school. They told me that they had just arrested my student.

As it turns out, his picture was on a "Wanted" poster in every post office in the state of Washington for some sort of larceny. The police put the two together when they saw the picture. In my scrapbook, I've still got this "Wanted" picture that I got from the post office. I never flew with him again because they put him in jail. I still can't believe that he had his picture taken. He was smiling and happy, and the next morning the police had him in the "cooler."

You should have gotten a reward.

His picture was my reward. He was a nice guy.

Any people have it against females?

I did not have very many problems. When the war got going, all of the civilian flying stopped on the West Coast. Our flight school had to move from Seattle, inland, so Mr. Kurtzer moved into Yakima. We all had to go inland from both coasts because there was no civilian flying allowed on the coasts.

This was January, and it was the last of my senior year, so I did not go with Kurtzer. I stayed and finished school, but in June, I was ready to go back to flight school, but Kurtzer needed no instructor. As a consequence, I ended up in Walla Walla at another flight school. There was a little bit of feeling there about this 20-year-old girl coming to instruct. Several men instructors—airport hanger on 'ers, older guys—were not sure if I would fit in. Eventually, they settled back and decided I was doing the same job they were. They were particularly happy because I took the 5:00 a.m. morning shift, which they did not want. I worked from 5:00 a.m. until noon.

There was a bit of a feeling against a young girl coming in, particularly when I was teaching a class of older guys and eventually boys that were in the Navy getting ready to become Navy pilots.

Was there one Navy pilot who stood out?

I've kept track of a couple of them. Several of the Navy boys did become fighter pilots in the South Pacific. When I went back to Seattle in 1994, I got an award at the Air and Space Museum. This one boy, Terry Dalton, who was in my first class, and whom I had not seen since he was a student, came out and had dinner with me. He became a Marine pilot during the war and served in the South Pacific. He was a couple of years younger than I. The boys were 18, and I was 20.

When I graduated that first class of five boys, they took me out to dinner at the Olympic Hotel in Seattle. We had a neat time. I got along well with all of them. They went on from there into the Navy, and then they started regular Navy basic training. The Navy was trying to give them their original 35 hours, which at that time was a private license. It was called NTS (Navy Training Service), which kind of followed behind CPT.

So you were an early bird?

Yes. When I was at Walla Walla, we started at dawn, and in the summer, that means 5:00 a.m. I lived in a boarding house with a family because I was away from home. The girl who worked in the office would pick me up, and we would hit the doughnut shop because they were just making the early morning doughnuts. Then we would head for the airport because my first student was at 6:00. It was early hours, but flying is always done early in the morning.

Ever had a forced landing?

Never. Thank the good Lord. I have gone almost 60 years of flying without a real emergency. And I flew almost every day. I was being watched over. There was no question about that. A lot of people who were a lot more confident than I am had problems.

Tell me about becoming a flier.

I was one of the original WAFS. Both Nancy Love and Jackie Cochran knew that there was a very great possibility that, if the war got critical enough, there were women pilots out there that could do the same job, at least domestically, and release the men for combat. Both of them were working on a program. General Hap Arnold had told Jackie that nothing was going to happen right away, so she took a bunch of girls and went to England with the ATA. I applied for that program and was accepted. I was ready to go to Toronto to take my flight check. All my paperwork had worked out. I was the right age, I had enough time. Also, I'd gone to high school. I was ready to go to Toronto to take a flight check when Nancy Love had convinced the ATC division that they should try a test group of women for the Army Air Corps. I got a letter from Nancy stating that if I had the following requirements and was interested and willing to come to Wilmington, I could try out to be in this experimental group of women pilots to fly for the Army.

I went to my boss, Herman Martin with Martin Flying Service, and told him I had a chance to fly for the Army. He said, "Go on kid, you've got a wonderful opportunity. Pack up and go. I'll write you any letter you need." He was a neat guy.

Actually, Herman could have made me stay. I was working for a government contract school, and he could have held me to that contract. Many of the girls who did not make the original WAFS group as I did, were unable to because their employers would not let them go. Any number of girls ended up in the third, fourth and fifth classes that were just as qualified as I was, but they were working for a contract school, and the contractor would not let them off.

I packed and drove back to Seattle and packed up everything. The girl who was working in the flight school as a secretary, Eleanor Dressem, decided it would be fun if she went too, so as the train went through Spokane, she climbed on and joined me in the upper berth. She was hoping to find a job in Wilmington too. As it turned out, Nancy Love had lost her secretary about the same time we arrived, so Eleanor ended up getting a job as Nancy's secretary.

We got to Wilmington, and then we took a taxi to the base. It was midnight and pouring down rain. The guard at the gate said that there was a BOQ 14, where the girls were housed. He took us to the BOQ. A housemother showed us two rooms and said, "Go to bed, and we'll check in with Nancy in the morning." So there we were on these iron cots with nothing but a three-drawer chest and a window with a big black curtain over it because we had blackouts during that time. We were 3,000 miles away from home with not 20 bucks between us, without jobs, wondering what we were doing there.

As it turned out, the next morning, I had them check my logbooks. I took a physical. Next, I took a flight check and was accepted, and within a week, Eleanor was hired as Nancy's secretary and we both had jobs.

Eventually, Nancy got someone else to replace Eleanor. Eleanor became my secretary for the rest of the war when I was in Long Beach. She stayed with me until the end of the war.

Barbara Erickson London receives Air Medal for
Meritorious Achievemnet as Pilot.

Did the fact that you were a pilot ever surprise any of
the men?

We all have experiences where we got out of an airplane and no one would believe we were girls. I remember taking an A-26 someplace and calling in and telling the tower I was on "downwind." The man in the tower said, "Well, we don't have you in sight, but we have an A-26 downwind, just follow it in." They would not believe that a girl's voice was coming from an A-26.

A lot of times you would climb out of a fighter and the guys would kind of gawk at you. The only time you ran across anybody that was jealous was when some guy was in an AT-6 and I was in a P-51.

Any specifics?

Everyone must work up the ladder. We started with Cubs, and went to Fairchild PT-19s and went to BTs, and AT-6s, and then BC-3s, and then B-25s, and then fighters. We worked our way up just like the guys. But if you are up in the fighter class flying P-51s and run across somebody that is still back down in the BT class, he might look at you and wonder why you were where you were, and he was where he was.

Did you ever verbally spar with any men?

They did not give us any trouble. We were all doing the same thing and we were all so busy. The average girl probably did not spend five days a month on the base. She was on a trip all the time. In the five months I spent in Wilmington, before I was transferred to Long Beach, I was probably on base a total of twelve days. It was hard to build up permanent lasting relationships. You could not make a date because you never knew if you would be there or not. Everybody was in and out. Just as fast as you were in, you were out again.

We were in a new location every night. Everybody was good to us. We stayed at military bases. We ate well. Though we did not get paid an awful lot, it was enough then. We got paid

$250 a month, and $5.00 per day per diem. How in the world did anybody live on $5.00 a day? That's what the men got. That's what we got. Besides, we stayed in military facilities most of the time. Ninety percent of the time, you landed and refueled at a military base where your billeting was free. Your mess hall was free, and the Officer's Club was inexpensive.

A favorite Jacqueline Cochran story?

I'm not really a Jackie fan. I was in long before Jackie was in the picture. She was still in England while I was ferrying airplanes. I didn't go to Sweetwater. I didn't go through her training school. I'm not one of the Jackie girls. She started a program, and she allowed a lot of girls to learn how to fly who hadn't flown before. It allowed them to serve their country. This was very admirable. Those girls all thank her for the opportunity that they had. But she did not start the program. She came in after we were already a functioning organization and started a training program. All of her trainees came back to Nancy and the Ferry Command. We were under Nancy's command for the first year.

Everybody that graduated from Jackie's school was a WAF up until August of 1943. She soon ran out of girls who had the requirements to get in. Our requirements were that we had to have a minimum of 500 hours. They had to have a 240-horsepower rating, which was the highest horsepower rating you could hold at the time, as well as a commercial license. There were only about 100 women in the United States that had those qualifications, and Nancy knew that when she started.

Jackie came in with the idea that every girl in the world could be trained to be a military pilot. She ran out of those experienced 100 very fast, so the requirements were dropped to 18-years-old and 35 hours. When the women graduated from the school in

108

Sweetwater, Texas, they didn't have the required time that the Ferry Command demanded to be a Ferry pilot.

Jackie had to find other places to put them. That's when they started putting them in the Training Command. They put them in to do test flights on airplanes and to do all these other various jobs around the country. In August of 1943, our name was changed to WASP which covered all of the various women's activities. Jackie was put in charge of all of that, and Nancy Love remained head of all those 300 that were left in the Ferry Command.

Nancy and Betty Gillies wanted to fly across the Pacific in a B-17, but were stopped. It is probably the most heartbreaking story because they had checked out in the B-17 and they were ready to go. The two had gotten the airplane up through Maine and were ready to "jump" across the ocean when General Arnold found out and stopped it. Nancy and Betty had to leave the airplane and let a guy take it across. They came home.

The women were very brokenhearted because it was a trip they really wanted to make. They had trained very hard for it. But, being civilians, we really were rather restricted to the United States.

This didn't occur because you were women?

I think Jackie found out and stopped it. Nobody really knows.

Was it politics?

It was all politics.

What about the end of the war?

Once the war was winding down, there were a lot of jobs

that the girls could have given up, but we did not want to give up the Ferry Command jobs. Every one of the girls in the Ferry Command was a fighter pilot. We had to be to stay in. The war was badly in need of those airplanes, so badly in need that we never got a break.

The Ferry Command pressured General Arnold very hard that if they disbanded the WAFS to at least leave the Ferry Command alone because they were trained and badly needed. But Jackie was not about to let Nancy's girls stay in and watch all of her own girls go home, so the mandate came down that we were all to go home. That was really sad.

The morning I left Long Beach, on the 20th of December, 1944, there were 60-some fighters sitting at Long Beach Airport that did not get delivered that day because we all went home. The boys that were doing the complaining about the women were Stearman pilots from the training school. In fact, the military had to go out to other commands, to fighter schools, to get boys that were checked out in our airplanes. Certainly, the government didn't fill our shoes that day. The boys could be trained to do what we did and checked out in it eventually, but we were already there and doing it.

It was sad that we had to go home, particularly those fliers that were crucial, and anybody who could fly a fighter at that point was crucial. At the time, some of the factories were building one and two planes a day. We had Lockheed, North American, Northrup, Convair, Boeing, Douglas, all of the big companies sitting right here in the LA basin pumping out airplanes. The planes were badly needed. We all volunteered to stay for nothing. What the military was paying us was not a dent in the debt anyway. Instead, we were sent home six to eight months before the war was over. We had to go home and sit on the sidelines.

It drives you nuts. I went home. I did not want to go back

to school because I was training to become a home economics, school teacher. That was about as wrong as anything could possibly be, but I did not want to go back to the department store and work. I stayed home a couple of months and my folks sent me back to California because I got a job at Ryan on a test program for one of their airplanes. When I returned to California, I came back through Long Beach and met my boyfriend there. I decided to get married instead. I just stayed in Long Beach.

What was your favorite plane?

I loved them all. When the government gives you a million dollar plane every morning, that is something! The planes all flew alike, whether a P-51 or a P-38. They were wonderful. I liked the A-26, a Douglas airplane. It was very maneuverable and was easy to fly. The P-51 had a nice small, compact cockpit. The A-26 was a real speeder. Very few girls got to fly it, because it was towards the end of the war when it came out.

Did you ever buzz anyone?

No, my halo was on too tight. I was very conscious of doing what I was supposed to do, right.

Never broke a regulation?

Never.

Were you tempted?

I danced around through the clouds, one billowy cloud to another, but never came close to another airplane and never came at all close to the ground either.

Explain "danced through the clouds."

There are big billowy, puffy clouds up there, and the only way you can tell how fast you are going is to race pretty close to a cloud. When it is standing still and you go by it so fast, it makes you realize how fast you are going. We were going 400 to 500 miles per hour. That was pretty fast back then.

What does flight mean to you?

I'm pretty down to earth. It is a mode of transportation. It is freedom and ability to get up above and out of everything. That's why it was fun to fly alone. That's why fighters were fun because you were in that airplane all by yourself on up there with the clouds, the sun and the rain. You had to make the decisions. You went places you had never been before. It was a freedom that you don't get any other way.

After the war, a few of us formed a small company in Long Beach called United States Aviation. It was a multifaceted business with a flight school, an insurance department, and a parts department. In fact, we were so multifaceted, we multifaceted ourselves right out of business. The company lasted about five years. Then we all went our separate ways.

Later, I worked for the Powder Puff Derby as Executive Secretary and flew in that for 20-some years. I instructed. I worked for a flight school. I went into sales working for Piper in 1966 and have been in the sales business ever since.

The Powder Puff Derby was one of the best training grounds there was for women pilots. There was nothing you could do that gave you better training than flying under the controlled conditions of flying across the United States, making eight to ten stops under supervision. It was a terrific way to get experience for cross-country flying, under conditions that were well managed. It gave hundreds and hundreds of girls very, very excellent training in planning, weather, and self-reliance.

Was one race more adventuresome?

The longest race was from Seattle to Clearwater, Florida. My daughter and I were flying a little Cessna 172 and were at the last stop before Clearwater. We got up in the morning and it was foggy. We finally got off through the fog, but we were running on a deadline. We had a choice of putting full power to it and running out of gas or pulling back and not making it by the noon deadline. Considering the swamps below us had alligators, we realized that we had to make up our mind whether we should try to get there on time and possibly run out of gas, or whether we throttle back, saved our fuel, miss the deadline and not finish.

We decided to go for it. We arrived at 12:10 p.m., just about out of fuel. It was a hair-raising trip because those Florida swamps are not very inviting. I did not want to go down in a swamp and be eaten. The native would say that the bugs would get you hours before the alligators.

Talk about your daughter, Terry, who flies professionally.

Terry is the older one. She always had a leaning towards flying. Very early on, she made up her mind that she would like to be an airline pilot. Earlier, I applied for the airlines when I got out of the service in 1944. (I think of all the airlines I applied for, two of them sent me back applications for a stewardess.)

They were not ready for women. My daughter, Terry, soloed

on her 16th birthday and got her license on her 17th birthday. Then she spent the next 10 years getting background enough to be eligible to be an airline pilot. She worked in flight schools. She instructed. She got her college degree. She got her 727 rating. She got her helicopter rating. She got several scholarships. She worked at it night and day. By the time she was 27, she was as qualified as the men who were being hired. She started applying to the airlines. Her approach was that, one of these days, you are going to have to hire a girl: best you look at my application and be ready because I am. When you have to make the choice, I'm here. She applied for every airline and upgraded her resume every 30 days to every airline. In 1974, the break came. She got a call from both American and Western. At that point, there were probably only about 10 women pilots with the airlines. Western (now Delta) hired her. She has been there 24 years.

I was proud of her. It was not easy. She worked in a flight school every night through four years of high school and four years of college to get her flight time. Nowadays, the average girl that goes to the airlines is from the military. They learn to fly in the military, and they are ready for the airlines.

Did you see yourself in Terry?

She had the same determination to do it and do it right. The reaction of some of the captains when she got hired was, "There's not going to be any GD woman in my cockpit." They eventually got over it, but she had lots of rough times.

Some captains would leave cartoons in the cockpit and make all sorts of remarks. Some of the captains would not speak to her. It was tough for the first few girls. It was hard to be accepted. She always said, "The only difference between a guy and me is our plumbing, and the airplane can't tell." It seems to me the only thing they never solved during the war and never have solved to this day is a relief tube for women. They can put us on the moon, but they have never solved that problem. (laughs)

How does it feel to be a pioneer?

Pioneers were the people who flew in the 1930s. Betty Gillies, head of the WAFS in Wilmington, got her first airplane in the 1920s. She had an airplane all her life. The girls who flew back in those days were the real pioneers.

You are a pioneer in the sense that you have made a substantial contribution.

I think what my girls did was outstanding. They did contribute a terrific amount to helping the war effort. That's what we were there for. Everybody was very patriotic. It is hard to explain what WWII really was. People know Vietnam and Korea but they don't understand about WWII. Everybody was involved. My mother saved grease. They picked it up once a week. We all were on ration stamps, but nobody complained. Everybody did something. I don't think we will ever see our country and our people as united again in any effort. I waited in line at the commissary to buy things to send home to my folks because I ate better than they did, though they did not complain.

I am proudest of being in the right place at the right time and being able to serve my country. I met some fabulous people that are my friends today. I still correspond with a man who is 91 years old, who gave me my first pilot's license in 1940. He is still alive and lives in Washington state. We still write. His name is Jack Feeny. He was the FAA inspector. He lives alone in Lake Bay, Washington.

I went to give a speech when they had the Battleship *Missouri* in Bremerton, Washington. I spoke to 10,000 people from the bridge of that ship. On that trip, we stopped by and saw Jack. Up until two years ago, he was still able to pass his physical. Now he doesn't fly. The FAA takes a dim view of us 80-year-olds flying. They'd rather we fly with someone.

When they stopped flying in January of 1942, I stayed in Seattle and went to work at Boeing. Why, I'll never know. I was going to school full-time. The same girl that eventually did not get in the WAFS because she was too short also worked at Boeing. We worked the swing shift. We went to school in the morning and then to work at five until midnight. The man who was my supervisor, Buren Reader, and I became very good friends. In fact, I kept track of him for almost 50 years. At Boeing, I worked on the wings of the B-17. I wasn't "Rosie the Riveter," because I didn't handle a rivet gun.

I remember when I had first been checked out on the B-17, I wrote Buren a letter and said, "Well, I finally made it from the time I was bucking rivets to a pilot of a B-17."

Buren sent me a little article from the Boeing paper about the fact that three former female Boeing employees had been checked out in a B-17. Betty and Nancy were the other two women.

There really was no reason for us to be checked out in B-17s. That was not the push. It was done to show the girls could do it.

What was the greatest compliment that you ever received?

There is not anybody I ever met that I would be afraid to meet today. I don't think I made any permanent enemies, and I didn't hurt anyone. I had a TV appearance on an "American Experience," which showed several years ago. We jokingly say that, as years go on and all the girls keep dying, our stories can get better and better because there are fewer and fewer to tell anyone that they are wrong. There are not too many of us left. Right now, of the original twenty-five, only nine are still alive. That is sad.

These girls came in and did their job. After the war, they returned to the same places they came from before the war. For example, I had a girl that was a buyer for Bullocks. She was an excellent pilot. The day the war was over, she was back to Bullocks and never flew again. In fact, ninety percent of the girls never flew again. Ninety percent of the boys never flew again. My brother-in-law, Charlie London, was the first American Ace in England in P-47s. He came back home and never flew again.

What would you be in your next life?

I have mixed emotions. Would I want to come back in the 1920s when they were doing barnstorming, or come back now as an eighteen-year-old, when the girls are flying the wonderful things they are flying, including the Shuttle. Then there are the girls flying all these new military planes. I am torn.

Just a few years ago, I knew a kid who had a tail-dragger airplane. He was going to sell it so he advertised it. A guy came to look at it, and he brought a girl. The guy liked the looks of the airplane and said he was going to buy it. "I'm going to teach my girlfriend how to fly," he said. The kid said, "You're not going to let a girl fly a tail-wheeled airplane like that? She'll wreck it." I said, "Where do you think I learned? They hadn't invented the nose wheel when I learned to fly."

Violet Cowden
"With the Women Airforce Service Pilots"

Violet Thurn Cowden saw a hawk and wanted to fly. Fly she did, as member of the pioneering WASPs, doing the important task of ferrying planes during WWII. It was work such as hers that freed up other pilots to fly in the many theaters of the war. Violet speaks to the pride and pain felt by the women who sought to fly in that time.

Violet was born in a sod house on a farm in Bowdle, South Dakota, on October 1, 1916. She attended Spearfish Normal School and graduated in 1937. Four years later she received her private pilot's license at the Spearfish Clyde Ice Airport. In

August of 1943, she received her silver wings from Sweetwater Training School, Sweetwater, Texas. She was a member of the class of 1943-44. At Sweetwater and Love Field, Texas, she flew a variety of planes, including the P-51 Mustang, which she described as her "great love."

She is a member of the Aviation Hall of Fame in South Dakota. She has served as WASP organization president and vice president, and represented the Air Force cutting the ribbon for the dedication of the Women Veterans Memorial at Arlington Cemetery in 1997. She is active in Women in Aviation. A city activist, she still manages time to work to save the environment. Married for 44 years, she and husband Scott have one daughter, Kim, and three grandchildren, Ferrin, Kiki and Quinn. An active and engaging speaker, this diminutive veteran spoke loud and compellingly in her soft, slight voice about the dedication and skill of America's female pilots, then and now. Vi was skydiving at 89 and paragliding at 90, the age at which she co-piloted the Collings Foundation P51c.

This sweet and wonderful lady, Violet Cowden, died on April 10, 2011 in Newport Beach, California, at the age of 94.

Were you interested in flying for a long time?

All my life. I was born in a sod house in South Dakota on a farm, and we used to have big hawks that flew, oh maybe one to two thousand feet in the air, and they would spot a little chicken, and they would just dive down on that chicken. I used to think, when I was a little kid, "Oh, if I could only do that. If I could only fly like the birds. If I could only zoom like that hawk did." I just knew that was something I wanted to do. It was like a kid's fantasy that became a reality.

Did you tell anybody? Were you outspoken?

I always said I wanted to fly with the birds.

You didn't want to be a predator and fly after chickens?

Absolutely not. It was like something that you say, and something that you do, and you dream about it. This fantasy that I just gave you became a reality. When we were in training, everyday we went out without the instructor, he would tell us that we had to practice on what we had to do (shoot landings and do chandelles). One day he said, "You can go up and just do anything you want to do." I went up. The Texas landscape is rather boring. I was flying around doing chandelles, lazy eights, and practicing landing. I saw a chicken yard. I zoomed down on that chicken yard and chased those little old chickens. Feathers were hitting the fence. I thought to myself, you know, I always wanted to do that, and here I had the opportunity. I think that proves that if you have something in your mind that is strong enough, eventually, it will become a reality.

Did anyone try to dissuade you from flying?

I used to tell my mom that I was going to fly, and she would say, "Oh no, you wouldn't do that." She didn't say, "You shouldn't do that." She just said, "You wouldn't do that." It was always in the back of my mind that I would fly. One day, I was out at the airport. I was watching my girlfriend's boyfriend shoot landings and I looked over at her and said, "You know, I'm going to fly." She said, "You're kidding." I said, "No!" So I went up to Clyde Ice, who was running the airport, and I said, "Clyde, I wanna learn to fly." He said, "Come on, I think you'll make a damn good pilot. Let's go." It felt natural. I just felt so natural it wasn't even funny. I don't know how old he would have been.

I thought he was an old man.

Clyde Ice must have been in his sixties?

Maybe not that old. He lived to be 103. I thought he was old. I remember what he said about flying. He showed me a few things and he said, "But you have to fly by the seat of your pants." Then he shot a couple of landings. The runway was evidently a gravel runway. He said, "If you can distinguish each stone, you better be down!" He was an excellent pilot. I learned to fly in the Black Hills of South Dakota in Spearfish Canyon. The cliffs run pretty close together. When we'd fly through there, he would turn the airplane sideways and we'd just breeze right on through.

He did not kid while we were in the air. It was a serious business up in the air. On the ground, he was very friendly.

Do you remember anything he told you?

No, the only thing that stuck in my memory was the "damn good pilot" comment. He was very busy. He was training many pilots at that time. That was 1940-41. I had my private license by the time war was declared on December 7, 1941.

Do you remember your solo flight?

Oh, yes! You are not supposed to know the day that you solo in advance, because if you knew when, you would probably be nervous. The instructor pretty well knows that maybe the next time you come out that you will be soloing. One day when I went out to the airport, they were playing on the airport PA system, "I'll Never Smile Again" and "I'll Walk Alone." I said to Clyde, "I'm gonna solo today." And he said, "What makes you think so?" I said, "Did you hear those songs they're playing?" Anyway, we went out and we shot a couple of landings. They kind of know that you are either on or off. Some days you have off days and could not make a good landing. He said, "Now, I'm going to get out." He weighed about 150 or 160 pounds. He said, "It's gonna go up real fast. You'll also notice that when you come down, and you will need to correct for that because it will take you longer to get down."

His son, Cecil, and I were stationed in Dallas, Texas. At that time, both his son and I were flying 51s. Clyde came down to see his son. I got to see him then. He said, "Boy, I really envy you. I taught you to fly, and look what you're flying when I'm still flying small planes." I didn't see him after that for maybe 50 years, and we had a reunion in Reno during an air show. Clyde was 100 years old and the airshow was honoring him. They would drive him around the stadium in a convertible giving his stats (how many flying hours he had without an accident).

In the mornings, at about 7:30, we'd have breakfast and we'd chat maybe for about an hour and a half because we had a lot of people that we both knew. We had a lot to talk about, namely what had happened in our lives within the last 50 years. In the evening, he'd come back, and be playing blackjack without glasses. He was absolutely an amazing man. I said to his son there, "You know, he really hasn't changed that much." Clyde had his arm around me at the time. His son said, "You know why?" I said, "No." Clyde said, "I never lost interest in women."And he didn't.

Which son was this?

It was his son named Howard. His other son, as I mentioned, was Cecil. He runs an airport in Pierre, South Dakota, and does crop dusting. When my mom was still living in South Dakota, I would go back quite often. I'd be landing at Pierre. I would always stop to see Cecil. Howard's wife, Jane, was my sorority sister when we attended Spearfish Normal School. I also taught there. Howard was the pilot for the governor of South Dakota for many years.

Did you choke up when you saw old Clyde?

It was like no time had passed. It was like yesterday, and then you see him today.

That's the feeling old friends experience when they meet.

Yes, it was just so natural. It was just like yesterday I saw him and then I saw him today, like no time had passed at all in our lives.

Any unusual things happen during training?

When I give my presentations to the different organizations, like women's clubs, schools, or whatever, I tell them that when you have a dream and you want to follow your dream, sometimes it doesn't come easy. When I took my physical, when I got my call, I took my physical and didn't pass my physical because I didn't weigh enough. I weighed 92 pounds, and I was supposed to weigh 100. I told the doctor, "Give me a week and I'll gain the weight." He gave me a week, and during that week I ate like crazy. I had heard that you were supposed to drink water and eat bananas to gain weight, so I did that. On the day that I was supposed to take my physical, I drank an awful lot of water and I ate a lot of bananas and I weighed 100 pounds. When I went there, I got on the scale, and he said, "By God, you've made it. How did you do it?" I said, "Look!" My stomach was extended like I was about five to six months pregnant. He said, "That is the funniest thing I've ever seen. Do you mind if I call another doctor?" I said, "No, not not until you sign this paper that I passed my physical."

You strike a tough bargain.

Also, when this woman whose husband was the movie producer, not Hal Roach, but somebody like that, wanted me to go for an interview, she asked about my past experiences. She said, "How badly do you want to get into this program?" I said, "I really want to learn to fly the Army way. You know, if you ask me to scrub this house with a toothbrush, I would do it." She said, "You're in." When I got my orders to report to Sweetwater, they said there would be transportation at the airport. When I got there with a little suitcase, to this sordid Texas town of Sweetwater, there was a cattle truck pickup with two benches in the back. Two Army fellows from Sweetwater had arrived to pick me up. Being the girl, I was always having somebody open the door and being real nice to me. I just figured one of the guys would ride in the back and I would ride in the front with the driver.

That didn't happen. They got in front, and I crawled in the back with my little suitcase and bounced all the way to Sweetwater. When I saw the PT-19 flying over, it looked big compared to a Cub and I thought, "No way will I be able to cut the mustard here." I realized at that moment that I was in a different field. I was going to be competing against men and I would have to hold my own. There was nobody going to open the door for me. It was up to me to do it. It was a rude awakening. Then, to sleep in the barracks with six women and share a common bathroom that had four shower-heads, with an additional six women in an adjoining barracks, I didn't think I was going to survive. A little cot with wire springs and a little thin mattress, a place to hang clothes, that was maybe not even two-feet wide, with desks in the middle and a waste basket. That was it.

Did you have any run-ins with roommates?

No. My focus was not to socialize. I didn't really make too many close friends. I studied like crazy. I held my own. I did everything I was supposed to do in the barracks. If it came time to clean up, I probably did more than my share. I was motivated to do the right thing. I had about 70 hours and a private pilot's license. I found out that some of these gals came in there with thousands of hours. I thought I would wash out competing against all this. I guess I had the desire to do a real good job, the best I could. Every day that I was in the program, I thought I've had another day to fly. When I found out that some of these girls that had many hours washed out, I really didn't think I'd make it.

Do you remember any instance when someone washed out and you consoled her?

No, in my barracks, no one washed out. Some people can't take check rides and they can't take tests. They just go to pieces almost. This friend of mine and I were in the same flight. There were usually four girls to a flight with one instructor. She just was beside herself. I had a check ride and came back. I said, "You know, it really isn't that bad." I just went up, and I told her I shot a couple of landings and I did this and I did that and I said, "Really, there was nothing hard. It was easy." The check pilot evidently overheard me. He said, "You didn't think that was hard?" I had a check ride every day for a week. It was hard.

He punished you for that?

He sure did, and to the point that I couldn't eat or even hold water in my stomach. He never told me whether I made it or not. You get three pink slips and you're out. I never knew whether I had a pink slip or not that whole time. Maybe I didn't have a pink slip. I don't know. I come from a German background, and my mom knew it all from the very beginning. She would say, "I don't think you can do that." I intended to show her that I could do it. I think it is that kind of a determination I have that pulled me through. Well, if I have a check flight, I'll show him that I can do it.

What was the greatest compliment you received about your flying?

I can't think of any one incident. Usually, when you have a check ride, they didn't say anything. That was the part that was the toughest. I know that some of the girls had instructors who said, "Yea, that was a good landing or that was a bad landing." My primary instructor was really tough. His name was Pace. I don't remember his first name. We called him "Ace" Pace. He would say, "Whatever gave you the idea that you could fly? That was the lousiest landing I ever had." Then he'd take the stick and whack it back and forth. He'd swear at you. It was really tough, really hard. He liked to fly upside down. Whenever we came in after practicing, he'd fly upside down. I used to keep money in my flight suit for Cokes. He'd fly upside down, and the money would fly out. Once he said, "Boy, are you stupid. Why don't you put your Coke money somewhere else? You're just scattering money over the Texas prairie." I think that, when the girls washed out, they did not wash out because they were

126

not good pilots. I think they washed out because they couldn't put up with the lingo. I found out afterwards that the men had the same lingo, and they used the same lingo on the men. With instructions, almost anybody can fly. But how do you act under pressure? When you have lots of pressure, can you think? Can you do the right thing? I think that's probably what washed out a lot of the girls. They just weren't used to this type of treatment. It wasn't harassment. It was just the way they did it. Of course, at the time, we didn't know that. I found out afterwards.

I guess another experience that probably you might be interested in would be, when I was taking my Pursuit training, we had 10 hours in the back of an AT-6. I was in a flight with three guys and myself. This instructor had never ridden with a woman before. He was always on the controls. He was flying all the time, and he didn't let me fly. Then the guys would say, "Well, how is she doing?" At that time, the men were so supportive. I needed a pillow to reach the rudders and things. Usually, some guy in my flight would save pillows for me. They'd say, "How did she do today?" He would say, "I don't know. I don't think she'll make it." Everyday, they'd ask and he'd say, "I don't know. I really don't think she's gonna make it." Then they'd tell me. This one day, when we came in for a landing, he said, "That was a very poor landing." He critiqued the thing, the angle of the approach and all this. I said, "You know something, I figured I was washing out anyway. That was not my landing." He said, "What do you mean?" I said, "You have been on the stick the whole time. You have not let me fly." The next day, he said he would let me fly. When we came in, one of the guys came up and asked, "How did she do today?" He said, "By God, if you guys could fly like that, I'd be happy." It just took a lot of determination.

On the day we graduated, a fellow came up to me and he said, "I want to thank you for what you did for me." Honestly,

I couldn't remember ever seeing the guy's face before. I said, "What did I do?" He said, "You know, I was so afraid of flying the P-47. Every day I would call in sick. One day I was standing out there watching everybody taxiing by, and you came by in the P-47, and all I saw was the top of your curly head, and I thought, by God, if she can do it, so can I!" I guess you never know when you're out there doing your thing that you are helping someone or influencing someone's life by what you do.

Did you have to fly some clunker planes?

I was in the best place that you could possibly ever be. I was at Love Field, Dallas, Texas. All the planes that we picked up were from the factory. We took them to training bases and to the point of debarkation. The only time we flew war-weary planes was when we were taking our pursuit training. A lot of those planes had been in battles and been misused. Those are the only planes I flew that were in bad shape.

Do you specifically remember a bad one?

No. Every time we picked up a plane at the factory, they were supposed to have been tested for an hour. One day I went out there, and I looked at the ship's papers, and there was no time on it. I went back, and I said, "This plane hasn't been tested." The mechanic went out and he got the ship's papers out and he wrote down "ONE HOUR TESTED." Taking off in that plane that day, I really did not know whether it was going to fly or not because I was the test pilot. You are going 100 miles per hour for take-off in the P-51. It was approaching 100 miles per hour, and I pulled it up, and it flew like a dream. I had such a feeling of wonderment to think that I was the very, very first person that ever flew that plane. It was like in South Dakota when the snow would fall on the ground, and I'd walk and think that no one else has ever stepped on this snow before. That's the way I felt with that airplane. It was wonderful.

Did you ever wonder what happened to your planes, your babies, after you left them?

Oh God, I wondered why I didn't leave a note in the plane just wishing them good luck. It was really like slow timing when you took the plane from the factory to the point of debarkation. It was really slow timing to know whether or not this plane was in good shape. We would have to write up things, like some of them would be a little sluggish on take-off, or we would hear a certain noise in the plane that did not sound quite right. Perhaps the motor wasn't synchronized well. We would write that up. I wish now that I had left my name in there or something. Anyway, I didn't do it. I wish now that I had. It might have encouraged somebody that was going to be flying them in combat.

We would pick up a plane either in Long Beach or Dallas, and we'd fly it to the East Coast and deliver it to Newark, New Jersey. Every evening we would have to send a telegram back to the base so that they would know where all the planes were. Once when I sent my telegram, I said, "Delivered P-51 so and so, Mother and Child doing fine." When I got back to base, this one guy said it was about 4:00 a.m. when he was reading the messages, and he had a good laugh over that. After we delivered our plane, they'd take us up to Buffalo, New York, and we would pick up a P-39 and fly it to Great Falls, Montana. From Great Falls, Montana, a guy would pick it up and take it to Fairbanks. There, the Russian pilot would come over to pick it up. The weather during the winter was really touchy up in that area. One time, I landed in Bismarck, North Dakota, and they had a rain and they had a freeze, and I had never taken a plane off on ice. I asked the operations officer, "Is there anything that I need to know taking off on this ice?" I knew that in a car, you don't put on the brakes because then you start spinning. He said, "Well, about the only advice I can give you is just to pretend the ice is not there." That's the help I had.

Just before Boris Yelsin took over leadership in Russia, about 40 WASPs went to Russia to meet the women Russian pilots. We met a fellow that had flown to Alaska to pick up the P-39s when we were there. The Russian women flew combat. They were called the "Night Witches" because they flew a plane not very much better than a souped-up Cub. They would tie a bomb on the bottom. The men would do the dog fighting during the day, and then the women would fly their sorties. They were 10 miles behind the line, and they would go over and bomb the Germans so they couldn't sleep. Sometimes, they'd do 10 sorties a night. These women were really something. They entertained us royally. The language barrier wasn't even there. When we came, they had flowers for us and hugged us. They cared about their families and their grandchildren and their country. The love of country and the love of flying were apparent. They loved to sing and we loved to sing. It was just great.

We met about 25 of the Night Witches. There are only nine still living. At the WASP Conference in Omaha, in 1998, 220 WASPs were in attendance. A producer from Britain wanted to film 200 women pilots. He shot the scene for a documentary of women pilots.

Give me a sense of when you came along. I assume that you happened to be one of the earlier pilots?

I was in 43-4. When the program started, there was 43-1, 43-2, 43-3, and I was 43-4. I was in the program three months after it started. There were 18 classes in all.

How unusual was it to be a woman pilot when you were first flying?

Jacqueline Cochran did not want publicity concerning the program. We were not supposed to say that we were pilots. Every night when we went into the hotel, we were just part of the group for the simple reason that, had they known that 38 women lost their lives, they would have cancelled the program. We did not say that we were pilots. This one time, I was checking in the hotel, and I had on my flight suit. We had little caps rather like baseball caps. This lady paused and said, "What baseball team do you play on?"

What did you tell her?

I didn't tell her that I was a pilot. Once I had the privilege of meeting General Stilwell when Truman called him back. The CO of the field asked me to be the greeter in the barracks because there were going to be some military women who were going to stay in our barracks that night. Can you imagine some of these society ladies and the Major's and Lt. Colonel's wives staying in the barracks with us? I wanted to go to the dance at the Officer's Club. They didn't come in and they didn't come in. I didn't even know who it was. About 11:00, in came General Stilwell's pilot, co-pilot, and a couple of the military men and their wives. They were to meet their wives there. They came with their black negligées. General Stilwell had no clue that the women were flying. He was so impressed to think that all these

American women were flying. He said, "Tomorrow morning, I want you to sit with us at breakfast. How am I going to get the women out of the barracks?" "Well," I said, "I'll tell you how it works. Guys have certain whistles and certain cat calls. They are outside and the girl inside recognizes the call of the person she is going to meet." He said, "Give me the call that ALL the women will come out."

I cried the day they scattered his ashes over the Pacific. I knew everything that he did. He was such a great guy. He was so real. You meet people like that you bond with right away and other people you don't.

Some other situations where you shed some tears?

I cried when the first girl was killed. Her name was Jean Rawlinson. She was in my class. We went to her service. I can remember, I don't know who said it, but they said, "We're not going to shed a tear for her because she is going to be living in our hearts." No one shed a tear.

No one?

Not one. I didn't think that way, but I think some did think that this could have been me. That didn't cross my mind. It never did. Hazel Ah Ying Lee, a Chinese girl in my class, was killed in a P-39. She and I had the same orders to fly P-39s to Great Falls, Montana. I was several stops behind her. This really bothered me.

What happened?

There were about umpteen people in this flight. There were a few girls. It was just before we were deactivated. I think it was her last orders. We were scattered all over the northern part of the United States because the weather was so bad. One guy was flying knowing that he didn't have a radio. He got a signal to land and then they told her to pull up or something. Anyway, it was because he didn't have a radio and she did. He ran into her because he didn't have the communication. They were both trying to get down.

Did you feel any survivor's guilt?

Yes, I did, mostly because I was on the same flight. We all had the same orders. Her uncle was mayor of Chinatown, New York City. If we delivered into Newark, New Jersey, we would go to Chinatown, and the mayor of Chinatown would treat us royally with Chinese dinners. Oftentimes when we would meet her, she'd cook Chinese dinners for us. Being that she was of a different nationality, I think we kind of looked out after her. She was special.

Were there any other minority fliers in the women's program?

She was the only one that I knew of. There were no blacks.

Do you have any Jacqueline Cochran stories?

I have a couple. She was visiting the base. Our class was the first class of women in Sweetwater. The other three classes were trained in Houston. There were still men cadets on the field. As the classes came in, they phased out the men cadets. We weren't supposed to be with them. We were supposed to pretend they weren't there. On certain nights, we could talk to the cadets at the PX. One time, Jacqueline Cochran was in the office. I was walking down to the PX. There was a cadet standing there and he whistled at me. I gave them a dirty look. They weren't supposed to do that. I didn't know that Jacqueline Cochran was standing at the window. She called me in. "You know," she said, "you're not supposed to be communicating with the cadets." I said, "I didn't. All I did was look at them." She said, "You're not supposed to even look at them." That was my first experience with her. I met her many times after this because she entertained the WASPs out at her ranch in Indio, California. Her bartender was Chuck Yeager. This one time, we were in her living room and we were singing songs and I was standing behind the davenport. I remember she came over and said, "You are so tiny. Had I known that, you would have never been flying."

What did you think?

What I thought in my head was maybe she wished she was that size.

How big was she?

She was not very much bigger than I was. I was, at that time, almost 5'2" and she was maybe about 5'4" maybe 5'5". I doubt if she was more than 5'5". The other time, we were checking in at Reno for a reunion and at that time her husband was quite ill with arthritis. He was bed-ridden for years. She came up in a motor home and had some parking arrangement made with the hotel. My eleven-year-old daughter was with me. I wanted her to meet Jackie Cochran. When Jackie came in, I said, "Kim, I want you to meet Jackie Cochran." Then Jackie turned around and I said, "Jackie, I'd like to have you meet my daughter, Kim."

Was she friendly to Kim?

Yes, she was nice to Kim. Jackie Cochran was a multi-faceted lady. She was wonderful. She was good. One time she flew a planeload of Christmas gifts to some families in Spain. She paid the way back for some of the girls, when they were killed. She bought wings for the first six or seven classes. She paid for them herself. She had whatever it took by way of money, for example. Her husband, Odlum, was considered one of the twelve richest men in the world at that time. She had the money power, plus she had a gift of guts that got her to talk to Hap Arnold and got her into Congress. She knew all these famous movie stars because her husband had Fox studios or something like that at the time. She had an "in" with people, but she also had the ability to get things done. Without her, there never would have been a program.

Do you have a Nancy Love story?

No, I only saw her once. She was then the director of the Ferrying Division. Jackie Cochran was the director of training. She visited Love Field one time. I didn't even talk to her. I saw her at a glance. I knew that she was there checking on how things were going. I was one of these eager beavers. I was so happy to fly. You were supposed to lay over for 24 hours. I never did. I would pick up some orders and clean clothes and be off the next day.

Did it ever get you in trouble?

No, because we worked seven days a week. I could sleep on the airlines where a lot of people couldn't. They would have to take time off. When we had the big push for the Normandy Invasion, they were saying how important it was to deliver as many planes as we possibly could. I never spent one night on the base for two weeks. I was on the road the whole time.

How many planes do you think you delivered?

I don't know. Could check my logbook sometime. I just picked up one plane and flew it. Came back, picked up orders, and picked up another plane, and away we went. I loved it. Let's put it this way. I wasn't doing anything that was hard. I was doing something that I loved.

What did you think when you had to quit?

It was the worst day of my life—one of them. I'll tell you what an eager beaver I was. I didn't even know we were being deactivated. I was so busy flying. I came in on Friday, and we were deactivated on Saturday. People said, "I cannot believe that you did not know." I was just too busy. I never was on base. I didn't hear the scuttlebutt. It was like the end of my life. I thought, "What am I going to do with the rest of my life?" I knew I didn't want to go back to teaching. Can you imagine, after doing what we were doing, then to go back to teaching little kids to read? It didn't appeal to me at all.

Were you in a depressed state for awhile?

Really depressed—I went home and there was nothing to do, so I went to Newark. There were a couple of WASPs living in New York City so I went there. I worked for TWA at the ticket counter for about a year. It just wasn't satisfying.

That must have been frustrating standing at the counter watching the pilots go flying by.

The only interesting thing was that I met Howard Hughes

and many famous people. That, I enjoyed. I worked for TWA, and I don't know who owned TWA before Howard Hughes, but he bought TWA. His flight was from Dallas to New York. That was La Guardia Field at the time. He had Jinks Falkenburg with him. I remember how thrilled we were when he came in. Talk about a good-looking guy; he had everything. He was tall and handsome and kind of rugged. As far as checking in people, the only thing that interested me at all or was challenging to me was at that time, there were 36 passengers on an airliner and I made it a point to memorize every passenger's name and identify them when they checked in. If they came back again, I knew them. I could call them by name. That was kind of a mental game. That was the only really exciting thing.

Did you get any funny responses when you remembered them?

Oh, they loved it. They couldn't believe it. This one guy, he didn't want anybody to check him in except me. I would recognize his voice on the phone.

Do you have a photographic memory?

No, I do not. I have to work at it. I play mental games. After the WASPs, I went into the ceramic business. That was very challenging to me because I didn't know anything about it, and all my life, whenever I get into anything, I go all out. When I learned to ski, before I flew, I drank, ate, and lived skiing. That was big stuff. When I got into flying, I did it full bore. Same way with the ceramic business—the mental game I played there— I kept the books. I would try to remember the checks that I wrote. Just how many checks I wrote—the date. One time, a business auditor came. He started asking some questions. My answers boggled his mind. The other night, I wasn't sleeping so I named the presidents in order.

Ceramics? What did you do?

We made television lamps. When television was first coming in, this was a lamp that gave an indirect light on top of the television. We also had ceramic classes. It was a fun business for about 10 years until I got pregnant and had a child. Then I went full bore on that. That's the way I am.

I just celebrated my 82nd birthday October 1st. I was born in Bowdle, South Dakota. When I think of my life, of how far and how much has happened, it is unbelievable. When I was born, my parents wanted to take me 14 miles to show me to their grandparents—in a horse and buggy. I had the experience of flying the fastest airplanes at the time. Now I know Eileen Collins, who is going to be the first pilot to fly the Shuttle. She was commander about a year ago. I've met all these young, wonderful women—Michelle Johnson, who is the first woman commander at Travis Air Force Base. On her final dine-in, she invited me to speak. We dedicated the WASP Statue at Colorado Springs. I was president the last two years of the WASP Organization. I sat next to Janet Reno at the dedication. I know the superintendent at Colorado Springs on almost a first-name basis. We've been corresponding so much. I can't even describe what that experience has led my life through. I wouldn't have met all these wonderful people.

Mentoring isn't the easiest sometimes. How do you feel about being a kind of mentor?

I feel good. I didn't really realize it until one time when we had a P-51 Conference in Colorado Springs. We went to the

Academy, and this darling little blonde girl came up and put her arms around me and said, "If it wouldn't have been for you, I wouldn't be here." The other day, we just returned from Omaha. We were flying along and I said to my husband, "Dad, they've got a woman captain." There are 600 women captains on United Airlines. Instead of going out, I went to the cockpit. I said, "Congratulations, I am so glad to see you in that seat." I introduced myself. She said, "You broke the barrier for us, and I want to thank you." I said, "I want to thank you for being where you are and congratulations." That was a conversation just last Sunday.

I spoke last Memorial Day to some young children. They were grades 1 through 6. Afterward, they were all lining up to shake my hand. This one kid came up to me and said, "You know, you're really a cool old lady." I said, "You know something, you're a cool kid,"

You retired from the pottery business to become a homemaker. Did you ever fly again?

I just flew the Goodyear Blimp on May the 5th of this year. That is the best story of my life. I've always wanted to fly the Goodyear Blimp, just to ride in it. The day that we went up, the pilot was going to marry the granddaughter of a WASP. The WASP is a very good friend of mine, Lila Mann. I knew her granddaughter, Alice.

Before we went up, I said, "Well, who is your co-pilot?" He said, "You're going to be my co-pilot." I thought that we would just go up, and he would put the earphones on me and let me listen to what was going on. When we got up, he said, "Over here are the rudders. It works just like an airplane but instead of a stick, there's a wheel. If you want to go down, you put the wheel down."

He was explaining all this. After he had leveled off (we took off at Carson and we were flying out toward the ocean), he said, "Would you like to fly?" I said, "Sure." I got in, and there were no controls on the left-hand side, so I flew the blimp for about 15 minutes. It was wonderful. It was great. Also, I did a taut sky dive on my 76th birthday in Perris, California. This was one of my dreams that came true because I had always wanted to make a jump. It was a great experience—much more than anyone could imagine.

Anything else? Any regrets?

No, I believe you have a choice. When you get up in the morning, you can be miserable or you can be happy. I try every day to do something nice for someone. Help someone or give them a phone call or do something nice for my husband or grandchildren or friends. I have had a few very hard things in my life. Whenever those come along, I think, what do I have to learn from this experience? When it really comes down hard, I find that in the long run, it was the best thing that happened to me, not the worst, because I learned from it.

What were some hard things?

I met the fellow in college that I thought was going to be my husband for the rest of my life. He was in the Navy. I had every intention in the world of waiting for him to marry him. After he graduated from officers' school, I thought we would be married. Then I received a "Dear Jane" letter that was a true disappointment. I thought it was the worst thing that could happen to me. That's when I picked up my boots and said, "I'm going to serve my country." That was the best thing that ever happened to me, because, look what it did to my life.

I have had a wonderful life, having had so many rich experiences in the service. I count my blessings by the friends and my family. I love my grandchildren almost as much as my only daughter Kim. My parents were my role models. They believed in the golden rule, honesty, service, and finding joy in whatever you do.

Ann Darr

"Poet and Pioneer"

In 1977 President Jimmy Carter approved veteran's status for the Women Airforce Service Pilots, thus ending a long arduous odyssey for this group of fliers. Ann Darr was one of those who served the United States as a WASP, training under flight legend Jacqueline Cochran.

The experiences during military service were often painful. When a member of the Women's Airforce Service Pilots was killed in a plane crash, the government refused to pay for the body to be sent home. To Ann—and her fellow WASP fliers—this was a shattering refutation, one she relates in the interview, which she could not force herself to speak about for years. Ann would later come to grips with the past and was part of the group that testified before Congress in the successful attempt to receive official recognition.

Born in Bagley, Iowa, she attended the University of Iowa

and later worked for NBC before joining the military. Ann Darr is a poet and teacher, and when one thinks of people who have written well about flight—people like Ernest Gann or Antoine de Saint-Exupéry—her name might well be added to the list. She has written about her flight experience in all five of her books, including *Cleared for Landing.* Her work celebrates the experience of flight and of those who have flown with an unflinching honesty and directness.

In person, Ann Darr was an introspective woman with piercing eyes and the active mind of an artist in freefall with ideas and feelings. Ann captures the experience of flight as few writers have. Ann, a dear friend and fellow poet, died December 2, 2007.

How did you become interested in flight?

My mother died when I was three. I was told she went to heaven and I knew the only way I could get to heaven was to fly. I had a myth that I would fly to heaven under my own steam. When it turned out I could to fly at the University of Iowa—when I got there—the myth turned into reality.

What was the program like at the University of Iowa?

It was the Civilian Pilot Training Program (CPT) and I took ground school work in the Engineering Department and flying lessons at the Iowa City Airport.

Did you get college credit for it?

I got college credit for the ground school work, but not for the flying. I got up at 6 a.m. to do flying before my 8 o'clock classes.

Did people think that was kind of strange? You would come rushing into the class from a flying course?

Yes because they thought I was dressed oddly.

How were you dressed?

In boots and jodhpurs.

What was the most interesting thing during training?

(laughs) Shall I say the tall handsome man that I fell in love with? I was always in love with somebody, especially teachers.

This was your trainer?

My pilot instructor. The instruction was given in a Piper Cub plane. One early morning, after we'd been practicing take-offs and landings, he hopped out of the plane and said, "It's all yours."

So you remember that solo?

Do I? Yes, indeed I do. I found myself singing at the top of my voice.

You were singing?

Yes, I say in a poem someplace, "I learned I sing when I'm afraid." One of my flying buddies, not long ago, read that poem and scoffed at the idea that I was afraid. I wasn't afraid of flying, but I didn't think I was ready to go up myself.

So you remember what you sang? "Go Down, Moses"?

That I don't remember at this moment in time, but it wouldn't have been "Go down, Moses" under any circumstances. (laughs) It was probably, "Up…up…in my flying machine."

What was next?

I graduated from college, went to New York and started working for NBC on the radio show "The Women of Tomorrow."

Then the war interrupted that?

Yes, but before that I went out to Idlewild Airport—Kennedy, now. I wrote a poem about that called "Kennedy/Idlewild—In a Lifetime."

You must have had really strong feelings going back there?

I was engulfed with memories. That once was the only time I ever flew over New York City by myself. I was scared spitless I would fly into one of those places I wasn't supposed to be and someone would shoot me down.

That was before the war?

That's right. The war—Pearl Harbor—came on December 7, 1941, our first anniversary. We had been married on November 7. My husband was in medical school and, of course, signed up for the Navy immediately. In January, 1943, while I was working for "The Woman of Tomorrow" program on NBC, I went to cover a fancy shoe show at Bendel's.

I ran into the other young woman who was writing copy for the radio show. We'd been sent to cover the same event by mistake. She was in a great state of excitement. She said, "I just have to tell somebody what I've done. I hocked some of grandmother's jewels she left me in order to take flying lessons. I've just found out about the organization WAFS." "Isn't that the British women pilots?" I said. And then she told me there was an American group of women fliers named after the WAFS and she was going to try to get into the group as soon as she had enough flying time.

How much was that?

The original requirement was 250 hours, but she learned that they had lowered the time to 45 hours. She thought it was because they had found that pilots with 250 hours had more trouble learning precision flying.

Precision flying?

Yes, in the Army you had to learn how to land on a dime, or to hold a specific altitude for formation flying. Pilots with 45 hours could be taught more easily that some of those pilots who had more time and were set in their ways.

So what happened when you heard what she was doing?

I was excited, I nearly shouted, "I've got 45 hours." She was dumbfounded when I told her. She didn't know until that moment that I could fly. Somehow, I just hadn't told anybody at the office.

Do you think you were embarrassed to?

Embarrassed, why would I be embarrassed? It just never came up.

So what did she say when you told her you flew?

She was agog and said, "You can get into the WAFS!" For whatever reasons the organization of the WAFS was kept secret, or it certainly wasn't advertised to any degree. I don't know to this day why that was the case, unless it was prejudice against it from the start. And it must have been partly that or it wouldn't have taken us so long to get veteran status.

Did you see some prejudice early on, in some ways?

Yes, we did, unfortunately. It was at the bases where we were sent. The male pilots—some of them—were not eager to have the women pilots around. Some of them simply thought women couldn't do anything as well as men. Some thought it was too dangerous a job for women. Mostly though, it was a matter of ego, I believe. As it turned out, our record for flying was better than the men's. Anyway, there were twenty-five thousand young women who did everything they could to earn enough money to get flying time, so they could apply. There were over eighteen-hundred who were accepted. One thousand-seventy-four completed.

And your friend from the show?

She washed out.

How did you feel?

Sick to my stomach. She called me up the night before I

was to leave New York for Sweetwater, Texas, where we were to be trained. In fact, this is a point I want to bring out. All of the women who were accepted into the program had to know how to fly before they were accepted. This was not true of the male flying cadets. They were taken in on the basis of physical and mental health—which we were judged on, too, but we also had to know how to fly.

Anyway, my friend was back in New York City. She telephoned and said, "I have washed out." I thought, "If she can't make it, nobody can." She was a bright, competent, and extraordinary young woman. She had made it through basic training, but had not been able to handle larger planes. I believe she was eventually qualified to teach male cadets in primary trainers, but I'm not certain about that.

So how'd you feel, really?

Glum. I thought, "What's the use of trying? If she couldn't make it, what chances have I got?" However, I got on the train and went to Sweetwater, Texas. I was picked up at the station in a big truck that they carried us around in. I arrived at Avenger Field.

Avenger?

It was named that because it had been turned over earlier to the training of young British pilots. In fact, when the first class of WAFS arrived from Houston—their earlier base—the British cadets were just finishing up. This was before I arrived.

There were, of course, three phases to training—in primary, secondary, and advanced trainer planes. If we failed, we washed out. If we passed, we got thrown into the pool that was at the gate of Avenger Field under a big Fifinella sign.

148

Did you say a Fifinella sign?

Yes, Walt Disney drew it for us—a flying woman in helmet, boots, wings—our own flying symbol.

Disney actually drew it?

That's what I understood. One of the women of our class had worked for Disney as a cartoonist. I always thought Fifinella looked like her—maybe she was the model for it. Anyway, Fifinella is still our emblem. We have it on our flight jackets and stationery and the like.

What was your class?

The way the course was set, first, we were in primary trainers, PT-19s; then we went to basic trainers, the old BT-13; then to advanced trainers, the AT-6, which was fast and had a lot of horsepower. Our particular class was the first one to go directly from the PT-19 to the AT-6, skipping the BT-13. This was done to see if we could do it. We were guinea pigs. So, when we were successful at it, that procedure became the standard way of doing it for men. After the war, I understand, cadets went directly to the AT-6 for all pilot training.

How about the planes that you flew. Any you remember, especially?

My old BT-13 rattled and thumped when you put it into a spin. It sounded like an egg beater. We took instrument training in the BT-13s—after we had jumped from the primary. That was when we flew under a hood so we couldn't see out.

They actually trained you that way? Under a hood?

Yes. Until I learned to do it right. It was one of the scariest things. Of course, we were also training, at that point, in the Link trainer, so we could learn to do this on the ground in a simulated version. That's when we learned how good our pilots—the friends, other women—actually were. Some were good; a few were not.

Talk about one that wasn't so good.

Someone once gave me a figure as to what our altitude was and she was off by a hundred feet—it was very startling. She was not aware that she had given me the wrong information.

How'd you manage to get out of that one?

I didn't fly with her again and I do believe she washed out.

What was the living like there?

The typical life of Army Air Force training. We lived in barracks—six women to a bay—a long row-house with bathroom facilities in between. A big room that served as a living room, bedroom, and study room. We got up to reveille and to bed by taps. We lived by regular Army rules and regulations, but we did try to have as much fun as we could.

We were not allowed as WASPs to socialize with our instructors, though as I remember, some WASPs married their instructors after graduation. On special occasions, carloads of male pilots would be brought from the Base at Big Spring for a dance. Once, I won a dance contest with a wonderful young dancer I had just met that night. Then they took the men back to Big Springs. I never saw him again. In fact, I don't even remember his name.

Later on, when we were sent to the Advanced Training Base in Stockton, California, we lived in the nurses' quarters and were not very welcomed.

What happened?

There was conflict with other women. The nurses didn't think the pilots were their equal. There was a competitiveness that made us uncomfortable. We were "wild women" because we flew planes—at least, that's how they seemed to feel.

Do you still keep in touch with any of your WASP baymates?

Oh, yes, of course, we have reunions. I haven't been able to go often, but I've kept track of several the women I was closest to in Sweetwater. Mary Cooper Cox—she had so many hours when she came into our class she practically took the whole flying course flying upside down while the rest of us were taught flying right side up. Mary DeBolt from California was another special baymate who is remembered particularly for her creative excuses for not getting up when the bugle blew. She's still flying her own plane on the West Coast. A young woman from New York, Cecily Elmes, a debutante I remember for being very generous with her wardrobe. Once, when my husband came as far as St. Louis to visit me, she loaned me some of her best civilian clothes to go meet him.

We were really very supportive of each other. Living in such close quarters we needed to be. Especially when bad news came from overseas or one of us flunked a check ride. We were like a big family of sisters.

What happened when you first lost a pilot?

That was the hardest of all. When one of our women crashed and burned in a trainer plane, it was as if we had lost a member of our family. We grieved, then we went back to the flight line.

We realized that this was war; this was no game we were in. That was the reason I was there. I wanted to do something for the war effort. I could fly—this was something I had—a skill that I could give to my country. By this time, we knew what a dreadful situation it was in Europe. We knew the Holocaust was happening; we knew there was no certainty that we were going to win the war.

Who were your flying heroes?

Lindbergh had been my idol. "Lucky Lindy flew all alone in a little plane all his own." Remember that old song? No, you're too young. I said in poems about sitting at my grandma's player piano and pumping away and singing—alternately singing and playing my brother's saxophone. There were several songs about Lindbergh when he flew.

And you knew them all?

Oh, yes. And Amelia Earhart, of course, was a dream woman as far as I was concerned.

Do you remember where you were when you learned the news that Amelia Earhart had been lost?

No, oddly enough, I don't. I do remember walking out into the front hall of my house and seeing on the floor the

Register-Tribune that had been delivered by the paperboy. The headline read "Wylie Post Crashes in Alaska." That moment I do remember. I can still see it.

Did Amelia Earhart show you that women could do this? Could fly?

Strangely enough, I knew I could do that. I knew that a woman could do that, I didn't know that being a woman was going to be a problem as far as anything I wanted to do.

But you did find it a problem?

In the actual WASPs, yes, I did. Once, when I did a cross-country from Sweetwater to California, I had barely made it over the mountains at El Paso when I set down my plane for an emergency—there was so much oil on the windshield. When I walked in the ready room, they made me account for every instrument reading before they would even go out and look at my plane. When they did go out and look, they said, "What kind of plane are you being sent off with? This is in terrible shape."

Did you fly an inordinate number of clunkers?

I can't put blame on anyone. We were flying everything we had and everyone was working hard—around the clock.

At Stockton, my job was to test planes. After a plane had been flown a certain number of hours, it had to be tested—all the instruments, the condition of the plane itself—or, after it had been in an accident and repaired, it had to have a check flight.

Where'd you go from there?

From there we were sent to Las Vegas to be checked out in the B-26s we missed in Kansas so that we could tow targets in the Gunnery School.

We towed the targets in B-26s while B-17s flew beside us. In maneuvers, what we did with towing targets was to tow this big sleeve behind us. The B-17s flew along with training cadets operating from their positions in the nose, the sides and the tail. First, they trained cameras until they had their reflexes under control so they could start firing, and stop so they wouldn't shoot down our own planes.

After they learned that control, they used live ammunition, which had been dipped in red or blue or yellow wax so their accuracy could be checked. You see, after a shooting run, we would drop the target on the ground and the ground crew would retrieve it and check it out. The colored wax left color around the hole in the target. Red, yellow, blue—very colorful. We used those discarded targets for bedspreads, curtains, everything.

Wasn't it scary flying targets? Did you ever get hit?

I was too intent on keeping that plane at a specific altitude—on course. I never got hit, but airplanes were hit. One went down with a WASP co-pilot. Both the pilot and co-pilot were killed. The pilot's body was sent home, but we had to take up a collection to send home the WASP.

The military wouldn't pick up the tab?

Correct. We were being paid by the Civil Service. Although we were flying under military orders with military rules and regulations, military punishment, if we went wrong. For example, we were dressed down if we didn't salute. Everything we did was military, but they said we were Civil Service, so the Army wasn't responsible. Civil Service said they weren't responsible, so we took up a collection among ourselves to send her body home.

That was pretty devastating?

I was so hurt and angry about the situation. I just didn't want anyone to know it for years.

You didn't?

My own country wouldn't. I was ashamed of what they did. I didn't want to admit it to myself that we were being humiliated.

When did you finally come to grips with it?

Only after the war. Are you aware we were disbanded before the war was over?

No.

We were told that we were being disbanded because more male pilots were coming back from overseas alive than they had expected. We flew over six million miles and did it all extremely well, and we were being disbanded. We flew every kind of aircraft they had from PT-19s to B-29s. Anyway, we were all dismissed from service before the end of the war.

You never refused because a plane was too dangerous?

No, I didn't. Once we flew UC-78s back from Stockton to the factory in Texas. Regulations said we had to have a pilot and a co-pilot—but we flew solo.

The UC-78s on our base had wings damaged by wind. They were not strong enough and needed to be reinforced. The Army wanted all of that model to go back to the factory, so we made the trip. I don't remember how many planes were in the group—maybe 20. I didn't want to do that trip, but I didn't feel I could refuse. I would have preferred to have a co-pilot along for that lengthy trip from northern California to Texas, but it led to a poem anyway.

Talk about the terrain in the Midwest where you grew up, all of those broad fields and spaces. There's a poem in my first book called "Gather my Wings" that talks about that. It should be called "Forced Landing."

Ann Darr

There is a part of me that looks
forever for a level land
where rows of grain run
straightway to the wind.

Once you have trained
these senses, they stay trained
and though I have no need
for landing, forced or free,
this noticing is part of me,

makes me check imprecisions of an eye,
correct for choppy heartbeats,
hear a whipping tongue as dangerous.
I must go out and gather in my wings.

Once prepared for landing forced,
one lives too much alerted.
One listens for a twitch of a snake
the thud of seedy apple.

*I think the idea of flight, which you've explored in the poem, is
interesting. Flight is really one of life's great metaphors.*

I think human beings have been wanting to take to air since
their eyes first sighted birds. You can't see birds flying without
wanting to join them. Flight is my metaphor—a personal metaphor—for flight in all of its meanings—from the power to dream
of rising and flying with one's own power—to the Phoenix rising
from the ashes—to flight as in running away from.

*You actually have one poem about running away from home as
I recall?*

Yes, it's called "Orders."

After I ran away from home and came back again
My papa said, Go, if you must but mind three things:
Stay away from water, stay off of boats and don't
Go up in an airplane. So first I learned to swim
Then I learned to sail, and then I learned to fly.

*Your father is in another flying poem of yours along with
another of your heroes. Can you tell us about that?*

I knew a flying poem was going to surface at some point or
another after those years. It happened when the invitation came
to put my name in a time capsule for the dedication in Texas
of Hanger Nine where many of the famous fliers learned to fly.
That was exciting.
"Hanger Nine"

Upon being asked to place my name in
a time capsule at the dedication of Hanger
Nine as an aerospace museum
because I flew with the Women's Air-
Force Service Pilots – or – the WASP

"...place your name in a time capsule . . .aerospace shrine . . .
dedication of "Hanger 9 . . ."
The morning mail condenses me
into part of the blue I want to become.

I dive to the bottom
of my old trunk
to retrieve my silver wings.

I come up goggle-eyed.

I put on another hat,
black cherries with a veil,
and Winston Churchill is dead
in the great cathedral.
"They buried the trees when your flyers came over . . .
let us eat our fill of strawberries
before they plowed the berries under,
and to make the runways,
they cut and buried the trees."

The cherry tree leaves are cherry red
and, I am wearing black cherries for the dead,

no, I am bare-headed
    and Wiley Post has crashed in our front hall
    black patch and all. I learn he traded his eye for his plane
(all right, used the insurance money.)
The headlines are squirming in the sun,
it is the Ides of August, and Alaska
has brought him down. Not alone. Will
Rogers went down with him, who never met
a man he didn't like

Wiley Post, born on a bloody date . . . a November
twenty-second . . . when a crashed career
drained the rest of us of dreams
we'd been afraid to dream since childhood,
that God was with us after all,
that faith and courage weren't mis-spelled words
in a computer, and suddenly joy was splitting apart like

old chicken entrails where my grandmother
ground off the chicken head with her heel
and threw the spastic body in the dust
that August afternoon where I, crouched
in the grape vines, stiffened like death
when the headless body went by . . . it was
Wiley Post. And I knew I was going to fly.

"place you name in a time capsule,"
just what I've been trying to do. My time
capsule was to be a poem to wrench your lungs.
Now here it all is so simply . . . because,
because, one January deep in snow,
an Alaskan day in Manhattan.
I thought I'd learned the reason I learned to fly.

I made my gesture to save Paris
I thought that Paris was where
I was trying to go.
THE GERMANS HOLD THE CITY OF LIGHT!
and copying the English girls
who pulled on helmets, parachutes
and boots and took to air, I threw
my lot in with the flyers.

WAR is now a dirty word
and I am marching marching.
When did WASP turn into
an obscenity? We flew
with honor for a cause:
people were being burned in furnaces,
human skin made lampshades exquisitely thin,

we cannot sit by. . .
"place your name in a time capsule"
would Will Rogers have liked Hitler?

"Lucky Lindy, flew all alone, in a little
plane all his own . . ." and I am pumping
the player piano in my gramma's cold parlor
and playing a saxophone . . . discarded by
my brother, who paid for it with nickels
and found he wasn't musical.

And I am standing leaden, astonished,
in the great Smithsonian hall, learning
for the first time that Lindbergh, flying
the Atlantic, could not see out.
There was no windshield! No windshield
at all! I wanted to run to tell somebody,
my god, what this man has done, he flew
into the unknown, blind as Wiley Post's eye,
blind as a headless chicken. But that was long ago,
and great drafted birds are flying over,
I hear their drone, and what one man has done
makes no matter. We are all flying blind.

Place your name. Amelia Earhart
with a touseled head was more than
a set of rawhide suitcases.
      I had a haircut like that when
      gramma cut it under a bowl
      and all those fat curls
      lay on the floor as if they had been killed.
      Did she die alone? Everyone dies alone.

Amelia Earhart . . . lost at sea . . . lost at sky,
coming on with a meaning
she never intended . . . luggage, luggage,
I wish that I could recreate her skin.
Bid her walk into a room again.
God, what a dream she must have had.

Papa's hand was big and warm to hold mine
When we watched the eyes of heaven,
Eyes of mother, and God, and maybe
   Abraham Lincoln.
I once knew a German boy who said
He had drunk from the Big Dipper.

And Michael Carmichael in her cocked hat
Flew all the way to hell and back while cancer ate
Her heart. Impossible! The impossible happens
All the time. Walk on water. . . walk on the moon.
     Kitty Hawk, Kitty Dove, Kitty Hawk . . .
     Go fly a kite!
and those bicycle brothers did.
They made their own music.

    You can still hear it,
    If your ear is cocked
    right in the cockpit.

Place your name. Edward White. Gus Grissom.
Neil Armstrong.
   Amelia Earhart. Wiley Post. Lindbergh. Orville. Churchill.
   Lincoln. Socrates. Icarus. God.
   Beelzebub. Papa. Place your name.

Freud would have said mine was a death wish
to join the conglomerate blue. That it was
heaven I meant to reach, not Paris,
that wanting to place my name
        Is grandiose.
I place his name. Freud.

    We walk in space every day of our lives,
       and our name is on that piece of space where
  we bolster the air, and live it however
    we dare,
           and dream of flying.

You've written some wonderful poems about flight.

Thank you. When the mail arrived, it was like a switch turned on! I sat at the typewriter and wrote for hours—pages and pages. It was as if all of the flying experiences finally took off and was flying under its own steam. Yes, indeed, it created friendships that last to this day; it gave me confidence that I wouldn't otherwise have had. Even with the mistakes I've made, I've learned from those. Maybe one learns more from mistakes, but the triumphs were rewarding too. When those silver wings with the diamond in the middle were pinned on me, it was as if I made a success of something I started out with.

You were active in the recognition movement of the WASPs, weren't you?

We were told not to get in touch with our Congressmen and we were supposed to act like ladies, quote, unquote. So we didn't fight it when we should have. When they said, "Go home, you're finished here," we went. It was a terrible time for all of us. We were being dismissed as if we had not done a good job— which we had. Yes, I became verbal later on. There was a quote I remember well: "The only reason I'm listening to the testimony of you WASPs is that I owe Senator Goldwater a favor."

Somebody actually said that?

Yes.

What year was that?

1977.

But you were finally recognized.

Yes, what we got out of it was recognition and a burial place.

No pension or anything?

We can have medical care from a V.A. hospital.

Are you satisfied with that?

What could I do? We did what we could do.

Claire Walters
Laughing and Flying All the Way

In a distinguished career, Claire Walters flew more than 38,000 hours and taught more than 2,000 students. She ran the Claire Walters Flight Academy in Santa Monica for some twenty-seven years. A founder of the Palms to Pines Air Race, she is a pioneer in the truest sense. Claire and her twin sister, Betty, wanted to join the CPT program, but because they were women they were not admitted. (The excuse used was that it was for second-year students only.) World War II limited flight possibilities, so they took jobs in a cannery. Each made thirty-five cents an hour and would work ten-hour days. With the proceeds, they would go out and buy a half-hour of flying time. Later, they went to Ground School after graduating from community college. Claire soloed on October 10, 1943. She raised one-quarter-million dollars for The Ninety-Nines. A book, *The Flying Life*, details further her amazing life.

Like others, Claire was such a sheer delight to interview, but it was her infectious laugh, which was both spirited and restorative, that distinguished her. This lively presence will be missed by all who knew her. As for me, I felt in this interview as if I had known her for years, as if we were best friends, a tribute perhaps to her openness and generosity. In short, she was a gem. Claire died at age eighty-five at Cedars-Sinai Medical Center.

How'd you get into flying?

I think it started when I fell out of my crib, the first time I fell on my head. No, I was born this way, wanting to fly. I never planned to do anything else.

Reactions of kids to you wanting to be a pilot?

I do not recall any conversations with kids. I knew (my plans) in kindergarten. I planned my whole life what I was going to do and when I was going to do it. In the sixth grade, the students built a balloon, and at the fiftieth anniversary of my high school graduation, some of the students said, "Remember the balloon we built?" (laughs)

What was it like?

It was a paper balloon and it seemed large. It was something we inflated and it would rise a little. It left an impression. Students never thought I was weird. I did know as I went through schools that my friends and I would not be going in the same directions.

Anything obsessive? Did you have your shelves covered with planes?

When I was about three-years-old, I took my little red wagon and all my dolls and went strolling on down the street. I wanted, I think, to buy an airplane to play in.

What kind of dolls?

The dolls were not priceless. I don't recall getting any takers (laughs), but I remember trying to.

Was your twin sister, Betty, interested?

I was more interested than she was. She went along with it. She later went into writing.

My mother and her twin completed each other's sentences.

Never seemed to do that. She lived out of town, and when she came up to visit me, we'd often find that we had dressed in the same colors. In school, I'd switch places with her in the classroom, and the teacher didn't know the difference. But the kids did, and they'd laugh all the time when I got called on by the teacher. One time, my sister's boyfriend saw me in the library and asked me for a date. She was mad about that. Another time, I was in a streetcar accident, so I was out of it awhile. During that time, she would take my place in pictures.

Most fun you had in flying?

In 1947, the first Powder Puff Derby took place. One woman couldn't get her A-26 started so only one airplane flew in the race. In 1948, I borrowed an airplane from a flight school in Santa Ana. There were six planes in the race. In 1950, there were thirty-three planes. Then in 1951, I took first place. Fran Bera and I flew together.

Anything unusual about that?

Fran and I flew in a Cessna 140, a two-wheel airplane. We planned to go from Orange County Airport to Detroit by way of Fort Worth, Texas. Everything went well, but in Fort Worth, we learned a storm was coming and found the participants tying down their airplanes and heading home or to a hotel. I told Fran that we could tie our plane down or take off and fly at the edge of the thunderstorm. She said, "Let's go." As a result, when we reached Detroit, we arrived a good hour ahead of the second-place plane. (Usually, the top ten would be within a couple of minutes of one another.)

Tell me about flying to Havana.

We left our Cessna in Miami and flew a Stimpson to Key West, where the U.S. Coast Guard gave us instruction on using Mae West life preservers and other safety tips. Cuba had invited us over as guests of the tourist commission. We arrived in Cuba and were met by soldiers with guns. They escorted us and we were worried. But when we reached the room, there were all kinds of people celebrating our arrival. The soldiers were just teasing us.

Talk about your philosophy.

I did my own thing. I knew the men's world and the women's world, at the time, were worlds divided down the middle. Anything that was fun and prestigious was men's world; slavery was the women's world. And if you don't want to be a slave, you have to ignore anything going around you and just go out there and do your own thing. And that was the way I lived.

Have any put-downs?

I worked for a man one time and overheard him say to someone, "You fly with Claire, but if you decide you don't want a woman instructor, then I'll change it to a man." Later, I went to him and said, "Jimmy, do me a favor and don't even put the idea in their minds." I had very few people refuse to fly with me.

Second "Leweys" are nice people, but there's nothing worse than someone who's just gotten his wings. By the time that same person has reached First Lieutenant status, he's turned into a good guy. And by the time he's a captain, he's a really good guy. I've taught a lot of people to fly because I was patient. I didn't talk down to them. They were always people.

Were you a born teacher?

I think most women are. If we're not born that way, we sure get a lot of training in it. I was very business-like in the plane, but I could be very good friends outside the plane. One time a fellow got in the airplane with a helmet on, and I ordered him to take it off (laughs). He took it off. If someone ever talked "smart" to me, he got it back. Another time, I got angry with a guy in his own airplane. He lit a cigarette. I said, "Either put that cigarette out or take me back." He took me back.

I used to go back east where I'd pick up a used plane to ferry. Going to the East Coast was interesting because I found a lot of professionals there. It's as if when you reach Arkansas it's different. It's because they're ready to make love instantly. And then as you got further west, the men were just friendly. I'm talking about when I was twenty to twenty-two years old (laughs).

So what about specifics?

It never did them any good. The opportunity wasn't there, because I was leaving the next day. Right?

Did you ever get really mad?

I decided early-on that anger was a waste of energy. You just have to be very professional or pretend you didn't know what they were talking about. That always put the guy off. The guy would then walk away, shaking his head.

Did you feel you had to be accepted in the men's clique?

I wasn't interested in making a living. At first, I was only interested in making enough dollars to buy a hamburger or a bottle of beer, but later it was different. At some point, I was working hard, overwhelmed with students, but the guys were just hanging around doing nothing. So one said, "Claire, you're making us look bad." I said, "You're making yourself look bad." I said, "I don't have a wife supporting me as you have. Why don't you get in here and work a little bit and help me?" At the time, I had to raise two babies. (I had married one of my students in 1951 and a year later had a baby. And then another.) He didn't want the responsibility. He ordered me to have an abortion or he would leave. I showed him the door. So I ended up raising my babies, but I had to work. I sure couldn't sit around playing cards. We made only four or five dollars an hour in those days.

I could not take time to worry about the men. In fact, I don't have time for negative people. If things are not going well, I try to figure out how to make them better. There's not time for the negative.

Any unusual stories about teaching?

Yes, one guy wanted lessons to see if he liked flying. So I explained how it worked and how this and that worked on the plane. I spoke of the dangers of ground looping. As we taxied out, I told him to ease back on the wheel, but he decided he wanted to pull the wheel all the way back. I put one foot on the rudder as we streaked down the runway and set the other knee against the wheel, pushing the wheel back, because, by now, he had the wheel back against his stomach. We somehow got under control. This was death or near-death because this guy was big and strong. We got back, and I landed the airplane. I never forgot that because he could have killed us.

Weirdest flight?

Three planes started out, and the wind started coming up. The first stop was Baker, but soon I could see we couldn't reach it. The other plane had the chart. (There was only that and one map between us.) Now, I looked around near Kelso and saw the second plane had turned around and that the third plane accompanying had disappeared. We were running low on fuel. I was scared. There was no good straight road below to land on. When I saw a playground, I landed. I walked over to the railroad tracks where some men were working. The men had one of these little, motorized carts and were surprised to see two twenty-year-olds there. I talked them out of five gallons of gas, had one of them put it in the plane, and went over and measured the space between the tracks. I determined there was just enough room between the tracks for my wheels. The men didn't think we could make it, but I talked them into lifting the plane up and putting it between the tracks. The plane had no brakes, so I revved the plane up and had the men hold onto the airplane till the throttle was full. Then the girl with me yelled for them to turn it loose, and we took off successfully. That was one of the weirdest flights.

Talk about a memorable student.

One of my students was John Gavin, the movie star. I didn't know who he was, because I didn't go to movies. I was working and had no time. He wouldn't tell me he was a movie star, and when I asked him what he did, he said he did some stuff in the movies. Neither did I know that he was "America's Secret Sweetheart." Ultimately, Mr. Gavin didn't get his license because he was busy in the movies. But he was so handsome.

Were you secretly in love?

Yea (laughs). Before and after each lesson he would give me a great big hug and kiss.

How would you be remembered?

That I tried to be safe, that I tried to make good pilots.

Betty Pfister
"Congressional Gold Medal Winner and Whirly Girl"

Betty Pfister's introduction to flight came at a small air show. At the time, she was attending Bennington College, and she and a friend decided to go to the event. After a flight, she says, "I knew what I wanted to do the minute I landed. There was no question." Immediately, she called her dad and said she wanted to leave college. The thought panicked her father who pleaded with her, "Please don't move, don't leave, I'll be up tomorrow." Her father came up from New York, and the two conferred and reached an agreement: If Betty would stay in college and keep up her good grades, her mother and father would pay for flight lessons.

After getting her private license, Betty was working on her

commercial license when she got a telegram from Jackie Cochran. Cochran had gotten the name of every woman who had a private pilot's license or better. The telegram inquired if Betty would be interested in a training program. Betty started with the WASPs in February of 1943.

Betty Pfister was born in 1921 in Great Neck, New York, and lived for many years in Aspen, Colorado. She was a member of The Ninety-Nines, the Women in Aviation International, the WASPs, the Colorado Hall of Fame and the Whirly Girls.

At age 70, Betty served as a member of the U.S. Helicopter team. A woman of flair, she would buy a Bell 47-G and have it painted like a butterfly and call it "Tinkerbell." She received the Federation Aeronautique International Rotorcraft Gold Metal for support of world-wide helicopter flight. Recipient of the Congressional Gold Medal for her work with WASPs, she was qualified in more than 25 airplanes.

A philanthropist and supporter of young, aspiring fliers, she died November 17, 2011 at age 90.

How did you get interested in flight?

I had a brother a year older than I was, and he started flying. He went into the Naval aviation at the start of the war, and then was killed, flying off a carrier. I was in the WASPs at that time, in the middle of my basic training.

What were your feelings? That's enough to make some-body quit.

I almost did. I went home for a couple of weeks, and my family had a big conference. My brother was the oldest one and the only boy. I had one younger sister. Finally, I guess they just decided that it was the thing I did best and I loved so I contributed to the war effort. They let me go back and finish my training, and I have always been happy because it has been a source of great pleasure to me over the years.

Tell me about your brother. What was he like? Was, and did, and just tell me a little bit about him.

Well, he went to Yale University and he was a terrific guy. We had a lot of fun together, and I don't know what else to tell you.

He was coming off of a carrier? What happened?

It was the catapult that failed to work and the Navy Torpedo bomber he was flying just went over the edge of the deck, and that was it.

Where did you train?

The first three classes of WASPs trained in Houston, Texas, but from then on, all of the training was done in Sweetwater, Texas. I was in the fourth class, and we were the first class to train at Sweetwater.

Did you have any unusual things happen during training?

Yes, I had just one thing. On my first day, I went up in a twin engine, UC-78 Bobcat, and there was another girl with me as co-pilot. I was to fly about an hour, and then trade places. About fifteen minutes after we first took off, we lost an engine, so we turned around immediately to go back to Sweetwater Field. About five to ten minutes later, we lost our second engine. So we, in effect, had become a glider. We just barely made it back to land. We did not land on the runway, but on a nice, flat dirt place. We probably totaled the airplane, but we weren't scratched at all. What had happened, they found out later, was that the man in charge of fueling that particular plane said the electric gas gauges showed that the tanks were nearly full. Our instructor had followed us and checked the plane out before turning us loose, and he felt we had plenty of fuel.

What did you say? Did you have a talk with your instructor?

No, no, no. He was just glad that we made it back to the airport and that we were all right. He couldn't have done anything differently.

Describe the landing a little more specifically.

There was a very steep embankment of rocks. I can practically see it in my mind. We had already lowered our gear, and we still had one engine going, and were getting ready for our landing when the second one quit. We wanted to go as slow as we could, and we needed every bit of altitude to keep us going above this big embankment. We finally just slowed up just enough to clear those rocks and sort of crashed on the field, but from a very low altitude—from maybe two or three feet. It did an incredible amount of damage to the aircraft.

Did you have any trouble getting out of the plane?

Not a bit, no.

You just climbed out?

Yes, but two WASPs had been killed the day before, so everyone was pretty edgy.

So then what happened?

Well, the ambulance came out. They had one on the field at all times. The poor flight surgeon had only been there about a week, and on his first day there, the fatal accident occurred. Then we called in with an emergency, and so he was pretty upset and pretty glad that we were fine.

We all worked hard and we loved to fly and some of the ladies, the girls, washed out and that was sad for them and sad for everyone.

Did you have any friends that washed out?

Oh sure, there were some in my bay. There were six girls to a bay, and we had one bed, I think, that nobody wanted to sleep in. This was crazy, but we were a little superstitious. I think three girls in a row that slept in that bed washed out.

After your training, where did you go?

I went first to Wilmington, Delaware, to New Castle Air Force Base, and to ferrying a lot of planes. From there, I transferred to Palm Springs, California, which is a wonderful base. I was there, totally out of season—I think it was something like May through September and it was extremely hot. It was so hot that we had to do all our flying between five in the morning and ten and then quit until about five p.m., because the heat burnt up the engines and the brakes and everything. It was pretty nice there, though. You would just go to the swimming pool and the

Officer's Club every day, and from ten to five, we had time off. We got paid for sunbathing, which was lovely.

So what did you do? You just developed that tan right? Did you meet young men over there or not?

Oh yes, there were a lot of guys there. I would say something like seven hundred men and thirty women, I don't know exactly, but you could have been cross-eyed and bow-legged and had a date every night.

Did you date over there?

Oh, sure.

You didn't marry anyone out of there did you?

No.

How close were the women in the WASPs?

Oh, very close. Physically close. Even during training we had six girls to a bay, six in a bay, and then we shared a bath, with two showers, two toilets, and so forth, and then six girls on the other side. So we were physically close and, I would say, close emotionally, too.

How many of those friendships have sustained themselves over the years?

Oh, a fair number. One of my best friends also goes to reunions, and I get to see her. We have some wonderful reunions every two years. We have conventions, and it really is fun. You look across the room and you see a face that even fifty years later looks familiar, and you can't possibly think of the name. Of course, a great many of us got married and that changes the name completely, too. Still, you can say, "Ah, you were with me when that B-25 caught fire that night over Chicago," whatever it was, and saw things you never will forget. I am just making up the bit about the B-25. As for my co-pilot, the one that was with me when I crashed the twin Cessna, I saw her about forty years later. I was sitting at a head table at a luncheon, and she recognized me. She didn't know my married name, but she recognized me and came up to me and said, "Didn't I fly with you that day when we crashed a twin Cessna?" It was exactly the same girl.

How many planes do you think you delivered?

Oh, I couldn't even begin to tell you. I'd have to go into the logbooks and add them up. A lot. We did an awful lot when we first got to Wilmington, Delaware. In fact, we delivered a lot of primary trainers. We'd pick them up in Hagerstown, Maryland, and deliver them to all kinds of places. The planes had almost no instruments in them, very basic instruments, not much. The PT-19 was an open cockpit airplane, and was it cold in the winter! We had these big teddy bear suits, big sheepskin lined pants and jackets and even boots. They were very clumsy, but very helpful in the cold.

You flew helicopters.

Not with the WASPs, but afterwards. It was 40 years ago that I got involved with helicopters. I got my helicopter license in 1961.

What number helicopter license are you?

I'm Whirly-Girl #52.

What interested you in helicopters?

It was strictly by accident. I was going to get my Airline Transport Pilot certificate (ATP) rating. I had taken the written, which was a really tough one. I passed that, but it was only valid for six months. I wanted to take the flight part of it while the written part was still valid. I heard their was a wonderful flight school in Fort Worth, Texas. I was in Fort Worth with my husband because I was going to start in flight school and finish my ATP. One of his customers was a man at Bell Helicopter, so we were out there one day. Normally, I would just sit in the car when I would go with my husband, which was very seldom. My husband said, "This is an awfully nice guy that I call on here. Why don't you come in with me and meet him?" And that seemed to be a nicer thing to do than to just sit in the car and read a book, so I went in, and this man and I talked for a bit. He wanted to know what I was doing, and I explained that I was there to start training for my ATP at the flight school the next day. He didn't say anything else, but he picked up his phone to call the flight line. He told them that he had a lady pilot, but that she had never been in a helicopter. And to take me for a ride and let me try and fly it. And we did just that.

I was wearing high heels, I remember, and first thing I had to do was to get those shoes off. We went up, and I piloted for about five minutes, though. We probably flew for about 45 minutes. I was just terrible, which everyone is when he or she first tries to fly a helicopter. But I just fell in love with it. We made a bunch of landings out in the field where some horses were grazing, and you could see grasses blowing. Somehow the horses never missed a bite; they just kept munching away. Then we came back and landed, just about exactly where we started. I knew right then that I wanted to learn to fly helicopters, and so I did. And I went to Oklahoma and found a wonderful woman instructor. It was too expensive at the Bell plant. They had instruction there, but it was $75 an hour, which is about like $700 today.

This was pioneering stuff, since helicopters had not been around all that long.

The Bell 47, which was one that I think they were producing the most of in the Bell plant, was just a wonderful machine and a pleasure to fly. It is the same one as you see in "M*A*S*H." with that big round bubble. In Oklahoma City. we also flew a helicopter called the Brantly. In fact, I think I'll start a club called "The Brantly Survivors Club." It was awful, a little, two-blade helicopter. It was so squirrelly, and if you learned on that, boy, everything else was very easy. I didn't really have much good to say about it, except that it was easier to operate than the Bell 47.

Did you have any close calls with the Brantly?

No, not really.

Did anybody else that was training with you have troubles with it?

No, there was just one guy that was there at the same time that I was, and we both took our flight tests the same day, and both passed; however, the FAA gentlemen who were giving the flights tests saw Brantlys crack up right and left. It certainly had developed a not-very-good reputation.

What made it so difficult?

The Brantly had to be landed absolutely. Forward motion was the only thing that was okay. But heaven forbid, if you did any sideways motion or any rear, because such motions would be just awful. Also, it had something else called "ground resonance" and though you could land with a little bit of forward motion, the best approach was just absolutely straight down. With anything else, it could self-destruct. It was not a very easy thing to fly.

It was a really good start because you knew that it couldn't get any harder.

Exactly. Everything else was relatively simple. I remember I smoked at the time, and I remember asking Dottie Young, my instructor, "Now where is the ashtray?" and she looked at me and said, "You are going to be a lot too busy to have a cigarette. If you want to smoke, you'll have to land somewhere." She was also a smoker.

Tell me about Dottie Young.

She was an outstanding instructor. I don't think that I could have had a better one. She was about five-feet tall, probably weighed a hundred pounds, if that, and was just a wonderful, wonderful pilot. My husband got his rating from her, too quite a bit later.

Did she have any tips or any kinds of things that she really stressed that made a difference down the line?

Oh, all I can remember is her telling me, "Now don't ever do that again." I'd look at her and say, "I'll never do that again." She was very emphatic about what would and would not work for the Brantly.

As soon as I finished the flight test for helicopters, Jean Howard in Washington, the one that started the whole "Whirly-Girls" organization, called and said I was number 52. There were only that many women that we knew about. There were many more in Russia, but now I think we are up to eleven hundred and something.

Did you have any close calls with a helicopter?

Not really.

Nothing? Never?

No, I had my own helicopter up until about fifteen years ago. I had a Bell 47, which I just had the most fun in. It was really a great running machine.

A lot of people think of helicopters as capricious and . . .

Dangerous.

Is that a bum rap?

No, they are fairly noisy and they have an awful lot of moving parts. They are quite a lot harder to fly, in my opinion, than an airplane. If you're not handling an airplane very well, as a student, the best thing you can do is take your hands and feet off the controls, and it will come back to level flight by itself. But, boy, in a helicopter, that isn't the same thing at all. It will crash in short order if you just leave it alone. Helicopters are hard to fly, and I think that makes it more fun. They are a real challenge, and the first day you kind of get ahead of the helicopter instead of the other way around—it's very rewarding.

How long did it take you to get to that point?

I can't remember how many hours I had. When I got my rating, it was too few, but it was a legal amount, something like fifteen or twenty, which wasn't very much. It was about enough to get into trouble.

Did you do commercial work then with your helicopter?

I didn't do any commercial work. I had it just for my own pleasure really.

Did people say, "How in the world do you that just for your own pleasure"?

It was very expensive because there was no revenue coming in and they're expensive to operate. But it was all that fun.

Tell me one of the fun trips that you took or one of the most memorable experiences you had while flying it.

Well, we have a ranch at Woods Lake that is at ninety-four hundred feet. It's only accessible in the summertime. We could get in there, usually, about the first of June and shut down and leave about the end of September. Anyhow, it used to take about two hours to go there by car on the roads that I find terrifying, so I was very happy to have the helicopter and make it in about fifteen minutes or so.

You actually find the helicopter safer, and you feel safer than riding on the road.

Oh yes.

What did your parents think of your flying? Particularly later on when you did the helicopter?

They thought that was fine. I had a little fighter plane after the WASPs was de-activated, though I never got to pursuit school. In fact, I got measles the day before I was supposed to go. Twenty-one years old, and suddenly I broke out in measles. As a result, I spent a week or ten days in the infirmary, instead of going to Brownsville, Texas, to pursuit school. That was the one thing I wanted more than anything was pursuit school. The only problem was that that was the last class scheduled to go to that school, so I couldn't just go to the next one a month later. When that happened, I called everyone. I think I called General Hap Arnold, and everybody I could get a phone number for, and I just begged and pleaded to go to the next month's school. So I didn't get to fly fighters like P-38s or P-51s. I flew quite a few bombers, twin engines and four engines. After the WASPs got deactivated, a friend of mine and I bought five AT-6 advanced trainers that the military were through with. At that time, they were available for civilians to purchase. I think that we paid about fifteen-hundred dollars for each plane.

We would fix them up and get the civilian license on them and sell them for about three thousand. We made a small amount of money, maybe four-or-five hundred dollars on each one. We kept one for ourselves—to fly. Finally, that one got too expensive to fly. I think it burned about thirty gallons an hour, something like that, so we finally sold it, and that meant that I didn't have anything to fly. Then I saw this Bell P-39 Aircobra sitting on the ramp at my home airport. I looked at it for a couple of days and then went in the office, and the secretary gave me the owner's name and phone number. The owner, it turned out, had bought it at the Cleveland Air Races and had flown it to New York, or Westchester County, which is where I saw it. Apparently, it had scared him to death. He had never flown anything as close to that powerful. So he had it for sale for a thousand dollars. It was a beautiful aircraft! The P-39 was a single-place, pursuit plane, so the only check out you have is someone standing there, telling you what the different controls are and what to expect. I will never forget, when I told him I was interested and wanted to buy it, but I didn't know for sure if I would like it because I had never flown one before. He said, "Well, why don't you give me your check ahead of time, in case you crack up?"

That makes you feel optimistic, doesn't it?

Then he said, "I will give the check back to you if you don't like the plane and just charge you for the flight time." I think it was forty dollars an hour and that seemed very fair to me. So I went and got a cashier's check and handed it to him. And I had never flown anything like it. The P-39 was something like a thousand horsepower. There was quite a lot of difference between that and the AT-6, with 650 horsepower. Anyway, I took off, and I remember I forgot to pull up the landing gear. At the time, I was only going about two hundred miles an hour, and I expected at least two-fifty. Finally, I realized I had forgotten to pull the gear up. I flew the plane for a half an hour and just loved it. It was the nicest little plane. Then I came in and landed and told him to keep the check. For about four years, I flew in some air races and had a wonderful time. The P-39 and the Bell helicopter were the two best aircrafts, I ever owned.

Tell me an air race story.

I did have one thing. I was flying a Navion in what was called the International Air Race. It started in Canada and went down to West Palm Beach, Florida. Just before I took off from Montreal, a friend of mine gave me a big chocolate milkshake, and it was in one of those cardboard cups or containers. I think it even had a lid on it. But anyhow, somehow it spilled on take-off and that plane smelled so awful. That chocolate milkshake was all in the carpets and everywhere. I was flying solo and got in some really bad weather, and the only thing to do was find a place to land because there was no airport anywhere nearby. I finally saw a big racetrack. And so I landed on the infield. Just barely had enough room. The plane had a hand brake and I still remember pulling on that brake as hard as I could, beginning from the far end of the field. I had no idea where I was, and then I saw a dog by one of the little buildings. I went in, and I found that I was on Alfred Vanderbilt's private racetrack. There were a bunch of guys playing pool there. I had to call the FAA and let them know where I was and that I was fine. Here I was, smelling of that milkshake. I can still smell it today. Finally, the ceiling lifted a little bit, and so I flew on down to either Ft. Lauderdale or Miami, to finish that race. And I won the race. Apparently, I had been on the ground for a shorter time than anyone else.

I raced the P-39 a few times, and that was always kind of memorable, just because it was the only one. But they didn't allow women to race at the Cleveland Air Races at that time.

They were the big deal in those days. So I had to have a man fly my plane. We didn't do very well because there were a lot of P-51's, and they are just basically a faster aircraft.

You must have been pretty frustrated that you couldn't fly at the Cleveland Air Races.

Well, I was.

How frustrated were you?

Well, I'd love to have flown it myself, but I found a pilot that liked the P-39. Not everyone liked them. Chuck Yeager particularly liked it, I remember.

Tell me what Chuck Yeager did.

I was flying in an air show there at Cleveland. They were paying me in a three-day air show to fly the P-39, supposedly doing a mock girl fight with a friend of mine who was flying an AT-6, which wasn't nearly as fast. It was a foregone conclusion that I was going to win this little dogfight. During our act, I didn't do anything too spectacular because I wasn't that good a pilot. I was okay, but nothing like Chuck Yeager. Anyway, Chuck saw my plane and asked me if he could fly it in my place. I think it was the third and last day at the air show. We were going to get him a wig so anyone who saw the plane taxi past would think it me, but we never quite got that act together.

That's pretty funny.

We made an arrangement that Gloria, the girl flying the

AT-6, would do all the radio for a flight of two, because we didn't want the tower to hear Chuck's voice on the radio. So that was easy. And I will tell you, on take off, I just sat on the grass and watched. I think he did three snap rolls on take off, and it went on from there. It was so spectacular that the announcer went crazy. He said, "Look at Betty flying! Wow! I've never seen a woman fly like that!" He went on and on, and that was fine, for about ten or fifteen minutes. Finally, when Chuck came in and landed, I suddenly thought, "Oh this isn't so good. They may be mad at us. They were paying me to fly, even though he did much, much better than I ever could have." I ran down to the plane as he was just getting out, and I said, "You know, Chuck, this isn't so funny now. We thought it was. But I wonder if somebody will get really mad." And here came this big, red convertible, with the top down and all these generals and people in it, and they were becoming down to congratulate me on what a wonderful flight. And so, Chuck got out of the way, and I looked as though I had been flying for twenty minutes because I was all hot and sweaty from running down the ramp. Chuck got the parachute halfway on me, and then the car arrived. And they kept bragging to me about how beautifully I had flown and I didn't say a word. Then they put me in the car—we were a long way from the grandstand—and drove me back there, but poor Chuck had to walk.

That's priceless. Have you been in touch with Chuck in more recent years?

Yes, I see him from time to time at different conferences and things.

Does he like to recount that story?

He'll never forget it. It was really funny. He had good things to say about the P-39, where a lot of people don't. It had a reputation, which I never thought it lived up to, for something called tumbling, which is the opposite of rolling, and it's nose over tail, tail over nose, whatever you want to call it. I think that if you just get it too slow, you might have problems. For example, a lot of the Russians, who never had any training at all, would do that. Though I never delivered the P-39 to the Russians, because I wasn't flying pursuit, a lot of WASPs did deliver them. I think Great Falls and Anchorage were the places where they landed them. The Russians would have some major problems with the tumbling, which is pretty hard to get out of.

Why do you think you were so interested in flying a pursuit?

I just kind of loved the idea of a solo experience. You don't have to get up in a bomber with a whole big crew, two, three, four people. I am kind of a fighter mentality, instead of a bomber mentality. But I enjoyed flying some of the bombers I checked out in. These included the B-25 and B-26. Also, I actually checked out in a B-24 and was co-pilot in a B-17 quite a bit. And it was fun. I didn't like the B-24. It was extremely heavy on the controls. We had two girls flying it, and then we would have a flight engineer, sergeants usually, some old guy, maybe thirty, thirty-five years old, married, usually with kids. Boy, these guys didn't want to fly with two girls at all! Still, after awhile, when they saw that we had a better accident record than the men, they were very happy to fly with us.

What's the worst treatment you've received from a man?

I was really lucky, I guess. The worst was when I left Palm

Springs and went to Williams Field in Arizona. I spent the last three months in the WASPs there, but our commanding officer there, Col. Grill, did not like women pilots. There were only about ten of us there. It was a small group, but our job there was interesting. There were a lot of men cadets—I don't know how many—maybe four hundred, and they were going through their normal training, and a lot of them cracked up planes. The school was a class for advanced training. When a plane was cracked up and then was supposedly repaired, one of our ten WASPs had to test fly it and find out if it was okay for the men to fly. Everything was wrong with those aircraft. Most of our good mechanics had gone overseas, and boy, if your gear didn't come up or come down, you weren't surprised. That was almost normal. If the wings stayed on, you were lucky. And if the engine didn't quit, I mean, it was almost that bad. I think 90 percent of our test planes needed more work.

Oh, that's tough, isn't it?

Well, I didn't care for it much. You had to really stay on your toes because you didn't know what was going to happen next.

What sort of things did the colonel say? Disparag-
ing remarks...

He did not say anything in particular. At Palm Springs, I think we had twenty-five or so WASPs, and the commanding officer thought we were great. We did the job as well or somewhat better than the men, and they treated us beautifully there. And then suddenly we got sent to Williams Field. It was a whole different atmosphere. We didn't feel a bit welcome. That's where we were when we heard we were going to be deactivated. Everybody was deactivated the same day, December 20, 1944.

Tell me your feelings though about deactivation.

We all just hated it. We would have flown for free, let alone for the very meager pay that we were getting, I don't even know what it was. But we loved flying the military aircraft, and then suddenly to be told, "Hey, it's over." It was very difficult.

Talk about your transition from flyer back to civilian society.

I was lucky in some ways because I got a few jobs. There were a few flying jobs, not very many. But I flew for a couple of non-scheduled airlines. I flew from New York down to Puerto Rico. I flew co-pilot on DC-3's mostly. Then we did some trips flying Brahman bulls down to down to Cartagena, Columbia. We took nine at a time—three rows of three each. That was really not quite legal because there was a law that said, when flying livestock, that they should all be able to lie down at the same time. If you know anything about cattle, you know they sort of get fatter when they lie down. So on our flights only two could lie down and the other one would kick the heck out of the ones lying down. And when it was his turn, he would get kicked. At the time, the company was scarcely making any money as it was. With eight cattle, we would never have been able to get to fly the flight. We flew out of New Jersey and we would go to Lumberton, North Carolina, because fuel there was something like five cents a gallon cheaper there. For that reason, all the "non-scheduleds" used Lumberton, and we would go to Miami and then on down to South America or Central America.

On this one trip, I felt really sorry for these Brahman bulls. We landed in Miami, and it was very hot, and the bulls had been cooped up for a long time. I was just the co-pilot, but I asked the pilot if I could take them off the aircraft and give them some water to drink before we took off. And he said fine. It wasn't so easy to get them off. They all were easy to lead on board, with a halter on, but getting them to turn around, was difficult. Then they practically galloped. You had to get out of the way when they saw that fresh air coming in the back door. Outside, I tied maybe one or two at a time to the metal fence. Then I would get buckets of water, and they were really happy to get a drink.

But at one point, I didn't make a very good knot, and the next thing I knew, the bull was loose and just galloping down the runway and all over the airport. There was a great deal of traffic in Miami Airport. They had Eastern and American Airlines there—you name it. And so the tower had to shut the field down for, I think it was, about two hours. The airport authorities finally got a professional cowboy in a truck with his horse, and he managed to lasso the bull and we loaded him up again. But it was pretty exciting for a while.

Did you get in any trouble for that?

I didn't get in any trouble, no. My pilot thought it wasn't the greatest thing that I hadn't tied a good knot, but, anyway, it worked out.

The unscheduled airline we flew for would go bankrupt, and the next morning, with the same pilot and the same aircraft, we would have a different name painted on the side. One was Puerto Rican Air Transport. We flew a lot of Puerto Ricans from San Juan up to Harlem. They would have some relatives in New York. In Puerto Rico, they had a lot of farms and they had fresh air and sunshine for their kids and chickens and cows. Then they thought America, or I should say the New York area, was the promise land. They'd come up in January, and the women were wearing sleeveless, cotton dresses, and it was just terrible. At one point, we were trying to get more passengers. Eastern Airlines was charging something like a hundred dollars. We were charging something like eighty or ninety. We kind of had a price cut so we could get some passengers. We'd have a mother, we'd have a four-year old on her lap and a two-year old and then maybe a baby, and the one rule we did obey was seatbelts for everyone. That would take another half hour before take off just to get everyone belted in.

So you were, in a sense, an early commercial pilot, weren't you?

It was non-scheduled, but you could say that. The pilot I think was getting five dollars an hour, and I would get three dollars an hour.

What year was this?

Well, right after the WASPs, and that broke up in '44, so about '45 or '46, I guess.

And you didn't have any adverse or unusual reactions to you as a female flying.

No, I was a good pilot, I think.

And just did the same job that a man would. But there wasn't any prejudice back then that you saw?

Not for the jobs that I had or the area that I was flying in.

194

I remember when the WASPs broke up that I wrote about fifty letters to every aviation recruiter of the airlines, but they weren't hiring any women. Of course, now there are a lot of women flying for the airlines, but in those days, there weren't any. And then I wrote to a lot of corporations that had aircrafts, to see if they would like to hire me to pilot, but I never knew there were so many ways to say no.

What was the lamest response you had from these people?

Oh, I don't know. All the responses read something like, "Well, we are just not hiring anybody at this time, but contact us again in another six months or a year." Those were the nice ones, and that was it.

Well, have you always liked a challenge?

I guess so.

Where do you get that? Do you get that from one of your parents?

No, not really. I was really glad my parents let me continue flying after my brother was killed. I've enjoyed it so much all my life, and I'm still interested in flying. I'm going to a conference called Women in Aviation next month in Reno, Nevada, and I'm going to be honored there in something called The Hall of Fame for Pioneer Women in Aviation. And all of us are getting on in years as you can realize at this point.

Can you imagine yourself not having flown?

Probably not. I have no idea what I would have gotten involved with. Well, I will be eighty years old in about four months.

You were born in '21?

Yes, July, 1921, I was born in Great Neck, New York. I had my first airplane flight when I was at Bennington College in Vermont. And they had a little air circus that came, and I guess I was about eighteen or nineteen years old at the time. I just went up there with a friend of mine who also went to Bennington. She's passed away now, but anyhow she thought it was fun, but I thought it was just marvelous. I knew what I wanted to do that minute that I landed. There was no question; it was just so black and white. And I called my dad in New York and said, "Hey, I just went for an airplane ride and I want to learn to fly, and I want to leave college and start flying tomorrow." And the only problem of course was money. I didn't have any money. I kept thinking my parents would probably have given me some sort of very minor allowance, for whatever I was spending it on, but nothing like the cost of an actual flight lesson. So I kind of panicked my dad, I guess. I was doing well in college and he said, "Please don't move, don't leave, I'll be up tomorrow." It's a long four or five hours from New York, and he came up and we had a big talk and came to an agreement. If I would stay in college and get good grades, he and my mom would pay for flight lessons. And I thought that was a wonderful thing to do. And that's what I did and that's how I got started. And then when I had about 150 hours, and I was working on my commercial, which takes about 200 hours, I got a telegram from Jackie Cochran. I had my private license, but not the commercial, and she had gotten ahold of every woman that had a private license or better and wanted to know if we would be interested in a training program, one very similar to what the male cadets had. I had my return telegram back before you could bat an eyelash. I think a great many of the other girls did, too.

And what year was this?

I started in the WASPS in February of '43, that was my senior year of college, and I finished college early and wrote my thesis early. They were letting us do all kinds of things because of the war. And I started in February of '43, and we were all disbanded in December '44. So I had almost two years, which was great.

So how many hours do you have total?

Something around nine-thousand now. My husband and I did a lot of flying and my license is no longer current. I quit flying, I'm trying to tell you, when I sold the helicopter. That was the last of my flying, and I think this was between ten and fifteen years ago. My memory is not great for some of these dates. They're not going to be accurate.

Well, that's amazing, though. Wonderful. How many air vehicles have you flown and checked out on, do you suppose?

Counting different models of the same plane at the base, we had the BT-13 and the BT-15. They were very, very similar. One would have a slightly different tail or something. But they were practically the same thing. I guess maybe twenty or twenty-five.

Wow. Do you have a favorite Jackie Cochran story?

Not really.

Did you really like Jackie very much?

Not at all. But I was always very very grateful to her and I am here today because without her we never would have had the WASP program.

I still remember the night my brother was killed. My mother called the base, I was in the middle of basic training at Sweetwater, and we were allowed to go outside of our bay, our room that we all lived in, I think until ten o'clock at night, or something like that, and then we had to be in the bay, if not in bed. I've forgotten the rules. But I went for a walk and that was perfectly legal. And then when I came back, one of the baymates of mine said, "Oh Betty . . . you had a call." We didn't have phones in the bay. The officer of the bay, or whatever, had been down there trying to find me because I had a phone call and it was important. But he couldn't find me, so they were going to talk to the commanding officer. Well, that was looking so bad, I just knew it. And the baddest thing I could think of was that something had happened to my brother. Otherwise, why would the commanding officer take my call? And Jackie Cochran was on the field at that point and she was talking. They were in a meeting—she and the commanding officer. And I guess some other people. And so I went with him up to the main room, which was quite a ways from our bay. And, that's where the telephones were, and I was going to call my family and make sure, if anything, was okay. I didn't think it was, but I was hoping I was mistaken. And so, the guy that was in charge, the officer of the day, or whatever he was, read my name tag and he said, "Oh I've had orders about you. You're not to make any phone calls." I thought "wow," and then I really knew it was something bad. And they went on with that meeting for maybe another hour. It was after eleven o'clock at night. And finally Ms. Cochran came out, she and the commanding officer. The two told me what had happened and that they wanted to be with me when I got the terrible news. And I always thought that was not great of Jackie, that it wasn't very understanding. You know, if you had the word, it would be, the sooner you know what's happened, the better. It was probably the worst hour of my life.

Katherine "Kaddy" Steele
"Trail-blazer and Ph.D"

Katherine "Kaddy" Steele has been a pioneering WWII flier, a chicken farmer, and an academic. Nicknamed "Kaddy" when her sister had trouble pronouncing the word Katherine, the name stuck.

Born in Marquette, Michigan, she graduated from Northern Michigan University in 1940. That same year, she had joined the Civilian Pilot Training Program (CPT), where she received her private pilot rating, after which she joined the Army Air Corps and became part of the Women Airforce Service Pilots, training a Sacramento at B-25 Transition, and at Biggs Field, El Paso, as part of a Tow Target Squadron, where she remained until deactivation. "Kaddy" has flown a variety of planes, including the following: PT-19, BT-13, AT-6, UC-78, A-24 (SBD), A-25 (SB2C) AT-7, AT-11, C-45, B-25, B-26, and P-47.

Her duties included tow target, simulated strafing (with the sun at the pilot's back, diving to buzz troops and gunnery), searchlight missions, flying at night without navigation, radar tracking, low-altitude night missions, laying smoke screens at low altitude, and occasional ferrying.

At the end of 1944, the military deactivated her. Katherine would continue to blaze trails after that. After the WASP years, she went to the Middle East where she was farm production manager at a poultry farm and hatchery in Beirut, Lebanon. She received both her master's degree in 1965 and her doctorate in

1969, from the University of Florida. After a stint as an adjunct professor at the University of Florida, she took a job at Florida Atlantic University for four years, then returned to an administration position at the University of Florida, retiring in 1986. "Kaddy" has also been an acrobatic pilot, control chief tower at Bartow, Florida, and a flight instructor.

She is still active in the WASP organization, where she says her deepest friendships still endure. Of them she says, "It's a camaraderie that I don't think you can get anyplace else. After all these years, we're as tight as ticks. I see my WASP friends at the meetings and correspond with them. We're very, very tight." A member of Women in Military Aviators, Experimental Aircraft Association, P-47 Thunderbolt Pilot's Association and Women in Aviation International, this bright and lively veteran served as chair of the "2000 and Beyond" committee of the WASP.

Tell me about your solo flight.

I had only seen two airplanes is my life before I got involved the Civilian Pilot Training Program. In fact, I didn't take it to learn to fly. I only took it because I needed two credits in Physical Education to permit me to graduate that August. Dr. Harold Bottom, who was in charge of the program, asked me to take it because they allowed one woman for every ten men. He felt sure that I would be able to succeed because I was athletic and he thought that my coordination would be okay. Then the first time I flew, I was hooked. At the time, we flew a side-by-side Taylorcraft. For my solo, Sig Wilson, my instructor, just got out of the plane after my eight hours of dual instruction and said, "Go around the field." I did and thought it was very exhilarating. I had a lot of confidence in myself at that time, I guess. I didn't think it was any big deal. I mean I wasn't particularly nervous or upset.

Where do you think you got your confidence?

I got it from my mother, who was a nurse and a very strong, confident woman. My father died when I was 13 from a ruptured appendix. It was right in the worst part of the Depression, in 1932. My mother went to work, raised us, and sent us both through college. She was born in Sweden and came to this country when she was 18 years old with her six-year-old sister and her nine-year-old brother. She didn't speak a word of English. They came to stay with her older sister, who lived in Omaha, Nebraska. Tragically, the day my mother arrived in the United States, her older sister died of a heart attack. That meant my mother was on her own from then on. She was just a very, very strong person and she just convinced us at a very early age that we could do whatever we wanted to do if we just worked at it hard enough. And I believed her.

The only reason we weren't on relief was because my mother was working. She was very capable; she really was. When I went to the WASP, I was 24-years-old and did not have much flying time—maybe about 75 hours. But it never entered my mind that I was going to wash out. I just did whatever I was supposed to do and I guess I did it well enough. There were 161 in my class and only 58 graduated. After we finished at Sweetwater and got our wings, I was sent with 19 others out to Mather Field in Sacramento, California, for B-25 Transition School. We were there for almost four months. I didn't have any trouble with that one, either.

Did you run into any tough instructors, or instructors who seemed anti-female?

When I first went to Sweetwater in that primary program, I

had trouble with my first instructor. A civilian contract company under the direction of the Army ran the field. We had all the Army personnel there, but the instructors were civilians. We got instruction from the civilians and check rides by the Army pilots. It was not that my first instructor was anti-female, but that I just could not understand him. I had never been south of Chicago in my life and this man was from Corpus Christie, Texas. I didn't think he was speaking English. A gentleman that I knew at the Detroit airport just before I came down to Texas, one of the flight commanders, called me in at the end of the first week and said, "Why are you doing so badly? Your instructor isn't giving you good grades at all." I said, "I don't know what he's talking about. He tells me to do something and I don't have any idea what it is that I'm supposed to do." So the flight commander gave me a change of instructor immediately. Incidentally, the new flight instructor was from New Jersey and I understood him perfectly. That kind of an accent was closer to what I was used to listening to than that Texas accent.

I know that many of the WASPs had a lot of trouble with regard to the reaction of some men; however, I can say that all the time that I was in, I never had anything but real good relationships with the guys.

What's the worst story you ever heard concerning the mistreatment of WASPs?

There's so much rumor and misinformation about it, I don't know how much is true. I was in Class 43-7, Camp Stewart, near Savannah, had women from earlier classes who had problems. The military sent these women down there, and I think one of the problems was that the people at the base didn't know that they were coming; they just sort of arrived. This threw all the men there into a flap because they didn't know what to do with them. It was a Tow Target Squadron and the men were very much opposed to having them there. The commanding officer opposed it too so, of course, everybody in the chain-of-command did. Not only were the women treated badly, but also some of the women thought that the airplanes were being sabotaged. One woman was killed. They didn't do an awful lot of investigation at the time. When they finally investigated the incident, they never really came up with any satisfactory explanation. It was then that Jackie Cochran came down and jerked them all out of there. Three of the girls that were at our field at El Paso also had been at Stewart. They said that even the enlisted men on the flight line treated them badly. I know that few of them had overt hostility. It was mostly covert: just being ignored or not considered or given the worst assignments. On the other hand, I was very lucky. I can't believe it. Our commanding officer, Major Richard Aikens, loved us all. He had been at Ascension Island, in the middle of the Atlantic for about two and a half years. When he returned and they made him commanding officer of his Buckeye Squadron with 27 women, he thought he'd died and gone to heaven. He was really wonderful to us. He really was.

Give an example of how he went out of the way for you?

I guess he must have been responsible for it, because before Aikens came we had a major who ignored the girls, and would always give them the least enjoyable assignments. The girls would get the trainers to fly or be assigned to rather dumb jobs. But when Aikens came, he made it very equal. We got to fly all the best airplanes, just like the men did. We alone didn't get the best planes, but they were on the line so when we did the rotation, we could fly them. The men didn't seem to object to that.

Aikens just treated us like we were equal, which was what we thought we were. He didn't want to alienate the men either, so he didn't show partiality to us necessarily. He had the idea that our jobs were rather boring and we had to have a chance to do something that wasn't quite so boring. From Friday night until Monday morning, he let us take any airplane on the line that was flyable and go as far as we could go as long as we got back. Consequentially, we had these wonderful cross-country flights to Los Angeles or to Dallas or to New Orleans.

Give me a typical day in your life as a WASP.

Our missions changed every day. Sometimes we had a lot of night flying. The squadron flying personnel was divided into three flights: flights one, two and three. We had required missions from 6 a.m. until noon: from noon until six in the evening, from six in the evening till midnight. We would rotate through that schedule. For an early morning mission, you had to be down there at six o'clock, and sometimes before six, because we were flying gassing missions that meant we had to take off before dawn. When we had to fly gassing missions, it had to be calm air, because they didn't want the gas to be sweeping away from the troops before they had a chance to complete their practice. So gassing missions were those early morning flights. If your mission didn't start until about nine o'clock, then maybe you were towing the sleeve in a single-engine SBD—the Army called them A-24s—but they were really Navy planes. You would be towing a sleeve for 50mm guns on the ground. All of our flying was for anti-aircraft. The sleeves had 2,000 feet of cable on them, but we used to call up and say, "I'm pulling, not pushing it! You're shooting too close to the airplane." Sometimes we'd come back with bullet holes. It didn't happen to me, but it did happen to other pilots. We also flew targets for the 47-mm guns, but that was at higher altitude. There, they used a two-engine airplane because they had to have a bigger sleeve and they had to let the sleeve out through the bomb bay doors with a winch on it, which allowed them to winch it back in—and winch it out, too.

We flew night missions endlessly. Sometimes we had to fly night missions for radar tracking two weeks in a row. The radar-tracking missions were connected to the searchlight training. We had to fly at higher altitude because the radar was tracking our aircraft and sending the information—our position—to the searchlights. We were flying Twin Beachcraft for that. The plane had a service ceiling of about 19,000 feet, though were usually flying between 16,000 and 19,000 feet. Usually there would be four airplanes separated by 1,000 feet. We would fly prescribed courses where we were constantly crossing each other. We flew with no lights on and faced some danger.

Describe a close call.

I can't describe one because you never knew what the close calls were. You couldn't see anybody. We were constantly saying. "What's your altitude? What's you altitude?" The two guys in the middle, especially, had somebody on top and on the bottom. The preferred place to be was either on the top or on the bottom, because if you were on the bottom you could drop down 1,000 feet, and if you were on the top you could go up 1,000 feet. We always drew straws to see who was going to get those middle spots—because nobody wanted to get stuck there all the time. It was very, very tense and nerve-racking. They were four-hour missions. It was all instrument flying. We just had to sit there and grind it out.

Did you lose any women?

We only lost one woman in our base, and unfortunately, we never got a chance to know her very well because she was in a later class. She was only there about two weeks before she was killed. She mistook the dive flaps for the wing flaps and the plane just went right in on takeoff. It's terribly upsetting, even though we didn't know her very well. Another crash on base proved to be even more depressing to us. We were a very small squadron on the end of an RTU B-24 base. RT stands for "re-training"— for replacing troops that had already been to combat. The base had 152 B-24s and each B-24 had a crew of ten. Just west of the airport in El Paso, there's a mountain that's about 5,000 feet. You have that T-setting that you would fly, which was to the northwest. Each time, the pilots would be reminded in a briefing of the mountain. We would hear, "Make your first turn at 700 feet to avoid the mountain because you have not got enough altitude to go over it after that point." Month after month, we all remembered that. During the winter months, when we go a lot of wind out of the northwest, one of the B-24s took off and went right into the mountain; never turned, never made any attempt to turn. It just went right into the mountain and killed all ten men aboard and so the military suspended flying. They shut down until everybody could try to get over the shock. They resumed flying and two nights later, another plane hit the mountain. We had three airplanes in less than two weeks that hit that mountain. They never had the funerals on base. Rather, they sent home all the bodies.

How did people grieve?

We were in shock. Unfortunately, most of the grieving took

place at the bar at the Officer's Club. When I look back on it, I'm much more perceptive than I was when I was there, because I was too young to understand what was really going on. When you think of it, these are 19-23 years-old. We didn't have counselors that would talk to you like they do now. But, nobody wanted to talk about it. They didn't want to mention it. And they just sort of tried to act as though it didn't happen. Even among us women, who didn't even know these guys, we did the same thing. We didn't mention it, either.

Do you think that's one of the reasons that people from WWII sometimes have chosen not to talk about the war experience?

I think that probably had something to do with it. But my theory about why military people, not only in World War II, but in other situations—maybe even in peace time—find it very difficult to talk to civilians is because civilians don't understand at all what it's like to be in the military. All the people who've been in the military will talk about it in the language and the vocabulary that we used. We used terms like TDY (Temporary Duty). These are expressions that we know about. We know exactly what they mean. I find when I talk to someone who is really a raw civilian, I have to do so much explaining. I don't think it makes any difference whether you're in the infantry or the air force.

It may ruin the story if you have to stop before the punch line to explain.

Now that we WASPs have become living legends, everybody wants everything talked about. I always tell people that there is nothing in civilian life that prepares you for the military. There's just nothing that I can think of with the exception of incarceration in a minimum-security prison. It's not like going away to college. It's not like going to summer camp. Because, really, your entire life is regulated. They tell you what to wear. They tell you when to wear it. They tell you where to sleep. They tell you how to get there. There is nothing in civilian life that prepares you for that, because you really don't have any self-reliance. You don't have to figure anything out. The give you a manual to follow for every operation that you do. And you better damn well do it that way. I mean, don't be creative, if you want to stay in the military. It was said, "There's a right way, a wrong way, and the Army way."

Was there ever a time that you departed from regulations?

There were a couple of times, but I certainly didn't let anybody know.

I did something when I was in training. We came to the cross-country part of our training. We thought most of us were going to go in the Ferry Command, and so we got a lot of cross-country time. At first, they would give us a prescribed course to fly. We would fly to maybe three different points on the map. We weren't supposed to land. We'd fly over these points and we had to radio in, report to the station, and go onto the next one, and so on until we got back to the base. We were flying BT-13s, which was a basic trainer with fixed gear.

After coming to Texas from Michigan where I had a lot of things to orient myself with such as Lake Superior, I found Texas looked like just a big flat piece of land where everything looked the same. I couldn't find anything. For example, there were very few trees and nothing that stood out to help you keep track of where you were. (That's what I like about Florida. You can't get lost in Florida because there's water on both sides.)

209

But Texas looked too much the same to me.

If you had a forced landing, you were supposed to land and leave the airplane there and then go call the base, which would send somebody out to pick up both you and the airplane. That was a very strict regulation. Once I went out on this cross-country flight and at about the second checkpoint, I got a little confused and had no idea where I was. I knew I was going in the right general direction, but I couldn't tell exactly where I was from anything on the ground. I didn't want to go down and buzz the town so I could find the water tower and read the town's name off of it. I feared the local people might catch the license number on my plane and turn me in. Finally, I saw a field that looked to be about 2,000 feet long. Someone had burned the grass. There was one tree off to the side of the end of one runway and a man who was plowing a field nearby. There weren't any buildings or other people around but a town was within about two or three miles of it.

I decided I need to know the name of that town because I found this out, I could figure out the rest. So I thought to myself, I don't want to wait until I run out of gas to find out where I am. And now that I've still got enough gas to get to where I'm supposed to be, the best thing to do would be to land, even though I knew I was not supposed to do that. I took a chance and I went in and landed. I thought: If I crack this thing up on landing, I'll tell them I had a forced landing, and if I crack it up on takeoff, I'll tell them that I tried to get in and missed the field. I had this all figured out in my head. A nice lie I had. I went in and I landed. I was in a hurry because I didn't want the people behind me to come by and see the airplane on that field, so I parked over by the trees. I ran over with map in my hand to the man on the tractor. When he saw it was a woman, the poor man nearly fainted. I said to him, "Where am I?" That's a nice leading question to ask.

And he said, "What do you mean, where are you? Don't you know where you are?"

I said, "No, I don't. What's the name of that town over there?"

And he said, "That's Breckenridge."

I said, "Thank you." And I turned around and ran back to the airplane and jumped in it and quickly took off.

I never told a soul about that, because I would have been washed out for it. That was a very bad "no-no." Regulations made a lot of sense because at that time, we were not really proficient enough to be making those kinds of landings and takeoffs. If it had been at an operating airport, it probably would have been a little bit better, but to land in the middle of a field like that was ridiculous.

Tell me a story that illustrates the courage of the WASP.

I think the courageous part of the thing was that we did our job. We did it well, and we didn't cause anybody any trouble. We did exactly what we were supposed to do when we were supposed to do it. Women, especially my generation of women, were better at mundane, repetitive jobs, because that is what women were raised to do: to make the bed every morning, to feed the family, to do the washing, those kinds of things. I think there's a truth to that, although that wasn't my particular background. I wasn't married and I didn't have those kinds of responsibilities, but I was raised like all women of my generation. That was what women did. I'm not so sure about that because in combat every day is a new day. It takes a tremendous amount of guts to get in there and get your head shot off. But to do the kinds of things that we did: the training of navigators, the training of bombardiers—those are

211

the worst jobs in the world. And so is flight training. It's the same thing, over and over again. And the tow-target business was the same thing. Ferry command pilots had much more excitement than we did. I don't know if there was any bravery connected with it, but at least they went different places and saw different things. I think it takes silent courage to do something when you have to do it over and over and over again. We didn't have to do what we did. We could have quit, which is more than the men could have done. If it got too much for us, we could have quit. And some women did: not very many, at least for that reason. Women did resign for other reasons. Sometimes it was personal.

Tell me abut the WASP who was killed.

That was at Davis Monter. There were 38 who were killed. That's the only one that I know of where that commanding officer wouldn't send the body back. And I have no idea why. When that woman was killed on our base, our commanding officer sent the body back, and he sent one of the WAFs (Women's Auxiliary Ferrying Squadron) along with the body to meet the family and try to console them about what happened. I don't think that there was anybody that got into that program that couldn't have made it if they'd had enough time. The problem with that kind of a program—not just that program, but anything that happened during the war—everything was accelerated. They had to get everybody through in the shortest amount of time that they could. The men told me the same thing about male cadets who washed out. If they'd only given the person enough time, things would have been different. I had been an instructor myself and I know that's true, almost anybody can learn it. I used to say I could teach a cow to fly if could get it in the cockpit. The instructors would tell us how to do something once, demonstrate it and then we would try to execute the maneuver. Most of the time, unless the effort was so bad that it wasn't even close, they would allow us to do it again. More often than not, they did it once and then they'd send you up solo and say, "Now, practice that." So you'd go up and, if you hadn't done it exactly right the first time, you probably were practicing it wrong to begin with. Then, they'd check ride you and they'd say, "Well, you didn't do it right." At that point, you were out of the program.

You have taught, so you know what learning theory is all about. Everybody doesn't learn at the same rate. You had to be really quick to get it the first time. I found out when I was being instructed that sometimes, if you asked your instructors at the time if they would demonstrate something again, they would. But most of us were so damn scared of their instructors. It wasn't that the instructors bullied. Somehow, we all got the idea that unless we said nothing but "Yes sir!" we were going to get washed out anyway. One of the things that may be indicative of that is that nobody I know of in that whole program ever got washed out for on-ground school. We were tested two or three times a week on our ground schoolwork. There was a lot of geometry for that navigation. Some of the girls were not very good in math and the geometry was a little sticky if you hadn't had it. I'd already gone through college so I guess I had a little more education than some.

Where there any complexities in terms of men and women working together?

The men just accepted us as guys. I don't mean so much in the military, because in the military we were separated. When we were in El Paso, for instance, we didn't fraternize with any of the men in our squadron. There were 4,000 men on the field, and 27 women, so we did not have to look for companionship. The base had a wonderful Officer's Club, which had a big swimming pool and a bar. As a girl, you just picked somebody you wanted to be friendly with. If somebody put a hit on you and you did not like it, you could say, "Bug off!" I think all this stuff that is going on now in the military, especially in the enlisted ranks, is because men are using their rank and position to intimidate women. They should be bashed for that. During WWII, if our commanding officer had demanded sexual favors, I don't know what we would have done. Of course, we had a net. If anything detrimental came up, we could call on Jackie Cochran. She had tremendous clout. If we told her, "These guys are giving us a bad time," the guys would hear about it, not from her, but from someplace at the top.

What has flying meant to you?

I don't think that this applies just to me, but I think for anyone in my generation involved in WWII, that it was probably the highlight of his or her life. It was such a turning point. It was more important than the other things we use as benchmarks, such as graduating from college and getting married. But to go through the experience of something of the magnitude of WWII and to be actually involved in it and maybe contribute, is something— although I get very annoyed when somebody calls me a patriot.

Why?

I did not do what I did for patriotic reasons. I did it because I wanted to fly airplanes. I was just fortunate to have a war.

But you're not an anti-patriot?

Oh, no. I'm not an anti-patriot. I think the concept of patriotism is very good. The people I think are patriots are the ones who lead exemplary lives as civilians. They do their job, raise their kids, vote. I think that's what a real patriot is.

How would you like to be remembered?

I can't think of any particular way. I hope they don't forget me completely. I don't know. I never thought of that. I think I would like to be remembered as someone who was very good at making a commitment. Once I started to do something, I did it. If I didn't think I could do it, I wouldn't even start. I think the other thing I'd like to be remembered for is as someone who had the confidence to do and accomplish whatever she started out to do. I never quit on anything. I never quit on my marriage. I never quit on my educational objectives. I never quit on my flying objective. If I decided to do it, I did it. I think that is something I wish more parents would stress with their children. It just seems to me that people don't make commitments like they used to. Maybe there is a generation gap, I don't know. Maybe that's not so important, but it was important to me.

Gladys Buroker

"Training at Farragut and Other Tales"

Gladys Buroker has flown planes, taught students, both military and civilian, and lived a glorious life of flight. She described that life during a visit my ten-year-old son, Sayer, and I made to her Athol, Idaho, home, set back in the woods from the Silverwood Theme Park. As Sayer moved stealthily as a cat about the room, sometimes sneaking photographs with his Olympus 35mm camera, we proceeded with the interview. Gladys seemed delighted to see the boy's newfound enthusiasm for photography. And I would soon learn of the enthusiasms of a woman who stands out as a Northwest flying legend.

Over the years, Gladys logged over 19,600 hours, eighty-percent of it instructing. But the breadth of her experience is what is remarkable. Her awards—too many to name—include Hall of Fame Pathfinder Award, Museum of Flight; National Aeronautic

Elder Statesman of Aviation Award and the J.C. Penney Spirit of America Woman Award. Gladys' life story is told in a book, *Wind in My Face* by Fran Bahar. This gracious lady passed in 2002 at the age of 88.

The year was 1932, when eighteen-year-old Gladys took her first flying lesson. I ask her if she remembers her first flying lesson, and the interview is off and flying.

She explains:

I remember it very well. It was in an OX-5 WACO 10. My instructor took me to the airport, which was in a cow pasture. He checked the oil but didn't check the gas—I guess he assumed there was plenty. He put me in the back cockpit and decided I needed a cushion to see out, so he got a cushion and showed me how to fasten my seat belt. He gave me a helmet that had two tubes, one on each side at ear level that came down to a "Y" under my chin. The single tube went down into the cockpit and up under the front seat. When he got ready to start the engine, he told me to hold the stick back. Of course, there were no brakes so you couldn't hold brakes. He went around and pulled the prop through and the engine started. He got into the front cockpit, put his helmet on, then pulled the tube from my helmet that had a funnel shaped at the end around his neck. This is called a Gosport. He could talk to me, but I couldn't talk back.

It's no fun if you can't talk back.

There were times I wish that I could. He told me to keep my feet on the rudder and my hands on the stick and throttle. I felt him open the throttle, and we started taxiing down the field. When we got to the end, I noticed he gave a real blast on the throttle, and we swung around. I learned afterward that's the way you have to do it when you have a tail- skid and no brakes. All aircraft today have tailwheels. He said, "We're going to take off," and I felt him open the throttle, wide-open, and I felt the tail come up. I was on the controls, and I could feel him on them, too. We were off the ground pretty fast and in the air. He said, "Using right stick and right rudder, make a right turn." I did that, and I thought, "Gee, this is neat," and then I was making left turns. After several turns, he said, "Hold your altitude." Well, I hadn't even looked at the altimeter. I knew to hold my altitude I had to keep the airplane from going up or down. From then on, it was just like riding over the waves in a boat, trying to keep it level. Anyway, before we'd hardly gotten started, it seemed that the lesson was over.

"Okay," he says, "it's time to go back—I'll take it." So I thought to myself, "I must have been doing some of the flying." Anyway, after he said that, I could feel the airplane diving, and it was just an instant or two before my head went down and almost hit my knees. He was pulling back on the stick, and we went up into a loop. After that, the next thing I knew I was upside down. I found out later that he did what was called a slow roll. I remember saying, "Boy, that's enough. I'm getting sick." He kept it up and I really did get sick. I pulled myself up so I could get my head out of the cockpit. The next thing I remember him saying was, "Well, we're going to land—follow through." By then, I could have cared less what we landed on.

We landed, and I never did tell him I was sick, but I went and cleaned up the side of the airplane. I was afraid, if I told him, he wouldn't let me fly again. During the next lessons, he continued to have his fun. I got smart and didn't eat on the days I was scheduled to fly. Once I started on takeoffs and landings, I was never sick again.

That's great. What did your instructor say when you first went to him and said you wanted to fly.

He just ignored me. In fact, I was working in a little combination grocery store and service station, and he came in for gas. I waited on him. I didn't know who he was, but after he'd left, the lad I worked for told me he was the pilot from out at the field. So I was watching for him the next time he came in. I tried to talk flying with him. I told him I wanted to learn to fly, but he was more interested in visiting with the gal who owned the store. I did find out what it cost for lessons: twenty dollars an hour. I had five dollars saved up the next time he came in, so I asked him if I could get 15–minute lessons for five dollars. And he said, "Well, I guess so," but he still ignored me.

My boss was a friend of his, so the next time he came in, I got her to go with me to find out if I could get a lesson. Of course, I had no transportation, but at that time he was teaching high school in the morning and then did his flying in the afternoon and evening. She suggested that he stop by and pick me up on the way out and give me a lesson, and then bring me back when he was through. That's the way it turned out. Still, he didn't think I was serious.

Do you remember the point at which he realized that you were serious?

I think so. I don't think I'd taken many lessons until he realized that I wanted to learn to fly and was working hard at it.

Why did you want to learn to fly?

I was born a girl, but with all the desires of a boy—shall

I put it that way? I liked everything that boys liked—anything mechanical, anything with wheels. As I grew up, I had pictures of little scooters and cars I built, and models I made. That just seemed to be where my interest was, rather than in the house, cooking and sewing.

You were really a pioneer of sorts, weren't you?

That's what they tell me now. I didn't think much about it back then —although there were no other women flying where I was. I was the first wosman to fly in Whatcom County, where I soloed. That was in Bellingham, Washington. However, there

were a few other women throughout the country that were flying. But there were not a lot. No.

Did you get any catty remarks from men?

No, if I did, I wasn't aware of it. I've had people ask me

this many times, but I always felt equal to anyone in my same experience range, and was always treated that way. The fellows always treated me as an equal. The only thing that I can recall was when I was training Navy cadets. There were places for the cadets to sit out in the sun, if they wanted. One day, several cadets were sitting just outside my window, and I heard one say, "I understand there's a gal teaching here." Another cadet said, "Yeah, and it would be just my luck to get her, too, wouldn't it?" (laughs)

What year was that?

Our first Navy cadets came in 1942. Our first government training was in 1939 in Olympia. Due to military restrictions on the Pacific Coast, we moved to Coeur d'Alene, Idaho, in 1942.

What was the hardest thing about training for you?

We had a certain amount of time to put in, and the students had to be at a certain level at that time. There were students we had to eliminate that would have made good pilots if we could have just had them a little longer. I think that was the hardest part for me. But I never really felt training was difficult. I mean, I loved every minute of it.

What about the earliest plane you flew in and what was it like?

I thought they were great for the period of time that we were flying. They had large wheels. You could land out in the fields, and you didn't get into trouble like you do with the small wheels of today. They had tailskids and no brakes, but it was all grass or sod fields that you were using. The skid just slowed you down so there was no really need for brakes. I feel it was easier to learn to fly back then than it is today. The sod is much more forgiving on landing. The airplanes were slower. The only minuses I can think of were that the engines were not as dependable and, of course, there were minimal instruments. The plane I learned to fly on had an altimeter, water temperature gauge, oil pressure gauge and a magnetic compass—that was it. No airspeed indicator, so you truly learned to fly by feel. I am very fortunate to have learned the joy of flying in the early thirties and not today—with your cockpit a maze of gauges and instruments. It has become a concentration of instruments rather than a feel for flying.

Did that scare you?

What you don't know (Laughs), doesn't bother you. And others seemed to be learning.

Beryl Markham talked about how lonely it was to fly by instruments and without radio. Did you ever feel lonely up there?

No, I can't say I have. I've made quite a few cross-country trips. There was always enough going on to keep me interested. Maybe she was in the clouds and flying solely by instruments. I have an instrument rating but have not done a lot of instrument flying.

How do you look back on some of those pioneer aviators?

Lindbergh was my hero.

Ever get lost flying?

Oh, yes. I guess I'm ashamed to say that, really. That was right here, leaving Coeur d'Alene on my way to Burley, Idaho. I had my own plane and had three nurses with me. We were going down to a convention. I planned to go direct to Boise, but when we got down around Grangeville, the weather was solid fog so I turned back and landed at Lewiston and took on more fuel. Checking the weather, I was told I could probably make it to Boise, if I followed the Grande Ronde River.

I only had a World Air Chart with me. Actually, I should have used a sectional chart for the trip I was making. I thought I was doing all right. The farther south I went, the better the weather got. Somehow I missed Baker, Oregon, altogether. I never did see it. I knew from the time lapsed that I had passed it. I didn't know where I was, and I couldn't locate my position on the chart. (Thank heavens the three nurses were all sleeping.) After checking my time and compass heading, I decided I had passed the Boise Valley. I took a compass heading that I figured would take me to the valley. I finally came out in Ontario, Oregon. I had about two gallons of gas when I got there. That taught me a lesson. Never say you're too old to learn.

How old were you when that happened?

I was in my sixties.

Any forced landings?

Yes, I've had several. I had two forced landings in a Tiger Moth. I flew one on takeoff, and one when I lost a cylinder gasket while towing a glider. I got down all right. Another time, the crankshaft broke when I was out with a student. In addition, I once lost oil pressure while flying with a student. While teaching three Army cadets during the war on cross-country training, one tank ran dry, so the student that was flying switched tanks but nothing happened. The students said, "What do I do now?" I said, "We have to land. Tighten your their seat belts." I took over and talked to them on the way down. I had picked out a stubble field and landed OK. There wasn't a sound from the students from the time the engine quit until we landed. It turned out to be a vapor lock, and the engine started after it sat on the ground for about thirty minutes. I had several others also but have never damaged an airplane.

Did you ever repair some of your planes?

I have done a lot of rebuilding, not so much maintenance. When I first started flying, they had a WACO biplane that had been damaged, and they were rebuilding it. My first job was cleaning the rust off the longerons on the fuselage. When I finished, they let me build the ribs for the wings. That led to making an envelope to cover the wings. Of course, my husband was a pilot and mechanic, and I used to work with him on doping the wings. I've also worked with my neighbor, Walt Redfern, who builds replicas of WWI airplanes.

Did you ever barnstorm?

Yes, in the thirties. I went with Jim Galvin, whose company is still running at this time out of Boeing Field. They took Eddie Brown along, who was a parachute rigger, to pack my chutes. Eddie fitted the harness on me and showed me where the rip was. He told me to get up on the airplane and practice getting in and out with my chutes on. I would be jumping from a Swallow, which was an open cockpit biplane with a Hisso engine. I would be sitting in the front cockpit and was supposed to get out and stand close to the fuselage and hang on until it was time to jump. Then I talked to the pilot. He said, "When I get on the jump run, I'll shake the stick." That meant I was supposed to get out on the wing.

Back then, everybody thought you had to pull the airplane up into a stall. You jumped when the airplane stalled. That way, you wouldn't hit the tail when you jumped. I practiced getting in and out of the cockpit with my chutes on before my first jump.

My chute was a backpack with the ripcord on the left side, so I would have to grab it with my right hand. While practicing, I found I could reach it fine, so I thought, "This is a piece of cake." Next day, when it came time to go, I can tell you the feeling is different. We were at 3,000 feet when I felt the stick wiggling, so I got out. I can tell you that standing on the wing on the ground and standing on the wing going about eighty-miles-per-hour is a little different. I was hanging on for all I was worth. I'd let go real quick and tried to reach the ripcord and, of course, I couldn't. I thought to myself, "Should I get back in and face the crowd a coward—or shall I kill myself?" (laughs) I decided I don't want to go back and face the crowd. When Jim pulled up into the stall and told me to jump, I jumped. I can tell you, I wasn't long in getting hold of that ripcord once I left the airplane.

Did you do a lot of barnstorming?

I had agreed to make twenty jumps on that trip. I was injured on the seventeenth jump, so that was the end of my jumping. I bought my own airplane after that, a Travel Air 2000, which was an open-cockpit, three-place biplane, and barnstormed the Olympic Peninsula. That was before I had a license to carry passengers.

Where the Wings Grow

What year was that?

That was 1935. I actually had enough hours of flying to get a private license, but somehow it didn't seem important to me. Anyway, I had a pilot friend who went with me. We liked to go to Forks, Washington, as that was a good spot. It seemed like the people there—the loggers and the Indians—always had money. As we approached Forks, I'd get out and walk along the front spar, hanging onto the flying wires. Near the end of the wing, I could hang on to the wing strut—it's a little more stable, easier to hang on to, at least. When I was out there, the pilot would come in low over town—or wherever he saw people—and I'd wave. By the time we landed, we would always have people there ready to go for a ride.

That was how you made your money—on rides?

That was the way it was parachuting, too. When you got them out, you'd sell them rides.

What did a ride cost?

I can't remember what they charged when I was parachute jumping, but with my airplane, I was charging five dollars a flight for two people, so it would be two-and-a-half a piece. I bought the Travel Air—it cost $400.00. I had three hundred in my savings account and had to borrow the other hundred. I remember I was able to pay off the hundred in nothing flat.

What exactly happened when you got injured? How did it happen?

At the time I got hurt, we had two airplanes. Frank Kammer of Wenatchee had joined us with his Curtiss Thrush, a six-place cabin monoplane. I would alternate my jumps between the Thrush and the Swallow. The day I got hurt, I jumped from the Thrush, and it was probably the best I'd done landing by the crowd. I could see I was going to land on the strip we were using. When I was about 100-feet from the ground, Jim took off under me in the Swallow. I have never known for sure, but I feel that the turbulence from the Swallow partially collapsed my chute. I know I hit the ground much harder than ever before. I ruptured the cartilage in my right knee.

Once I was assisting on the rebuilding of the plane I told you about, and was asked if I'd like to fly to Boeing Field and pick up rib tape and cord they needed? Everett was as far south as I had been—I had never flown to Seattle. I said "Sure," if he thought I could do it, I was game. I'd never been out of a five-mile radius of the field. "How will I get there—I've never been there?" He just went over and got a road map and handed it to me. I collected my gloves, helmet, goggles, and jacket and went out and got into the airplane before he changed his mind. I asked about fuel. His reply, "There's plenty." When I got out of the five-mile radius, things were not familiar.

I had lived in Bellingham all my life, so I knew the highway south. I decided to take a look at the map. I took my gloves off and sat on them. I held the map with one hand, and the wind vibrated the map so I couldn't see a thing. I held the stick between my knees so I'd have two hands, but it was useless. The wind coming through the front cockpit made it impossible to read. I remember thinking at the time, "He just thinks I can fly by the seat of my pants, but how do you navigate by the seat of your pants?" I remember thinking that (Laughs). I knew the highway went to Seattle and I was sure I could make it to Everett. I had been there by car. I soon became apprehensive. I couldn't recognize anything, but still I could see what I thought was the highway —which was the only paved road at the time. I finally saw smoke up ahead. Then I knew it was the mills of Everett. The highway was easier to follow once I was past Everett, and I did make it to Seattle and Boeing Field.

What was your next most ambitious trip?

By '36, I had owned two motorcycles. The first one I owned was a four-cylinder Indian Ace, which I traded in for a new Harley 45. I had a girl-friend, and we thought we should see more of the country than northwest Washington, so we decided to take a trip and see every state in the United States. We both worked and saved until we had a $150 apiece. We left the first of September 1936 and were gone three months. We visited every state, up into Canada and as far south as Mexico City.

That must have been unusual for the times.

Well, it was, in fact. Very few people we saw realized we were girls. We slept in sleeping bags and always filled our gas tank in the morning at good-looking service stations so we could clean up.

One morning we pulled into this station, and my friend went into the restroom. The fellow waiting on us, a middle-aged fellow, started laughing. He said, "You know, I thought she was a fellow, too." So I just laughed with him. After I paid him, I headed for the restroom, too. When we came back out, he was standing in the door shaking his head and laughing. When we got to New York, we wanted to see the Empire State Building, so we pulled up and backed into the curb. We got in the elevator—it must have held 25 people—and as we started up, I could see this fellow staring at me. I finally turned and looked at him. He said, "Are you girls or boys? I said, "That's an insulting thing to ask a fellow." Everyone in the elevator just roared.

What else happened?

In Mexico City, before they had traffic lights, the police directed traffic on the corners. We were just leaving the city on our way back to the United States, when a policeman pulled us over the side of the street. I told my friend, "If he speaks English, act like you don't understand him. I don't know what I've done." He talked Spanish, and we couldn't understand him. He finally started pulling at his ear. He didn't act mad or upset. People started gathering around and, after about ten minutes, I realized he was trying to find out if we were girls, so I said, "Si senoritas." Everyone laughed, and he sent us on our way.

You flew planes across country too, didn't you?

Yes, especially during the war. Most of the cross-country flying, to start with, was picking up aircraft that had been assigned to us for training. We taught primary, secondary and cross-country courses. We'd take three students at a time for the cross-country course for a three-hour flight in a four-place cabin airplane. The student would change every hour, alternating with the flying, the radio work, or navigation.

Any tough situations on those flights?

I had a couple of forced landings. We were flying Fair-childs —they have two wing-fuel tanks. When one tank went dry, it would form a vapor lock, and the gas would not run from the full tank. The first time this happened, I landed in a field in Missoula, Montana. As soon as I was on the ground and tried the engine, it started. I found transportation for the students to Missoula Airport —not wanting to have them with me for the takeoff. I flew to the airport and picked them up. We returned home—I wanted the engine checked before another flight. This happened many times, especially during hot weather. We finally got smart. Every time he had to switch tanks, we made sure we were over an airport.

Of all the planes you've flown, what was your favorite?

I'd have to say the Fairchild 24 with a 165-horsepower Warner. It was just such a smooth, comfortable airplane to fly. For fun flying, I'd choose any of the open cockpit WACO biplanes.

Were you good at judging the length of clearings?

Yes, or maybe I was just lucky. You get pretty sharp after one or two forced landings. I think I've improved even in my old age, because the last twelve years I have done a lot of soaring and gliding. That makes you really conscious of wind direction and velocity. I've also had my own balloon and did quite a bit of ballooning. I think it's kind of what I said in the beginning, which is I've always liked anything with a challenge.

Any balloon stories?

I think the time I laughed the most was right after I got my balloon license. I started to teach my son-in-law. On our second flight, we were heading south. About the time we got over the rimrocks, the wind really started picking up. I was really inexperienced—even though I had my license. I really didn't have enough experience to be teaching someone else. So I told Doc we'd have to land. We kept looking, trying to find a field that we would line up with, because with a balloon, you have no control, except vertically. You just go where the wind takes you. We saw a field ahead where I planned to land. We were going so fast that it was going to take both of us to land. So I said, "I'll handle the burner, and when I tell you, pull the ripcord." That opens the top and lets the hot air out.

Just as we cleared the fence I yelled, "Pull the ripcord." I closed the burners and we hit the ground hard—throwing Dick out of the gondola. Here he is on all fours, trying to keep ahead of the burners. I mean it was funny—at the time anyway. The wind was so strong that it dragged the balloon, even though the apex of the balloon was wide open.

Do you feel like you've learned anything about the winds from flying gliders?

Yes, I'd say you become more conscious of the wind in a glider. Let's say your glider comes in on an approach for landing at 60 miles per hour. If you have a 10 mile-per-hour wind as you turn into the wind on your landing approach, you have to increase your speed to 70 miles per hour, in order to penetrate that wind and get to your runway. You do really have to be aware of the wind, and your correction that way. To me, gliding is the safest type of flying there is.

Is there any most engaging image you remember from your flying in those earlier days?

I think the thing that impressed me the most and has stayed with me the longest was my view of the earth while jumping—it's always a great sensation. You're just floating, and then I was always amazed at when you get down to about 100 feet above the ground, you don't have any sensation of falling at all. It just looks like you're standing there still, and the earth is coming up to meet you. It's a different sensation.

I've had a few pretty things. Three times in my flying career I've had a rainbow completely surround the aircraft. Not all pilots get to see that. It's being just in the right position between the clouds and the sun when atmospheric conditions are right that the rainbow is a complete circle. The last time that happened was a few years ago, while giving a young girl a glider lesson. The clouds were about 2000 feet, but there were holes in them. I had them tow us up through a hole, and we went out on top with the glider. When we released from the tow plane, we just happened to get in a spot where the sun was right on the moisture and the clouds. No matter where we turned, or where we went, the rainbow followed us. She was so excited about seeing it —she still talks about it when I see her.

I have never forgotten the day flying over the Cascade Mountains, flying from Kennewick to Seattle. We were above the overcast, and I spotted something ahead of us. I noticed I was gradually gaining on it. When close enough, I could see it was an eagle, and it was just going for all it was worth, looking back to see we were gaining on him.

What were you flying?

A Curtiss Thrush. One time in 1935, my husband-to-be, Herb, was going from Everett to Wenatchee to pick up an airplane. A young fellow that owned an airplane was flying Herb over to get some cross-country experience. The fellow's wife and I were took the bus over to Wenatchee and would fly back with them. When we got to Wenatchee, there was no sign of them. We stayed around for awhile and finally got a call from Herb, saying they had cracked up in the Cascade Mountains, and we'd have to come back home. They were flying above the overcast. This was before airplanes had carburetors with heat. It turned out the plane would lose power and let them down into the clouds, and then the engine would pick up power and they would lift up out of the clouds. That happened about three times. When the engine continued to lose power, they knew they were going down. The clouds stay pretty milky, but if you're close to the ground, it turns dark. When it turned dark, they came back on the stick, to slow the airplane down. Just about the time they came back on the stick, a big pine limb brushed by the airplane, and they pulled all the way back on the stick to stall it. One wheel hooked over a limb of a big tree and they just slid up against the trunk of the tree, stopping with the wheel hanging on one side. They were about 40 feet up in the tree. They had tools with them and were able to disconnect one of the control cables to help them get down from the tree. Neither of them got a scratch. As they were getting down from the mountain, they both got blisters on their toes.

That's pretty remote country.

Yes, for a number of years afterward, the Civil Aeronautics Authority (CAA) would get reports from hunters who saw that airplane up in the tree.

What were the worst flight conditions you've flown in?

Well, I've had a few things that kept me on my toes. One

happened when we moved to Coeur d'Alene from the West Coast. All my past flying had been along the West Coast, and I had never flown in snow conditions. I'd never even been in the air when it snowed. In order to get airplanes over here, they had to be ferried, and it was decided that I would take the six Piper Cubs that we were using for primary training. I would fly one, with five student pilots following. None of the students had received cross-country training. We couldn't come direct because the pass was closed, so we left Olympia, flew south to the Columbia River, then went east to The Dalles, in Oregon, where we refueled. The weather was minimal—this was in February 1942. As we headed east, my main concern was the responsibility of the students following. Before we got to Sprague, Washington, it had started to snow, and I was concerned. I had never flown in snow. There was an airport in Pasco, but when I did some figuring, I knew we would not have enough fuel to get back.

The conditions were getting worse, and there was no airport before Spokane. I knew we were going to have to land—and believe me—I had been looking. I was over Sprague Lake before I saw it—a field I figured would be all right. I made a circle to make sure I had all five airplanes behind me, and I did. I circled out around and came in and landed. I got out of the plane, stood on the ground and signaled to everyone as they'd come in, whether to land or go around again. The place had big cottonwoods that the students had to come in over. Eventually, they all got down.

How did you learn to deal with that stress?

Well, I'm not sure that I did. That's one thing about instructing —there's certainly a lot of stress. I think I felt it all my life, but I do think it got easier with time. I've done enough instructing to where I feel I'm a better judge of what students can do or what they're ready to do. One day out here, about six or seven years ago, when we were flying passengers in the glider, an airline pilot and his son came out and wanted to go for a ride, so I took his son up. That was a two-place glider, one passenger and the pilot. When we got back, I took the dad up. I always put the passengers in the front seat, so they could see much better. Just after take-off, I could see big rolls of dust off to the west. I thought, "That sure doesn't look good." We go to 2,500 feet before we release, so we went right on up to 2,500 feet, and I could see that a storm was coming. When I released, the tow plane went back to the field. There's lots of lift in front of the storm, so I was watching the tow plane and saw him try to land. He was drifting clear off the runway, and I never did see what happened to him, but I knew that he never landed on the runway. I knew I had to land and could see that there was a direct crosswind. I started losing some altitude and told the captain, "We have a real strong crosswind—a glider can't handle the crosswind that we have and land on the runway, so I plan to come in between the hangar and the cafe and land crossways on the runway." He turned around and said, "You can't do that. Look at all those trees!"

There were a lot of trees, but I knew I'd never get to the trees, even if I planned correctly. Well, here's an airline pilot, and you know how long a runway they have to have. But the guy was upset, petrified. He sat there and never said another word. I said, "I don't really have another choice—it'll be all right." I wanted him to know what I was doing, so he might be less frightened. I was heading into the wind sideways, until I turned in for landing. It was summer, and there were a lot of people out there watching to see what was going to happen. Fortunately, we got down all right and didn't roll ten feet when some of the Henley Aerodrome crew grabbed the wings.

What was the main change over the years in flying?

When I learned to fly, the air was free from the ground as high up as you wanted to go—and horizontally the same. Today, you can hardly go ten miles without invading some type of airspace. Things are so controlled now that there just isn't any freedom anymore. That's what I notice. I'm not saying it's bad, but I sure am glad I lived and flew when I did.

Do you ever long for the good old days?

No, not really. I think I've finally adapted to the change. It is kind of fun to tell people how it used to be. Sometimes, I think they think we're exaggerating, but I'm sure that aviation—the way I saw it back in the early days—was pretty much like it was for the pioneers who came west on the wagon trains. Now they have highways, and so on. We had no airways. The first airways I remember were towers with beacons on them. They had them between Missoula and Spokane and clear to Seattle. About every 25 miles, they had one of these towers with a beacon on it. The pilots could fly at night and follow those beacons. I took up nursing in the 1960s. And worked at the hospital. After work, nothing was more therapeutic than getting into the airplane and going flying. It was restful and I enjoyed that. But whenever I'm out flying, I'm thoroughly enjoying myself. I love to go out—especially with the glider. I do lazy-eights and wingovers and just kind of float around like a bird.

Do you think you have some secret wish to be reincarnated as a bird?

Maybe.

Beryl Markham, again, talked about developing an intuitive sense—or a fatalistic approach—and she said that most pilots she knew were like that.

I think most people who fly for any period of time have a fatalistic approach all right, but I really never felt pessimistic. I feel that, if I got killed in an airplane, it would probably be a mid-air crash. I just don't feel like there's any reason for having a problem otherwise. Of course, there are circumstances. My brother was killed in an airplane. He was only 1,000 feet in the air when the horizontal stabilizer let go—and he wasn't high enough to parachute out. He tried to, but the airplane hit the ground before he could even get out. So there are things that one cannot control.

That must have been tough, losing your brother.

Yes, it was, and especially so because I had taught him to fly. We were real close. Yes, it was hard.

You don't get over things like that.

No, you don't.

But you continued to fly.

Yes. There again, the thing that was hard for me was that my brother more or less idolized me as he was growing up. I was doing everything he wanted to do. And, as I said, I taught him. He was a fighter pilot in WWII. When he came back from WWII, he and Clay Henley, who were friends, built a midget racer. They went back to the Cleveland Air Races to fly it. My brother was doing the flying. They did so well that they decided to build another one and make it better—faster. They built this one with a cantilevered horizontal stabilizer. My husband, who was an aircraft mechanic as well as a pilot, told them they should put brace wires on the stabilizer, as a safety precaution. They didn't want to do that because it would cut down the speed.

In the meantime, my brother told Clay he would help finish the airplane, but he didn't want to fly this one because his wife was expecting a baby and he just felt he shouldn't. That was fine with Clay—he said they would make the cockpit a little bigger, and he would do the flying. Milton Chester, an engineer, stopped by to see the airplane and ran some tests on the stabilizer and told them it was fine, so they didn't even consider wires after that. After the plane was finished, Clay still couldn't get into the cockpit, so my brother changed his mind and said he would fly it. The plane had been flown about eight hours and was making one more flight before heading to Cleveland. It was on this flight that he crashed.

It's been quite a life of flight.

Yes, it has. Not many people can go through life earning a living at what they love to do and still have a nice family—I have three children and six grandchildren.

Do you think you'll ever stop flying?

I plan to fly as long as I can pass my yearly physical examination. I have a couple of airplanes down there in the hangar, and I sure don't want them to get covered with dust.

Doris Watson Thomas

"He Flew: She Flew"

Doris Watson joined the Air Force in 1941. As children, she and her brother—who were only 18 months apart—used to try to outdo each other. When her brother became a bomber pilot in WWII, Doris followed. Doris says, "I wasn't going to let him fly, if I couldn't fly. I just had to prove to him that I could do anything he did." So when she had a chance, she started taking lessons. By this time, she was married to Gordon Thomas, an Air Force pilot who also lived for flying. She would earn a 2nd Lieutenant commission in the U.S. Army Air Corps.

After moving to Orlando, Doris's husband bought a printing shop and then gave it to Doris, who ran it for a while before deciding to sell it. Along the way, she worked as a private detective, she says, "because I wanted to see what it was like." Later, she became Executive Director of the National Kidney Foundation. An exercise enthusiast, she was frequently found at the gym on the treadmill, lifting weights, or on the rowing machine. She and Gordon, the flying couple, lived in Orlando, Florida.

During her colorful life, this wonderful woman would work as a private eye and later own a café/bookstore and fine restaurant in Winter Park with her husband.

She died on July 28, 2011 and is buried in Arlington National Cemetary.

What did your brother say when you got your license?

He congratulated me and was happy for me.

*Did he have any big celebration? Do you remember anything
he told you?*

He was stationed somewhere else. Not too long after I got
my license, he was killed.

What happened?

It's a very sad story. He was at Hunter Field in Savannah,
and they were going to go on a training mission. The pilot and
my brother were flying. The pilot was a nervous person, who
at the slightest thing that might look like smoke would freak
out. Anyway, the pilot got the go ahead from the tower and got
into the pattern but then he decided he was going to come back
because of what he thought was smoke in the cabin. He got permission to turn around and started letting down. This was about
8:15 in the morning. He was landing right into the sun from the
Atlantic Ocean. A Gooney Bird was landing ahead of him, but
it landed on a taxiway, instead of the runway. This pilot with my
brother was so perturbed that he must have just lost everything,
because he followed the Gooney Bird in. A taxiway doesn't
stop a big bomber. It has to be pretty long before you can get
the plane stopped. So, they went on in. Unfortunately, he didn't
jet some gas, which he should have done. When the plane got to
the end of the taxiway, it tipped over into a ditch and the JP fuel
exploded and caught fire. The three of them jumped into the fire.
This occurred at the edge of the base, so that the firemen came
right away with the flight foam. The crash didn't kill them then,
but all three died later.

The sad thing about this is that the day my brother died I

was in the hospital. A woman came along and kneeled down in front of my mother and asked us for forgiveness. We said, "For what?" She said, "Well, I knew my husband was upset about fires, and I know he should have gone to the flight surgeon to get checked out, because it might not be right for him to continue flying. But he just couldn't give up his flight time."

Was there a tendency for you to not want to fly then?

No, when I got back to Kansas City, the first thing I did was go up. My brother would have told me to do that.

Did you sense your brother was with you in a way?

Yes, I was feeling more and more how he felt flying. He didn't like me to be a quitter and I never was. I went up twice before I finally started to do the round robins and other things I had to do. I felt better about it and I was not afraid to fly. I've been flying commercial planes. I told you that we had fighter planes on the base and that it was hard to get to take off because there were so many planes coming and going. That's how I came to start going over to that Olathe Field, where we were landing on those ruts in that plowed up field.

What year was this and explain a little about this story.

That was in 1958. I was stationed at Richards-Gebaur AFB. I didn't have my license yet when I went over to Olathe. I went over with my instructor because that's where I was going to start my first school of flight. It was a little field with a gravel runway. The instructor let me go ahead. I got up in the air and thought, "This is wonderful." Finally, I thought, "My God, I've got to land it." I had been taught that landings and takeoffs were the most dangerous times. I was a little nervous about it, but I made it down all right.

What the instructor taught me was to be careful of my speed, because you could really wreck the plane if you weren't careful with it, and this was my first time landing alone. That is what made me nervous, but it never happened again, because the time I got lost, I went through all kinds of thing when I wasn't nervous.

Did the guys treat you all right?

I had a real strange thing happen to me. I was in St. Louis. That's where I met my husband. We were doing a War Bond sale. We had some movie stars there. We had Errol Flynn and Victor Mature. We also had a big play in a big arena in which all of us played a part and wore our uniforms. When Victor Mature would come in, a line would form in front of him so that everyone could come up and shake his hand. He was a very arrogant fellow and the women didn't like him, but he said to me, "What do you think of me?" Teasing him, I said, "You're just another hooligan." What happened after then was that, when the play went on in the big room, he got on stage and lambasted the idea of women in uniform. He said nasty things about them. He said they were worthless. He said they had no business being there, and that they should be at home minding their children. He said that, in fact, they just slow everything down. What he didn't realize was that there was a Navy captain in the audience. Victor Mature was in the Coast Guard. That captain got hold of Victor Mature after the show and told him that if he ever heard of him acting or speaking like that again he'd spend the rest of the war in the brig. So, Victor Mature came looking for me. He was blaming me for what happened to him. He said, "You got no damn business standing in uniform. It got me in trouble." It just passed over my head. I'd been worrying, though, because I knew that he'd get something for it, and he did.

You mentioned to me that you believe men think women are so darn dumb.

A lot of them do, and we'd have a little trouble between men and women when we got in uniform. We had a booth in a movie theater in St. Louis, where we were recruiting in the lobby. I had three other women in uniform with me. We were giving out brochures and talking to them about the service. A woman came up to me and she said, "You should be ashamed of yourself." I asked, "Why?" She said, "Because you know that they only let you in the service to service the men." Of course, being in uniform, I could not snap back at her, and I was absolutely livid. That's the kind of thing that happened.

When we were in basic training or OCS, the women would be marching; the men would be on the by-line. They couldn't stop from making remarks. We had to learn to take it. They got stopped frequently. The thing that made me feel best was an old master sergeant who had been in the Air Force for years. When I took over a job with the air inspector—we needed a lieutenant to go into combat—he was the biggest help to me. I could not believe how nice he was to me, although he did not approve of women in uniform.

What did he do?

My air inspector was an unusual person and one of the things I used to do in the air inspector's office was to go out and check the offices to see if their regulations were in order and go to the

PXs and things like that. The first thing that happened to me that upset me occurred when I was checking out that day. I went over to a barbershop that was at the end of the PX. Normally to check out, you have to ask the barber if the men's room is clear, so you can go in and check it to see if it's clean, etc. The barber told me that it was clear. I walked in and there were no doors on those cubicles. They just open. I was horrified. There was a poor G.I. with his pants around his ankles, a cigar in his mouth, and this woman walks in. I thought he was to swallow the cigar because he was so horrified. I was upset because I didn't think they should send me in to do that. Later on, this is true—my husband remembers it, too—the assistant inspector said that we had railroad tracks down at the end of the airbase that had freight cars parked there, which had come in with supplies of some kind. The colonel said, "Doris, those men are bringing prostitutes into those box cars. I want you to go down there tonight and check it out." I said, "Yes sir." I went back and the old master sergeant was in the office and he said, "What's the matter with you?" I told him what happened. He said, "Doris, you stay in your office. I'll go down there and make a report and it can be yours." They had no business sending me down there alone. Some of them were nicer to us.

Did you ever want be a WASP?

By that time, I had children. I didn't want to do anything that might in some way separate me from the children. I had three children.

During the early days of the war, when did you have your children?

I had my first child a year after we were married which was 1945. The second child came 17 months later—another girl. Then I had our son, who was also a pilot. He booked his way through Embry-Riddle College.

Tell me about losing him.

Well, he worked for the post office and saved his money. He was able to not only pay all his tuition, but he was able to buy himself a little Aeronca Champ. He bought that and went into Embry-Riddle over at Daytona Beach. He was on the Dean's list. He did great. He would come home with that plane, and he and I would get up on Sunday mornings and would fly somewhere. We'd stop somewhere for breakfast and he let me fly. So I got to see his flying; that was great too. He just wanted to fly, because he was a good pilot. It was a shame that had happened to him like that. He left five children.

What happened?

Oh, yes. The only thing my son flew was that plane of his from here in Orlando out to Arizona to the Prescott campus. He got his plane out there and finally sold it to help pay the rest of his tuition. My son came back to Orlando and to Daytona to finish his course there. Next, he went to work up in Chattanooga for a company. He flew a company plane for them for a while. That's the sort of thing he continued to do. Then, he went to California. His sister was in California and the two of them formed a company together. It was a management consultant company and that kept him from doing too much flying because he was busy. They still live out in California. My daughter flies a lot but not as a pilot. Her business takes her all over the country. She's responsible for everything west of the Mississippi.

Tell me about your solo flight in detail.

In my first real round robin, I was supposed to go from Kansas City to Topeka. I got in the plane and got my instructions from the tower. When I took off, I got a weather report and weather was fine. I made it to Topeka and got a new weather report. They said that there were some clouds but nothing serious. They gave me clearance to take off. After about twenty minutes in the air, I noticed there were dark clouds gathering to each side of me, and also in back of me. I thought, "I won't be going into them." In order to get away from them I wouldn't be reaching where I'm supposed to reach, but I kept going and, of course, remembered my lesson that every time you see a place where you can land, keep it in mind. I kept flying and flying and I finally saw sunshine shining on some water on concrete that was ahead of me. I headed towards it. It was a long-long runway. It was an emergency landing for commercial planes. There was a gasoline pump there and a little brick building with smoke coming out of it. So, I landed my plane there. There was no tower or anything there. After landing, I went into the building. There were three men playing cards. I said, "Where am I?" I was supposed to be in Chanuteas, but he said, "You're in Oklahoma." Oh boy! I asked him if he had an aerial map, but he only had a road map. So, I called my instructor on the telephone there to tell him I was all right and where I was. He said he'd come get me. I said, "Don't do that. I've got to do this myself." I got the road map and had to fly by just looking for tanks and for railroad tracks and that sort of thing, but I made it home.

How many miles do you think?

Oh Lord, it took me a while. Well my logbook isn't handy right now. I guess I was flying a good hour really, but I got home like I said. It was a good experience. It taught me something.

What did your instructor say?

He wanted to come get me. He thought I was scared and I wasn't. He didn't want me to be nervous because then he was going to come get me, but I said, "Don't you dare. I'm coming back myself." So I went back myself. My husband was pacing the floor at the Arrow Club and my poor instructor was scared to death that my husband was going to eat him out, because he worked for my husband. They had people out looking for me.

How long were you out there before you were able to contact him?

When I landed at that country spot, where the commercial planes stop, I went in there and they had a phone in there. I thought they'd have aerial maps but that's when I found out they didn't. I did get to call though and tell the instructor that my husband shouldn't worry because I was coming home and I did.

What was the greatest moment of flying with your son?

It was a special time. We got up one Sunday morning and headed up towards Jacksonville. There were these great white fleecy clouds. The sky was full of them and it was the weirdest feeling to be, not in them, but so close to them. I felt like I was in another planet or something. You couldn't see anything on the ground and he was just calm and cool. I trusted him. He let me take over for him, but we did that several times. Of course, my husband also let me fly in a private plane. We flew down to Florida in a Mooney Mark 20A and had quite a time. We got a weather report in the Panhandle that told us that storms were coming up. We headed for a little strip, with a hanger, and no tower. We landed there and this man came out and took our plane and put it in the hanger. As soon as we got it in there, the biggest hail you ever saw started falling. Now, we had fabric wings on the plane. Who knows what would have happened to us had we not found that place.

What did you do? Did you go pray?

I couldn't even talk. When that hail hit, I knew there was no way we were still flying.

How big was the hail?

Well, some were like little marbles and some were uneven chunks, but they were pelting pretty hard.

Describe how close it was. Was it just seconds or minutes since you got down?

It was very short minutes before we got that into the hanger. It took all three of us to shove it in there.

Describe a traumatic moment.

Well, this was probably my fault in a way. I was starting on another round robin. I took off from Richards-Gebaur Air Force Base and stopped at the international airport there in Kansas City. Then I taxied up, so as to top my tanks. This sergeant came out and opened my cowling and looked inside. Everything seemed all right, so I got permission to taxi and take off, but as soon as I got into the pattern to get away from the airport, the cowling came up and started smashing against the windshield. That could have broken because they are heavy metal. So, for the first time in my life, I hollered, "Mayday" in the radio. When I did, air traffic controllers stopped all the commercial planes and got them off the runways because of my little plane out there with that thing banging my windshield. So, those are hairy things that the F.A.A . inspectors are really rough on you when you try to get your license. One of the things they told you was never to land in a crosswind. My instructor told me that it could flip you over. I went to get my license and passed everything: navigation, takeoff, and landing. We flew around a couple times near Topeka but, on the way back, the wind started to shift. I tried to land it. I ended up with a crosswind landing. I made it, but it scared my instructor, the F.A.A. man. I thought he'd turned green. He said to me, "I can't give you your license because of that procedure of landing in the crosswind." Sometimes, you won't be able to do anything else but land in a crosswind.

So what happened? Did you finally take another flight?

I went back and took another test, but when I got back to the field where the Arrow Club was, my instructor made me do some crosswind landings. When I went back to get my license, he didn't even ask me to do one.

Why did you quit?

One reason I quit was because of the children. I was flying one time, and tower contacted me to tell me that my son had an

249

accident and I should come in. I came in and he'd fallen and split his head open. They had fifty-six stitches in his head. There was blood everywhere. I felt guilty flying around while that happened to him. Then, as the children got older, I had to be there to be sure they had done their lessons. I didn't feel you could just walk away and leave your children to do what they want to do. There was a lot of flying I didn't get because of having children.

Did it also get expensive?

Very expensive, the insurance alone was ridiculous. Gordon and I had talked about getting a little light plane, but when we started figuring out the money, we thought, "Is it worth it?" I could, if I wanted, go out to the Executive Airport in Orlando and get a check out toward a new license.

You ever think of doing that?

Yeah, I do, but right now because of Gordon's physical health, I won't leave him.

Your husband's suffering, isn't he?

Yes, he is and I can't leave him. He's fallen seven times from his sciatica and spinal sclerosis and I won't leave him alone in the house.

You couldn't fly as much as you wanted, but isn't it better to have flown than to have never flown at all.

That's true. I'm so glad I had the opportunity and took it. Some of my women friends thought I was nuts, but I didn't care.

What's the strangest thing your women friends said to you?

They said that they'd be afraid to fly. They said that if you hadn't been taking lessons for very long, suppose you crash and all this stuff. "Another plane's going to hit you." I don't know what was wrong with those women.

They just didn't have a lot of confidence, huh?

No, they didn't. They wouldn't even take lessons.

Who were these women? Were they in the military?

They were wives of military men in Kansas City.

What was it like having a husband and brother who flew?

Well, things like that give you more in common. You know, we're pilots. It's just like being a fisherman. That's what me and my husband and I do a lot of. Or hunting. I do that too. My brother did it. My husband did it, and I have to do it.

But you don't look upon it as a big chore though, doing those things?

No, it's fun. I've had fantastic times fishing and hunting.

Did you ever fly out and do some hunting or land on a private strip?

We were in Incirlik Air Force Base, down in Adana, Turkey.

That's where I learned to fly anyhow. The Navy had a ship in port at Iskenderun, down south of Adana. I hired a tutor that came three times a week so I could pronounce the Turkish names. I learned the language!

What happened is, the commander of the ship invited my husband down to the ship. Gordon was not only in command there on Incirlik, which was a classified base, but they had things in common to talk about. So he said to Gordon, "Is there any good fishing?" Gordon said, "There certainly is." So he said, "I'll tell you what I'll do. I'll send one of my choppers halfway up there and you meet us in the road. Then we'll go up and fish." So we did. We got our fishing gear together, drove down the road and parked the car. There, in the intersection of a dirt road, comes a helicopter. It was a big red thing and it blew dirt everywhere. We climbed in and started up in the mountains to go fishing. I was the only woman in the group and we landed in a potato patch up in the mountains and we had tents that we put up there. The gypsies used to go up to the glacier and bring ice down to keep fish from spoiling. We caught German brown trout. We had a wonderful time. The Turkish people don't do a lot of fishing like we do.

This Turkish colonel took my husband down to the Mediterranean near where we had a little place in the summer. He told us that we were going fishing. Gordon said, "Well, how are you going to do that? You don't have any gear." He said, "Yes, I do." So he kept telling Gordon to go out a little further. He said, "Keep your stance." At that, Gordon got out to where he was up to his waist in water and the colonel was back near the shore. All of a sudden, that fool picked up a piece of dynamite and threw it in the water. A big explosion came. I'll tell you, it's a wonder my husband didn't turn out being a soprano. It scared him to death and here come all these dead fish. That's how they fish.

What year was that?

That was in about 1958.

Tell me about your husband.

I didn't know him when he was in combat. I was stationed at Lowry Field, and he was there to pick out some female officers and some enlisted people to go to St. Louis for recruiting. I didn't know anything about him. I hadn't seen him. There was a big bank in Denver outside the base. They had a defense command stationed there. I came in from Lowry Field, and my husband was agitated and standing up in the mezzanine looking down on the lobby. I didn't know him from Adam. I didn't see him. Anyway, he said to his aide, "Go down and find out who that girl is. She looks like she needs someone to take care of her." That's how he picked me to go recruiting. I didn't even know it then.

Tell more about going into the plowed-up field.

That's the scariest thing that's happened to me. We were in a C-150. The year was 1957. My instructor was with me. It was getting dark, but we took off and headed west. He was just having me do some little maneuvers and, all of a sudden, the electricity went off in the plane. I had to hold the flashlight up to the dials so he could see what we were doing. I said, "Well, where are we going? There's no airfield here." He said, "Well, there's a small airfield. I know just where it is and we're going to land there." He kept flying and in about 15 to 20 minutes, he said, "It's down there." I said, "It's dark down there. I can't see anything," but there was a lighted road. He said, "Right past those lights. I've landed there many times." So we proceeded to land there, only to find that the whole thing had been plowed up. We were in ruts like you wouldn't believe. I thought we were going to smash up that C-150. There were no lights or anything. We had to push that little plane up near that little building that was there and then hitchhike out on the road, because we had no way to get home. A farmer came along with a station wagon full of chickens. He looked at us and said, "What the hell are you doing here?" When we told him that we flew in, he thought we were crazy. He took us in to the nearest town where we could call somebody.

What's your secret for old age?

I don't know what would happen to my body if I just vegetated. I work on Fridays at a bookstore. I keep busy.

Betty Wood McNabb
"Flying Civil Air Patrol"

Born in Spring Lake, Michigan, in 1909, she saw a plane take off from the airport in Albany, Georgia, and was hooked. Early in her flying career, Betty Wood McNabb decided she was without promise as a pilot. Nothing she seemed to do met with approval from her instructor, or her husband for that matter. While on her way to the airport to "bow out gracefully," a huge tractor-trailer truck slid out of control and came right at her. Betty aimed for the ditch to escape him. The driver of a logging truck followed her into the ditch, spilling logs everywhere. Enormous logs flew in the air, some only inches from her head. No one was injured. Betty proceeded to drive to the airport and when she saw her airplane, she says she hugged it and "got up into nice, safe air."

With the arrival of the Hill-Burton Act (1948), many small hospitals were built around the United States. The hospitals needed guidance in many areas, so Betty Wood McNabb became a consultant for the Georgia Department of Health Administration and flew about assisting them, principally in the area of medical records. During her travels she has landed planes in all forty-eight contiguous states.

Ms. McNabb has obtained ratings for multi-engine aircraft, single-engine sea glider, CFI-I (aircraft instructor and instruments), and ATP. Over the years she has owned seven airplanes. In later years she flew a Grumman Tiger. She was the eighth woman in the western hemisphere to have flown through the sound barrier, in an F 100F Super Sabre. Her public service side shines in the work she performed as a member of the Civil Air Patrol (forty years) and the Coast Guard Auxiliary (twenty-five years). She was also a member of Angel Flight, which flies ill or injured patients to the hospitals. She has served as president of The Ninety-Nines, the Association of Women Pilots, and was a member of the United Flying Octogenarians, the American Yankee Association, and the Grumman Aircraft Owners' Association.

Betty Wood McNabb graduated from the Florida State College for Women in 1930 and a year later graduated with a master's degree from the University of California in Berkeley. I ask her if she took physics or anything that might have helped with flying. "No," she says, "I didn't. I can't put two and two over yet." .

To this woman whose history reaches through her father to the first flight at Kitty Hawk, the Coast Guard recently offered an aviation award in her name, "The Betty Wood McNabb Aviation Award."

Have you inherited your love of flying from your father?

Not really. I learned to fly without having any reason for doing it, except my job. I was working for the state of Georgia. The roads were terrible in those days, and I had to drive. They were red clay. I got stuck. I got flat tires, and I was by myself and it was dark at night. Oh, I didn't like that at all. I thought I either have to learn to fly or give up this job, which I was enjoying very much. So I learned to fly.

What was the job like?

I was a health records consultant for the state of Georgia, and I had to get up in the morning and leave the house at five.

256

I got home at seven at night. My husband got to where he was saying, "And who might you be?" So I thought, "Well, I can't do it this way." And you know that Georgia is the biggest state east of the Mississippi River.

What did your husband think of your flying?

My husband would have had a fit if he had known I was learning to fly, so I didn't tell him until I soloed. It was my money—I mean, I was working. I figured he wouldn't go anywhere with me in the plane. But when he found I had spent that much, he said, "Go ahead, finish. You are a nitwit." I said, "No, I just can't drive those horrible roads in Georgia anymore, and I love my job." I was right. He didn't fly with me for a long time; then I think he built himself up. One day I heard him on the phone—he was consulting for the state of Georgia education people—he said, "Bill, I'll come if Betty can bring me, but if she is too busy, I won't be able to make it." After that I took him everywhere he went.

Your father has a place in aviation history.

Well, he was at Kitty Hawk.

Tell me about that.

I think it's kind of interesting. His father had gotten him a job he had to worry about, and one day he sent his son—my father, Frank B. Wood—to Washington, D. C. In those days you couldn't call and say, "I'll be over at such and such a time." So Dad went to D.C., where the people he wanted to see were having a meeting. Dad was just sitting there, mad as a wet hen, trying to decide what he would do for the next two days. All of a sudden he heard someone holler to him, "Hey Tudy, Tudy." Why they called him that, I don't know. "Tudy, what are you doing?" The man was Barney Oldfield, who was famous at the time for bicycle races.

Oldfield and Dad had known each other for many years. Barney said, "What are you doing? You're not doing anything? Well, let's go down to Kitty Hawk, North Carolina. I need to get a much better bike. My legs are too strong and I keep busting things." At the time, of course, the men who were doing the airplanes were also makers of racing bikes.

So the two men got into an automobile and headed to Kitty Hawk. Of course, Kitty Hawk is on an island and, in those days, they didn't have much of a bridge. That didn't matter because the car went bad, so they got in a horse and buggy and went on their way. When they got there, they saw some people, including the Wright brothers, messing around. Barney told Wilbur and Orville, "Hey you two, when you get through with what you are doing, will you make me a stronger bike?" They said, "Okay, but that will have to be when we get back home. Come up here and help us get this thing up on top of the hill." So Barney and Daddy helped them get it up there. Daddy even did something with some of the inside parts that weren't working.

After the Wright brothers flew, Barney and Daddy got in their car, which had been fixed, and headed back to Washington, D.C. Dad had to go back and tell these people why he wasn't there. It turned out there was a reporter there that had been at Kitty Hawk but had apparently not seen Daddy, and he asked, "What do you think the Wright brothers are going to do with that thing? Do you think it'll ever be any good? Do you think people will dare to get in it?" Daddy said, "Yes." The reporter said, "What's going to make it work?" Daddy said, "What's going to make it work is that they'll give it to the military, and they'll make it work." The Wright brothers actually did go to the military, didn't they, and began selling them?

I'm not sure. Daddy thought that is what they would do. When they invited us to come to the fiftieth anniversary at Kitty Hawk, we decided to go. There were a lot of people that just didn't believe that Dad was there. Anyway, Daddy stood up to the questions of the people who were running the fiftieth. Finally, he said, "This does not look like the place where I was. It was much closer to the water." The man said, "I guess you were there. It's all been pulling in, pulling in." The particular hill that they were using for the ceremony had moved over the years. Nobody ever asked him questions again. Knowing my dad, I don't think he would really tell a whopper. That's the story of Dad at Kitty Hawk.

When I went down to Kitty Hawk the next time, there was a picture of three men, whom they didn't know, but they put it on the wall. One of them was dead; one of them was Dad.

Any other things that your dad told you about Kitty Hawk?

Oddly enough, he didn't tell us much until he got this letter saying, "Mr. Wood, would you come to the 50th anniversary?"

That would have been 1953, and you just started flying a couple of years earlier. How did you go about learning to fly?

In those days I lived in Albany, Georgia. All you did was get a man who was an instructor, and he did the whole thing. I went to Chicago in my little Aerocoupe. Of course, we didn't have any radio or anything like that. I just went by IFR. That means, "I Follow Railroads." I went anywhere I wanted to. Finally, I put my airplane in every state in the United States, except the two of them that aren't hitched on.

You've flown in all but Alaska and Hawaii?

Right, and I would like to do that. I started with Florida and with Georgia, of course. Medical records work was just kind of growing up in those days, and I had apparently grown better at it than the rest of them, so I went all over the U.S. doing medical records for other states.

One day I stopped in Arizona at just a little airstrip. The wind was blowing strong against me, so I stopped. I didn't see a soul. I got out of the plane and there was a little old house, and I walked in. There was a little old man there. I said, "I'd like to have some gas, please." He said, "Well, we don't sell car gas at all."

"I don't want car gas. I want fuel for my airplane."

"You do? Well, all right, but your pilot will have to pay for it."

"Well, all right, here she is. I'm the pilot."

"Oh, you are?"

"Go out there and see if you see anybody there."

He did. He walked right out and looked to see if I was actually telling the truth, then he came back in and was so embarrassed. He said, "I just never happened to see a lady pilot. I'm going to remember you. And I want to know what your name is." He apologized and said, "Here's your gas. You don't have to pay for it."

Any other stories like that?

I was coming from the West to the East Coast. It was horrid. It had been raining, and I was afraid to be out in it anymore. I thought, "It's getting toward dark. I'm going to spend the night right here." I landed and went in and the man said, "Where did you come from?"

"Wherever it was, I have forgotten."

"Well, you'll have to get out of here, we're going to have water."

"I can't. It's bad to the north; it's bad to the east and everywhere else. I've just got to spend the night here with you."

"Well, all right, you will make a nice person to have around to talk to because no one is around and no one can get to us."

He found a place for me to sleep. The next day he said, "You can't go yet. You are going to have to just sit here and do nothing."

"What?"

"That's what you do when you fly. I got some things we can eat. I've still got the phone, but it's apt to go." Then he said, "Excuse me, I have some work to do." He had to do some typing, but he said, " I can't use a typewriter, but I'm going to have to."

"No, you don't."

"Why?"

"Well, over the last forty years it seems to me I might have used one. I'll do your stuff for you."

So for three days I lived with that man. We did his paperwork and ate up all his food. Finally, the weather got good enough so somebody could get in.

Where was that?

Probably Arkansas, but wherever it was, he was a real nice man.

One of the times when I flew my little airplane to Chicago, I had a problem. There was a little place where you could stop there, and I never figured out why they did it that way because it was always against the wind. I managed to put the plane down there and tied it down. When I got through with my business there, I came back to find my airplane halfway full of water. Water had come from the bottom. It took hours and hours to get that thing dry enough for me to go again. Everybody in the place tried to get this little plane clean and dry and make sure it was going to fly, and somehow we did get home.

Tell me about your solo flight.

I was always scared the first two years I flew. When the instructor, John said to me, "You are ready to fly, aren't you?" I said, "No, not yet." I made him let me have two more days. Then, when I got into that plane, I thought, "Well, let's just play like John is here." So in the air I talked to John the whole time. We didn't have radios in those days. But it was all right.

You talked to someone who wasn't there?

Yeah, I played that he was there.

What did you say?

I said, "John, what do I do now?" Then I thought what he would tell me. Of course, I knew how to fly, but I was just scared about the whole thing and going by myself.

How long were you actually scared?

For two years. I found out that if you treat the airplane the way it should be treated, it will treat you right, and I've been doing that ever since.

One time I was taking a bunch of teachers down to go to a seminar. It was all teachers and they were all old to me. All of a sudden we got into bad weather—terrible weather—and we climbed and climbed. Pretty soon all these old folks but me and one other girl got sick. So the two of us ran back and forth with boxes and things for people to get sick in. You know, I was amazed, but those things happen. I can stand an awful lot, even as old as I am. I can stand stuff better than ever, better than most people. I don't know why.

How many hours do you have in the air?

Nine thousand three hundred and forty-two.

You've got it down, don't you?

You bet. I wanted to get to twelve thousand before I had to quit, but I don't think I will.

Any forced landings?

Just one. We had been up to Atlanta. We came out and all of a sudden the plane began to sputter and cough, and I said, "Suzy"—I had a girl with me who was a student pilot—"find me a place, we've got to find a place, I've got to get on the ground." Me hoping, and she looking. All of a sudden she said, "Oh, hey look, there's Atlanta and the airport." Their airport then, of course, is nothing like it is now. So I landed in the airport without any radio and without telling anyone anything. I just looked to see if there was a place I could get in on. When I got that airplane on the ground, about three or four minutes, it quit cold.

Do you remember any unfair competitions you were in?

Yes, I actually do. It was Powder Puff Derby. Women were not allowed to fly in bad weather—I mean, real bad weather. You'd have to wait. I was coming in to put my airplane down, and coming right at me through the clouds and trees—four or five airplanes saw it—was the woman who had won many, many races. She came in through the white clouds. Thick, I mean, thick clouds. You first saw her nose, then you saw her come out. She was in ISR weather, and she wasn't supposed to be. She was absolutely wrong.

She was trying to get a jump on you?

Yes, unfortunately, even though there were several people who saw it, not just me, they decided not to do anything about it. She later got in a bad place and was killed. I think that kind of shows you that she was used to being bad during bad weather. I mean, she just did what she wanted to. I don't. I'm scared to death to do things that you are not supposed to do in an airplane.

Did your dad tell you any stories about WWI?

Daddy was in charge of airplanes in WWI. He had to see that they were working all right, which he did. He talked a lot about them. One of the stories isn't about an airplane. It's about the surveillance balloons they sent up. This was in France, and they used it to spot airplanes coming in from Germany. Anyway, Daddy and the balloon man were up there looking. All of a sudden somebody came in that they didn't see and shot them down. They both landed in a tree. They weren't high enough to kill themselves. Daddy broke a leg.

They had a bunch of balloons, about twenty-five of them, near the beach here, and they told me to come at five o'clock in the morning so we could have a run in the balloon. There was a man in the balloon who just didn't know what he was doing, I don't think. In the first place we didn't take off from the beach, which we were supposed to. The weather was not right for it. I knew that myself. Then I was surprised to have the head man say, "Oh, we've been waiting for you because we knew you would have all this information on what the weather was doing." I said, "I do, because that's the way I live. You know now how to find out, don't you? You don't start along without knowing, do you?"

"No, but when we knew you were going to be here, we thought we would ask you. You did get the weather, didn't you?"

"Yes, and I can tell you people what you can do. You have two alternatives: you can either go to Cuba or to the other side of the United Sates. You cannot go where you want to go. Look at the weather."

"Well, we though that was going to happen, but we wanted to ask someone else."

They took the balloon over to some place where we could get off from the right direction. It was a real hot, and we were on a level place, with no trees around for a ways. So we floated, and the man apparently didn't know that when he was getting over the trees, it was going to be cooler and he was going to drop down. Well, I wasn't a person who knew that much about balloons, but I knew that much. So because of his inexperience, he went down into the trees three times, and every time he would do it, he made it out, thank goodness. He'd say, "All right, put one hand over your head, your face and head, and hold on with the other. You're going in again."

We would go into those trees, but he finally got it out. He then said, " This is a big thing for anybody to do—but me doing my first run—Mrs. McNabb, you are a pilot. Is there any place I can get this monster down on the ground?"

"No, I can't tell you much because I don't fly fifteen feet off the ground."

Then I remembered. I said, "I know there is a little place over there on the right. You can go that way if you want to." It was wet and we got to this place, a messy place full of water, which I knew would be there. I noticed two other balloons were in there. He crashed in. We just got to the edge of the trees and went right into the place.

He said, "Don't move, don't move. We will get out all right," just as the balloon came flat down with us in the middle. He said, "Don't move until I tell you." Well, I was on top of all of them. He was underneath me, the other man was next, and I was on top of him.

Finally, the man running the aircraft said, "Mrs. McNabb, if you get off please, the other two of us could get off" (laughs). You know, the other man—I never found out who he was and never saw him again. When I looked around, he was running as fast as he could away from there. I'm sorry to say the guy tore up his balloon, but we weren't hurt at all, which I thought was remarkable.

Did your dad fly?

He had never flown the birds that he took care of in France, but he always wanted to. He used to go with me many times. One time he said to the man who had been my instructor, "Hey, do you think I could possibly get up and down in this airplane?" I was fifty or so at the time, and he was eighty. The man said, "Yes, sure you can do it, if Betty will let you." Well, I certainly had to let him. He helped me pay for the airplane. So Daddy got into the airplane. He wasn't trying to do it, really. He was trying to get familiar. He certainly didn't mean to solo. But one of Dad's cronies came in one day and saw him getting out of the airplane—he didn't notice that Dad was in the right seat not the left—and he said, "Fine. You old fool, are you trying to learn to fly at your age?" Daddy said, "Why not?" He got in and went right to the man and said, "Look, Joe, do you think I could possibly solo?" Joe said, "Yeah, if Del lets you; if Bets will let you." I said, "I have to help. He helped me buy the airplane."

He'd help you buy another, maybe.

Yeah. I don't know what they do now, but long ago you were supposed to take three runs. So he made three. He did a good job. Then he made another, then he made a fifth. The instructor got on the horn and said, "Frank, Frank, what's the matter, why don't you get on the ground?" Well, you know, the FAA doesn't really like people to swear. Daddy said, "Hell no, I'm not getting on the ground. I've never had such a damn time in my life. I love it. I'm going to do a whole lot of these. Don't bother me."

That was at age eighty?

That was at age eighty. He kept going as fast as he could, six or seven times, then he got on the ground.

How did you feel when he was up there?

I knew he was going to be fine. I loved it. He was the cutest man in the world. He lived to be ninety-two. At eighty-nine he was still coming with me in the plane.

What about the earliest time with planes and with your father?

I remember that, years before, we had seen a barnstormer in a field. Dad was taking us from school to home and he saw an airplane in a field. I was eleven, and my brother was seven. Daddy said, "Hey, let's look at this airplane." So we walked over to see who this man was. He had his nose under the hood and was working on the plane. The man turned around. You know how he felt: "Go to the dickens! Who in this place is going to know how to fix this?" It was one of Dad's people from World War I in France.

This same man stopped in Albany once and invited my dad to go for ride with him. So Daddy did, and when they came back the man said, "Anybody you have that would like to fly?" Dad asked, "Are you going to go anywhere near Tallahassee? My daughter is there, and she would love to have a ride with you." So he stopped. I think he had some business there. He looked me up and said, "Hey, would you like to take three or four of your friends to Pensacola? I'm going over there and could take you if you could get yourself back."

I said, "I'll do it if I have to walk." It was terrible trying to get everybody's permission to do such a terribly awful thing. Goodness, getting into an airplane! We had to have a chaperone. Have you ever heard of anything so silly? So we got a chaperone. That was Tallahassee in those days. The chaperone was a lady who taught geography, and she was scared absolutely to pieces. She had never been up before. She held both hands together with her eyes closed, praying all the way there. Now, of course, the flight takes a short time now, but it took quite a while then. It was just a beautiful day. He took us over the water. We four or five girls were just going crazy. We got out and, as our chaperone stepped out, she said, "Thank you, God, for getting me out of this place in one piece." Just then, she fell and broke her ankle. Wouldn't that be a note? How could we not laugh? We just died. We had to get away from it because we laughed so hard. It wasn't anything to laugh at, but I still laugh at it.

Do you remember the first plane that you saw crash?

Yes. It was just a little airplane, and it was down in the trees. They had a plane down in Florida. They looked and they looked, and they called the Florida and Georgia people in to help. Finally, a man found it. He called and said where it was, and he landed his airplane on the ground and said both men were dead. He got back into his airplane and could never find it again. He couldn't find it. We didn't have LORAN then. They sent me and a policeman who knew his way around. I am on the left side, and we are going around one of those little bunches of trees. Then all of a sudden, I saw it. I said, "Look, there it is." The two people on the other side and doing nothing didn't see it, and I did. They said, "I don't believe it. I don't know what you saw, but it was junk." Well then I started flying, looking for it again, and we flew and we flew and we couldn't find it. Then, all of a sudden, I saw it again. So we stayed right there until we got people there.

The reason I guess why they couldn't see it was the wings got stuck up in the air, and the two men in the airplane were still in it, and they were sitting down there and the way they looked was just like some junk. It didn't look like anything and didn't show any sign of being an airplane.

You are a member of The Ninety-Nines?

Yes, I was president of it for two years, and I enjoyed it. Back in my day, I kept complaining to the girls that all they were doing was having lunch and I wanted us to do something that would be good for aviation. So gradually we did. We do a whole lot of things. Most of us are either in the Civil Air Patrol or the Coast Guard.

Ever feel a little sad that you spent the first half of your life not flying?

You bet I do, and what I feel worse about is that I know it isn't going to be much longer that I can fly. I just don't know what I'm going to replace it with. I don't think about it anymore than I have to. I know at eighty-one I'm going to have to quit soon. I'm losing weight, losing words, etcetera. I don't think my reactions are slow because I can still pick things up before they hit the ground. But I just think it's not going to be a good idea for anybody to keep on going. I might hurt somebody. I just won't do it. I don't know what I'm going to do. I've loved it so much so many years. Thirty-nine, to be exact. I've been in races, but I've never won.

What happened?

One time I beat fifty-four airplanes in a race. Don't ask me how many I didn't beat. That was fun, and a very good thing for us women.

What does flight mean to you?

It means so much. I can't tell you what, except that I love it. In the air, it is like nothing else. I am closer to the Lord.

Flight Image Gallery

Following is a collection of early pioneer pilots. Photography taken in the early Twentieth Century.

Harriet Quimby. First licensed female pilot in the U.S
and the second in the world.

Gladys Ingle. Stunt Pilot. Wing walking on a Curtiss JN-4 Jenny circa 1920s. She would change planes in mid-air with no saftey gear.

Gladys Ingle. Stunt Pilot. Wing walking and perfoming an archery stunt on a "Bon" MacDougall's Curtiss JN-4 Jenny circa 1920s.

Gladys Ingle pulling herself onto the wing of a Curtiss JN-4 Jenny, during a stunt, circa 1920s.

Ruth Law. Pioneer, 1910s b.1887

Bobbi Trout by Golden Eagle (Bone) P-2 Parasol Monoplane circa 1928-1929
Endurance record holder; first female pilot to fly all night.

Katherine Stinson AKA "The Flying Schoolgirl" b. 1891 Alabama
First woman known to loop the loop.

Laura Ingalls. First flight over Andes Mountains by an American female. Set distance record for women fliers—17,000 miles. B. Brooklyn, NY.

Meli Beese b.1886. Germany's first woman pilot.

Bessie Coleman. In 1921 she became the first ever African–American in the U.S. to be a licensed airline pilot.

Ruth Nichols. The only woman ever to hold simultaneous world records for speed, altitude and distance for a female pilot.

Pancho Barnes b. 1901 Known as "Fastest Woman on Earth."
One of first women to be licensed in U.S. Flew stunts for major Hollywood
motion pictures.

Helen Richey first woman to be hired as a pilot by a commercial airline in the
U.S. Held endurance record with Frances Marsalis when they stayed airborne
for ten days.

Hazel Ying Lee gained her pilot's license in '32. A native of Portland, Oregon, she joined WASPs and died in service of her country.

Eileen Collins. Test pilot and NASA Astronaut. first female pilot/Commander of a space shuttle.

Ellen Ochoa. Engineer, Astronaut. First Hispanic woman in space.
Former Director, Johnson Space Center.

Mae Jemison. Physician, Engineer, and Astronaut.
first African–American woman in space, having gone into orbit on
the space shuttle Endeavor. Holds innumerable honors including
many honorary doctorates.

Evelyn Bryan Johnson
"Teaching and Flying"

Evelyn Bryan Johnson has totaled 57,000 hours of flight time in her amazing career. She says, "I don't know what number was in The Guinness Book of Records last year, because I did not buy one. I'll probably buy one this year, and I'll write and update the number of hours."

Evelyn's parents came from Tennessee and moved to Corbin, Kentucky, where Evelyn was born some 90 years ago. Evelyn's husband, W.J. Bryan, borrowed $250 from his father, which enabled them to open a dry-cleaning plant in Jefferson City, Tennessee. It was the time of the Great Depression, and times were tough. Evelyn explains: "Had Franklin Roosevelt not come up with the National Recovery Act (NRA), we could not have survived. The NRA froze wages (that did not matter since we had no employees) and prices. That mattered a lot, because it kept competition from cutting prices." In five years, Evelyn and her husband were able to buy their own building and had fifteen employees. "We were even able to pay W.J's dad the $250 back," Evelyn says. At that time, the cost to clean a pair of pants, jacket or sweater was twenty-five cents. When Evelyn's husband went off to WWII, she began to look for a "hobby." That hobby, which would become far more, was flight.

Evelyn taught more than 3,000 students to fly since 1952. As a flight examiner for the FAA, she has given more than 9,000 flight tests. Her numerous honors include National Flight Instructor of the Year, 1979; Elder Statesman (N.A.A.) 1993; and a Carnegie Hero Award. She also was a member of the National Flight Instructor Hall of Fame and Women in Aviation and Pioneers Hall of Fame (1994). She was enshrined in the Kentucky Aviation Hall of Fame as well as the National Aviation Hall of Fame.

Evelyn was small of stature, just five feet, but this pioneer was clearly big of heart. Her nickname, "Mama Bird," suited her persistence. Evelyn continued teaching and managing an airport at age 100. She died on May 10, 2011, at the age of 102.

You've been flying for 56 years.

Yes. October 1, 1944, was when I got started.

How'd that happen?

My husband was in the military, and I was operating his laundry and dry cleaning plant. I just got so worn out. I thought I should get myself a hobby, which would get me out of the laundry two or three hours a week. I thought that way I would feel better. But I didn't know what I wanted to do. One day, I saw an ad in the paper that said, "Learn to fly." I said, "I believe I will." So the next Sunday afternoon, I got on a train in Jefferson City, Tennessee, and went to Knoxville, got on a city bus, which went to the end of the bus line, and walked down a road along the river for about a quarter of a mile. I then crossed the river in a rowboat, where I took my first flying lesson. I've been flying ever since.

Were you a little apprehensive before taking your first lesson?

No, not really. I wasn't. I don't know why I wasn't, but I didn't get scared. In fact, I really enjoyed it.

The most difficult person you've taught or flown with?

I had a student once about whom I thought, "If I had two like this, I'd quit instructing." But he turned out to be a good pilot. It just took him awhile.

What was the problem?

I think he may have had some family problems about that time, but later he picked up the techniques and was doing much better.

Have you ever had a student who froze at the controls?

No, not a one.

That's good.

I guess you're right about that.

What is your secret to teaching?

I love to teach. There's nothing more exciting than to teach someone who knows nothing and teach him or her to fly.

On October 31, 1997, I was on my way to Oshkosh, Wisconsin, where I was to be inducted into the National Flight Instructor Hall of Fame. We had to change planes in Cincinnati. As we taxied out, the pilot came on the intercom with the usual message and ended by giving his name. He said, "My name is Max Roberts." When I heard that, I told the lady next to me, "That sounds like Eddie Roberts to me." So I sent a note up with the flight attendant and said, "Max Roberts, are you the Eddie Roberts I taught to fly?" It was. When he got the message, he said he nearly fell off the chair. He was so excited. He got on the loudspeaker and said, "We've got a special passenger onboard—my very first flight instructor." Then he told who I was, where I was going and why. Then he said, "I think it is so neat that I am getting to fly her up there."

When we got to Oshkosh, he was standing down at the foot of the stairs with a red carpet and bouquet of flowers. It was really exciting. At the induction I had to deliver a two-minute acceptance speech. I knew what I wanted to say, but didn't know how to end it. The thought occurred to end the speech by telling about Eddie, which I did. Everyone liked that.

I've taught two airline vice presidents—Gene Sharp of Piedmont, then U.S. Air, and Greg Gibson, who is now with U.S. Air. I'm real proud of these boys, but I'm also proud of all the rest. Also, some of my girl students are now airline pilots. One of my students, who was just about as old as I, was Fran Davis. She sent me a Mother's Day card back in the sixties. I wondered why in the world she would send me a Mother's Day card. Then I opened it. She had written, "You look after the students the way a mama bird looks after baby birds. So Mama Bird—that's your name." People have called me that ever since. My biography, which one of my students, George Prince, wrote, is titled *Mama Bird: Biography of a Flight Instructor, Evelyn Bryan Johnson*.

Have you had some forced landings?

I've had my share, but I haven't even put a scratch on an airplane—or hurt anyone. My flight instructor, Mr. Herbert Neff, was very cautious. He kept on giving me simulated forced landings, which is all right. But right after I got my private pilot's license, I had an engine failure. In fact, I'd only had my private license for a week. I was up practicing stalls, slowing the plane down, when it quit. Now there's nothing bigger than a wooden propeller sitting out there not going around! Some people say you can dive it down and get the prop spinning. Well, you can't. So I knew I was going to have to land. I picked out a field. It wasn't the greatest one in the world, but I landed it safely. Actually, the owner of the plane and a mechanic came down, and got it running, though I don't know what he did. He then was able to fly it out.

The other failure occurred off the end of our airport at Morristown. I was not high enough to turn back to the field. I figured I had to land, so I turned slightly to the right and there sat a pretty good field. I set the plane down there. I didn't hurt anything or anybody. On that flight I had a student with me on his first lesson. I thought, "This will be the end of him as a student." But it wasn't. He found out you can make a safe landing without an engine, if you have to. In fact, he kept on until he got his license. I was real proud of him.

I've had a fire in the air. At the time, I was checking a young man out in a Tri-Pacer. He had a friend sitting in the back seat. We got up to about 1,200 feet when the cockpit filled with smoke. The pilot reached over and opened the window. Suddenly, the space down around our feet burst out into flames. The guy in the back is screaming, "We're gonna get killed. We're gonna get killed." I said, "Not if I can help it." I took over the piloting and handed over the fire extinguisher to the young man. Finally, we got the plane back down, but the fire was not all the way out. Unbeknown to us, we were still feeding the fire. Now you would not have thought of this fire coming from the engine, but it was. The fire occurred at the exhaust pipe where the heater goes around. The exhaust pipe had a weld, and that weld had come loose. Then flames came through like a blowtorch. The flames burned a hole in the little aluminum cover and put a flame on the firewall. But we hadn't known this at the time.

On the ground, I managed to put the fire out. Fortunately, the fire did not do too much damage. The funny thing was that when we landed, so did a Bonanza. A man got out of the Bonanza and came over, and I told him what had happened. He said, "You're in luck. I'm your insurance man" (laughs).

Talk about your first experience with helicopters.

New England Helicopter had come down to Lakeland, Florida. They did this every winter. I went down there and got my commercial license. At that time, because of insurance and because the FAA did not require it, none of the people in the class got to solo. Later, I went out to Ft. Worth to take training at Bell Helicopter for helicopter instructor. The instructor there went out with me for about 30 minutes, then sent me out alone. The guy didn't know he was going to solo me. That was the first time I flew a helicopter by myself.

You saved a man once.

Yes, that man died about a month ago. I was sorry to hear it, but he got 42 extra years. This goes back to the day I got back home from Ft. Worth in April of 1958. My business partner was sick and tired of having to look after everything while I was gone, so he did not come out to the airport that day. As a result, I was the only one there until two little boys came up to look at the helicopter. After awhile, this Bell 47 helicopter landed. I gassed it up and also filled the two extra G.I. gas cans on the side of the helicopter. The pilots were doing power line patrol over in Virginia, across the hills from here. We chatted for awhile, and then they took off, right across in front of where I was standing. Then they turned and went out over what would have been the runway, but it was being paved, so it was all plowed up. Suddenly, the helicopter lurched up and made a sharp turn to the right. I could see the pilot trying to gain control, but he couldn't.

The helicopter crashed and hit hard, with most of the impact on the right—or passenger—side. When the helicopter hit, it squashed it down to half-size, but the rotor continued to go around and around and around. It was hitting the ground. I grabbed a fire extinguisher, carried it out and then laid it down. Then I lay down and crawled under the rotor and shut off the helicopter. Then I emptied the fire extinguisher on it where the transmission was beginning to burn. I checked on the people and found that the man on the right side was dead. There was not much blood—about three drops from his nose, but he had no pulse. It turned out he was dead. The pilot was unconscious, but he was breathing. I started to pull him out and remembered something in a first aid class I'd had a few months before about not moving someone who might have a broken back. I called for help and waited till help came. When they arrived, it took about five of us to pull the pilot out. I rubbed his hands to keep his hands warm, and continued to talk to him. He was just moaning. When he reached the hospital, he found out he did have a broken back. He was in and out of the hospital for three years. Meanwhile, he studied to be an FAA test pilot and passed all the tests, so he became an FAA employee, based in Atlantic City after he was well.

Later, I was up in Atlantic City acting as a timer at a Powder Puff Derby. (I had to stop racing when my husband and my business partner died, because I could not be off for but a few days at a time.) Anyway, I was timing the race, when someone came running up and said, "Evelyn, Evelyn, come watch me takeoff—but not like the last time" (laughs). It was John Ryan, the man we got out from under the rotor. Ryan was really a Czechlosovakian, who had come here under the auspices of Secretary of State John Foster Dulles. He had changed his name to Ryan. I got a letter from his wife recently saying he had died.

A few years ago, I went to the Whirly Girls meeting in Las Vegas—to what's called "The Hovering." I had just passed 50,000 hours of flying, so that was mentioned. Then the moderator told about the helicopter crash. She asked me if I had kept in touch with the man in the crash. I said, "Yes, I hear from him and his wife maybe two or three times a year." She said, "Was his name John Ryan?" I said, "Yes." All of sudden, there he was like on the television show "This is Your Life."

That's an awfully brave thing you did to climb under a turning rotor.

I've got it figured out. You do what you need to do. If something has to be done and you're there, you do it. The adrenaline builds up and out you go, and you could do a lot of things you would not have thought you could do.

Tell me about your check out in the Bonanza.

Tommy Moore had gotten a Bonanza and was going to check me out in that. I was raring to go. I had always wanted to fly everything I could get my hands on. I don't recall him ever mentioning the Vernier throttle, which works by twisting or pressing a button. Anyway, we flew around the field together a couple of times. Now I would never check anybody out in a plane by just going around the field a couple of times. But he did. When I got back and was coming down real good, I pushed in the throttle knob, but had not twisted it, so I had more power than I needed. I looked down and realized there was no way I was going to get down on that field. I said, "God, please help me." It's almost as if someone pushed my hand and I got that throttle in and just barely cleared the fence, flew back around and landed safely. When I got down, Tommy said, "I never really thought to tell you how different that throttle was."

Did you ever feel the ghost or spirit of Rev. Murrell at Murrell Field?

No, but I'm very interested in him. Murrell was a circuit rider preacher, who got a patent on the American Flying Machine in 1877. When he became a preacher he decided that he would let the flying work drop. He went back to work on it later, and about 1911, he got it to fly. Of course, the Wright Brothers had already flown by then.

The man was a visionary.

I understand that he got on a barn with two great big cabbage leaves and tried to fly. Of course, he fell off the barn (laughs).

Talk about the Transcontinental All-Woman Race.

Nineteen-fifty-one was my first race. I had never flown to California before. As I flew out, I ran into what looked like a rain shower and turned around to go back. But the storm started behind me, so I climbed up to 13,000 feet in my Piper-Pacer and got across the mountains. That way I was able to avoid the storm. The funny thing in racing was that I wasn't going to open my throttle wide. I figured if I did, it would ruin my engine, so I flew cruising throttle, racing across the country from California. All the rest of my competition flew throttle wide open. Of course, flying with the throttle wide open does not hurt the engine at all.

Where do you think you got that idea that you needed to use the cruising throttle?

I don't have the slightest idea, except that somebody must have told me that. I don't know.

In that first race, I think my main objective was to get there. In all the races I was in, I was never disqualified and never came in last. So it worked out all right. In the last four races, I was in the first ten or so.

You like the poem "Unstable Mable." Have that handy?

I've got it in my head:
I hope that I will soon be able
to learn to fly "Unstable Mable."
Now one of us is so unstable.

I hope and trust that it is Mable.

Tilt the rotor
Raise the collective
Rev the motor
Add torque corrective.
These things I cry
 I know how to do.

I will make Mable fly
Before I am through.
 Evelyn S. Bryan (Later, 1965, EBJ)
And I did.

You have a great memory.

I don't have such a great memory. I just happen to remember that poem.

Tell me a story about a trip.

Once I was ferrying a Navion out to a doctor in California. I had gone over Gastonia, North Carolina, and picked it up, but couldn't go to California for a week or so. As a consequence, I flew the plane around here for awhile, to see if it was okay. It seemed fine, but when I got to Memphis and stopped for gas, it took five quarts of oil. At the time, the mechanics had all gone to lunch so there was no mechanic there. I thought, "Must have left the oil cap loose." I took off and stopped in Texarkana, and again it took five quarts of oil. I put the oil in. There was no mechanic at the airport, so I headed for Dallas, where I stayed a couple of days during which I spent a lot of money supposedly getting the problem fixed. Then I left and flew up to Mineral Wells, and suddenly the oil pressure went down. I landed and spent a couple of days and a whole lot of money there to fix it. Finally, I took off and about 22 miles out, over a little place called Palo Pinto, the engine and panel started vibrating. I say it was vibrating over a foot, though that's probably overstated. It was only an inch. I kept fooling with the throttle and that managed to stop the vibrating, but it still wasn't flying too well. I told this girl with me that I felt we could make it back to Mineral Wells. She didn't think we could. I told her to watch the oil pressure and to keep an eye out for some place to land. As we headed back, we couldn't find anyplace to land in that area. One might think of Texas as big and flat, but it has a lot of lumpy little hills, too. Finally, we saw a place. Because we still had power, I kept flying till we got to the airport. Once at the airport, the engine quit—dead. The plane had swallowed a valve, and the piston looked like someone had taken a hammer and chiseled the whole thing out. We chatted with the people at the shop and told them that we had found only one place to land. Someone spoke up and said, "It's a good thing you did not land there. That field is nothing but quicksand." We were very fortunate.

Did you say your prayers after that one?

I always say them. God's always with me when I'm flying. Anyway, we had to leave the plane and go back on the airlines. It was several months before I met the doctor. Eventually, my mother and I went out to Texas for my helicopter instructor training, and every day we went over to Mineral Wells to see if they had fixed the plane. Finally, it was fixed. I went out to check on progress one day and finally met the doctor. The doctor looked just like my father! The next day I had my mother go with me, because I wanted her to see. She agreed that he looked just like Dad.

Later, the doctor came to visit my husband and me. It's a good thing he did because in another month, the doctor died. Then in another month after that, my business partner died, and the next year, my husband died. And all three of them had taken this doctor out. Within a year they were all gone, and it just seemed so strange.

Tough to abide. How'd you sustain yourself?

It was kind of hard. When my partner died, I was left to run the airport and the Morristown Flying Service. When my husband died, I still had the dry cleaning plant. As a result, stupid me ran them both—for twelve years. As a matter of fact, I told people during that period—1962 to 1974—that if I was ever going to have ulcers, I would have had them, because I was going through a lot of pressure. Finally, I sold the dry cleaning plant in 1974.

How old were you then?

I was between 54 and 65 years of age. I'm 90 years old now.

You've received a lot of recognition, including at home. It is nice to be appreciated at home.

Yes, I'm in the Hamblen Women Hall of Fame in Morristown. The Girl's Club recognizes people they think will make good role models for girls. I've been inducted in that. It's very small. But I appreciate it as much as the other honors and awards I've received.

Of what are you most proud?

I was given a Carnegie Hero Medal for saving the helicopter pilot's life. I'm rather proud of that. Some people in Morristown recommended me. Then someone wanted to show the medal to his wife, and I did not get it back. I don't know why I let him take it. Luckily, the Carnegie people gave me a replacement. I mounted it in a big square of Lucite. And I don't take it to the airport any more.

How would you like to be remembered?

I hope I'd be remembered as a pretty good pilot and some-one interested in aviation safety. I always say flying is as safe as the pilot makes it. Of course, being honored as the very first Flight Instructor Hall of Fame was wonderful. The fact that so many people have given me so many nice honors—I get amazed sometimes.

What's your secret for old age?

Staying busy and loving the work. I don't sit around and watch the grass grow. People say, "When are you going to retire?" I say, "I'm not old enough—I'm just 90."

Your eyes are still good.

I've had cataract surgery. Also, I don't have to, but if I want to hear, I have to wear these hearing aids. But I get along just fine—because I've got spare parts.

What does flying mean to you?

The flying has just been wonderful. This year my flight hours are down a bit because I was sick. I came down with double pneumonia and was in the hospital for 26 days and came close to dying. But in the last four weeks, I've given about fifteen flight tests. Flying to me is a whole different world. It's so beautiful. I tell everyone that I don't see how anybody could be up there looking at this world and not believe in God. It's so majestic—so enormous.

Do you ever think of your dad when you fly over a train? After all, you're doing something similar, in a way.

He used to take us as kids down to the rail yard, and sometimes the men would be switching trains in the yard. We rode on engines, boxcars, and cabooses, and got quite an education on the train. But strangely enough, my dad never would go up in a plane with me. Mother did, but my dad wouldn't. I suppose he was scared.

Did that disappoint you?

I would have liked to had him fly with me, but I couldn't force him to go.

Do you think the influence of the train early on could have had some effect on your flying?

It could have—I don't know. And I loved the cabooses. They don't have cabooses anymore.

Fran Bera

"Air Racer"

Fran Bera soloed in 1941 at age 16, without even the consent of her parents, in a Piper J-3 Cub. Today, many years later, a hip replacement hasn't slowed her down and this distinguished "pioneer" still waxes poetic about the flying life.

Her flying life encompasses charter flight, chief pilot work, flight operations, testing, instructing, as well as working as a pilot examiner for the Federal Aviation Agency (FAA). In 1969 Governor Ronald Reagan appointed her to his Aviation Education Task Force for the state of California.

Fran continued to hold records, including the altitude record in light airplanes for many years, beginning in 1966. She is also the first woman to have flown a helicopter with no tail rotor.

As a racer, Fran won the All-Woman Transcontinental Air

Race (Powder Puff Derby) seven times, and placed second in that same race six times. Also, she has placed at numerous other races, including Reno National Air Races and the Great Race between London, England, and British Columbia in 1971.

The Silver Wings Fraternity has chosen Fran as the "Woman Pilot of the Year." In 1975, Representative Don H. Clausen placed Fran's name in the Congressional Record as one of America's distinguished female pioneers of aviation. In 1978 her name was placed at Memory Lane on a plaque at the International Forest of Friendship in Atchison, Kansas. In 2011, she received the Katherine Wright Award from the National Aeronautic Association.

As instructor, ferry pilot, pilot examiner, experimental pilot for Beech Aircraft, she has just about done it all in the aviation field.

Another five-foot bundle of energy and talent, she's an inspiration to those who admire the American entrepreneurial spirit.

Do you remember the first plane that you saw and what you thought of it as a child?

The first plane I saw, I don't know what it was, but it was an old bi-plane. There was nobody around and I went up and peeked in it. Then I went away. That was the first plane I saw.

How old were you then do you suppose?

Probably 13 or 14.

What did you think when you peeked in?

I just knew that I wanted to fly. I had known this probably from the time I was 13, almost as long as I can remember.

What do you think attracted you to flight?

I have no idea; no idea whatsoever. I did have a brother-in-law whom I guess, used to fly in the 1920s. He wasn't flying at the time, but I'd ridden in this old Ford Coup, or whatever he had. He'd pull back on the steering wheel and say "Now we're going up." And that probably put the idea in my mind. I was probably 10 or 11 at that time.

You used to skip class in high school to fly, didn't you?

The same brother-in-law had taken me to an airport in Kalamazoo when I was fifteen because I said I wanted to learn how to fly. He went in to the office. I didn't go in. Finally, he came out and said, "They said you can't learn to fly until you're 16." So then I just waited until my 16th birthday. There was no airport at my town. This one kid in school said there's an airport over at Grand Rapids. I had been saving my money for five years or so. By then I think I had $80. I hitchhiked over there and asked about lessons. It was $9 an hour dual; $6 solo. I said I wanted to learn to fly. And I gave them all my money. I used to just hitchhike over, and some days I would skip school.

You hitchhiked over. That wasn't a dangerous thing then?

In the 1930s, people hitchhiked all the time. Nobody had any money for cars. And I didn't have a car. My dad had one, but I couldn't very well skip school and take his car.

So, did any of your teachers catch you or find out about where you were yesterday, young lady?

Oh, no, they didn't at all.

You were a good student?

I was a good student.

So it didn't catch up with you?

I lived out in the country. I would climb on the school bus and get off up at the next corner, where the main highway was going off into the city of Grand Rapids. That way my folks didn't know I hadn't gone to school. I'd just get off there. Then I'd hitchhike over to the field and take my lesson. Sometimes I would go on weekends. I only took a half-hour of lessons a week. Sometimes I'd get over there and the weather would be bad so I would not be able to fly. I didn't know about weather at that time. So this went on until I had eight hours.

Then I was ready to solo. So my instructor said, "You have to have your parent's permission on this piece of paper to solo." I said "Oh, I do?" And he said "Yes." So I took the paper home and told them what I'd been doing. They were amazed.

Were they mad?

No, they weren't mad. They were just amazed. They saw the permission form and my dad signed it.

Do you remember anything they said when you first told them?

He said, "You're flying what?" I said, "An airplane, an airplane up in the sky." Nobody had ever been up in a plane. And he said, "What are you flying? That tractor up there?" Then he said, "Okay. Do it well." And he signed it. My parents taught me to be very independent. I was always very independent.

Were you an only child?

No, I was the youngest one of eight children.

Did your brothers and sisters know about your little secret?

No, I didn't tell anybody.

Gee, that's pretty amazing. Did you ever get your parents up in the air?

Oh, yes. My mother loved to fly. I think I never took them both together. I took my mother up. She loved it. I did stalls and loops and all kinds of things. It was right after I got my license. At that time you had to be 18 to get a private license; today it's 17. Then I flew around solo for two years. I flew from Michigan to Florida and all over. That was during the war years. Anyway, my mother liked to fly. I took my father one time. He was going to another town on business, and I said, "I'll fly you over." He said, "Okay." He'd never been up in the air, either. But he threw up on the downwind leg. And he got airsick. I flew him home and he laid down for the rest of the day. He never went up with me again. But I did continue to take my mother on little trips.

Did your daddy ever fly again, period?

Finally, he got to where he would fly on an airline, later. But he didn't ever fly with me again.

What was your dad like?

When he said do something, we kids minded him. I never had a licking in my life. I was never touched as a child. I was loved very much. But when he said "do" something, you did it. You just knew that you did it, that when he said "jump," I said "how high?"

What was your mom like?

She was a little more lenient that my father, of course. I think all mothers are. I could talk her into things I couldn't talk him into. But my father always said, "You can do anything you want to."

You ferried aircraft after World War II?

There were five of us that went down to Cape Girouroux, Missouri, to pick up some surplus Stearman airplanes. Anyway, I was in the one airplane and was following this other guy. Back then, we had no radios or anything. I guess I had a map. Anyway, I was following the other guy and lost sight of him. It was starting to get dark, so I knew I had to get down. I landed in this farmer's field and got stuck in the mud because it had rained. I stayed the night at the farmer's house.

The next day, he pulled my airplane out of the mud with his tractor and got me to a dry spot in the field. He helped me start the airplane because it didn't have a starter and you had to crank. It was complicated. He didn't push the prop or anything. The old Stearman planes started with a hand crank. You would get on the wing, and the one person would crank it and engage the starter. Then they would pull the crank out and throw it in the plane and jump off. So I told the farmer how to do this. I finally got on my way.

After I had the Powder Puff Derby in 1963 and my name was in the paper a few times, I got a letter from this lady that said "Are you the same person that landed in our farm field?" I wrote back. She had sent me a picture of me with her girls. We were standing by the plane. I had this big fur-lined jacket on because it was winter and it was cold. It was an open cockpit.

Did you fly any military aircraft?

Only the ones that were surplus.

What were some of the kinds you flew?

There were mostly trainers: Stearmans, PT-19s, Ryans, PT-22s, Fairchilds, and that sort of thing. I later bought a twin-engine UC-78 from surplus. I got my multi-engine rating in that. It was a twin-engine trainer, military.

Did you sort of wish that you'd flown during the war effort?

I tried to get into the WAFs. In fact, I had learned to fly a year before the war broke out. Then, by the time I got out of school, they had already started the WAFs. So I tried to get into that. I went to Detroit and filled out an application. I put down that I was five foot two. When they first started, they didn't have a height limit. Anyway, I got a telegram that came back and said, "We have changed the height to five foot four, so you're not eligible." When they started, I was too young and didn't have the time.

So you must have been very disappointed. What did you feel when you got that?

I was disappointed, but I just went on and did other things. I didn't stay disappointed for too long. I just kept flying and got my instructor and commercial ratings. After that, I immediately had a job.

Any stories about getting your ratings or anecdotes or anything unusual happenings?

I probably should tell you. The ratings were a little illegal. When I went to get my instructor rating, you had to have a recommendation from an instructor, but there weren't any instructors around where I was. So I wrote my own, and copied some guy's name out of my log book who was an instructor I had flown with back in Detroit. He recommended my rating.

I don't think they can catch you with it today.

I did some things back then. This was the 1940s. The training I had was very, very hit and miss. We weren't trained like you are today, or as they were in the military. After this incident where I landed in the farm field, took off again and was lost, I saw this great big airport and I landed. Then this Jeep came up and said, "Follow me," which I did. It turned out to be a military airport. This was in the Midwest somewhere.

What did they say to you?

The soldier said, "You've got enough gas, and there's an airport across town. Go over there and get gas. But you'll have to file a flight plan." I said, "What's a flight plan?" I didn't know what a flight plan was. Anyway, he showed me what a flight plan was. I did have enough gas to get across town.

I'll tell you this funny story that happened. I think it was still during the war. Back in the Midwest they had these little triangular fields that students went out in their Stearman. The students would do touch-and-goes there.

Anyway, by then I had a job as an instructor. A girl friend and I were flying from Michigan to Texas to a Ninety-Nines meeting, in this old little two-place Porterfield. We were sitting behind each other and flying along when pretty soon, right up beside us, came a little yellow Stearman, this light little plane that those guys trained in. When they flew real close to us, they were able to see that we were girls. At that point they waved and started down, signaling for us to follow. We refused to fly down with them, even though there was this little strip right under us. Of course, their plane was faster, so they would fly up beside us again and wave. Pretty soon we said, "Oh, what the heck." So we followed them down and landed and sat on the grass and talked. The guys asked us to go to a dance that night, but we had to go on because we had to be at this meeting. I often wonder what would have happened had we gone to the dance. I have said that I think we were the only girls that were ever picked up in the air. I was always going to write that in *Reader's Digest,* but never did.

Have you ever had any really tough mentors?

I had one instructor in the beginning. But I didn't have any mentors, really. I used to come around the corner and I guess I shoved in the bottom rudder, and he would say, "If you keep doing that you're going to kill yourself." But that's the way he talked. I made a landing with another instructor, and of course he was in the front and I was in the back. When I did, he would put his head up and hold his nose with his fingers. You know, when you gesture like, "That stinks." I felt so awful when he did that. I just felt terrible.

Have you had any strange reactions from males, from the opposite sex, about your flying?

No, I have been very lucky. I never had any problem with the opposite sex. I like the opposite sex. A lot of girls don't. I never had any problems. I always had a job. I always got a job, because I was well qualified. With one job I had, I left town as the chief pilot, but when I came back the other guy was chief pilot. He'd talked the boss into hiring him. But that was okay. I didn't care. It wound up that I got the chief pilot job back again.

Tell me about how you got it back.

I don't know. I think the boss finally realized that I did a better job. I don't have any strange men stories. I always got along with men. I always had a good job and I got paid the same that men did. Of course, they didn't hire women on the airlines when I was at the age when I could have gotten on there. At the time, I did what I could do and what I was qualified to do, and what I was allowed to do. That was it. So if they wanted a man, it didn't bother me. That sort of thing never bothered me. In other words, I didn't know that I wasn't liberated. I always thought I was. I had always worked with men and I just don't have any stories about men holding me down or any of that. Sometimes I used to have better jobs than they did.

I got to be chief pilot when I came to California in 1951. I went to work for a school where I was hired as a chief pilot over

306

nine instructors. I was just a kid, 25 years old. But I had more ratings, more experience than any of them did.

What was it that you like about air racing?

Oh, I like the competition and camaraderie. I've met so many women that I can communicate with, you know. It's just a lot of fun. I hired several women as instructors. I have always helped other women get jobs.

Even today, I'm still flying. I'm 75 and I am still flying. I still help young kids out. I have a retractable-gear airplane with a high-performance engine and if some young person is working on a particular rating and they need this type of plane, I sometimes help them. I still have an instructor rating. I just don't charge anything anymore. I do it when I want to. But I might help somebody out that way. I like to help the young people, the young girls, get their start, as well as young men. For example, there was a gas boy who was learning to fly. I would see him out there at 7 o'clock, when I had to fly across town to the sales meeting. So, whatever airplane I took, I'd let him fly it. He built up some airtime that way. Today he is with one of the airlines somewhere; I don't know where. He was working as a line boy.

You're a seven-time winner of the All-Women Transcontinental Race. Describe one of the more exciting races.

They were all hard to win. I don't know which was the most difficult. I think the second race I went on was difficult. We were flying east to west in an old Stinson. I flew about 100 feet off the ground for the whole trip, except for one leg where I went up to 12,000 feet. I did win because the winds were predominantly from the west, and early in the morning down on the deck, there wasn't much wind. In those days, there was no autopilot, and not much in the way of radio. I had a student pilot with me. I just told her to hold the map.

Who was she?

She was my boss's wife. Her name was Marcella Duke. She never did go on to get her license. I think her husband had her quit flying.

That must have been very suspenseful down there that low.

That low is very tiring, very tiring. You pull up to get over the power lines.

What year was that?

It was 1953.

They wouldn't let you do that today would they?

Sometimes we can get down there over open country. You can't do that over towns. You can get down there today and do it. Some of them still do. But more obstacles exist now. There are a lot more TV towers sticking up around and there is more air traffic. It was easier to do back then because it wasn't as congested. Back then, when we came to a town, we would have to pull up to 1,000 feet.

Did you have any close calls with towers or anything over the years? Have you ever had any forced landings?

Back in the 1940s. I don't have forced landings anymore. But then, I flew a lot of junk. On the first job I ever had, which was right after the war, I took off in three different beat up airplanes. The first two of them quit. One of them landed back on the runway and into a corn patch. I've had forced landings.

This on the same day?

Yes, this was the first school I worked for. I had to take one off and it wasn't operating. The second one quit on takeoff, but I got back down on the field, but the little runway was right next to the cornfield, so I went into that. The third airplane worked all right. I've had some other forced landings.

How many of do you think you've had?

I can't remember. I've had several where the weather got bad and I landed on a field. For example, when I was a student, I took off and ran into this snowstorm and got lost and landed in a farm field and walked up to the farmhouse and said, "Where am I?" And I had lunch there.

Sounds like a great way to meet friends.

But I wasn't far from my home field, so my instructor came over because I'd ripped a hole in the bottom of the airplane. He said, "That'll fly." It was a fabric plane. One time I was in a race and the engine quit, just before I arrived at the airport. I was going to New York. I looked down and I saw what looked like a great big field, so I turned in and went down and realized it was a great big runway and so I just landed. Of course, it might have been La Guardia, I don't know.

An airplane went around me at the time. It was probably a DC-3. The airport people charged me a $2.50 landing fee, and that made me mad. Two dollars then was certainly a whole lot of money.

What year would this have been?

That would have been about 1952, '51 or '52. I didn't win the race. I didn't finish it.

That would throw a crimp in your budget, wouldn't it, $2.50?

Yeah. That would be the whole race. Gas was like 15 cents a gallon or 20 cents a gallon back then.

As I say, I've had some other forced landings. But today, I don't. Today is a whole different world. I turn on my automatic pilot and my GPS. I never get lost. Those were little Cubs that we were flying back then.

You've flown pretty well the range of aircraft, haven't you?
How many planes have you checked out in?

Oh, my God. I couldn't even tell you. I have flown all the Pipers, all the Cessnas, all the Beechcraft, plus all the Stinsons and Bellancas. When I finally got my type rating, it was at the ripe-old age of 70. I got my type rating at the age of 70.

Is there a story about that?

No, and so I just then decided that I needed something more to do.

What's your favorite plane you've flown?

The one I have right now is my favorite. It's a Piper Comanche 260-B.

What do you like about it the most?

It has long range, high service calling. Maintenance is not that expensive. I love Beechcraft airplanes. But my favorite plane happens to be the one I own. I don't own a Beechcraft right now. I have owned Beechcraft Bonanzas and lots of others. I've owned a lot of different planes. One I really wanted to get rid of was that twin-engine Cessna UC-78 that I bought. I got my multiengine in it, but I was short on money. Another one was that DC-3 that I owned. I was really glad to get rid of that, but I wish I had it now. I had a lot of money tied up in it—not a lot of money in today's dollars, but back then.

What would you do with the DC-3—if you had it today?

Today it would be worth several hundred thousand dollars. I'd sold it for $25,000. Today, I'd just play with it. I'm old. I don't do anything but play. I fly some in my business, too. I have real estate that I fly to Texas for. I wouldn't use a DC-3 today. Other than just for air shows and stuff. That's all they're used for now.

You tested for that astronaut test, didn't you? Did you have any stories about that?

Actually, it was just a week-long medical. I tested for it, but nothing came of it. I was not chosen. I don't know if anybody was chosen. But there were 13 people out there that, I guess, supposedly passed. The officials never told me if I passed or not. I just did the test and went home. I waited but I never heard about it again until 20 years later when a group had what they called the Mercury 13. But they did the same thing I did.

In our initial group, there were only 25 of us, and we went individually. But Jeri Cobb is the one that got me into the group. She asked me if I wanted to join. She was a sort of the instigator and head of the whole thing. It was her little baby.

Are you in touch with her these days?

Oh, yeah. In fact, I saw her last summer. I few to Cape Canaveral to watch Eileen Collins. And Jeri was there.

Were there any unusual tests or anything you had when tested?

They put ice water over your ears. The worst part for me was taking castor oil every morning.

Why did you have to do that?

It was a big physical exam, and you had to take castor oil to clean out your system. I haven't taken castor oil since. We had to take it every morning. It was a total physical exam. I was there alone. I wasn't with anybody else for, I think, five days or a week.

Where was that?

That was in Albuquerque, at the Lovelace Clinic. I said at the time, "I guess I was just a reject."

You've been in practically every aspect of flight, from aircraft sales to charter flight operations.

I owned and operated my own flight school. I was chief pilot at several flight schools. I had my own airplane sales business. And worked as a salesperson for Piper working in new airplanes. During the last 15 years of my working for money, I worked for Beechcraft, at sales. And then I was also an FAA examiner, and did check rides. I enjoyed working for Beechcraft because I was dealing with all new airplanes. I would never fly anything old, except when I would give a check ride to somebody with an old airplane.

When I retired, I went about four years without owning an airplane. Unfortunately, when I wanted to fly, I would go out to rent one and it would be gone. One time I had a trip scheduled in one and something interfered. I had thought, "I'd better buy my own airplane or I'll quit flying." So I bought a 235 Cherokee and flew that around for four years. And then I said, "I'm getting older—I've got to go faster!" At that time I bought the Comanche. Also, I am having a new hanger built that will be open on both ends and include a ramp.

Where will this be?

This will be at Gillespie Field. The pad for the hanger is poured. I've had a deposit on it for a year and a half. You know how those things go. There are going to be about 20 hangers there. They'll have side buildings, offices and grass around it, full bathroom and the whole thing. I'm looking forward to that. Right now, when I have to get my airplane out of the hanger, I have to go find somebody to help me. Even with an electric tow, I can't do it.

Do you have a favorite pilot experience, a favorite story from charter piloting?

There was one that was really crazy. This pilot worked for a fellow that had a twin-engine Cessna. So he couldn't take this trip. He called me and said, "Fran, will you take this trip? This old man here has this twin-engine Cessna and he wants to go back to Wisconsin." I said okay. His regular pilot said, "Now don't order anything more expensive than a hamburger steak because he's tight with his money." I think he might be dead, so he probably won't read this. We began the trip and the man I was flying told me, "You can't go over 8,000 feet because I have heart trouble. And I've got to go through Salt Lake City." He had this girl and her brother with him. I guess it was his sort-of girlfriend. Boy, she was a trooper. She could swear like a sailor. Anyway, we squirmed through the mountains at 8,000 feet, going up through the passes and everything, and we got to Wisconsin. Then, it turns out, the rest of her family worked at the fair, so we ended up there. And, all of a sudden, the two of them wanted to go someplace and I was left at this booth selling — it was one of these things, you walk through at 10 cents a ride. They took off and left me there.

I'd say, "Step right up. Ten cents." It was night. I think they went off to the bar. It was crazy. Anyway, finally they came back. He had gotten a motel with two rooms: one bedroom, and a bed in the front room where I was supposed to sleep. All of a sudden, all of the relatives came in and they were up all night. I didn't get much sleep.

So then I took her over to her family in some other town. I left him and these other guys here, and he says, "Take her over there." I took her over there, and I was there for a couple of days. And then he called. They got into a fight. So he got onto the phone and he said, "You can leave her there. You can come back here, where I am." I can't remember what it was. It was in Wisconsin. I jump in the 310 and I got back to this airport, but he's not there. I've got ten bucks in my pocket. I knew this motel. It was the Blue Moon Motel, where they were staying. So I called over there and I said, "Is Mr. So-in-so in there?" And she said, "No, and as for his party, good riddance!" Anyway, finally he showed up at the airport with nobody in tow. He and I flew back alone to the West Coast, by ourselves. I will tell you that was the most hilarious trip I've ever been on.

Tell me another charter story.

In the early fifties we had an Avion airplane at the school at Santa Monica. The plane wasn't very fast. This old guy, I think he was on an inheritance, would come out to the airport. Nobody wanted to fly with him around. So, anyway, he decided he would charter my airplane to Chicago. During the trip he talked all of the time. I think he was on dope or something. I didn't even know what "drugs" were back then. He must have been on something.

Every time we'd stop, he'd get in big conversations with the gas boys at the hotel or whatever. I think, "Oh my god!" and I'd pretend I didn't know him. I'd say, "Now, come on." Finally, I got in the airplane and said, "I'll bet you can't keep your mouth shut for five minutes — and not talk." He said, "Okay, we're not talking." Before the five minutes were up, he was writing me notes. He wouldn't shut up. I left him in Chicago. I went to Michigan to visit some of my relatives. Then I picked him up in Chicago. When I did, he was a changed man. I guess he had visited his family and was off whatever drugs or medication he had been taking. He was a changed person. I wouldn't have known him On the way back, he had me stop in Riverside. He said, "I have to see this doctor in Riverside." So we stopped and he went off into town, and before we got back home, he was jabbering away again. I think he'd picked up something. He was really weird though. Nobody wanted to take him.

Did you ever meet Jacqueline Cocheran?

When I won the Powder Puff Derby in 1953, the Inglewood Chamber of Commerce had sponsored me. She came to the banquet for the Chamber of Commerce and gave the speech. The banquet was in honor of me winning the Powder Puff Derby. I met her then. Other than that, I didn't really know her.

Was that kind of inspiring?

Oh, yes.

Do you have another story about racing?

We went on a race with Margaret Mead. I went as copilot/navigator, across the Atlantic. We took off at midnight from Oxford, which is near London and landed at Prestwick, Scotland for fuel. We didn't have time. We were on the clock the whole time. It was raining and we were throwing money at the people and saying, "Put the fuel in! Put the fuel in!" I ran in with the paperwork.

Margaret accidentally hit the string on her life jacket. Of course, we had them on because we were starting across the water, so she had to fly the whole trip with that thing inflated. I thought that was pretty funny. But it stayed inflated, because we didn't want to deflate it in case we needed it. That was kind of uncomfortable.

You flew to Serbia too, didn't you?

Yes, I took my Cherokee. I had never flown to Alaska. I had my 235 Cherokee then.

So, I had asked my friend Margaret to go with me, but she couldn't go. So, I was out at the airport one day and ran into the guy. I had met him a few times. He was a mechanic and had a private license. I said, "Hey, John, do you what to go to Serbia with me?" He looked back at me and said, "Well, I don't know. I had a family reunion back on the East Coast that I was going to go to on that date." I said, "Let me know in a day or so, because I want somebody to go with me just for company." I figured he'd be real good because he's a mechanic, too. There was no maintenance over there.

The next day he came back and said, "I'll go. My mother said, 'You can always go to a reunion. You might not get another chance like this again.'" I decided to go, and we took off. All the way through Alaska we had terrible weather. Then we went to Nome and across the Bering Sea. And you had to go at the exact time because of the weather. The trip also involved a lot of paperwork. I had to get permission from Moscow for the airplane to go over. The paperwork was more work than the flying over there. We stayed in Provadenia, Russia, for three days and came back. The trip had been arranged through a fellow in Nome, who knew him. So, this guy in Nome said, "Oh, they'll give you the altitude in feet." We get over there and we're on top and we had to go in IFR. And the radio tower says for us to let down whatever number of meters. I said, "John, how many feet are there in meters?" He says, "I don't know, maybe three." I was concerned about getting down before we hit the shoreline. It was a spooky approach, because you went through a canyon between two mountains. I knew if I got down early over the water, then I could see. So I made a very steep let down. When I first started letting down, I was on top of the clouds, 6,000 feet and on the top of the clouds. I started letting the VFR and the tower started screaming at me, "You can't let down." Then the tower said, "Okay." By the time I was finally cleared for the approach, I really had to dive fairly steeply to make it.

It was kind of exciting, being there in Russia. There was nothing there; no trees, no nothing. We stayed in this little building. Some of the engineers and navigators lived in apartments. And below there were just some rooms. Anyway, we were sitting out in the front one day and this woman came out and got me. She couldn't speak English, so she just grabbed me and said, "Come on in." They were having a party in her room. So I joined the party.

Drank a little vodka?

Yes. I forget what they had with it. God, I think they had champagne with it. Jeez they drink a lot of vodka over there. The woman said something about grandma. I don't know if she said I looked like her grandma or what, and we managed to communicate through hand signals. We had taken gifts over for them, too. The Russians were real nice, sweet people. A lot of fun, too.

You tested a helicopter without a tail rotor. You were the first woman to do that. Can you tell that story?

I knew this fellow who was building this helicopter in a garage. One day he said, "Fran, will you test fly that for me when I get it done?" I said, "Oh, sure." I never thought he'd get it done. But lo and behold, one day some time later he did. On the first test flight, we kept the helicopter tied down so I would just lift off a little bit. The men put it in this big truck, and we took it way out in a place that there weren't a lot of people and would test fly it there. It was not a very stable machine, but I flew it around all summer. They gave me a hundred bucks an hour. So, for that, I'd do most anything.

What year was that?

1966.

Were you ever frightened in that?

Not really. I wasn't frightened, but I cracked it up eventually. For that, I didn't have time to get frightened.

What happened?

I was close to the ground, and it ran out of lift and hit and it just tipped over and got the blades. That was our last flight.

So nothing much happened with that design, did it?

I think some of the people that were designing it worked at Douglas. Anyway, during the testing, I had one fellow ride with me. He worked at Douglas. He said, "Fran, this is a very unstable thing." Ultimately, I don't think the helicopter had enough power. We'd flown it all summer without the body on it, and then put the body on it and that made it a little bit heavier. Anyway, it was certainly some kind of experience.

Do you ever wish you'd just been a test pilot?

Oh, sure.

You did some testing?

I did some testing on little things. I think it was when they were testing some kind of radar thing. And I was flying this Stinson. It had a big engine thing in the back. They'd taken the seats out. I was followed by the twin Cessna. They had aluminum foil around it. I don't know what they were doing.

My job was to fly this along. One day they said, "We have rigged up a system where if you have a fire back there, a bell will go off." The system involved a string. If the string burned, a bell would go off. Anyway, I was up there at 12,000 feet and the bell went off. And, man, I got that back down on the ground quickly. It turned out that it wasn't on fire. The string had just broken.

We would fly out in the mountains. I was called, "Red Fox Leader." I'd talk to the men on the ground, and they would do their thing. I was testing equipment for this company. That was kind of a fun job. That was in the early fifties.

What's the most difficult student you've tried to license? And how many students have you licensed?

I've licensed over 3,000 students. They were not difficult to license.

Was there ever one that was difficult or quirky or that you had a terriable experience with that's still in your mind?

Well, those I flunked.

One guy came over with a twin. He wanted to get multi-engine ratings, but he would come over in some poorly maintained airplanes. So we would get in and usually one of the engines wouldn't start. He wanted to go out and prop it to get it started, which is fine. We would do that. Finally, I said, "What's going to happen on the test when I go up there (because I shut off the engines) for the multi-test? What's going to happen up there when I shut off the engine?" I said, "Are you going to get out and prop it?" We didn't even go up, and he flunked.

It's been a great life of flight.

I've enjoyed it. A great life of flight. And I'm still enjoying it. This past year, though, I've had two artificial hips put in. I've had a few other problems, but I am still flying and I intend to fly as long as I can get in the airplane.

I am not going to let just somebody do the hip replacement. I wanted to know how many such operations he had done. He said, "Oh, about 1,500. Not as many as you've flown." And I said, "Do you have any recommendations of anybody you've done?" He said, "Sure." So he had this guy call me. He was an airline pilot—younger, maybe 50. The doctor had operated on him and he said the doctor was the best. So then I said "Okay. Do it."

I couldn't, when I had the hip done, the first one, I couldn't get my foot up into the airplane. I almost cried. But we solved that. My friend said, "Oh, you've got this little stool here. We'll drill a hole into the middle of the stool and put a rope in it." And so, for the past year, I've just reached the point where I could get rid of the stool. Over the past year, I'd put the stool up there, step, hold onto the rope, step up onto the wing (the Comanche doesn't have a step and you've got to lift your leg up) and then I'd pull it up behind me and throw it in the back. Then I'd get out the same way. I called it my retractable step. So that's how I flew.

I won the Palms Pines this year. Last year I was between hip operations and I was with a cane and my stool. Then I came in second. I said, "I guess the old lady's still got it in her." It's probably the last race I'll win. But I enjoy the girls. I enjoy competition. It's just been my life.

It's been your life. What does flight really mean to you as a kind of metaphor?

Well, to me, it's been my life. That's what I've done all my life, what I've enjoyed. It's always there for me, no matter what else happens, or whatever hardships or things happening that might not be what I would wish. I always have my airplane and I can go back out and fly it. And then I'm okay. It's been a source of joy.

What was your greatest hardship?

My second husband died. They include things in life that happen when you're 75. Deaths in the family and different things like that.

As far as hardship, I grew up in the Depression days. If you don't know you haven't got it, it doesn't matter. I mean, if you don't know you're poor and everybody else is poor, you're just as happy. Money does not bring happiness. I did learn that. The happiness comes from other things besides money. I have earned a lot of money in my time, not in flying; but investing in real estate. And I can do whatever I want now. In fact, I'm going to Tibet in November.

Gene Nora Jessen
"The Mercury Program and Beyond"

Gene Nora Jessen illustrates the role of determination against odds in her pursuit of a a flight career.

Gene Nora was born in Springfield, Illinois, and grew up in Evanston, Illinois. She graduated from Evanston High School and attended the University of Oklahoma where she graduated in 1961. She married Bob Jessen in 1964, and because Bob wanted his own business, the couple sought out possibilities. After looking around the country, they decided on Boise, Idaho. She and her husband have owned and operated Boise Air Service. At Boise Air Service in the early years, Gene Nora ran the flight school and charter. The couple had two children: Briana (whom Gene Nora taught to fly) and Taylor, and Gene Nora stayed home to raise them. She says, "I've done a lot of speaking to school groups, and I have always advocated to young girls to be selfish and do the career thing. For me, it was important to do that first and not have any regrets about being home and raising children." At the time of the interview, Gene Nora had recently competed in the Air Race Classic, finishing sixteenth out of forty, in a Bonanza. (All of the top ten winners were small airplanes.) Active in civic affairs, she worked hard to develop the new Ninety-Nines Women's Aviation Museum in Oklahoma City.

When Dr. William Randolph Lovelace offered the opportunity for performance tests for NASA astronauts, it opened the challenge to 13 women, one of whom was Gene Nora Stumbough (Jessen), the now-famous "Mercury 13." What a powerful legacy!

Was there anything curious about how you got interested in flight?

I think the significance of that is that, when I was in high school in the Chicago suburbs— I grew up in Evanston—I joined the Civil Air Patrol and would go out to the airport on the weekend and would hang around and get a little 10-minute ride. There was a senior, with whom I am still in contact through the years. This would have been about 1953. We must have been flying a Cessna 172—I don't know exactly what it was—but anyway some light airplane. He let me handle the controls a little and he said to me, "You're a natural" and that made a great impact on me. Of course I've been an instructor all these years, and I know that you say things to encourage students, and I don't know exactly what he meant by that, but it did cause me to believe that I could actually fly the airplane. In the mid 1950s, I had no idea that I could ever expect to have a actual career in aviation, but it caused me to pick a university where I could get a degree in airport management, an aviation program.

I came from a very modest home. I certainly could not afford to learn to fly and go to college. But I always had this idea in the back of my head that maybe I'd be good at that because of what he had said.

So that really affected your teaching over the years?

Yes.

It's a pretty simple statement: "You're a natural."

Yeah, it doesn't mean a thing, but I took it to mean that I had some ability and that it was not out of the question to think that I could be in this field. So when I did my sophomore year in college, I did dredge up $280 and got a pilot's license in this Champ, and then I was totally hooked. I was in and out of college then, earning money to go back and take more flying.

How did you dredge up money?

My parents helped me with it, and I would drop out of school and go to work, and then I'd go back. I was six and a half years getting a degree.

Did anyone say, "You must be nuts, dropping out of school"?

No, I was the only girl in the program. I would periodically go see Mr. Kraetly. Mr. Kraetly was the University of Oklahoma money lender guy. This is back in the fifties. It was pretty primitive then. They didn't have any kind of a formal loan program.

I'd go see Mr. Kraetly and say, "Mr. Kraetly, I want to take some more flyin' lessons." The maximum they'd give you was $500. He'd say, "Here's this girl who wants to be a pilot. There are no jobs for girl pilots." He would act like that was perfectly normal and give me $500. Then I'd buy some more flying lessons, and then I'd drop out of school for a semester and I'd go to work and earn the money and pay it back and earn a little more and go back to school, then go borrow some more. I think I did that three times. He acted like that was okay.

Did you ever get a chance to thank Mr. Kraetly?

You bet.

What did you tell him?

I just wrote him a letter and told him that I thought that was pretty brave of him to stick his neck out for some young girl who wanted to be a pilot. He lived to a ripe old age. He lived into the age where you have all the government forms and loan programs and all of this formal stuff that they have now. Back then, you just go in the office and see Mr. Kraetly and say, "I need some money." And he'd say, "okay."

What is there about Oklahoma? Isn't flying akin to being a cowboy of sorts?

I don't really know. They had a very excellent flight program there. My mother was an Oklahoman and she encouraged me to go to school there, but the Flight School is what drew me. Being the only female in the program, I really can't relate to whether they were good to the girls or anything like that. At that time, college was pretty formal. You always wore dresses, skirts and sweaters to go to class. I had to go to my professors and tell them that I was flying an airplane with a stick, and I had to wear pants and that's why I was coming to school in pants. You did not dress that way then. Hard for people to imagine that now, but that was the way it was handled then.

Did any of them have trouble with that?

Oh, no. When the university hired me at 160 hours, I was already a commercial pilot and a flight instructor and I was teaching people how to fly. When the university hired me on a three-quarter basis, I continued to go to college until I finally got a degree, but it was very formal.

How did the students treat you?

My maiden name was Stumbough. The students called me "Miss Stumbough." I was the same age, but they treated me with respect.

I can't believe you are saying that nobody ever disparaged you at all over all those years?

Not that I knew about.

What did you do after the University of Oklahoma?

I finally graduated. The way I did it was, I knew I didn't have enough money to fly and get a degree so I presumed I was not going to get a degree. Still, while I was there, I kept going to class, and since I wasn't going to get a degree, I just took all the classes my two favorite professors taught. They happened to be in the English department. One day I checked my transcript and the adviser said I had enough courses for a major in English. They said, " If you'll get a little foreign language, we'll give you a degree." So I did and they did. So finally six-and-a-half years later, I have this degree.

I heard that there was another lady in Oklahoma, Wally Funk, who was learning to fly at Oklahoma State University. We would run into each other once in awhile. She told me of Dr. Lovelace's program at Albuquerque and how he was giving women the astronaut physical exam. I thought that sounded interesting so I wrote them a letter. I said that I understood that you had to have 1,000 hours flying time and a college degree and that I wanted to get into this program, that I fit those qualifications, and I just didn't see how they could run this program without me.

He wrote me right back and said, "Come on." Janey Hart, who was the wife of Senator Phil Hart of Michigan, arrived at Albuquerque at the same time and we went through the tests together. We were the 24th and 25th women, the last two to take the tests. Of those women who took the tests, 13 of us passed.

We were to go on and take further testing at Pensacola. The Navy was going to do the jet orientation and centrifuge and all that for two weeks. We had our airline tickets and we were already to go. I asked my boss at the university for two weeks off work to go take these astronaut tests. It was all very secret. You were not supposed to tell anybody. He denied permission because it was the first two weeks of school. Of course, you have this big influx of students and we'd each get 12 new students to start, and he said no, he couldn't spare me for two weeks, so I quit my job at the university so I could continue the testing. He hired somebody immediately because school was getting ready to start, and two days later they canceled the tests. I got a telegram, which was how they did things. Here I find myself burdened with college debt and I am unemployed.

Have you since learned why they canceled? Was there pressure to get rid of the program?

People have written books on that subject. It is very complicated. I think NASA got wind of it and the astronauts got wind of it, and there was a congressional investigation. Janey Hart had some political clout. "Was NASA Prejudiced against Women Astronauts," which they were, but at the time it didn't really do much good to point it out to them. They decided that if you were not a jet test pilot, you could not be an astronaut. That was the end of the program.

What was the toughest part of the test?

It was a week of pretty severe physical exams, and if you read *The Right Stuff,* that was pretty much right on what happened. They did every test that they could possibly think of.

Was there one that scared you?

I don't think so. We had no idea what we were getting into, but we were here to do well. We had a great attitude. I think in the book, *The Right Stuff,* the guys kind of play around and do practical jokes. We were very serious. We wanted to do well.

When you are a pioneer in a field, like a woman pilot, you always feel like you are paving the way for other people and you need to do well. We were pretty intent on doing well in the testing. The tests were compressed. You just raced from one test to the next one. There were very serious eye tests, lots of eye tests. They did probably 75 X-rays of the body and lots of stuff that could have been determined to be dangerous later on—but what did they know in 1961? They tested everything they could just to see what you could do.

Do you remember anything that seemed weird at the time?

I think one that they abandoned pretty quickly was putting ice water in your ear and holding it there to measure the amount of time it took for you to have vertigo.

How secret was all this?

We were asked to not tell anybody. We could tell our families but no publicity.

Was it hard keeping the secret?

No, I went there on the spur of the moment. I did not have a lot of time to worry or think about it. When we finished the tests and got the word that I had passed and that I was going to go to Pensacola, my folks had moved to Colorado and lived at 8,500 feet, so I went to Colorado between semesters and did a lot of pretty intense walking at altitude. I did not know what else to do, except to try to be in pretty good shape.

I was very skinny. I was about 120 pounds and they flew us up to Los Alamos, put us in a human counter machine, which was a long cylinder that they rolled you into and they measure the lean body mass. They do that today in water. I did not have any fat on me. I was pretty fit already and had done this walking at altitude, trying to get in as good a shape as I could be for that. I would walk up Pike's Peak, as well as up the various mountains around there.

How many hours a day was that?

I didn't work a lot—maybe a couple of hours a day. I was familiar with that country. During the summers, I had worked in those parts for the Chamber of Commerce. In my job, I'd stand out along side the highway dressed in cowboy clothes by a covered wagon and people would stop and say, "How do we get to Pike's Peak?" and I'd tell them.

They would ask some pretty phenomenal questions. "How high is Pike's Peak?" I'd tell them. Then they'd say, "Is there any way you can get to the top without going that high?"

How'd you feel about leaving the University of Oklahoma?

I was very happy there. I really liked U.O. I felt very comfortable there. I liked the people. The airplanes were maintained very well. I'd probably still be in Oklahoma. It was a dead-end job, but I was happy.

I got an interim job. I called the head of the aviation program at Oklahoma State University, and told him what had happened. He said, "You mean old Joe let you go just because you were going to miss the first two weeks of school to go to the astronaut program?" And I said, "Right!" He said he would call me back. He called me back in five minutes and said, "Get yourself up here. We want you to work for us." I taught flying at Oklahoma State University for two semesters. In the meantime, I wrote everybody in the world looking for a job because I suddenly had an incentive to do something else.

My letter arrived at Beech Aircraft Corporation in Wichita just as they were getting ready to introduce a new model airplane, the Musketeer. They were going to fly that airplane, a formation of three Musketeers, in the 48 contiguous states, for 90 days,during the summer of 1962, in order to introduce the airplane.

They had a girl pilot at Beech. Her name was Joyce Case. She had been the Women's National Aerobatics Champion, a really fine pilot. She was going to fly one of the three airplanes, and two guys were going to fly the other two. When my letter came in, this vice president thought they could probably get more free publicity if they had two girl pilots, so they hired me—absolutely dumb luck and perfect timing.

You must have been pretty startled at that.

I was thrilled. It was rather interesting. This vice president said, "If you are the lady, this picture appears 'ladylike.'" "Ladylike" was always important at Beech. We always flew in high heels and dresses. I flew up to Wichita in a Cessna, which was all we had at the university, to sign up for the job and meet the people.

Beech was a fabulous place to work. We had all new airplanes. They never did fix planes; they just replaced planes. You always had brand new airplanes. Also, it was very important for them to be able to say: "Our girl pilots fly the line." So we flew everything. We flew the Twin Beech, the Twin Bonanza, the Baron, and the Musketeer. Whatever they had, we were checked out in. It was interesting. This vice president who hired me told the men who worked there, "We have these two girl pilots. You are going to be traveling with them. There will be no problems." The whole atmosphere was terrific. The dealers and the distributors accepted us as experts, which we were.

No one had ever flown this plane before, and we were flying three in formation for 90 days in all the contiguous States. We flew in all kinds of conditions. We always had a chase plane with us with photographers and public relations people.

Any unusual things when you were flying formatiom?

Yes, that's the reason I'm trying to finish this 1929 Air Race Book. I think enough time has passed. Mrs. Beech is deceased. They do not make the Musketeer anymore. I think it's probably time to tell the story of the things that happened on that trip. For one thing, we made 280 changes in that airplane the first year. It is rather startling to realize how a new model develops.

What change are you most proud of helping bring about?

I think the first thing that went bad relates to the fact that Beech had never built a cheap airplane before. Beech was known for their quality, so to build a less expensive airplane was tough for them. One of the things they did was, instead of putting a shimmy dampener on the nose gear, they put a centering spring on it. As that spring wore, it weakened, and we're flying these planes every day—all day long, and so we are putting a lot of time on these first three airplanes—plus the production test airplane. The first four airplanes are getting a lot of time on them. We are finding out where the weaknesses were. This centering spring started to loosen up. The nose gear would shimmy on landing. When flying, we got really good at holding the nose off as long as possible, but as the centering spring loosened up, the nose gear would shimmy and that vibration would go back to the tail and would loosen the tail. They ended up making a change there and putting a shimmy dampener on the airplane. There were a lot of things we learned on this tour about the airplane, and changes came about on the airplane.

The Three Musketeers Tour was a fabulous experience.

We were on TV and in the news in every state. But the tour was tremendously tiring. We flew the planes between the stops. We visited every dealer and distributor. We demonstrated the planes. We always flew in high heels and a dress.

In 1962 you did not have wash-and-wear clothes. You are wearing wool, silk, or cotton dresses. The ease of traveling was not there like it is now.

What would you do?

You would carry enough clothes so that you could always look fresh. Then on trips where you were two days in one place, you could have everything cleaned. You had lots of cleaning bills. Now this is in 1962 when women went to the beauty shop once a week and had their hair done and had it all backcombed; then a week later, they went to the beauty shop again and had their hair done. You had lots of Spraynet in your hair, and it got very dirty before you had it done again. When we flew, we were in the wind and the weather. Our boss said, "You girls can have your hair done as often as you want, but I don't want to have any discussions with the accounting department about beauty shop bills, so I just want you to take lots of taxi cabs." You did not get receipts then. He trusted us to not mention the hairdos, but he said to go ahead and have our hair done. He did not want to have to defend beauty shops for his two girl pilots.

It was a fabulous experience. The Beech years gave me my instrument rating, my multi-engine rating, and I checked out in all the airplanes.

Just recently, I have had a lot of publicity about this astronaut thing, which is nothing, but I do take pride in the years I flew for Beech. I guess that was not nearly as exciting or romantic as being involved with the astronaut program, even though the astronaut program was only for a week.

What was your favorite Beech plane?

I fly a Bonanza now. I loved the Bonanza. I loved the Staggerwing. I've only been in one once. I've never flown it, but I
love the Staggerwing. I loved flying the Twin-Beech. That was
fun and a challenge. I have a very strong prejudice for the Beech
airplanes. I love them. Nice place to work. Nice people. The
distributors and dealers always treated Joyce and me very well.

Any unusual questions asked of you by distributors or dealers?

I suppose that this vice-president maybe gave the dealers and
distributors the same speech, I don't know. They treated us well,
though. There was one interesting thing that happened. If you
landed the Musketeer airplane with full flaps and hit the brakes,
you would hydroplane. You would get up on the nose gear. It was
important to retract the flaps before you ever touched the brakes.
Eventually they placarded the airplane: "Do not apply brakes
until flaps are retracted" because of the hydroplaning. Eventually,
they changed the configuration of the flaps so the problem went
away. However, at one time, people were hydroplaning with the
airplane and going off the runway. In fact, I spent a year of my
life traveling around to all the distributors and dealers, and my
assignment was to teach everybody involved with a dealership
how to land that airplane.

I was flying with people who had no interest in flying that
model airplane. When I arrived at a distributorship, I was supposed
to fly with every pilot they had. I was to show them how to land
the airplane so they could train their customers properly. It was
an interesting experience because the "high time pilots," like the

King Air pilots, had no interest in flying a Musketeer. Still, they were wonderful students because they respected the fact that I knew how to land that airplane, and I could show them something about the airplane even though they had lots more flying time than I did. The "high time" pilots were terrific students because it was easy for them to accept that they did not know this airplane. A real "low time" flight instructor was usually very defensive about my teaching them how to land the airplane.

You studied Airport Management. Any outrageous principles that they taught you in school that we would laugh at today?

They dropped the major my freshman year, so I never did take airport management. That's why I ended up in English. First, though, I decided I would major in business. I did not like that. My second year, I got my certificate and decided that I had to fly airplanes. Then I decided that I could not afford school and flying. I'll just fly. That's when I was in and out, taking more and more flying classes until I had 160 hours, and they hired me to teach flying. That's when I decided to take classes on the side, and since I couldn't afford to get a degree, I'd just take classes and I kind of came in the backdoor.

In your reading, did you like stories about Icarus?

I discovered the aviation writers, particularly Ernest K. Gann and the ones who could really write. *Fate is the Hunter* by Ernest K. Gann is what really introduced me to the excitement in aviation. Today, I have quite an extensive aviation library. I think my favorite at that time was Gill Robb Wilson, who was also the editor of *Flying* magazine. He was a Methodist minister, so there was a lot of religion in his poetry, just pure beautiful aviation poetry.

Any stories from your early days as a student?

I remember particularly some of the people from the industry who were so supportive of the student. Grover Loening was alive then. He dates clear back to the Wright Brothers and was known for the Amphibian. He used to love to dance with the girls at the National Intercollegiate air meets.

Was it inspiring to be around someone who goes back to Wright?

It is now. At that time, these were just guys who came to the intercollegiate competition. They were big names in aviation, but they were down to earth people who mingled with the kids and were just there. We had to get a little older to appreciate how unusual that was.

Among those that you met, who moved you the most?

I don't know about moved, but I'll tell you a funny story. It had to have been about 1963. I was flying a Bonanza into Lunken Field—"Sunken Lunken"—in Cincinnati when I heard this woman's voice. The woman was flying a Lockhead Lodestar and had just called the tower. I was impressed. Man, that's a big airplane! Furthermore, that was a woman flying that airplane. I wondered who it was. When I got on the ground, I kept the radio on. I was listening to what was transpiring. Pretty soon the tower tells this Lockhead that she is lined up on the wrong runway, but that she was cleared to land on the runway of her choice. This voice came back and said, "I'll land on any goddamned runway

I please." I thought, "Wow! I did not know you could say that on the radio." It was Jacqueline Cochran. Of course, she was the one who paved the way for the women to take the astronaut tests. Anyway, I stood right next to her when she came in and paid her gas bill. I stood there, but never spoke to her. I was too awed. I don't know who else could get away with talking like that but her. That was typical Cochran.

Where did you get your confidence?

I think probably from my parents. Although they could not support my flying financially, they always were supportive emotionally. Mother said to me that she had friends who thought she was an unnatural mother because she did not worry about her daughter flying airplanes. I was just stunned to hear that. Why would she worry about me flying airplanes? I always thought it was great. It never occurred to me that there was anything unusual or dangerous.

Do you remember a time that they were most proud of you?

I cannot come up with one. I think they bragged to their friends about their daughter, the pilot. Mother still does that today. I know that they were proud.

Have you had any forced landings?

No, really not. I had an engine stop on take off with a student in this little field in Oklahoma on a dual cross-country. It was a carburetor adjustment. We came right down and landed on the field.

Any unusual student stories?

I had a niece who went to school at Oklahoma State University. I was flying by and I stopped to see her. I was at the airport waiting for her to come in from class and was talking to the secretary there. I told her that I used to teach flying here back in 1961, but I don't imagine that there is anybody around that I would know. No there wasn't. But there was this fellow watching, and he went off and returned with this old, dog-eared student pilot log book. He opened it up and said, "Is this you?" And sure enough, it's my signatures in there. I taught him to fly. He'd gone off to the Vietnam War, flown helicopters, been in the Army, and retired—and was back at Oklahoma State University—flying charter. I am thinking I can't be that old. He said to me, "You taught me something that I've never forgotten." I thought that I must be a pretty good flight instructor. I taught him something that he never forgot.

He tells me that we are on our first lesson in Champs. I tell him all about the airplane and tell him to fasten his seatbelt. We finish the lesson. Next day, he comes back for another lesson. We go through all of this, and he forgets to fasten his seat belt. I tell him that I've told you twice about your seatbelt and I'm not going to tell you again. The next time he comes for a lesson, he does not fasten his seatbelt. We are up flying and I pop the stick and he went up and hit his head real hard on the roof. He said he never forgot to fasten his seat belt again. Egad! What a thing to be remembered for!

Patty Wagstaff

"Stunt Flying"

Patty Wagstaff

By the time she was five, Patty Wagstaff had crossed the country four times by train and car. She was, she says, a good traveler. Patty has traveled a long ways since. She was the first woman to win the U.S. National Aerobatic Championship, which she won in 1991, 1992 and 1993. She is also a five-time member of the U.S. Aerobatic Team and a consistent medal winner in Olympic-level competition. In 1994, the BF Goodrich Aerospace Extra 260, which Patty flew to victory in the 1991 U.S. National Aerobatic championships, was inducted into the National Air and Space Museum, Smithsonian Institution. The plane takes its place beside Amelia Earhart's Lockheed Vega in the Pioneers of Flight Gallery.

Patty was born in St. Louis, the daughter of an airline pilot. Over the years, she has tried her hand at an unusual mix of jobs, including abalone diver, waitress, limo driver, office manager, as well as courier for a messenger service. Finally, she returned to the comfort of the family occupation—flying, a place she has stayed ever since. At one time she wanted to be an astronaut; now she continues to set high standards for herself and for women in the once-male dominated world of flying and looks to other challenges and other venues. One of the few pilots in the world who combines professional air show flying with competition aerobatics, Patty's skills have been admired by audiences the world over. She currently runs the Patty Wagstaff Aerobatic School in Saint Augustine, Florida.

Remember your earliest dreams of flying?

I had been around flying with my dad, but I don't remember when I really didn't want to fly, or at least, didn't think about it. I really liked to fly with my dad, but I think I was a little afraid of it when I was about four or five years old. When I really, really started dreaming of doing it myself was when I started reading Ernest K. Gann books. I was probably about twelve years old. That is when I started getting a feel for what it was like. It's funny because Ernest Gann was pretty sexist. For example, the women in his books are flight attendants or babes. Aside from that, I read his books and romanticized flying.

Remember any scene or book?

I remember *Fate of the Hunter.* I liked it very much. It was a kind of revelation to me. I just remember the feeling of camaraderie that the pilots had with each other. I also remember the feeling that you were not just a cog in the wheel—you were the wheel. You could control the airplane. In addition, I recall seeing the movie, *The High and the Mighty*, when I was a kid. Of course, it was corny, but John Wayne was so cool. I remember the end of the movie when he kicked the tires on the ground.

Part of my interest in flying came from the fact that my dad was an airline pilot, and girls idolize their dads, but it was more than that; it was romantic. It's funny, though, because at that time, there were not opportunities for women to fly. It was only a romantic idea, really. I didn't sit there and say, "I'm going to study hard physics in school so I can fly."

Remember any special flight your dad took you on?

When we moved to Japan for him to work for Japan Airlines, I was nine years old. It was always a real treat if I got to fly with Dad on a trip. Two or three times a year I could take a day off from school. The country didn't have the rules at that time that we did in the United States, so lots of times my dad let me fly, and he let me do turns. I remember flying around Mount Fuji, and he would say, "Oh, go ahead, you fly it." We'd be doing circles around the mountain. The crew would all be laughing because this little girl would be flying the plane. The experience was so comfortable. A lot of people get involved in their parents' profession for that reason because it is comfortable.

Your parents supposedly told you girls can't be pilots, but it doesn't sound as if your dad believed that.

I didn't come from an academic family or a family where the women worked. In fact, career women were thought as oddities. I wasn't raised to think of a career. I remember my mother saying to me about someone, "Well, she's a career woman," as if it was kind of weird. None of the women in my family worked, except in volunteer work.

When I got to the age where other girls say, "I want to be a wife," or "I want to be a mother," I didn't say that ever. I remember vividly saying to my mom, "I want to be a pilot!" Dad looked at me and said, "Oh, Patty, women don't become pilots."

What did your father say when his daughter was up in the air performing aerobatics?

He has been real supportive. My family's funny. I've done a lot of jobs, tried a lot of different things. Everything I did that way, they never really understood. They'd say, "Why don't you do something else?" But, when I said, "flying," it was the first time I had done anything they could relate to because that was perfectly normal. Plus my sister, Toni, had started flying when she was fourteen and helped pave the way for me. She had total dedication to flying for the airlines. Since she was about ten-years-old, she was an inspiration for me. When I started flying, it was good and brought me closer to my family, to my dad and my sister, especially.

Did you ever worry about being better than your father?

Never, that's one of the things I like about flying. There are so many types of flying, and people have so many different talents. You can have a person who is the greatest glacier pilot in the world, but maybe he has no interest in flying helicopters.

For example, I have a float rating, but I have no desire to be a float pilot; even though, I spent a lot of time in Alaska on floats. (My husband did most of the flying on floats.) I started in floats, but I don't care much about it. I'd rather be doing aerobatics or flying warbirds or flying helicopters. My sister, who flies for Continental, doesn't have a big interest in aerobatics, but she loves airline flying.

My husband—we're not together now—taught me to fly, and we were together for a long time. He was a great instrument pilot and a great float pilot, and I don't care about either one. So there has never been a competition with him. That's the way it has been with my dad. He flies out in the forest of Central and South America, now that he's retired from JAL. But we just like different things. It's really neat that aviation is like that.

Did anything unusual happen flying in Alaska?

When I first moved to Alaska, I hadn't started flying yet. My girlfriend and I were waitresses in a hotel, way out in the sticks. This guy invited us out on a trip one day. I was smaller than my girlfriend, so I got in the back of the plane. Now this guy was drinking, though he was not a wild drunk and could hold his liquor. I remember saying, "Cathy, don't give him any more. He's not supposed to drink and fly." She said, "It's okay." We got stuck on a mud flat and had trouble getting the plane out. We buzzed a big grizzly bear, a mother with babies, and it stood up and almost knocked the plane out of the sky. This was my introduction to Alaska flying.

My next introduction was when I got a job at Bristol Bay Native Association, a non-profit organization that administered government grants, among other things. My job was to fly around to twenty-nine villages to talk about economic development. They said, "Tomorrow, you will need to go to Portage Creek." So I called up this airline. We went up to this village and picked up another guy. I was sitting in the front seat. The pilot must have been twenty-one years old, and again, I didn't know a lot about flying, but you sense things. He took off the middle section of an 1,800-foot muddy strip during spring breakup! I just remember hanging on and thinking, "Oh, my God, we're never going to get off!" We got to the end of the runway, and the plane flipped over. It was actually standing straight up. That was another introduction to Alaska flying.

You didn't get hurt then?

No, we didn't get hurt.

Have you ever made a foolish mistake when flying?

The first time I used the instrument rating, I knew, I could survive, but I knew it wasn't my forte. I flew out to a small town to pick up my girlfriend in a Cessna 185. We had planned a trip to Yukon, Fairbanks, down to Mt. McKinley, to Anchorage—about halfway around Alaska. On my first leg up to Bethel, we got lost, and the weather got bad near Togiak. There's nothing there—no roads, no nothing. I got totally lost and turned around, and the weather got worse and worse. There were mountains all around. I had two choices: either put the airplane down in the tundra and maybe be stuck there with the bears, or climb up and try to go back to Dillingham IFR. I saw a big alley, so I started climbing. I climbed up to about 10,500 feet where I knew I would be above the highest peaks in the area. It isn't that exciting a story, but to me it was exciting at the time. I'd flown instruments with Bob but never done any myself. I just remember looking at my girlfriend

346

and saying, "I can't screw up because I care about you." And she was sitting there with total trust and total faith in me. She had no idea how nervous I was. I remember how we were picking up ice on the wings and wheels. There was no one to talk to on the radio because it was uncontrolled airspace. I couldn't get anything on the DME or DOR, so all I did was pick up a heading back toward east. It seemed like forever, but I finally got a signal. It's just as well there was no radio contact because I don't know what I would have told them—we had no radar.

We flew all over Alaska. The weather there is so unpredictable, and it comes up so fast. I remember losing friends for the first time in my life up there — people that I knew died in airplane accidents. I had never known people who died. Growing up, you might know one kid who gets in car accident. With the airlines, accidents weren't common. I remember I had a lot of recurring dreams of airplanes flying low over cities, not being able to climb from growing up. But you never did think that your dad was not going to come home. My flight instructor, Dean Kurtz, was killed on Denali.

Ever think of quitting?

No, I just tried to learn from it. The more I could learn from each of the incidents, the longer I could stay alive. Even at the worst, several years ago, when I lost my close friends within a short time, I felt a little flicker of doubt, but I knew that I was not going to quit.

I lost a friend named Jan Jones. She was my age, a little older maybe. Her husband had flown, and Jan hadn't, but she came to the air show at Oshkosh with her husband, John, and saw me perform. She said, "That's what I want to do. If she can do it, I can do it." So she always told everybody I was her inspiration. (Even in her PR materials!) She was very nice, and we were friends, though we didn't spend a lot of time together. Still, I always tried to keep up with her career and keep an eye on her. She was anticipating her first real air show season. Being a woman was a real advantage. If you're talented and have a good routine, you can go far quickly. There are only a few women and there is really a demand for them in aviation. Anyway, I'd been talking to Jan a lot. She was frustrated from the airplane problems. Even if the problems are under your control, there is no air show performer for whom such things aren't difficult.

I was on my way to Poughkeepsie, New York, for a show. We were both looking forward to it, for this was to be our first show together. I got to Wichita from Tucson, made some calls and heard about Jan going down in a field. No one knew why. I headed up to Cleveland. The weather was really horrible, and it took me long while to get up there. Her husband said he felt she was going to die. I just wanted to visit her before she died, even if she wasn't conscious. Besides, you don't know if the person has some kind of sub-conscious recognition. I had this vision of coming in to her room, putting perfume on her, fixing her hair, something like that. Anyway, the weather was bad, so I didn't get there until three o'clock and found she had died at noon. I saw her mom and dad, who were quite elderly, in the waiting room. A sister and her husband were there. Her mother said, "You were her inspiration." I said, "Oh, God, don't blame this on me!" I mean, it was real flattering in one sense, but I had to deal with that because I had some guilt feelings about it. I felt, "God, if this is what I inspire people to do, maybe I'm in the wrong business." But later, I talked about it with some friends, and they all said, "Look, you may inspire people to start flying, but they don't have to take it to the extremes that you do. Most people won't. It's their choice." So we deal with it, and go on.

What's the most extreme you've flown?

Honestly, I don't like to scare myself. I have never done anything wild, down low that I haven't tried many times up high. I fly low, and I do a ribbon cut, and I race these jet cars at air shows and go inverted at 20, but it took me years to get down there. I've just taken one step at a time.

Your limits change from day to day. Some days, you're really sharp and on target and can get closer to the ground, but some days, you're not as sharp—for whatever reason. I scared myself only one time in an air show. I was going through a difficult time in my life, personally, and got too low on a maneuver. I think only a couple of my friends picked up on it. I don't think anybody else knew the difference, but I scared myself.

What did you do?

I just got too low, and I was too slow. But that was only one time. That was a wake-up call to me. I'm not going to let that happen again. I won't let my personal life interfere again.

Isn't that easier said than done?

Maybe it is. I'd never had personal upheavals while flying until separating with my husband. I'd had a very stable environment, and I didn't realize how personal instability could affect me. I thought, "If this type of thing happens again, I'll either stop flying, or I'll change the situation." What I did after I scared myself was, I just flew the next few events a little higher. Nobody knows the difference.

Who influenced you other than your father?

The one person who influenced the most in aerobatics, was Leo Loudenslager. He was the one I'd heard the most about. I really didn't know anything about competition aerobatics or air shows until I'd been flying for a couple of years. In Alaska, I couldn't find an instructor who was teaching aerobatics, but I knew I wanted to do it. One day, I was sitting in an FBO, and I found a copy of *Sports Aerobatics* magazine, put out by the International Aerobatic Club (IAC) and thought, "A whole organization dedicated to this!" I began subscribing. A couple of years later, a woman in Alaska, named Darlene Dubay, started teaching me aerobatics. Then, I was lucky to fly with Duane Cole later that year, and he helped me a lot.

Are you by nature competitive?

By nature, I'm not very competitive. That was one of the things I had to learn. At first, I didn't care if I won a contest. Once I accomplished what I wanted, I have to teach myself to want to win. Competition is competition. Some of the people who fly aerobatics are very competitive; some are backstabbers. While there are very few people in the air show business with whom I don't get along, I have a few, in competition, that I don't get along with at all for all the petty jealousies and such.

How do these jealousies manifest themselves?

A lot of it is subtle. People make up stories about you. They say you cheat. I remember people saying, "Of course, she's good. She can afford to do it." And I tell you, it's the women who are the worst. I've had more support from the guys than I have from women! But the backstabbers are the reason I did so well, so you have to thank your enemies.

I found that in aerobatics, there are many things I could do. It really annoyed me when I started that people didn't think women could do it. These people were in a rut. You'd hear, "Well, they'll never let us win the Nationals!" At first, I only had people competing against me who were very competitive, but I also had a good motive to do well—to be the first woman to win the Nationals. I lucked out, for if another woman had already won the Nationals, I wouldn't have had the same goal to shoot for.

What about your championship? Talk about it.

It's all a mind game. By the time you get to the contest, you've been training, and you are a certain level. There are a certain number of people who can win the contest. In the world contests, it's probably the top ten who are capable of winning. In the nationals, there are maybe three or four.

The mental preparation starts early. You think, you visualize months beforehand. When I won the Nationals the first time, I had a lot of mental prep. I talked to a number of people. I surrounded myself with only the best people. Bob, my husband then, didn't come to the contest because he would tend to get nervous. In short, I had to set up 100 percent for success. When I won, 99 percent of the people were happy. I got a standing ovation at the awards banquet. But when I won, I didn't feel, "This is all there is." I immediately felt, "I've got to do it again." I knew, I had to for reasons, such as people saying, "It's a fluke," or "Oh, sure, yeah, a woman won." I knew that, only if I won it three times, it would be enough to convince them. Nobody can argue with that.

What were your feelings about being a torchbearer for your gender? Any burden?

Sometimes. You are reminded of it constantly because you're under lots of scrutiny. A man can have a bad day because, well, he's a man, and he's having a bad day. Women can't afford too many bad days. That annoys me. In one sense, I've had incredible opportunities because I'm a woman. In the other sense, I've had more responsibility to do well. Because I've been given certain opportunities, I've had to live up to that. I've had to be careful not screw up and not make mistakes. I don't mind it because I think it makes me a better pilot. I always cared about people and being a good person, but I didn't have anything to focus on. I was drifting around and trying different things. I thought, "Why have any discipline? Why do anything?" I didn't see the need for it. And when I started flying, all that changed.

For me, it's about talent. For me, I can't just be happy being good about something or being the best at something. Once you are the best at something, then what? What do you do with it? Where do you go? You can't stay static. You have to stay open to challenges. That's important. I'll always love to do aerobatics and always be good at it, but I have a lot of things I want to do. As far as reaching a new level is concerned, even though I didn't win the Nationals this year, I did reach a new level in my flying. I was in the first place until the third flight when I blew my maneuver. Big deal. I got on the team, which is what I wanted. Now, my main focus is going to be on the world competition. That will be my last contest. Even if I didn't win, I know what I did. I want to branch out. I have a lot of planes I'd like to fly.

What's flight a metaphor for?

Freedom. That is the biggest part of it. Completeness. When you fly, you take off; you land. You've completed a process, and it's real fulfilling. You've done it. Anyone who's soloed, that's an accomplishment.

It's not unusual for me to fly coast-to-coast without ever using a radio. I listen to music on a stereo. It's freedom. I don't have to talk to anybody. Sometimes, I choose to. I don't think, there is any country in the world where you can fly 3,000 miles, and not talk to anybody, and not tell anybody where you're going. For one thing, I never file a flight plan. It's not because I think, I'm too good to have a problem, but because these little aerobatic planes don't have much range, and with the wind, you don't always know where you're going to land.

What prompted you to start a school in St. Augustine?

A school was something I had always had in mind, but wasn't sure when I would do it. When I started our school, things just came together at the right time. Office space was available at Southeast Aero Services, where we are based; a friend offered to sell me his airplane for a good price; and I had a couple of people who were anxious to train with me,

Without naming anyone specifically, who's the student that you relish telling the other students about as an inspiration or person who overcame?

All of our students are amazing. Taking aerobatic or upset training lessons is an "elective" and not an FAA requirements, so everyone who trains with us really wants to be here to improve their skills, widen their envelope and to become a more confident pilot. We have attracted some wonderful people we have become friends with. It's been really fun to see people who come just to improve their flying ability, and find they unexpectedly fall in love with aerobatics.

What was the toughest part of starting it?

It wasn't tough, but I had no idea where it would go. I had the vision but didn't have every detail figured out. I just knew if I would start it, things would evolve and I could take care of the issues as they arose,

You're a detail person. Ever feel so detailed out you want to escape somewhere? And where, if that's the case?

Sure, I love to escape! Everyone needs a vacation from time to time. I like the ocean and warm water so am most attracted to places like that. Sometimes an escape is just going to the movies.

How's it feel to fly over the city of Saint Augustine, what with its amazing long history? It's almost like a meeting of the old and modern.

St. Augustine is a very special place with an interesting history. They say there are a lot of ghosts here, but I wouldn't know. It's a great place for a school because students can enjoy the town, the beach, the restaurants, etcetera, in between flying. People sometimes bring their families with them for that reason.

You fly cross-country sometimes and enjoy doing so. Strangest flight you've taken across country?

I fly cross country all the time. I've always enjoyed it. To me it's a great way to enjoy the freedom we have as pilots in this country. I really value the fact that if I choose to, I can safely fly from coast to coast without ever talking to anyone or filing a flight plan. This just isn't the case anywhere else. I've flown a lot of cross country in the U.S. and to and from Alaska, but some of the more interesting flights have been in Central America and Mexico.

Where do you get your confidence? Were grandparents a source of strength?

It took me a long time to gain self confidence. I knew I needed to excel in something on my own terms to feel self confident. Learning to fly, getting my ratings, and flying cross country by myself gave me self confidence. My grandmothers were a big influence on me and really helped shape my belief in myself.

Proudest moment, to date, in terms of flight?

Probably winning the U.S. National Aerobatic Championship for the first time. I had set it as my goal, worked hard to achieve it.

Proudest aerobatic maneuver you've undertaken?

The snap rolling 360 degree circle.

What would you say to the little twelve-year old, you once were, who dreamed of flying?

I'd tell her about all the people that said you couldn't do these things. "You'd never have the money. Women can't do these things." I'd say for all the rebelliousness and all the trouble I caused, being myself and not letting any of those people get to me, I'd say, "Good for me!" because I was right, and I knew it.

Emily Howell Warner
"The First Female Airline Pilot in the U.S."

Emily Howell Warner was a single-mom with a six-year-old son, when she went for a critical interview for a job as a commercial pilot. She would make aviation history: In 1973, she became the first permanent female pilot for a regularly scheduled airline—Frontier—in the United States. She took her first flight with Frontier on February 6 of that year—to Las Vegas and back to Denver. When she arrived in Denver, she was met with red, white and blue carnations, as well as a telegram from Turi Wideeroe, the Norwegian who was hired by SAS in 1961, congratulating her on the flight. In the interview, Emily talks at length about the experience of trying to get a job. In 1976, she was the first female to achieve the rank of U.S. airline captain. She flew for United Parcel and later worked for the FAA. Emily is soft-spoken, modest to a fault, perhaps, but remarkable in her persistence and determination, a model for many. To date, she has flown 21,000 hours and has done more than 3,000 check rides and evaluations.

She is a member of the National Aviation Hall of Fame and the National Women's Hall of Fame.

Do you consider yourself a stubborn person?

Yes, I suppose—stubborn in the fact that I set out to do something and usually don't give up.

Did you get that from your parents?

Yes, especially my mother.

Tell me about your mother.

Both of my grandparents are from Ireland, and my mother's an Irish-Catholic mother. If you know anything about the Irish, you know that they are very strong and family-oriented, and they kind of run the family, in a way. They do so, especially with the discipline. Mother grew up on a farm and she then moved to the city. She worked her way through college, studying music. She had a beautiful voice—mezzo soprano—and she tried to make her life better, and she did through her years. She ended up with a good career in singing. She wasn't famous but was in local operas and churches. She made sure that out of six kids, at least two went to college. We didn't have a lot of means, so I wasn't able to go to college. I was always interested in flying, so I took flying lessons.

You noted that your sister wanted to be a nurse, but when you graduated in 1957, you were not sure what you wanted to do.

Right, I thought I wanted to be a nurse because my sister was going to be a nurse. Actually, I went to her job interview and my sister said, "I don't think you're cut out for this," and I knew she was right. It was after that that I thought about what I was going to do. Then that's when I started thinking about being a stewardess.

Tell me about the Emily Griffin Opportunity School. That's a great name.

Yes it is. Back in the twenties, Emily Griffin started a school in Denver for people who could go take classes and learn how to read and write and take business courses. The school has prospered, even to this day. It even has an aviation mechanics school now at one of the ex-Centennial airports.

What courses were you taking there?

I was taking mostly tentometer—the forerunner of computers. Basically I was taking secretarial and bookkeeping skills, that sort of thing.

Would you have been a good stewardess, do you think?

I don't think so. I think I would have felt the same way if I had been a flight attendant and saw the cockpit, because as soon as I saw the cockpit, I knew that was where I wanted to be.

I was thinking about being a stewardess. I was living at home at the time. I started writing airlines and I found out right away that you had to be 20 and a half to be hired. I figured out later that you actually had to be 21 to serve liquor. Well, I was too young at the time. I was working at a department store in Denver and I was thinking about how glamorous it would be to be a stewardess, and how I'd get to travel. I had a first cousin who was a stewardess and that kind of inspired me. One of the gals asked me if I had ever flown in an airplane. I said, "No!" We started talking about that, and she had a daughter going to Western State University in Gunnison, Colorado. Eventually, she got me together with her daughter. I went over to spend a weekend with her daughter and go to a dance at the college. That meant I had to buy a ticket and take a flight. Ironically, the flight was on Frontier Airlines and on a DC-3. My family saw me off at the airport—I was the first person in the family to fly. Anyway, we went through Pueblo, Colorado, which is a short distance and then on to Gunnison. The ride was kind of bumpy, but I didn't get airsick. During the flight, I watched the attendant do her duties, and I looked out the window. On the way back, I was the only person on the airplane. It was a Monday morning —a beautiful Colorado morning with snow on the mountains and blue sky.

We took off, and right after take off, I was talking to the flight attendant and asked her what the cockpit was like. In those days, security wasn't so tight. She said, "Well, do you want to see it? I'll see if the pilots will let you come up." She got permission, and I went up into the cockpit. When I walked through that door and looked out the front window and saw the difference between looking out the side window and looking out the front window at the mountains, I was hooked. I liked hearing the noise from the cockpit, and seeing the dials. They explained a lot of things going back to Stapleton Airport. We landed on runway 12 at Stapleton. They explained the runways and how they were numbered. They just did a lot of talking about flying, and as I listened then, I found myself just absolutely fascinated.

If you hadn't been told all that, would you still be interested?

Oh yes, I was still interested. I made them talk. I started asking questions.

Do you remember what you asked them?

I asked them how long they'd been flying. I asked them how you get started and things like that. After we got into that conversation, later on, one of them said, "If you're so interested in flying lessons, you should take flying lessons." I remarked to them, "Gee, can a girl take flying lessons?" We didn't feel like things were open to women in those days. It just didn't dawn on me that you could go out and take flying lessons. They told me to go over to Clinton Aviation at Stapleton Airport. Before the next week, I was out there on my day off from work, and I went out and talked to them and signed up for flying lessons. My flight was in January of 1958, and I was taking flying lessons by February.

Did you have any close calls while learning?

No. I didn't think I was going to make it on a solo, cross-country flight. Actually, I ground looped a Cessna-140. That's the only accident I ever had. I got caught in a cross wind and it was only about my third solo flight. It was a Cessna-140 with a tail-dragger. If you let up on that yoke at all, you had to hold it all the way back. In a crosswind the tail will pick up and the plane will make a 180-degree turn. It's sort of like a skid on a highway on ice. Anyway, the plane tipped over and I caught a wing tip.

How did you feel after that? Were you upset?

Oh yes! I thought that this was the end of my career. I was so scared because I had to talk to the FAA.

What did you tell them?

I didn't know what happened.

Were they sympathetic?

Oh yes. As a matter of fact, the man I talked to became a friend, after that.

What was his name?

Jim Prendergast. He ended up retiring in Boise, Idaho. He was an FAA inspector for years.

What were your feelings and apprehensions about your first solo flight?

I became a flight instructor, so I kind of know how I must have felt then. You know what's going to happen, but you don't say anything, and you know that the instructor is getting you ready. I remember that my instructor was really working hard a couple hours before I soloed to make sure that he had covered everything. I remembered that point years later when I was soloing people and had the same reaction. I remember my instructor getting out of the airplane. I knew this was it. I was nervous, excited—everything all at the same time, and I wanted to do it. I remember him closing the door and making sure that his seat belt was in the airplane. If he had left his seat belt out, it would have banged on the outside of the airplane and distracted me. He said, "I'm putting this seat belt in here and it will be a little lighter when you take off and you'll notice that." Sure enough, it was lighter—a lot lighter. The drill is to make two touch- and-go landings and a full-stop landing on your first solo and then pick up your flying instructor. I got the job done and I was so excited. Then I made another solo. You make three supervised solos and then they turn you loose. I guess it was on my first flight that I was turned loose. The wind came up on the way back. It was a little more wind than I anticipated. Unfortunately, I wasn't real sharp on crosswinds yet, so I ground looped. That day, my mother drove all the way out to Sky Ranch, which was about ten miles east of Stapleton at the time, and she watched me solo. Then, I went back to Stapleton, and that's when I ground looped. I'm glad I didn't do it in front of her. I never told her either.

Keeping secrets seems to be part of the game!

Oh yeah.

Your mother must have been very proud.

Oh yes, she was. After I soloed, she felt better about it because she was a little nervous about me flying.

What about your dad?

My dad thought it was just great. He thought I'd amount to something some day if I kept it up.

How important was it to have the parents there?

They were very supportive and the family was, too; however, they got a little tired of me talking about flying around the dinner table at night.

What did they say to you?

"Don't you have anything else to talk about?" It was that kind of thing. I wouldn't buy records like most of the kids. I just saved my money to take another flying lesson.

Do you remember a time when you begged, borrowed, and stole to take a lesson?

About six months after I was flying, I was anxious to get a job at Stapleton. The bug really had me then. I had looked around and tried to get a job at different places in the terminal. I wanted to be there all the time. My flight instructor said, "I think they are looking for a receptionist right here. Why don't you apply?" I did and it was just a part-time job. She called me back and I told her I wanted the job and I'd take it as part-time. I gave a ten-days notice and quit this job at the May Company. That's all I could do because they wanted me right away. The May Company people told me I was making a terrible mistake because they were priming me to be an assistant buyer. I told them I knew that, but I really wanted to do this. Years later, this same woman, Juanita Beaty, wrote me a letter that said, "Boy, I guess you knew what you wanted to do." Once I got to the airport I was there every day and got to know people. After I got my private license, I started to fly airplane parts and do different things like that. Eventually I got to ferry new airplanes from Wichita to Denver.

Tell me about the toughest, unusual, or most interesting flight that you took that way.

On one of my solo cross-country flights, the weather was getting worse and the wind was really blowing. I got about over Ft. Morgan, which is east of Denver. There's an airport there. I was looking at my fuel gauge. I just had the feeling that I wasn't going to make it to Denver. I only went a little distance, and I kept thinking about that and figured that I better turn around. About the third time that I told myself I had better go back to Ft. Morgan, I did. I turned around and went back. It was starting to get dark, too. I landed and it was really windy there. The Bristol brothers had a spray plane operation there, and they saw me land. They came out in a truck and got a hold of the wings and walked me back to the hanger. I was safe, and I called Denver to let them know where I was. My flight instructor was upset. I was already checked into a hotel. He said, "Oh no, we can't leave you there." He sent up another flight instructor, another airplane, and two other people to come up and get me and bring the airplane back that night. I could have gone back the next morning, but here I was, a girl, and they were being very protective.

You didn't have any aversion to that at that point, did you?

Oh, no, no. That was part of the culture at that time. I just kept doing my flying and got to do air watches in Denver—traffic watches—one of the first ones in Denver. I got free flying time there. After all, I got most of my flying time doing this and doing that, but it was free flying time. Before, you had asked me how I scrimped and saved money. I lucked out and got in a place where I got lots of free flying time. I worked toward my commercial. After that, the flight instructors would say, "Well, aren't you going to get your flight instructor rating?" I was with a group of people and everybody was encouraging everybody to work on their next rating. I decided I was going to get my flight instructor rating. That really changed my career path, because when I started instructing, I really started a real flying career. Then I was training and making my living on flying.

Talk about being a flight instructor. Did you ever have any trouble with men objecting to you teaching them?

No. The only person who really didn't want to be assigned to me was another woman. That's really the only person. I'd get assigned students and then I started getting a lot of referral students, people who wanted to fly with me. You kind of have a captive audience in a Cessna 150 or any small airplane that has two seats because you're the one that knows how to fly. You develop a relationship like you would as a ski instructor or college professor. You are the professional, and they want to learn how to fly. It's really a unique situation. I really enjoyed flight instructing.

Was there anything you thought you were especially good at?

I was a good flight instructor. I related to people very well. The woman was the only one that ever didn't really want to fly with me.

Tell me the story about that.

My instructor became the flight school manager, and a married couple wanted to take flying lessons. He said, "I am going to set Mrs. So-and-so up with you." She absolutely refused and didn't want to fly. He said, "Accept that, once in a while, someone isn't going to want to fly with you." That was really the only person that refused. I taught many women how to fly. We have what we call a "pinch hitter" course, and that's from the group, The Ninety-Nines. We would encourage women whose husbands owned airplanes to at least take enough flying lessons so that they would know how to land the airplane and how to use the radio and fly the airplane in the air, if they had to. I got most of those women past that into a private license. They would get so enthused.

I found that women were more timid about flying. They didn't know much about the mechanical end of it. But once they got to the point that they knew they could do it, there was really no stopping them. They caught up really fast with the men who seemed to have an edge because they understood the mechanical end of it and how things worked.

Who's the most interesting student you ever had?

I have taught a lot of people who went all the way to the airlines. I remember that about the time *The Flying Nun* was on television, I actually got a nun. Her uncle had bought her flying lessons and she was assigned to me. It was the perfect set-up because they didn't want her to be with a male flight instructor. The deal was, in those days, nuns never went anywhere—downtown alone—they didn't go anywhere without two nuns being together. So this other nun came along. We took a 172, which had a back seat. One nun had to ride along while this other nun was taking her flying lessons. The one taking the flying lessons absolutely loved it, and she was doing a great job. She said that, that summer, she would take as many lessons as she could, but that she'd probably have to quit at the end of the summer as she'd be going to another assignment. We were flying along, and this other little nun, about two or three hours into it, got airsick in the back. I really felt sorry for her, and I said, "Is there any way you don't have to go along? You could sit right in our showroom and have a cup of coffee. You'll be just fine." I'm Catholic, and I told her there wouldn't be any problem. She asked me if I thought it would really be all right. I told her yes and that I thought she really hadn't liked it that much anyway. She said, "No, I really don't feel very good when I'm in the back seat there." We made the deal, and I told her that nobody would ever have to know anything. "You can tell your priest what we are doing, and I'm sure he'll agree with it," I told her. That's how she got out of the back, and then the other nun and I kept on going with the flying lessons.

There was a couple in Nashville—a kid that grew up across the street from me in Denver and his sister. His sister was my very good friend. She was about a year younger than I was, and he was about a year younger than she. Anyway, he came out to the airport after I was flying out there. He was a fireman at the airport. He said that he wanted to take flying lessons. He was real young. He was a natural—sort of like a Robert Redford. We got in the airplane, and I could have soloed him in three hours. He had it. Where he got it, I don't know, but it had to be just a natural thing. I finally soloed him in about eight hours. You are supposed to give them eight hours before you solo them, but I fudged a little. He did great. I just encouraged him and told him that he should go right through this and go straight to the airlines.

He didn't. He had gotten married. He had young kids, and his wife didn't want him to continue toward a career in aviation. But he would have been a natural. A few years later, his sister came out to see me. She had married a jet jockey in the Air Force. She said that she'd like to take some lessons because her husband talked about it all the time. I told her sure. We got in the airplane, and we were like two peas in a pod. She was exactly the same as her brother. She was sharp and just had it.

When you say a "natural," what did she do?

If you showed her how to maintain straight and level flight, she'd do it. If you showed her how to make turns, climbs and glides, she'd do it. It was like a one-time deal. It's like learning to ski. If you can imagine getting on skis and having it all down in three hours of lessons—it's similar. There are natural sportsmen and natural flyers, and so forth.

Were you a natural?

No, I wasn't. I worked hard at it.

You weren't far from natural.

No, I wasn't too far. I recognize that something was coordinated in the minds of certain people, and that the way they did things made them more of a natural than I was. I had to work at it a little harder.

Give me another instance—maybe someone you persevered with who didn't think they had it but you knew they did.

Oh yes. There was a man who ended up being a Frontier pilot who came out and said he wanted to learn how to fly and was assigned to me. Right away, we were only out about 20 minutes, when he didn't feel good. He said, "I guess we'll have to go back. I'm not feeling so good." We got on the ground and I said,

"Do you want a cup of coffee?" We sat down and we talked for a while. He said, "You know, if you stay with me—I know I'll get airsick—but I want to learn how to fly but if you'd just be patient with me and see if we could work it out." I said, "Sure!" We'd go out and fly till he wasn't feeling too good, and we'd start landing at Sky Ranch Airport, which is the field we'd use for our practice. We'd sit on the ground for a while and then we'd go again. I worked him up to an hour and then an hour and a half. Then, when the cross-country came, we had to work that out. But there were three legs with about 40 minutes on each leg, so he could fly an hour or two hours at the most without getting sick. He ended up being an instructor right at Clinton where I worked, so he got over it. He built up his time and eventually got hired by Frontier Airlines.

One day somebody from Frontier was talking to me about flying. He said, "I had this guy last week who was my co-pilot and he'd get airsick every once in a while. I couldn't believe it!" I said, "Who was that?" It was my student. He was getting a little airsick now and then. I said, "What do you do about it?" He said, "He just goes out and upchucks." I didn't tell him that I knew him and had taught him how to fly. He actually retired with the airline, and I think he eventually got over it.

At one point, you have 2,500 hours, and you're flight instruct-ing—but you're not quite qualified according to the attitudes of the times. In your words, you are "anatomically incorrect."

Well, things were happening. In the the 1960s—with Martin Luther King, women's lib, the first flight into space—there was a lot going on in the country. I had 2,500 hours or so, and in 1966-67, Clinton Aviation, where I worked, got a contract with United Airlines, which involved hiring pilots with commercial licenses. That meant they had to have at least 160 hours at that time to get a commercial license. They had to have a college degree. It was a pilot project. The pilots would be hired by the airlines, then the pilots would be sent to us on contract, and we would work with them to get their instrument rating. I was assigned three students every three weeks to assist them in their instrument ratings. We'd fly two-hour blocks of times, and we'd get them through the instrument ratings.

The first couple that I flew with, I found that their basic flying techniques weren't very good. So we spent a lot of time doing some VFR flying to build up their flying skills, let alone their instrument time. One of them practically took me off the runway one day, which got my attention.

He practically took you off the runway—what happened?

On take off, he practically went off the runway. There, you are not using any rudder. You are supposed to have a commercial license, and you have to steer it down the middle of the runway to keep it on. Here we go off—headed for the side of the runway. He wasn't doing anything, so I had to kind of take over and recover.

Were you scared?

No, because you're a flight instructor, and you have to be ready for those kinds of things.

You have a limit if a student gets more than 10 or 15 degrees left or right of the center line, and you know right away that they're headed off—and they're not correcting—you correct for them, because there are dual controls on the airplane. Here he is, he has his job with United Airlines, and I'm teaching him how to fly! That sort of got me going.

It got in your craw?

Yeah, it did. That's when I started applying to the airlines. I picked out three airlines: United, Frontier, and Continental. I started applying in 1967, but it wasn't until 1972 that I got some interest. It took me about six years.

Tell about the worst rebuke you had during those six years.

Most of the airlines, like Continental and United, never would answer. They'd send me a form letter. Frontier never answered any of my applications. I knew some people at Frontier, and one day I talked to the chief pilot. I knew his wife was a member of The Ninety-Nines because I'd see her at meetings. I'd asked her about the airlines. She told me to go see her husband, who was John Meyers, the chief pilot at Frontier at the time. So I did. By that time, I had 3,500 hours and had an updated application, which I presented to him. I caught him in his office. He knew me and knew my flying time. He was real nice but he said, "You know, Emily, I have 3,000 applications here." I knew he was exaggerating. He said, "You're qualified—you have a lot of flying time—but you need more multi-engine time. If I were you, I'd get your airline transport rating." I had enough flight time to do that then. I took his words, but the biggest thing he said, was, "This is what I would do if you want to continue toward being an airlines pilot, but I don't know if an airline will ever hire a woman." He actually said that to me. I said, "Well, thanks for the advice." That put another thing in my craw and made me more persistent.

I hammered in on Frontier and found out where their offices were. Next, I started to meet people in the business offices. People started to know me by name and would ask me what I was doing there today. I would just tell them that I was looking around and visiting people. I was kind of campaigning. Eventually someone invited me into an aircraft simulator. People were getting to know me.

What's the most outrageous response you had when you were standing around?

I had one captain who said something. This was after I had filed an application and the airlines were looking at it. I guess the captain had heard about it, and he stormed to the personnel office and, after that, to the chief pilot's office. He said to them, "You're not thinking of hiring a woman?" I got all this back from people I knew. He used some foul language and said, "It will be the ruination of the airlines if you ever do that!" I was hired anyway. He was actually the only pilot who blackballed me in ALPA (Airline Pilot's Association). I was accepted anyway and became the first woman in the ALPA in 1974. I don't think I had anybody that was really bad to me—to my face anyway.

How important is personality? You seem to have a very pleasant demeanor. What if you had responded negatively?

I would have lost a huge amount of ground, if that had happened. Luckily, I got a good Irish sense of humor from my family and I've always liked people. I think that helps a lot. Ed MacMiller was a writer, a United Airlines pilot, and he also ran a radio show in Denver. He wrote a book called *Wild Blue Yonder* It was a picture book about the Air Force Academy. Ed was a well-respected pilot. I met Ed through his radio talk show. One day he called and said he had heard about me flight instructing at Clinton. Of course, he was a pilot and wanted to get people on his show to talk about things he liked, but I got on his show and we talked about it. After his show was over, we had a cup of coffee and he said, "Emily, you're qualified—why don't you apply to the airlines?" There was a Mr. Bob Green (I think his first name was Bob), who had just been hired by Continental Airlines, and he was the first black man in the country to be hired by an airline. He actually went through legal methods to get his job. He was a very good and professional pilot. Ed encouraged me to do what Bob Green did and get some legal help. I said, "You know, Ed, I'm just not that type of person, and I don't want to do it that way." I know I could probably get on. But then you are facing a brick wall when you get in there, I feel. You've got pilots to contend with, and if you come in that way, they're not going to like you right off the bat. It would probably make your life very difficult so that's why I didn't do that. I felt, if I kept prodding the way I had been doing, that I could probably achieve my goal.

Tell me more about hanging around. This is a riot. What did you do—bring a sandwich and hang around?

Oh yes, you got to know people that would talk to you, and pretty soon, you've got two or three people. Then, when you go back there, you can say, "Hey how you doing today?" Then you start using their first names, and they start to know your first name. You know where the coffee machines are and you say, "Do you want a cup of coffee?" You just do anything to talk about flying! I knew it was getting close. I kept updating my applications, but in 1972 a pilot who was a flight instructor—and by this time I was the chief pilot and flight school manager—whom I supervised, came to me and said, "Emily, I just want to let you know that Frontier is hiring again." I had updated my applications and there was a time when the airlines weren't hiring—in about

374

1968-69—but they had a lot of furloughs. John came to me and said, "I got a call from Frontier and they are hiring again. I just want to let you know I've got an interview next week." Well, I didn't get any call from them. That did it. He was just a year younger than I was, and he had less flying time than I did. I said, "Well, gee, that's great John. I hope you get the job!" Inside I was saying, "Ohhh!" I went home that night and got my applications out and got everything updated and went to Frontier the next day with my applications in hand. I had two. I wanted to give one to the chief pilot and one to the personnel office. I went to the personnel office and she said, "What position are you applying for?" I said, "A pilot!" She said, "A pilot? How much flying time do you have?" I said, "I have 7,000 hours of flying time." It was a long time from the first time I had talked to John Meyer. By now, I also had my Airline Transport Rating. She said, "Well, just a moment." She walked back to an inner office and came back out. She said, "Just a minute, I want to talk to somebody." She went back to this inner office and this gentleman came out. She introduced me and said, "This woman wants to be a pilot. Here's her application. She has a lot of flight time." The guy looked at me and said, "Well, we'll get back to you."

A few weeks went by—about two or three weeks—and I didn't hear anything. One day I was flying over to Stapleton with a student. We were on an instrument approach in Stapleton. The tower said, "Hey, Emily." Everyone knew my voice on the radio because there weren't too many women flying as often as I did, so they recognized my voice. The controller said, "We heard you got hired by Frontier Airlines." I said, "Gee, I think that's great, but they haven't told me yet!" That was encouraging and I knew the word was getting around.

So, you hadn't actually been hired?

No, no. Then, I started calling some people I knew. A fellow called me whom I'd known. He had done some flying over at Clinton and was a captain over at Frontier. He said, "Emily, I just want to let you know that they are hiring another class for Frontier and your name came up, but they dropped it like a hot potato. They don't know what to do with it. If I were you, I'd get over here and talk to Ed O'Neill." He was Vice President of Flight Operations. I said, "How do you suggest I do that?" He said, "What are you doing this afternoon?" Then he said, "Do you know where the coffee area is?" I said, "I sure do." He said, "Well, meet me there." I met him in the coffee area, which was right outside of the main office. There was an outer office to Mr. O'Neill's office, with secretaries in it. I knew a couple of the secretaries. I had talked to them, but I had never seen Mr. O'Neill.

He said, "I'm going to go in and see Mr. O'Neill. I'm going to go into the inner officer, and you give me about five minutes and then you just walk in." I said, "What do I do then?" He said, "Just watch for my cue!" I said, "Okay!" I gave him about five minutes and walked into this inner office and said hello to a couple of the gals. Jack was standing there. He was poking around in a file cabinet. He said, "Emily Howell (my name was Howell at the time), what are you doing here?" I knew that was my cue, and I said, "Well, I'm here to see Mr. O'Neill," or I said, "I'm here and I'd like to see Mr. O'Neill," or something like that. Jack said, "Ah, just a second." He walked right into O'Neill's office. He said, "Hey Ed, there's somebody here that wants to see you." I don't know what he looked like, but he must have said, "Well okay." Then Jack came out and said, "Come on." He ushered me in there and introduced me and said, "Ed, she wants to be a pilot at Frontier." Then Jack left the office. So, I sat down and here was Ed O'Neill, V. P. of Flight Operations, and here's this gal. I could tell he didn't know what to do.

Were you pretty nervous?

No, but I knew I had to start saying something. I told him who I was and that I had several applications at Frontier. I told him that Jack had given me this opportunity to meet him. We talked for about 30 minutes. I did most of the talking, and it seemed like the biggest sales job of my life. He said, "Well, thanks for coming in, and we'll get in touch with you." I thought, "Yeah, I've heard this before." But the next morning, I did get a call from Frontier, and they said, "Can you be over for a formal interview this afternoon?" I said, "I certainly can." That was my first interview. If I hadn't had a chance to meet O'Neill, I don't think I'd ever have had that opportunity.

Is there ever a time when you talked to him that you thought you had said the wrong thing or that you blew it?

No, but I could feel my voice getting real hoarse, and I knew I was doing an awful lot of talking. If I did anything wrong, I thought I was probably talking too much. He was Irish and I was Irish. Between the Irish, there's a way of communication. I had him—I could tell. I felt like I was kind of in control of the interview. He wasn't asking me all the questions. I was doing most of the talking.

You didn't resort to an accent did you?

No, no—I've tried to get one but I can't!

You actually got on the simulator then?

I went over for the interview, and Mr. O'Neill and an Andy Hoshuck kind of cross-interviewed me. They asked me what I'd do with my son. I told them that I had a good family and that was no problem. He'd be well taken care of when I was on a trip. Andy asked me what I'd do for a uniform. I said, "I don't think that's your biggest problem, but I'd wear a pant suit—similar to the men's." Then I said, "This is probably going to attract some attention, if you do desire to hire me. I'm sure you'll want to talk to your president, Mr. Feldman, at some point." Mr. O'Neill said, "We've already talked to him. In fact, if he's not busy, we'd like to take you up and have you meet him." Mr. O'Neill made a call on the phone, and we went up to Mr. Feldman's office, and I met Al Feldman. He was really an interesting man. He asked me how I'd handle publicity. I said, "Well, that's kind of up to Frontier." He said, "If you have the job, we'd let you handle it in your own way. We are sure you'd do a good job." Then he said, "Would you mind if I called my wife?" I said, "Well, not at all." So he called his wife. Her name was Rose Emily, I found out later. She had been an engineer with Convair. He talked to her and said, "I have a young woman in my office." I couldn't hear the other part of the conversation. He said, "She wants to be a pilot." Then they were talking back and forth a little bit. He hung up and said that his wife wished me well. I thought that was very interesting, and I think that helped that she had been an engineer with an aircraft company.

She must have put in a good word.

I think she told him that he better hire me or else—if she was pro-woman! She probably gave me some encouragement, I'm sure.

378

So you got Mr. O'Neill to go up with you in the simulator. I wondered whether you had to talk him into that.

No I didn't. We were still sitting at Feldman's desk and Ed said, "We think that Emily should see this simulator." I had been in a simulator—it's just that other people had invited me to watch. Now this is the first time that they wanted me to go fly it. Ed said they'd like me to get in the simulator and see how the pressures are and see what I thought of it. That related to me—"flight check." I said, "Certainly, I'd be happy to. I just want you to understand that I'm not familiar with your standard operating procedures that every airlines has and your emergency procedures and that type of thing." He said, "Oh yes, we know that, of course. We would just like to give you the opportunity to see what you think of the Convair." I said, "That would be fine." He said, "Are you busy right now?" I said, "Not at all."

This was a lucky break for me. He made some calls and the simulator was busy. It was going to be open at six that evening though. He said, "Can you come back this evening?" I said, "Yes, I certainly can." This was about two in the afternoon. I went home and called a couple of friends at Frontier. One was Jack Gardener. I called another person who had been an instructor at Clinton who was a good friend of mine and a pilot at Frontier. Over the phone they related information about Frontier's center operating procedures, what to expect, certain call-outs they like to do—such as when departing an altitude and approaching an altitude and different things.

One of them suggested I read the Navy manual on basic instrument flying—which I had—just to review good instrument practices. Then I went back and met Ed in the lobby at 6:00 p.m. It was 6:00 p.m. and was dark in Denver because it was in January. This gal came out, and she was the little gal that had taken my application. She said, "I remember you. You're Emily, aren't you?" I said, "Yes." She said, "We all heard you were getting in the simulator tonight!" I said, "Really?" She said, "Yes, and we're all rooting for you!" That gave me a real burst. I was really charged. So Ed came into the lobby and we went back to the simulator and got into it.

You wanted Ed to go with you?

Yes. There was an instructor there. We talked about flying and looking at charts and everything. They asked me if there was anything I wanted to know about the airplane. I said, "No, let's just go fly the simulator." I said, "Is Mr. O'Neill going to be in the left seat?" Someone is always in the left seat and someone is always in the right seat. The co-pilot is always in the right seat. I'm not being hired as the captain, so I said, "Is Mr. O'Neill going to fly in the left seat?" Jack Robbins was the instructor, and this was the first time I had met him. Jack said to Ed, "Hey, Ed, I think that's a great idea." Since Ed was the Vice President of Flight Operations, he probably hadn't flown an airplane or been in a simulator for three or four years. They're running the business and aren't out flying airplanes. Ed said, "Well, I guess so." He got in the left seat. That was also a lucky break for me because at that point I was probably more current at flying than he was. We started off and did some basics. Everything was going well and I had started feeling more and more comfortable in the airplane. We were going to do some single engine work, and the Convair 580 is a pretty heavy airplane—so on the first V-1 cut (V-1 is when you lose your engine when you're taking off), I didn't quite get it off the ground.

What were you thinking now?

I said, "Gee, I didn't quite get it off the ground, can I try that again? I think I can do it the next time." They said, "Sure, not a problem." So the next time, I got it off the ground. Once I got it off the ground and we were flying and came around, we made a single engine approach in the landing. Then they said, "Is there anything else you'd like to do? We can continue on if you'd like." I said, "Whatever you'd like to do." By this time, we had been in there several hours, but I didn't want them to think that I was going to chicken out. I was tired, though. I said, "If you want to continue on that's fine with me—whatever you want to do." Then Jack Robbins said, "Oh, I think that's enough, Ed. We'll call it a day."

Then we went to the simulator at a long table. It was one of those conference tables. Ed O'Neill sat on one end of it, and I kind of leaned on the other end of it, and Jack was kind of in the middle between us. Jack was going on about how tough airline flying was—long days, lots of bad weather, away from home a lot, and so on. Finally, I just ignored him and looked at Mr. O'Neill. I said, "Mr. O'Neill I know I can do it and I want the job." I just kind of ended the conversation with Jack, and Mr. O'Neill said, "You've got the job, but I want you to think about three things and call me tomorrow." I said, "What's that?" He said, "Is it going to be good for aviation? Is it going to be good for women in aviation? Is it going to be good for Frontier Airlines?" So that was easy. I could have answered him right then. But I said, "Yes, I'll call you first thing in the morning." So I called him first thing in the morning, and I said, "Mr. O'Neill, I still want the job." He said, "Well, you're hired." About an hour or so later, the PR Department at Frontier called me in a frenzy, saying they didn't even know it had happened until they got the word. They were trying to put together a press conference. They said, "Can you get over here this afternoon at 2:00 p.m.? We're trying to put together a press conference or media thing." I said, "Sure." So that afternoon I met them, and Mr. O'Neill was there. We got in the cockpit of the 737 and photographers took pictures. One photographer was down on the ground, and wanted me to open the window and I didn't even know how. Ed showed me on his window and said, "Just push the button and pull it." So I pushed the button and pulled open the window. That was my first flying lesson in a 737.

Any unusual questions asked at the press conference?

Not a lot—just a few. A lot of them were, "How do you think the public is going to react to this?" The media wasn't as tough as it is today. I wonder how it would be if I was the first today. It went along fine. My background was pretty impressive. I was hired with 7,000 hours. I remember one of the reporters said, "How many hours do male pilots have?" I said, "They can be hired from 1,500 hours and up." She said, "Wow—what took you so long?" I said, "They just weren't hiring women yet!" That's how it went. After that, the Navy hired a woman pilot. The Air Force then started promoting women to be pilots. The next woman hired was with American Airlines. I was hired in January, and they hired her in March. After that, Western Airlines hired eight women pilots. United couldn't hire any women pilots because they had 600 pilots furloughed. They couldn't get on the bandwagon until they got all those back. Then they hired their first women pilots in 1978.

What's the greatest compliment that you've received?

Everybody knows me by my first name. Also, sometimes I hear nice things like so and so told me about you. The thing that I'm proud of, though, is that I've helped a lot of other young women get into aviation through mentoring and through ISA scholarships and also recommendations to The Ninety-Nines scholarships. Also, United has a mentor program through Metropolitan State College in Denver. I've helped several young women there.

Tell me the most touching thing that a young woman said to you.

They keep in touch, and that always thrills me. One of my biggest thrills was when I learned how to fly, and I met a gal that was taking flying lessons with me. She was a Western Airlines stewardess, named Jackie Mattus at the time. We both got our private licenses. I was working at Clinton, so I continued flying and she continued being a stewardess. She got married and went that direction. I ended up living across the street from her for many years. In fact, I was living across the street from her in Denver when her daughter, Kelly Marcotte, was born. When Kelly went to high school she was very bright and intelligent. She went on to Metropolitan State College, and she decided she wanted to learn how to fly. They asked me if I'd give her a ride in an airplane, and I told them I'd give her a flying lesson. So I gave Kelly her first flying lesson in 1991, and she went through Metropolitan State College and got a 4.0 average all the way through. She continued all her flying and got her flight instructor ratings and ended up getting enough time to be hired by Great Lakes Commuter Airlines, who are a commuter for United Shuttle. She has been flying with them and just made captain about a year ago. She's a captain at age 25 in a commuter airline and she has 3,000 hours. I was really happy about that.

So the baton is passed?

Yes, the time has come for her to get on with a big airline.

Tell me about the FAA job.

I was called an aircrew program manager with the FAA. I'm assigned to the 737-300 fleet. There are about 170 airplanes in that fleet. My main job is to watch the flight operations end of it. I have a partner who's the maintenance end of it—he's the mechanic end of it, but I do the flight operations. I watch new airmen, new captains, new evaluators for the training program, do en-route checks for new line-check airmen—I help any of the changes they make in their training program and approve them. We work together on that. I work with my partner in San Francisco on any changes to the maintenance book.

How many hours have you logged as of now?

I've logged 21,000 hours as of this interview. I do a lot of the simulator work and I do a lot of flying of the simulator myself. I don't do too much airplane time anymore because you can't fly in a 121 airline operation unless you're hired by the airline.

You are a legend in your own time, yet you seem modest.

I really am kind of a humble person. I don't like too much showered on me. My husband says, "Sometimes you've got to blow your own horn." Most of my friends take care of me anymore.

384

Ellen Paneok
"Bush Piloting in Alaska"

Photo copyright by Roberta Degenhardt

Ellen Evak Paneok has flown as an Alaskan Bush pilot, often flying 1,000-1,400 hours per year and flew over 15,000 hours. Ellen started flying at 16 and got her private pilot's license at 21. Her first flying job came in 1984. For years, Ellen flew out of Point Barrow, specializing in off-airport landings, which included landing on sand bars, beaches or gravel and tundra, wherever she made her own runway. She has flown into gold mining camps, hauling dynamite—wherever the adventure has taken her. During her flight career, this mild-mannered pilot has served as a pilot certification violation investigator and aviation safety inspector with oversight of air taxi operators and commuters. She worked for the FAA as operations inspector and for Alaska Aviation Safety Foundation. She also volunteered for Alaska Aviation

Heritage Museum.

A multi-talented woman, she was recognized for her art, as well as her community work, which included encouraging young people interested in flight.

Ellen spoke in an easy, candid manner with a trace of an accent. Daughter of a full-blooded Eskimo mother and German-Irish father, she was a role model for other women and other members of the Eskimo culture. In her spare time, she investsed her energies visiting schools and villages, attempting to share her enthusiasm for flight with young people. In the interview, Ellen speaks about her troubled youth and how flying changed her. I asked her where she would be today if she hadn't flown: "Probably in jail or working in a grocery store—I don't know. That was a long row to hoe," she said with a measure of pride showing in her smile.

Tragically, she died in March 2008 at age 48 of Hepititas C.

As a woman flier, what was the strangest reaction you got from someone?

I was one of the first, front-running women out there flying in the bush. We were very rare then. The reactions were interesting. I'd get this old, old Eskimo couple getting on board, and they'd look at me and say, "Eskimo woman pilot." They'd look at me with little grins. Then they'd say, "Oh, cool," because it was such a novelty. I never had anyone who was rude to me or refused to fly with me. I remember one drunk being rude—but he was drunk.

What'd he say or do?

He must have chugged a bottle of vodka before he got on

the aircraft because he was intoxicated when I picked him up at the airport. He had alcohol on his breath. I could smell it. Still, he wasn't swearing or slurring his words. He was just kind of quiet. I'd say he must have chugged a bottle, because it apparently took awhile to take effect. Suddenly, he just went ballistic and started saying, "Women pilots shouldn't fly." He then unbuckled his seat belt and started making a lot of rude comments. He tried to go in the back. I told him to sit down and shut up, but he wouldn't. Finally, I took the wheel and shoved it down as fast as I could, then shoved it back as fast as I could, so he was slamming himself around in the cockpit. Things were flying all over the place. At that point, I turned around and looked at him and said, "Next time, I'm going to turn you around." From then on, he just sat with his hands on his lap, looking straight ahead. He never even turned sideways.

How did you get into flying?

I was interested pretty early—when I was fourteen years old. To tell you the truth, all I did was pick up a flying magazine, which listed flying careers. I said, "This is going to save my life." The reason I said that was because I was in a girls' group home. I'd been in about five different foster homes by the time I came to the group home. In all, I ended up in seven different foster homes. When I announced that I was going to fly, the authorities sent me to a counselor. The person who sent me said, "Ellen, you're screwed up in the head. You'll never amount to anything. You need a counselor. Where in the world are you going to get the money for eagle flying?" The experience was horrific.

The counselor actually said that.

387

Yes, I was still fourteen, and they sent me to this guy, and he just sat there and waited for me to say things, but I didn't. I'd gotten to the point where I thought, "I'm just not going to say a thing." So I just looked at him and didn't say a word. He didn't bother to ask me any questions. I decided that even if he did ask me something, I wasn't going to answer.

In Alaska, we have this Native Settlement Act, which began in 1971. It was designed to insure that Alaskan Natives didn't get screwed the way the American Indians did. The act allowed for land or dividends. I was sixteen at the time and was going to school in Anchorage. Anyway, because I'm half Eskimo, I received a dividend check for $1,500, and when I did, I took the money and plunked it down on the counter and said, "Teach me how to fly."

It was a jumpy start, in the sense that I was still in a kind of survival mode. But when I got going, it was fine. There was one problem. The kids at school would ridicule me because I had to take a bus to the airport. I didn't know how to drive a car. In fact, I flew airplanes for two years before I finally knew how to drive a car. The car I drove was actually a truck—a stick shift model, and the first thing I did when I got in was starting to use the pedals as rudder pedals.

That created some problems.

It was weird and hard to get over the fact that I was in a truck, not an airplane.

Once my aviation career took off, I ate, slept and dreamed flying.

Did you have any close calls in the beginning?

My third solo flight was a close call. You go out in the practice area and practice. I was practicing at about 2,500 feet when I put the airplane into a stall, and it went into a spin. I had no idea what a spin was, but the airplane just kind of whipped over. The nose dropped down. I was holding way back on the wheel and, miraculously, everything stopped spinning. After I landed, I headed back to the instructor. He saw me and said, "You look white as a ghost. What happened?" When I told him, he said, "Okay, we'll get in that airplane right now." The irony of it is that I wanted him to teach me to do spin training, but he wouldn't. Back then, the FAA didn't want spin training. They had taken it off the requirement for a private pilot's license. Needless to say, when I taught flying after that, I made my students do spin training.

What did you do for a living at this point?

I never had a real job when I started flying at sixteen. I began doing silkscreen for a kid's school. Then I started doing ivory necklaces and earrings. Ivory was what took me through the rest of my flight school and allowed me to get my commercial, instrument and CFI. I literally supported myself on ivory. At the time I lived on a 160-acre piece of land and just flew like mad. I got all the ratings in 1983—in one year. I just went ballistic about it. My first aviation job was in 1984. I was twenty-four years old. That took me to the bush in Alaska.

Visual flying was still pretty new to me, which is what you do in bush flying. I was testing my mettle with my own airplane. I got this job, and I was working with sandbars. I would go out in the bush. The weather was totally new to me, too. I had never experienced it this way. One day I was coming back empty of passengers and experienced a whiteout. I never did trust the

389

instruments, so I kept tying to look outside. I kept trying to see, and finally I looked down out of the window but I had too sharp an angle. Anyway, I turned the plane around and just dived through the trees, which was a pretty stupid thing to do. At the time I didn't have very many hours flying. I forget how many I had, but somehow I managed to get myself out of trouble. Once I had dived into the trees, I found some visual bearings. At the time I didn't trust instruments because I was afraid I was going to hit the mountains. Obviously, I was a young, greenhorn dummy. I had exceeded my limitations. That's what I learned from that—not to push myself too much.

You've been caught in weather a few times, I'd bet.

Yes, once I was flying a Cessna 207 and had just dropped off some passengers near Barrow. I was about halfway between Port Lee and Wainright, flying at about 7,500 feet. At that point, I got a call saying that the weather had gone down to an eighth of a mile. I asked the guy about some of the other places like Dead Horse, and they had gone to an eighth of a mile. Meanwhile, I kept talking the whole time to the Barrow Flight Service Station. Still at 7,500 feet, I was watching the ground turn from brownish green to white. I was now 45 miles from the nearest airport and there was nothing I could do.

The North Slope of Alaska is 88,000 square miles, but there was no clear area I could reach with the fuel I had. (I had a full tank when I left Barrow.) As I flew along, I felt helpless watching the whole North Slope as it got covered up with fog. I called up to Barrow to try to get a continuous run-down on the weather. I thought to myself, "Well, I can't land in Wainright because there's no navigational." Anyway, I thought I'd find that place in the fog, too, so I headed to Barrow and followed the VOR inbound. There was a heading there. It was a 190 radial of the Barrow VOR. The first 20 miles ran parallel to the beach. So I bee-lined for that. When I got there, I descended until I got about five miles off of Barrow. Now I got a call from the tower, and the guy said, "It's getting worse." When I first called him, it was about a half-mile visibility, but now he had called me up to say it was one-eighth visibility. I said to him, "I don't have a choice. I'm in an airplane that doesn't have much fuel." It was almost as if I was declaring emergency. I had to make it or else die. There was absolutely nothing I could do. I was screwed big time.

At the field they had pilot-controlled lighting with strobes. Using radio navigation, I began my approach. The conditions were just nasty. The operator called me up on his unrecorded radio and said the level was 600 feet. I just called back and said, "I have no choice. Here I come." Just then I saw a piece of building go underneath me. At that time the visibility was so bad.

So what are you thinking?

I was focused because I knew I didn't have a choice. You do what you have to do. I just aimed my plane between the trees and went for the gusto. I managed to get the plane on the ground and began to taxi back when the flight service station operator said, "Ellen, are you on the ground yet?" The runway was only four hundred yards from the building where he was. When I landed, I was just shaking. You are concentrating very hard and have all that adrenaline. Then when that adrenaline has no place to go, it makes you shake.

Did you sit there for awhile?

No, I just hopped out of the airplane and went home and

had a beer (laughs). I figured it was safety-beer time. Besides, I knew I wasn't going anyplace else. That fog ended up staying for three days.

What about forced landings?

I was flying an old rickety, green Tri-Pacer and was halfway between McGrath and Fairwell, on the west side of Alaska. The flight usually took about an hour, but after a half-hour, my engine started running so rough that the instrument panel was bouncing up and down. I yanked the throttle all the way back. As soon as I did that, the propeller, which was wind milling, just seized up. It felt as though the airplane wrenched around when it seized up.

The guy who was with me on the flight started singing, "You picked a fine time to leave me, Lucille. Four hungry cylinders and a prop in the field…" He was making these words up as he went. At the same time, I was punching him in the arm and telling him to shut up. Finally, I just went down lower and aimed between the trees. You could see where the trees were. I slammed into several trees and the wings came off, which is what you want to happen anyway, to slow the excess energy. Then this big bunch of trees mushroomed in my windshield. I pulled back on the wheel, but it didn't do anything. The nose gear caught this one tree and yanked the airplane around. The whole time this is happening, I was holding the wheel. Then I could see this mud come up and slap me in the face. It was splattering me and I was thinking, "Why in the world is mud slapping me in the face?" After all, the windshield isn't broken. We could hear everything creaking, tweaking and cracking. Finally, I got the airplane to a stop. You've never seen two people jump out of one door so fast. We found ourselves in knee-deep swamp water. That's when the mosquitoes came after us. It was pretty bad.

A big, black cloud of them?

Yes, black clouds of them. In the bush the pilots have this saying: "The visibility is one-quarter mile through the mosquitoes." In just a second or two, they were upon us. We ran for about 20 yards in this mucky swamp, which was about as far as we could go. My back was really hurting. Anyway, we stood there and just stared at the plane for awhile to see if it would blow up or burn up, but it didn't. Luckily, I had about a half bottle of DEET mosquito repellent. We used it up in four hours.

What happens if you don't have the repellent with you?

Mosquitoes can literally drive you nuts. That's no joke.

How do Eskimos handle the mosquitoes?

The Eskimos burn different things, and the smoke keeps the mosquitoes away. I took black spruce, which burns smoky, and took the oil out of the engine and used that to start a fire. And that kept the mosquitoes away.

We had gone in at 3:10 p.m. We had an emergency locator transmitter. I waited until my flight plan was out at six in the evening to turn on the transmitter. After that, search and rescue might come looking for us. I kept it on until 9:00 p.m. I figured no one would come out at night to rescue us. The next morning at 6:00 a.m., I turned on the transmitter again and left it on. This was before satellite systems.

When the rescue people found us, they buzzed the heck out of us, and then dropped a rescue radio down in a parachute. We talked to them and asked when we might be rescued. They answered, "It might be awhile." We wanted desperately to be rescued, but it would take eight hours to get a helicopter back up.

You had hurt your back badly?

I was hurt. I could move for three days, but then when I got into a relaxed environment, that's when I stiffened up. But I didn't know why, and I certainly didn't know my back was broken. It turned out I had cracked three vertebrae.

I am one of these people who do stupid things. Once I popped my shoulder out doing something stupid, and then flew this airplane for three hours. Then I got into another airplane and flew for another half-hour, and then I drove a Jeep with a big stick shift for an hour. Finally, I went to where I lived and realized I was in too much pain, and that I should have done something for it a long time ago. This time, though, I was able to rest my back.

This time you were really incapacitated, weren't you?

Yes, I couldn't walk and lie straight. I couldn't bend or twist either. I was totally out of it for flying.

How is the injury now?

I have arthritis big-time. I also have bone spurs growing here and there. My neck still hurts badly from being kicked around in that crash, but I just keep on truckin'.

Describe the rescue for me.

It was really weird. When they came to rescue me, they were at 10,000 feet. Then it was almost as if they did an emergency power-off dive, and then they buzzed right over the top of the trees, which were only about 40 or 50 feet high. After the aircraft went away for a second, the place got deadly quiet. Then a few seconds later, the turbulence on the tops of the trees made them go, "Whew-whew-whew." It was the eeriest sound and feeling that I have ever experienced. It was really weird. I knew what the sound was, but to me it was weird to hear that in dead quiet. You've got a dead Tri-Pacer sitting in the trees. And there you are sitting in swamp water.

Then the rescue people talked to me on the radio. They said, "We understand that you have three passengers." I said, "No, we only have two." They asked if anyone was injured or dead. And I said, "No." When I said I had a problem with my back, they misunderstood and thought that I had said one person was dead. After that, they called my mom and told her that I was in an airplane accident, and didn't know what condition I was in. Of course, you know what parents are like. Later, after they came and dropped us off at Fairbanks International, the airport police picked us up and took us to Alaska Airlines and we flew from Fairbanks to Anchorage. There they dropped us off. I got in a relaxed environment and called my mom up. My mother answered, and I had to hold the phone out like (gesturing away from her body), until she would get done yelling at me. At the time she was totally devastated, and I can understand that.

Are your parents proud of the fact that you're flying?

Oh, yeah, they are proud.

You must be a wonderful role model for Eskimo kids.

There was a kid I flew that affected me a lot. I had just

borrowed an airplane from a company to attend this Whale Festival in Wainright. I was sitting there visiting with my great uncle, spoon-feeding him Jello and eating Eskimo food, when this little girl, who was probably about two-and-a-half-feet tall, came up and stood there just staring at me. I knew I had seen her, but I couldn't begin to tell who she was. Then her mom came up, and I realized I knew her mom. At that point, the little girl points to me and said, "Pi-let." Her mom said, "Ellen, you remember Katie. You took her on an airplane ride about a year ago. She remembers you and wants to be a pilot." Just then the little girl pointed to me again and said, "Pi-let." The experience was really strange to me because until that point, I just wasn't kid-oriented. I just thought they all looked the same (laughs). I can't tell one from the other. That experience just affected me. Now their parents actually try to get their kids to fly. I like to visit schools and tell kids how they can learn to fly.

You were in aerobatics.

Yes, I used to be able to do slow rolls with 250-degree turns, and maintain altitude, but I can't do that now to save myself. That's a hard maneuver. I did all kinds of aerobatics like that, but once I was flying and doing the super-decathlon. I had just gotten down with one kind of maneuver. I don't remember which one, but it was at about five or six g's. As I came out of the maneuver, the stick whipped out of my hand, and the airplane just made a dive down. I grabbed at the stick to try to get the plane right side up. I was holding onto the stick with both hands. I was sitting there thinking, "I have a parachute, but how am I going to jump out of a diving airplane?" I slowly looked back at the elevator on the left side. The tail looked normal except that I was using all the pressure I could to try to keep the stick from going forward. I was thinking, Why in the world did this happen? On the way down, I chased three airplanes out of the pattern and had to make an emergency landing. I had gotten tired of holding the stick because I had to hold the stick with my other hand to keep it from going forward. Anyway, when I got on the ground, I got out and was looking at the tail. It turned out the seat-deck parachute straps had come loose and the rear stick had gotten tangled up in the straps. I don't know how it happened, because I know these things were tight when I went in. I don't know if it was because I was doing heavy maneuvers, or what.

So you don't do maneuvers any more?

Nope, and I don't want to. When I started out, I had about 200 hours of aerobatics, but I started having these nosebleeds and seeing little sparkles in front of my eyes. Then when I got done with a maneuver, I'd get these bad headaches. Then, when I did a maneuver one time, I grayed out. That's not where you pass out—it's where your vision turns gray. At the time I could hear everything I was doing with the airplane, but I couldn't see anything, until I reduced the g's. So I went to the doctor and told him that I did this and that everything had turned gray, and then I said, "Can I stick with aerobatics?" The doctor looked at me and turned white as a ghost, and he said, "Hell, no." I was only twenty-three years old when this happened, and I'd been practicing aerobatics for years, spending two or three hours per day, morning and evening. I was gearing up for air shows and competitions and was hot and heavy on it. Then I had to quit. That was one of the hardest things I've ever had to do: quit flying aerobatics. Even to this day, when I see someone doing aerobatics, it really hurts me. It's funny, though, because in recent years, the doctor has said that it's okay for me to do aerobatics. It was a problem of high blood pressure, and I've gotten that under control. I take medicine for it. Still, I'm reluctant to get back into it, because if I do and have to stop again, it would be even more devastating.

Then you focused on antique aircraft?

Yes, I had to concentrate my energies somewhere, and finding, owning, and maintaining antique aircraft is a logistical nightmare—at least for me in Alaska. Part of it is that not many antique aircraft reside in Alaska.

Tell me about the complexities of getting an antique airplane.

I'm a real horse trader at heart, so this skill worked for me here. First, I do scrimshaw, so one day some people came along and wanted me to do a little bit of it with their ivory. I did the artwork on their scrimshaw, after they had polished it. Some people had this lynx hide. I told them I wanted that hide. It was big—forty-six inches from nose to tail. I proceeded to trade them my ivory for this hide. Then I turned around and took the hide to a taxidermist. I had him make the hide into a rug—an open-mouthed lynx rug. I kept the rug for awhile. One day I was at a craft show selling ivory and this guy came along who loved that lynx hide. I traded the hide for nine hundred dollars worth of ivory carvings—really pristine ivory carving. I turned around and took those ivory carvings and traded them for a polar bear hide, straight across. (This was in 1981; the lynx hide I had gotten in 1977.) The polar bear hide was a legal one, which means the hide of an animal taken before 1971. In fact, the hide had papers to prove it.

So I was sitting there and wondering what I was going to

Photo copyright by Roberta Degenhardt

do with this polar bear hide. Then someone came along who had an airplane—an Aeronca Chief. When he professed to liking the polar bear hide, I offered to trade him straight across for this '46 75-horsepower Aeronca Chief. He agreed to the deal, so now I had an airplane. I had the airplane for some time and was going to rebuild it, but it got banged up a bit so I never did bother.

One day I decided I needed a truck, so I put an ad in the paper requesting to trade a plane for a truck. A guy called me from another airport and requested I fly the plane over to his airport. I did. We ended up trading and I walked away. That was in 1985.

I had a Volkswagen diesel pickup, a little gutless wonder. I drove that around for awhile, and then I moved to Anchorage. This guy had a 1928 Fairchild-24. He let me fly it around, and I flew it a lot. All of a sudden, though, his life changed when he ran into his old high school flame. He was about seventy years old at the time and was leaving the state to be with her. I convinced him he didn't need to take the airplane with him. I traded him the truck as down payment for this antique airplane (laughs). That was in 1986, so my trading spanned a nine-year period.

What does flying mean to you?

I'm an incurable romantic when it comes to flying. After more than 25 years, I still get a big grin on my face when the airplane under my hand takes off. To me, flying is like putting on a glove. It's not like a machine. It becomes a part of me when I fly. I can't come up with another metaphor.

I live on a lake and all kinds of airplanes take off every day. If I hear an engine take off, I still jump up and look at it—even if I've seen that stupid airplane five times already that day.

Genie Rae O'Kelley
"Instruction Flights"

Genie Rae came from a traveling family. Her father traveled a lot in his job for Standard Brands, Inc., and often took his family with him. Though Genie Rae was born in St. Paul, Minnesota, she left there with her family after only three months. Her father's job then caused the family to move to several states, ending in Birmingham, Alabama, where she entered second grade. She remained in Birmingham and graduated from Howard College, now Samford University, in 1948. Later, she pursued graduate studies in Educational Psychology at the University of California, Berkeley, where her husband was studying for his Ph.D. degree in chemistry. Through the influence of her mother-in-law, who maintained that Genie was a born teacher, Genie pursued education—a career that would ultimately lead to teaching people to fly.

In the mid-60s, Genie's husband, Dave, decided he wanted to learn to fly. On July 4, 1965, Genie Rae took her first flying lesson. Although she confesses to some early trepidation during those first few hours in the air, she developed an intense love of flying. Along with teaching school, Genie began flying on weekends. While still a student pilot, her flight instructor, David Hiltz, offered her a job if she would continue her training and obtain the Certified Flight Instructor (CFI) Certificate. She has flown more than 20,000 hours and has received numerous awards, including National Flight Instructor of the Year for 1986, only the third woman to receive such an award. For her dedication in advancing the cause of aviation safety and education, she was honored in 1984 by the Tennessee Department of Transportation with its Certificate of Merit and by the Governor of Tennessee with its Certificate of Commendation. Genie Rae has been based at McGhee Tyson Airport, Knoxville, Tennessee. In 1982, she founded Volunteer Aviation of Knoxville, Inc., as president and majority stockholder. In addition to flight instruction, Genie Rae has served as a teacher of aviation ground schools for credit and noncredit, in basic and advanced training. Since the 1970s, she became responsible for the aviation ground schools at the University of Tennessee, Knoxville. She also has been active with the Girl Scouts and with their Wings program.

In 1976 she flew in her first air race, the All-Woman Transcontinental Air Race, popularly known as the Powder Puff Derby. By 1999, she had participated every year except three in the derby and in its successor, the Air Race Classic. Genie Rae placed among the top ten contestants three times and has received numerous "leg" prizes at other times. Genie Rae is author of numerous articles on the subject of aviation and is a co-author, with William Kershner and Daniel Juchta, of the Student Pilot's *Groundschool Manual,* published by Iowa State University.

At the time of the interview, this couragous woman, burdened with eyesight problems, still continues to fly.

How did you get started flying?

My husband Dave wanted to learn to fly. In the 1960s he became involved in developing methods for analyzing the first samples to be returned from the moon. The National Aeronautics and Space Administration (NASA) was designing the Lunar Receiving Laboratory at the space center in Houston, Texas, to examine the lunar samples, and it was going to be necessary for Dave to make any trips to Houston over a period of years. Learning to fly would make scheduling the trips easier. Earlier, my dad had passed out from a virus while driving a car, and I was determined that, if Dave learned to fly and took us all with him, then I needed to learn at least to land the airplane. So, on the day of his first flying lesson, I took my first lesson immediately after. I was scared to death, but soon learned to overcome this fear and have been flying ever since.

You studied with Evelyn Johnson?

She wasn't my primary instructor at the time, but was the FAA Designated Flight Examiner for my private pilot flight test. Then, of course, through the years, we have become very good friends. She was also one of my instructors for the multi-engine rating as well. Through the years, Evelyn has been the mentor and role model I strive to emulate.

Any Evelyn Johnson stories?

In the 1960s, my first student cross-country solo flight was from the Powell (Tennessee) Airport, north of Knoxville, to the Morristown Airport. When I was on final approach at Morristown, I noticed a small figure on the ground, just to the right of the active runway. It was Evelyn Johnson, watching a student flying the traffic pattern on his very first solo flight. What Evelyn did for this student, she has done for many others who have flown with her. She has earned the nickname "Mama Bird," because she watches over her fledglings.

Evelyn Johnson administered my flight test for my private pilot certificate, on a cold, January day with snow everywhere on the ground around the Morristown, Tennessee, Airport. Evelyn and

I took off toward the southwest on my simulated cross-country flight. I was planning to circle over the airport, while climbing toward a course for Roanoke, Virginia, my destination. Over the airport, I said, "Evelyn, we're off our course." She sat up, surprised, and asked, "How do you know?" I showed her the chart and said, "We should be going northeast and, instead, I am going almost north. I should be following that road, but I am going to cross it at a 60- degree angle." She was satisfied that I could read the chart and fly the airplane, so she said, "Take me to Newport, Tennessee." As I turned toward the southeast, on a course for Newport, I saw nothing but snow. I set up a radial off the Knoxville VOR and explained to her that I was aware that radio navigation was not very accurate in those days, but when the needle centered I knew that Newport would be nearby. She was satisfied that I knew radio navigation, and we had not left the traffic pattern. We then proceeded to carry out the maneuvers required for the rest of the flight test. We both agreed that I had had one of the shortest "cross-country" flights for a check ride.

Through the years, as we became friends we have taken many trips together to aviation-related meetings, and together we have spoken to groups of teachers enrolled in summer aerospace workshops at the University of Tennessee. It is always great to share the stage with Evelyn, as she is very gracious and helpful. I am now legally blind, which caused me to give up flying as pilot-in-command about five years ago. Evelyn often comments that she is my eyes—and I am her ears. I have not had to do much on the hearing, but she has been wonderful to help me with reading such things as menus in restaurants and display cards in museums.

So, you're still involved with aviation?

I am still active with aviation ground schools at the University of Tennessee and Volunteer Aviation, a company I founded in 1982. In spite of my vision problems, I can still legally teach advanced flying students and give flight reviews, under VFR conditions.

Have you had any unusual responses to your blindness?

Most people are unaware that I am legally blind. It's just that I keep using what sight I have left. I have been a ground school and flight instructor since the 1960s. Sometimes, in speaking to aviation groups, I tell them that I'm flying "partial panel." You know what that is—when one or more instruments are inoperative, you must rely on those that remain. I just tell people that I can see the big picture and don't worry about little things. Actually, almost everyone has been helpful and encouraging.

How blind are you?

I am considered to be "legally blind," which means that, on an eye chart, I can only see between 20/200 and 20/400, both eyes. The cause is called "macular degeneration." For those who do not know what this term means, I would describe it as an aneurysm of blood vessels in the retina of the eye. It was not painful for me; my vision just deteriorated.

Through the years, I have found various ways to adjust and compensate for the condition. Although I am legally blind, I have shown that I can land an airplane and still navigate, using my peripheral vision, adjusting for my blind spots. It doesn't slow me down, as the FAA just renewed my CFI certificate. I have been active in the FAA "Wings" safety programs, particularly as an instructor of "Pinch-Hitter" courses.

My one regret is not being able to teach primary students. I loved to teach beginning students and watch them develop their first pilot skills.

You're involved in safety counseling.

I have been a safety counselor since the 1970s and am still active today. Although I have given talks and organized safety seminars, I also believe that one should stay alert for any dangerous situations and do what you can to prevent accidents.

One such case developed as a student, and we were taxiing out for takeoff behind a Cessna 172. I noticed that the baggage door of the other airplane was open and flapping. I asked ground control to alert the other aircraft to the danger of losing articles from the baggage area in flight. The pilot stopped, then proceeded to stomp to the rear of the aircraft, slammed the baggage door shut, glared at me as if it were my fault, then got back in his seat, and finally slammed the door with a large part of his seatbelt and shoulder harness hanging outside. When he called the tower for takeoff clearance, my student turned to me and asked, "What are you going to do now?" I said. "I'm going to call again, because in his state of mind, he's an accident waiting to happen. Besides, he must have his seatbelt and shoulder harness fastened for takeoff."

Did you have to muster a lot of courage to make that call?

No. As an Accident Prevention Counselor since the early 1970s, one of my responsibilities is to correct unsafe problem areas. I have had to correct many unsafe practices through the years.

Have you ever had any forced landings?

No, not really. One time, a friend asked me to go with him while he checked the radios in his plane after maintenance. I said, "Sure, I can do that." This was, by the way, after I was legally blind. We planned to go to the practice area. However, when we took off, my friend commented that the controls just didn't feel right. I was checking everything on the panel, and everything appeared normal. I had already found several radio malfunctions, so I said, "When things aren't right, land as soon as possible!" We remained in the traffic pattern, and, at first, the controls appeared to respond. As we were in the last stages of landing, he remarked that the control yoke would not come back very far. After observing that the plane was almost in level flight, I advised him to add a little power to raise the angle of the nose, but not enough to takeoff again. We got the nose up, about ten degrees according to our maintenance mechanic. Our tricycle gear wheels all touched the ground at once, and it appeared we had landed uneventfully. But then, the nose wheel hit a pebble and began to wobble, causing the nose gear to collapse. We were left sitting in the middle of the runway, tail in the air, and a Delta airliner going around.

One of the instructors from my flight school met us when we returned to the office and repeated the old pilot saying about retractable gear landings, that there were "those who have and those who will." I commented that I had done it the hard way, in a fixed-gear airplane!

We later found that the loss of a screw from the transponder mounting resulted in the transponder partially blocking the yoke guard.

You have a teaching background.

Yes, Evelyn Johnson and I are both teachers. I taught school in Alabama, California, and Tennessee, mostly at the junior high school level. I also originated aviation ground-school courses at several community colleges in East Tennessee, as well at the University of Tennessee, Knoxville.

I just like to teach. When I first became blind, I must admit that I was discouraged. Then, one of my students said to me, "Genie, you've got the knowledge upstairs; you don't need your eyes." I found I could teach and still enjoy teaching because I love flying and enjoy sharing.

What makes a good instructor?

A good instructor is interested in the student, and cares. To me, when you teach school, you're never sure whether you are getting through to the children or not, or whether the material was something they learned elsewhere. But when you teach flying, the results are immediate. You can see the response, and I am usually as excited as the student when something new has been learned.

Any time you could not control your enthusiasm?

No. However, if the student has problems, I just try different techniques. I usually use background experiences to aid in learning new skills.

Name a student of whom you are especially proud?

I have had many. Dana Wooten Moser is one. I have raced with her across this country many times. On our first race together, she had never been west of the Mississippi River. Now she is an enthusiastic and accomplished traveler and still a great friend.

408

Evelyn Johnson was responsible for getting me into cross-country air racing in the first place. She told me it would be a great way to learn about flying different types of terrain. She was right. It really is a great learning experience that I have shared with Dana and other students.

Tell me about how much you were set back by deteriorating vision. How did you get through it?

When it first happened, it hit me pretty hard; but not long after maybe fifteen minutes I thought, "Well, I'm otherwise healthy." The doctor had said that, within five years, I would be blind; actually, it was only about three years. I felt I should resign my many aviation activities. At the time, I was the president and chief flight instructor of my own flight training school and had been elected to serve on two international women's aviation boards. I was an active FAA safety counselor, and was teaching aviation ground schools at my own flight school, the University of Tennessee, Knoxville, and at several local colleges. As many of my friends and associates reminded me, I found that that I did, indeed, have the knowledge and experience in aviation to allow me to continue most of these activities.

The retina specialist, who told me I would be blind, remarked that he had many patients with eyesight not nearly as bad as mine, but who appeared not to see as well as I did. I said, "Well, I think I try." He replied, "Yes, and that's why I say it's attitude." He said to remember attitude, and that's what I tell my students.

You do seem like an optimistic person.

Yes, I am. My husband calls me the oldest Polyanna he knows.

Where the Wings Grow

Where do you get that?

From my dad, I guess, more than anyone. He was that way. When I was just a year old, he had a problem with his heart and was given a year to live, but he just would not let it get him down. He lived a full and active life and did not die for many years, until I was in my 60s. He was always interested in new ideas and in planning ahead —that's how he faced life and I do, too.

So those were lessons for you?

Absolutely.

Did your dad like the idea that you were flying?

Well, yes. They were both very enthusiastic about my flying activities, but they would never fly with me.

Do you know why?

Yes, I think so. It took me a long time to realize this, but my dad had taught me to ride horseback, taught me many games, including golf—and he taught me to drive a car. But he had not taught me to fly, and there he was a bit concerned because he had not taught me that.

Any unusual student story?

One time I was flying with a teenage boy. He panicked and froze at the controls. I used to teach lifesaving, so I knew that you could hit a little spot on the hand and it will let go. At the time he had one hand on the throttle and the airplane was pointed down, so I had to make him let go. I lightly touched the spot on his hand, and he let go. Of course, I took over then. When we got back to the office, he said in a voice everyone could hear, "She hit me!" This was greeted by laughter from the old-time instructors.

In the early 70s, a nice young man came in and told the secretary that he wanted a one-hour dual cross-country lesson. He was told the only instructor available was Genie Rae. He looked over at me and asked, "Do you have anybody else?" The secretary said, "No, she's the only one free at the moment." He replied, "All right. I'll take her on approval." We went out to fly. I felt he wasn't going to pay much attention, but I would do my best. As we came in to land, as luck would have it, the wind gusted suddenly, and we were pushed sideways toward the edge of the runway. When he did nothing to correct the situation, I took control of the airplane. This was one of the very rare occasions when I have ever found it necessary to take over the airplane. As he taxied in, I said, "I know you want to go cross country, but you need to get an instructor to teach you more about crosswind landings." He asked, "Are you free?"

You met his approval?

Yes, and he went on and got his training with me for the private and commercial certificates, as well as his instrument rating.

That gets us to the issue of the female flying. Do you have any stories of poor treatment?

Well, no. That was the only one. Everyone else has been so very helpful to me. Men, including my husband, have pushed me when I would have been more reticent to take on some of the opportunities that came my way. In the early 70s, we flight instructors realized that the Air Force ROTC students at the University of Tennessee, Knoxville, did not understand a lot of the required ground-school work. Colonel Daniel Kuchta, who was in charge of the program, asked if I would come and help him teach the first ground school at the University of Tennessee. Not only that, we went on to set up aviation courses at several community colleges in East Tennessee.

Another person who has been very helpful through the years has been William K. Kershner, noted aviation author, respected mentor and friend, with whom I was privileged to co-author a book. When I was flying in transcontinental air races, Bill helped me test airplanes that I planned to use. One situation illustrates what a safety-minded person he is. I had gone to Sewanee, Tennessee, for some flight instruction and was preparing to fly home. It was getting dark, and my preflight inspection showed that one of the navigation lights had burned out. Bill insisted on having a bulb removed from his plane and installed in mine, so I would have operating navigation lights and be legal to fly at night. I thought that was great!

How many years do you want to fly?

Now I no longer can be pilot-in-command (PIC), but I can fly as an instructor with any advanced student who can serve as PIC and who wants to earn an advanced rating or certificate. One young man came to me recently and asked if I would fly with him because he wanted to do some mountain flying. I said, "Sure, I can do that." Moreover, I enjoy it!

Did you ever meet a student who reminds you of yourself?

No, not really, although when I have taught fear of flying

classes at the University of Tennessee, several of my students have had fears similar to mine when I started flying. I still hear from some of them, who are now flying all over the world. This is very rewarding.

Was there anything pivotal that allowed you to get over your fear?

My primary flight instructor was very patient with me. Since turbulence bothered me, he asked me how many bumps in the road I had encountered on my way to the airport. He suggested that I count them on my way home. I was amazed at how many bumps there were. He remarked that, as I flew more often, I would not notice the bumps as much. Therefore, he scheduled me to fly more frequently, but for shorter periods. It did help.

How scared is scared?

When I took my first few flying lessons, I was in a state of shock. I really was. Nothing registered for a long time.

It seems you would have been ready to quit — if you were that frightened.

Oh, I was, several times. My husband kept urging me on a little bit.

How competitive were you, when racing?

I always thought I should do my best and improve my skills. While I was on the board of directors of the Air Race Classic, I was instrumental in beginning a program called "Motherbird," to help the inexperienced racers. In the program, the more experienced racers would take the newer ones under their wings and share racing tips. The Motherbirds also would advise their fledglings in flight by radio of unusual weather or other hazards.

How does it feel when someone comes up to you and refers to you as a pioneer? It must happen a lot.

Yes, it does.

What do you say?

Not much. I just say that I am glad to still be here and be teaching flying.

It sounds like you place many demands on yourself.

When I get interested in a subject, I try to do my best. My mother-in-law, who was active in the field of education, called me a "born teacher." I realize that she was right. I love teaching, and especially, teaching a subject that is as interesting, exciting, and continually changing as aviation. I'll always be excited about flying, and I still enjoy learning new things about the field of aviation.

Is it sad to go up in the air and not be able to see the beauty of nature?

I can see the parts that are important. I just can't see the details. I see the mountains and the green valleys. That's the beauty of it.

One of my former students, a man about 72 years of age, I

guess, wanted to fly with his wife to meet Evelyn Johnson. He asked me if I would go with them. I offered to sit in back, but he said, "No. You sit up front, because I know if anything goes wrong, you can land this airplane." On the trip back, he asked how I wanted him to return. I said, "Do you see that ridge across the valley, about 30 miles away?" He was amazed that I could see that. Throughout my vision loss, I have been blessed with good peripheral vision, which helps me see more than people expect.

You seem an inspiration to people without sight, as well as young fliers—all sorts of people.

I just know that you need to do the best you can and use what you have. What really counts is attitude.

Attitude is everything, isn't it?

It is. It truly is.

Martha King
"The Flight Business"

Martha King was born in Big Spring, Texas, in 1945. Her father was in the Air Force, so they moved a lot. She attended Indiana University in Bloomington, which is where she met John. They married while they were still in school. After taking summer school classes to finish her degree in three years, Martha could graduate with John. Previously they had started a business in Bloomington. It was a fueling service and an onsite lubrication service for truck fleets. After running the business for five years, the Kings sold it and moved to San Diego. Then they started franchising the same business but went bankrupt in 1974 during the energy crisis. After that, they began a business teaching flight, and their story is as meteoric as any aerospace effort. They have taught about 15,000 students, face-to-face in live classes, but in Martha's words, "maybe 250-300,000." A remarkable couple and their remarkable flying careers are revealed.

Tell me about your solo flight.

The solo flight is not my most vivid memory. The most vivid memory I have is my first solo cross-country flight. Up until that time, I was basically going along with the whole flying bit because John was very passionate about becoming a pilot, and I didn't want to sit at home while he was out hanging around the airport. I was learning to fly but was doing it as a duty and with determination—not with any joy.

Then I went on my first solo cross-country. It was all the way from Indianapolis to Richmond, which is probably not more than 100 miles. I left a little bit later in the afternoon than I should have. This was November, and there were some rain showers around and I ended up detouring around them. Then when I got to Richmond, I took a while on the ground having a Coke. Then after that, I went back, and again there were rain showers, so I did a big detour around that. The net effect was that I showed up back in Indianapolis after dark.

I had not had any night instruction or anything. This was back in the days before you even had to have any to get the private pilot license. It was a beautiful, calm evening. The lights just came on gradually underneath me. This was our own airplane—a Cherokee 140, and I was pretty familiar with it—as much as a student pilot can be. I knew where all the switches were and what lights to turn on, and so on. I came back in, and I made probably one of the prettiest landings that I'd ever made. It was particularly amazing since this was the first time I was ever up at night. That's when I got hooked on flying.

Were you hooked mostly because of the glorious beauty of the experience or because you could do it?

I was hooked because of the beauty of the experience. I knew all along that I could do it; it's just that I didn't get any enjoyment out of it, up until then.

I'm trying to understand that concept a little more. Were you doing it more as a family obligation?

Yes, John and I were in business together—we did everything together. Later on we learned to ski together, scuba dive together, and we just would do things together in our life. I could see that this was something that he very passionately wanted to do, and it wouldn't be really fair to him for me not to get involved. I also was concerned that it might end up with him out at the airport and me not. So I was going at it with a kind of determination up until that point. Then, on this particular flight, it was so beautiful and awe inspiring that it totally changed my attitude.

How did John respond when he found you'd changed your whole focus and feeling?

Oh, he was very excited, of course. It started out that he was very worried because he was out there at the airport waiting for me, and here it was dark and I hadn't come back yet. He was very concerned that what he'd get back was an hysterical basket case on his hands who'd never want to go up in an airplane again. He heard me call on Unicom. I did my downwind base and final and lined up on the runway and came in. He could hear the wheels squeak when I did that beautiful touch down. I taxied up, got out on the wing of the airplane and said to him, "That was beautiful."

Did he just about drop in his tracks?

Yes he did. He was very surprised because that is not the reaction he expected from me at all. We had sold the business in Indiana, and we got our pilot licenses. We were going to get into another business, but between the two, we both got our pilot licenses—interestingly enough— two days apart, at two separate airports, with two different examiners because that's how we could schedule it. Somebody in the FAA must have put them together because we have sequential pilot license numbers. That was a kick. About a week after we got our private pilot certificates, we took off in this Cherokee 140, and we flew down to Florida. This was basically Christmas and New Year's holiday time.

That was 1969.We spent probably four, five or six days in Florida, and then we headed back to Indianapolis. We were going to go back and settle in and start this other business, and the further north we got, the more snow there was on the ground. We finally both just kind of looked at each other and said, let's go west instead, and we made a left turn and went west along the Gulf Coast and ended up out in California. We had been talking for years about moving to California. We had gotten married out here because my father was in the Air Force and stationed out here.

We flew the airplane out to California and flew it up and down the coast looking for a pretty place to live and ended up in San Diego. We rented an apartment, went back to Indianapolis, packed all our stuff up, and shipped it out. We had somebody drive the car out, and we flew the airplane out and settled in here lock, stock, and barrel.

Did anything eventful happen while flying out?

Here we were, brand new private pilots, and so we had some

adventures. We did not have an instrument rating. We got caught by bad weather in the panhandle of Florida and ended up circling an airport having trouble getting lined up on the runway to land because the clouds were so low. In Houston, Texas, at Hobby Airport, I got confused by all of the runway numbers. I ended up landing on runway 2 when I was supposed to be landing on runway 2-0. Then we had our first introduction to night flying going west into the Tucson area, which scared us because there are mountains around there. We hadn't really been taught how to avoid mountains at night, and we were adventurous. We probably pushed our limits more than we should have. We don't do that any more but we were very eager for the aviation experience.

Were there any close calls in the early days?

We had an accident and a forced landing in 1974 in a Cessna 210. That's the only one.

Basically what happened is, at that time, we had changed businesses again and we were in the weekend ground school business where we traveled out to different cities from San Diego to teach a weekend ground school class. Then we'd give the FAA written exam on the following Monday. We were going to places like Billings, Montana, and Fargo, North Dakota; and on this particular trip, we were going to Sioux Falls, South Dakota. We had stopped for fuel in La Junta, Colorado, and after we took off and were headed for Sioux Falls, we had an electrical failure. We ended up having to let down in the Sioux Falls area through the clouds, with no navigation and no communication. They had weather there that was not forecast. They had freezing rain and an ice storm going on. When we got under the clouds, the weather was too bad to find an airport, and we put it down in a cornfield.

That was a pretty harried experience, I bet.

Yes, it was!

Describe the landing precisely. Did you take out a half- acre of corn?

I think that we probably took about 100 feet. When we went down through the clouds we picked up a load of ice and we got under the clouds and it was starting to get dark. John looked at a road—he was flying—and said, "Let's land on the road." I thought I saw power lines across the road, so I said, "No, there are power lines across it." So, John said, "Okay, were going to land in this corn field," and he just pulled the power back and landed. Because of the freezing rain, they had 18 inches of snow with a crust of ice on top. So we landed and rolled for about 100 feet on the crust of ice and then the airplane broke through and came to a very abrupt stop. We went up on the nose and rocked over on the left wing and back onto the gear. It broke the wing spar on the left wing.

Any farmer story out of this—what did the farmer have to say?

Well, we didn't see the farmer that night. Actually we didn't see the farmer for about six months. The insurance company took care of getting the airplane out and all that kind of stuff. We found out later that he was driving by the next morning and saw the airplane in the field and got very upset. We had some tools go through the windshield that broke the windshield out. We wanted to make sure that the snow didn't pile up in the airplane and get it wet, so we put a cushion up in the windshield to block the snow and freezing rain. It was a red cushion, and when he saw it from a distance, he thought it was blood that he was seeing and that someone was still in the plane and very badly hurt. He got upset about that, but eventually he learned to fly and came to one of our ground school classes in that area.

Did he say it was a direct cause and effect because of you folks landing there?

Yes.

Tell me about a memorable student.

We had one student in the class who had both hands blown off in Vietnam by a hand grenade. He had hooks where his hands had been. We were very concerned about whether he was going to be able to keep up on the class or not. He was about the fastest one going through, and he was doing just an absolutely beautiful job. We had another student—when the FAA showed up on Monday to give the test, they said, "Is so and so in your class?" We said, "Yes," and they said, "Well, that's great," because they had told him that he needed to get his license right away. What happened is that he had gone out for a lesson and the instructor was not there. I don't know why, but the airplane was. The student had gone up in the airplane with a friend of his. As they took off, the wheel came off the airplane. This kid, who had soloed but not more than one or two lessons beyond that, ended up having to land the airplane missing one wheel. Apparently he did a beautiful job and landed with no further damage to the aircraft. The FAA inspector was very impressed. The kid had gone up without his instructor's approval and with a passenger, which are both illegal, so the inspector, rather than penalizing him, told him to get his license by a certain date and we'll forget that this ever happened.

Commonly, we had people in our class who would be flying around in these areas of the country: Alaska, North or South Dakota, Montana and places like that. They'd own their own ranch, they'd fly their own airplane, they would fly their own airplane around on their own ranch. These people didn't really see what the FAA had to do with anything. Then, one day, they'd fly their airplane into town and they wouldn't know the right communications procedures, so they'd get in trouble. The FAA very typically—rather than trying to come down hard on these people—would simply say, "If you get your license by such and such a date, we'll forget this happened." The problem these people would have on getting their license was never the physical control of the airplane, but passing the written test. A lot of them had dropped out of school at various grades, before high school or during high school, to work on a farm or ranch, and weren't that comfortable taking written exams. So we'd come in and have a class for two days and give the test on the third day, and we were a real solution for these people.

There must be a lot of satisfaction in that.

There was, very much so. What we had the opportunity to do was to be a part of people's lives when they were doing something that was about the most important thing in the world to them and certainly the most important thing at the time when they were taking the flight lessons. That's a very special opportunity.

When you were starting to do that, what was the biggest obstacle that you had to get over? Did you have misgivings about whether this was a practical approach or whether this kind of business would work?

We had worked for another company for about four months that was doing something very similar. They went broke in it and we got laid off. We had been looking at their business and thinking that we didn't think they were making money in this but thinking that we could. We looked at what we thought they were doing wrong, which was not paying enough attention to what part of the country and what cities they had big classes in. They were trying to go to too many cities without paying enough attention to whether they had big enough classes there. They were trying to get big instead of trying to get profitable. When we got laid off, we took a look at that and said, "Well, we've really enjoyed doing this; we've had a wonderful time here; what we can do is do this ourselves and focus on making sure we go to places where the class sizes are good and drop very quickly those places where they're not." Our specialty, where we ended up focused, was medium-sized to small towns in relatively rural areas where there was a lot of distance to cover, a lot of airports, but not enough population to have really good services.

Is there a funny story about rejection, or some confusion when you first started doing this?

We had an office manager working for us. We had one or two occasions where she would get mixed up and would schedule one hotel for the class and then put a different hotel in the brochure that we mailed out to people. We had a couple of times where one of us would be at the correct hotel registering students and the other one would have to be at the other hotel getting the walk-in students and sending them to the correct hotel. We are teaching in places like Fargo, North Dakota, and Billings, Montana, and we had a couple times where we were teaching classes immediately after a holiday. We'd show up at the hotel, and all the restaurants would be closed, and there would be no place to eat. We went to Billings, Montana, in February—I'm not sure what year this was—and we were taxiing into the ramp. I was looking at all the snow around on the sides and there was snow blowing around in the air, and I said to John, "We forgot one big item for this class." He said, "I thought we packed everything. What did we forget?" I said, "Our coats!" It was about 10 to 20 degrees there, and when we left San Diego, it was warm and sunny—maybe 65 degrees—and we just totally forgot about the idea of needing to take coats.

So, did you run down to the store?

No. We were in a hotel, and we kind of scurried between the hotel shuttle van and the hotel. We were kind of cold when we got back to the airplane to pack and go, but we could stay inside the hotel other than that. We managed, but we did get cold when we were trying to leave.

Was there ever a time when you gave up or when you had to dig? Or was the business an immediate success?

This was pretty much an immediate success. We had watched the company we worked for previously and had seen where they had big class sizes. We thought we'd picked a pattern out of rural areas, with lots of small airports, but not much in the way of services. We did well from the beginning, and we loved the business. We couldn't imagine anything any better than flying around the country and talking to pilots about aviation. They were wonderful people. We had a great time getting to know them; we had a great time flying our airplane around, and it was just fantastic.

Tell me about another interesting character that you've taught— maybe someone who had an attitude about you as a woman.

We only had one incident of that. It was a class, I think, in Spokane, Washington. We were doing the registration. The way that we divided up the classes was that John would teach the private class, and I would teach the instrument class. John had a guy come to him towards the end of registration and say, "I understand that this woman is going to be teaching the instrument class." John said, "Yes, she is." The guy said, "Well, I had a woman instructor once, and she wasn't any good." John said, "Well, I very much doubt if the two were related, at all! Here's what we can do. If you're at all concerned about this, go ahead and take the class. On the other hand, if you're unhappy at lunch time and feel that you're not learning what you want to be learning, we will give you a complete refund, you can get your course fee back, and go ahead and leave at that time." The guy went to him on the first break and started apologizing for questioning whether I was going to be able to teach him well. He went to him at lunch and said he was so sorry that he'd ever questioned it, so I managed to make a convert in about the first hour and a half.

That's pretty impressive. What did your dad, the Air Force guy, think about you flying?

He died before I started flying. He died in 1966.

Has it ever been your regret that he didn't get to see you fly?

Somewhat. I don't know how much that would have meant

to him. He didn't do any civilian flying. All his flying was in the military. I don't know whether it would have meant a lot to him to have a daughter that flew. I don't know that aspect of him well enough.

Do you ever imagine or dream of taking him up, just for curiosity's sake?

You know that's interesting—no I really haven't. I guess because he wasn't involved in it on a civilian basis and didn't talk about his flying. He was commander of a couple of different bases during World War II, where they were doing a lot of training. During the war, at the training bases, they had a lot of accidents because they were pushing a lot of people through pretty fast. In some ways, I think that might have turned him off, at least as far as introducing anyone else to aviation.

That makes sense. Where were the bases, do you know?

The bases were in Big Spring, Texas, and Liberal, Kansas. There were others, but I'm not sure where they were. I remember those two because that's where my sister and I were born.

What about your mother—what were her feelings about it?

Mother died in 1979. We had been in the business since 1974. Interestingly enough, her attitude was "Why don't you quit this silly traveling around the country, settle down, and get a real job."

Was her attitude more that females didn't do that particular thing, at least, at that time?

It was more of an attitude of—you don't have a real job unless you work for a big company—the government or some big bureaucratic company. Then, you've got a real job. You have all these perks, and you can see your career path, and so on.

So other than John, you really didn't have a lot of support from your family.

That's correct.

Was that hard?

No, not really, because of the strength of the support I got from John.

Do you remember a time t hat you and John talked seriously about it, in the sense that you needed a pillar of sorts—at any specific time?

Not a specific time. We didn't particularly get along well with my parents because of their attitude about jobs and the feeling that we ought to be doing something more conventional for a living.

So you just did your thing, didn't you?

Yes, we just went off and did our thing. We weren't in a fight, but we weren't on the same frequency about how we should relate to people, how we should live our lives, how we should make a living, and other things. It's interesting because my grandfather on my father's side was a country doctor. My grandfather on my mother's side did all kinds of businesses. He owned a farm, ran a store in a small town, and all kinds of stuff like that. On both sides, they were more entrepreneurial.

Have you ever been competitive with John about any aspect of flying?

It's very difficult for two strong-willed people, who have about the same amount of flight time, to fly together uneventfully. Whether you're sitting in the left seat or right seat, you tend to want to be in control. We've had to work on that. It's actually easier, since we've been flying the Citation, because it requires two pilots. There are very clearly defined roles for each pilot, depending on which seat you're sitting in. You've got very definite pilot responsibilities and very definite co-pilot responsibilities. So from that standpoint, it's actually easier to relate in the cockpit when flying the Citation.

The biggest disagreement you had before the Citation?

I don't remember any particular incident because nothing's ever happened and nothing's been big. Basically, the friction would come because I'm probably a little better instrument pilot than John is. I visualize things in 3-D a little bit better. So when we're on instruments, I'd be—particularly when sitting in the right seat— a little bit ahead in my thinking and awareness than John would be. I'd be right there to remind him or suggest things to him, about 15 to 20 seconds before he would have figured it out himself, which can be a very frustrating thing to do to someone.

We guys don't like to be told directions a lot of times, too.

Yes, but it works both ways. John is somewhat a better pilot, if you're looking at pure physical control of the airplane, than I am. When I would be in the left seat and John in the right seat, he would be able to see and visualize whether I was on the correct descent path and lined up right. He could tell whether a particular maneuver was going to bring me out exactly where we both knew I ought to end up. He could project and visualize that better than I could, so he would know maybe 30 seconds ahead of me if it was going to work out or not and whether I was going to need a correction. In each case, if we commented to the other about that, we would end up—whoever was the pilot— a little bit irritated, because we both figured, "I would have caught that but you didn't give me time!" It worked both ways—I did it to him and he did it to me, but about different topics—about different aspects of flying.

I know lots of husbands and wives that just can't work together. They have good marriages but they can't work together well. Yours seems to be pretty remarkable. You work together, though you are strong-willed.

Yes, in some ways. It's something that has been very important to us from the time we first started dating. We were planning on working together in business from day one, and it was just, overall, extremely important to us that we work out ways to make sure that we got along well, not only in our marriage, but also in our working and then later on in our flying. We put a lot of time and energy in it. Which is not to say, in any way, that it's always gone smoothly or been perfect. As I said, we are both strong-willed people, and when we get passionate about things, neither of us tends to be as careful as we should be with the other person's feelings. But we work very hard on trying to be very

430

considerate and are very aware of giving each other room to be important and to be people in our own right.

Tell me the proudest moment in your flying career.

Oddly enough, getting the commercial rating in an airship. An airship is very, very, very difficult to fly because basically what you have is the equivalent of a powered balloon. Unlike an airplane or a helicopter, when you ask it to do something by putting in certain control input, an airship tends to think about it for a while and then say, well, maybe so, or no, I don't think so. It's responding very strongly to any wind effect on it and a lot of other influences—thermals—and just a lot of weather influences. So you have to be thinking quite a bit ahead of it because you have to anticipate if the wind does this or the thermals do that. The ship is going to want to do this, so I need to do that to be ready for it. You really need to be thinking ahead of it.

Were there any particular stories or anecdotes about learning that or gaining those credentials? Did anything unusual happen in your training?

Nothing unusual. It's just a very disconcerting thing. You have a ground crew of about 18 people that help launch you and retrieve you. It's a little disconcerting as an airplane pilot to, all of a sudden, have a crew of 18 people standing around waiting for you to get ready and do all your checks and decide that you're ready to go. The process of getting the airship ready to go off the mast or go on the mast, at the end of a flight, is about a 15-minute process. By the time you get all the engine checks done and all the other checks that you need to do, you really feel very self conscious when there are 18 people standing around waiting for you to get all your stuff done. You feel so fumble-fingered, and you know you're taking a lot longer than someone who flies it on a regular basis and is very proficient at it. That is something that took quite a bit of getting used to.

How long did it take you to get used to that?

Well, I wouldn't say that we're really used to it, yet. It took us quite a while to get the commercial license because, basically, we were doing the training when the blimp wasn't being used for other things, and we had to fit it in between events, and we had to get a lot of night time in it, which is hard to get in this particular airship because it doesn't fly at night very much. It took us over a period of two years, that we worked on getting the license, before we finally got the commercial license. Not steadily, obviously, but off and on over two years.

How many qualifications do you have?

Every FAA category and class of license, which includes seaplane, land plane, balloon—both hot air and gas—gliders, helicopters, gyroplanes, and airships. Also, I have all seven of the flight instructor ratings.

That's incredible. There must not be very many people have these credentials.

I believe I am the only woman. There are other people that have all of the flight instructor ratings, but I don't believe there's anyone besides John and me that have both every category and class and all seven flight instructor ratings.

Do you feel like full-time students?

Yes, but you know, the reason that we did get all those categories and classes is because that's what our business is. We're in the business of helping people to pass written exams and helping people to pass flight tests. It was a way of staying in the student mode—knowing how a student feels emotionally. It's easy if you don't have to take any check rides or aren't getting any new ratings, over a period of years, to get away from the stress and the emotional impact that a student feels going through training. It was important to us to keep that kind of emotional connection to what our customers were going through.

I believe that you have to actually do certain things to really understand them. My simple example is: I was a college basketball player. I feel I know a lot about the game, from having played, stuff that the non-participant may not. Could you give me an example of how your specific training in one of these areas has enabled you to understand—so as to be able to teach better.

It's tough, because we don't teach students in the airplane. Part of how it interacted is, when you're a glider pilot or learning to glide, you become very aware of what the wind is doing and what the thermals are doing. You become very aware, because you have no motor, of judging your glide path and your landing spot. Then judging your glide path and your landing spot carries over to when you're trying to work with someone in airplanes— as far as emergency landings and focusing on the attitude of the airplane and how to judge where you're going to be landing and how far you're going to be able to glide as you come down. The whole awareness in a glider of wind and thermals and so on carries over to the airship operations, and some of that carries over to seaplane operations because when you're operating off the water, you need to be very, very alert to where the wind is from because it affects your landing and how the waves are going to be. Being a seaplane pilot makes you alert to being able to read the trees, the wind ripples in the water so that you can tell where the wind is from, and that carries over to an airship and being able to look at a lot of things and knowing what the wind is doing and also somewhat to airplanes—just in terms of your total awareness of your environment.

Have you any seaplane stories or any unusual things that happened while training or flying seaplanes?

One of the interesting things about seaplanes—and the way that the FAA regulations are written—is that if you're an instructor in airplanes (land airplanes) and you go and get a commercial seaplane rating, you're automatically a seaplane instructor. This seems a little odd, but that's the way the regulations are written. So we got our seaplane ratings down in Southern California over on the Salton Sea. At the time, we were going to Alaska every two months to be able to teach these weekend, ground-school courses up there. We had friends who were flying seaplanes, and they had more time in seaplanes than we did, but we were much higher-time pilots, and we were instructors. Although we didn't have as much seaplane time, we had a better feel for the attitude of the airplane, and so on. We would be asked very frequently to fly with these friends because, in Alaska, all winter long, everything's iced up and nobody flies on floats. The planes are in the hangar or they put them on skis, and then when things thaw out, there are people who haven't flown very much for six months, and now they want to go out and they want someone with them

434

to keep them out of trouble. So we did a fair amount of that kind of flying. One summer we were up in Fairbanks, and a friend of ours said that they went up a week ago and dropped some friends of theirs off on this lake, on the north slope, and said they wouldn't get up there for another week. They asked if we could go up and pick them up and bring them back. So we did, and it involved taking his 185, on floats, up and landing it on a lake that was right near the Arctic Circle, taking off some barrels of fuel that we'd flown up there, refueling the airplane, going from there to another lake north of the Arctic range up on the North Slope, picking the people up, coming back, refueling again, and then going back into Fairbanks. We spent the night out in a cabin on this lake. It was a very special, very spectacular experience.

Do you ever find yourself flying in maybe a fixed wing and you say, "Oh, I wish I was in a glider now, or I wish I was in a helicopter now?" Do you ever cross-reference like that?

Between airplane and helicopter quite a bit. We have a lease on and we fly a small helicopter, a Robinson R22, and that is our low and slow "look at the countryside" kind of airplane. There will be times when we're flying, and we think, "Boy, it would be really fun to be down on the deck sightseeing in the helicopter." We kind of have the two ends of the spectrum—we have the Citation for when you really need to get somewhere and the helicopter for when you want to sightsee and just have fun.

What's the most extravagant beauty you've ever seen from the air? What's the thing that almost made your knees shake, you were so inspired?

We've seen a lot of them. I don't know that I can name any

one. Some sights to behold are the glaciers up in Alaska, the Grand Canyon, and the mountains, in southwestern Colorado, when the aspens are turning color in the fall. Those are probably the things that stick in my mind the most. Also, just taking the helicopter up and down the San Diego coast, as the coastline is beautiful from the helicopter.

Did you see whales or anything?

Yes, you do. Actually, we chased whales more in the airship than in the helicopter. We would take the airship back and forth between Oakland and southern California, and we'd go down off of Big Sur and down the coast around Vandenberg. Very commonly, you see whales on that route, quite close into shore.

Were you adventuresome as a young girl? What were you like?

I was a tomboy. I was always playing Davy Crockett. I had my coonskin cap. I liked to ride horses. I played ice hockey.

What would you be doing if you weren't flying?

Before I met John, I was going to be a college professor and teach English. That's a little bit hard for me to believe right now.

That's what I do, and you have more fun than I do, I'm sure!

Well, I don't know. Like us, you're working with people and getting a chance to watch them as they learn and be an important part of their lives. That's very, very rewarding.

You must have a lot of patience, too. You're talking about helping people.

Where was your patience most taxed with the students?

When we were teaching in Alaska, we had a number of students who were Athabascan Indian or Eskimo. They had very poor education. It was difficult for them to understand a lot of the concepts involved in the written-exam part of learning to fly. They didn't have any difficulty with the physical task of it, but getting the regulations down, doing the math—as far as the weight and balance calculations and the navigation problems—that kind of stuff was a problem for them. We had some people that came back probably six or eight times before they got it. The thing, I guess, that tried our patience the most, is that some people would give up. They'd come to class one day and not show up the next. Then three months later, they'd be back and come to the class the first day and not show up they next. They wouldn't give you the chance to work with them clear through the program and get the job done. The people that would keep coming and stay for the whole class, and work at it, and give us a chance to work with them would eventually get through. Although, as I say, sometimes it took them six or eight times to do it. So I guess the biggest thing that tried our patience was the people that wouldn't stick to it and give us a chance to get them through.

It's been a great life of flight for you, hasn't it?

Yes, we've had a wonderful time. The most special thing about it is the special people that you meet. It's interesting because flying has so many little, separate worlds. They all touch in some area, but gliding has a whole different society and group of people and attitude than the balloonists do—than the helicopter people—than the airplane people. In the airplanes, the people that fly seaplanes have a totally different mindset. In many ways, they operate in a totally different world than the people who fly turbine aircraft. We've had a chance to be a part of all these different worlds and get to know the people in them who are very different from each other but share a lot of common characteristics and are all very special people. That's been the real wonderful fun of it.

Greatest support you've received from John?

Always backing me up and respecting my authority as pilot- in-command, in our own relationship and when interacting with other folks in aviation. Calling me "Captain" when pilots and line service folks ask him for instructions about the airplane.

Is there anything in flight you wished you could have done?

Not really. We have been very privileged.

Proudest accomplishment?

Achieving every category and class of pilot and instructor certificate.

How often do you fly these days?

Usually once a week, either in the Falcon 10 or in a Robinson helicopter, an R-22.

Any anecdotes in past few years, any touching moments?

Most powerful experience is a two-week flying safari in southern Africa (South Africa, Botswana, Namibia, Zambia), in a Cessna 182 that John and I flew ourselves. The view of the countryside and the animals—elephants, giraffe, etcetera—is extraordinary, and the experience is life-changing.

Will you ever give up flight?

Probably not. It has been an enduring passion for over 46 years now. Nothing else comes close to the pleasure and sense of accomplishment I get from it. Even when I can't pass a full aviation medical, I expect to fly under sport pilot rules.

Are you still unique in the number of categories and classes of licenses you have? Have any women surpassed you in this?

To the best of my knowledge, no other woman has equaled or surpassed me in the categories and classes of certificates.

Proudest you've been of a student?

When we were teaching live, weekend, ground schools for the FAA Knowledge Tests, we taught every two months in Alaska. In Fairbanks we had an Athabascan Indian named Tommy come to the Private Pilot ground school class. He had only about a 4th-grade education, and did not know how to multiply and divide. He kept coming back to the class each time we came to Fairbanks, working doggedly, and finally passed the FAA Knowledge Test after his 5th time in class. During our class he learned the concepts of multiplication and division. It was thrilling to be part of his success.

How would you like to be remembered?

As someone who helped people make their dreams of flight come true—made aviation accessible to many people, and helped them learn to manage the risks of flight so they and their loved ones could finish their trips safely.

Ilovene Potter
"Helicopter Flights"

Ilovene Potter at Boeing Field in Piper Aztec. Early 1970s.

When Ilovene's husband became interested in flight, he decided to buy an airplane with three other fellows. At the time, Ilovene would tag along with the fellows just for fun. Her interests grew and, in exchange for keeping the airplane clean and the logbooks up to date, she could fly the airplane. I mentioned that not many women were flying when she started. "None that I knew of," she answered. Since earning her private pilot's license in 1941, Ilovene has flown more than 10,000 hours, 3,000 of which were in helicopters. She earned her ATP and got the job of chief pilot for Boeing Field Flight School. She served as a charter pilot and did traffic watch. In 1973, she served as captain of the U.S. Helicopter Team.

A native of Tacoma, Washington, Ilovene attended high school there and two years of college at Pacific Lutheran University. She was inducted into the Washington State Aviation Hall of Fame and was a member of Whirly Girls—and was the 50th woman to receive her pilot license for helicopters and the first in Washington State. She was also a member of The Ninety-Nines.

She died in Puyallup, Washington, February 14, 2006 at the age of 87.

Did you ever compete with your husband in flying?

Yes, almost constantly. Later on, he encouraged me to get my instrument rating since we were so many times in weather. We had arguments about taking and changing channels on his plane when I was flying instruments. They were the usual husband-and-wife things.

But nothing catastrophic?

No, we never came close to blows.

Describe your style of flying as opposed to his style of flying.

He didn't care about rules and regulations and things like that. He just wanted to get in the airplane and go. And I was more on the conservative side.

How conservative were you? Can you give me an example of how careful you were or how detailed you were?

I was always very careful about checking weather and making sure I thought I could make it. I don't think I took many chances. I taught all three of my boys to fly. I didn't teach all of them everything, but I did share in their learning.

Did you ever come close to crashing?

That seems to be what everybody wonders. But no, I have not had very many close calls. We had a twin engine Aztec, and one day when my husband and I had two of the kids flying with us, both of the engines quit. What happened is that we had iced up over the mountains going to California, and the fuel had siphoned out of the caps and down underneath the wings which meant that we couldn't see it. The plane was out of gas. At the time, we were flying over Lake Bereson in north California. I had to tell everybody that both of my engines had quit. My husband said, "Say it again," so I said, "My engines both quit." That's a mouthful when you're scared to death. Anyway, we made it in to a military base that was close by. By the time we got on the ground, I couldn't walk. I was just paralyzed with fear for what could have been the consequences.

That was just a freak situation, wasn't it?

It turned out there were several other airplanes at that time that had the same problem. So I guess that it was common with that particular airplane. They had this thermostat bottle cap on this airplane. When we left Seattle, we had 144 gallons of gas, and we should have had plenty to make the trip, but all of it was gone.

Did you give your boys their solo flight?

443

No, I never did. I just gave them part of their training. With my youngest son, I just couldn't get to first base with him, so we finally hired another instructor. He wouldn't pay attention to what I told him to do. He'd say, "Mother stop raising your voice." My husband said that, too. He said, "If you don't quit raising your voice, I'm going to quit letting you teach me." But I taught him most of his helicopter flying.

When you raise your voice, you don't really raise it very much, do you?

I had to, because I don't have a very loud voice, and I would raise my voice so they could hear me when I thought they didn't hear me.

They interpreted as it being loud?

Yes. When my husband and I used to fly instruments, I would talk to the air traffic controller, and quite a few times, I couldn't get any answer. Then my husband would pick up the microphone and say something, and they would acknowledge him right away. So I know I've had a little trouble with my voice.

You don't think it was because you're female?

No, I don't think so. It might have been something to do with being "Mother." I used to fly for KIRO-TV and then for KOMO-TV. I guess it was for both TV and radio. I never broadcast, but I would fly. They would have a passenger to broadcast. All I did was fly the helicopter.

Did anything unusual happen while flying for the media?

444

It was pretty boring. Nothing happened, nothing exciting. I circled a fire one night. Otherwise, it was just routine things.

What was the toughest thing you encountered when you were flying for one of the stations?

Fighting the weather. Paul Brendel, served as a pilot for KIRO-TV, always was gone between Christmas and New Year's, and so I flew in his place. Then the weather was always a challenge. I had the helicopter bubble ice up one time, so I couldn't see out ahead, but could see out one side. That's just part of the game.

Was it affecting the weight very much?

Yes.

How many sandbags did you carry with you?

I had three. Two ten pounds and one five pound.

So you couldn't fly without a certain amount of weight?

No. The helicopter I learned to fly in back in the early 1960s was a Bell, and the minimum weight of the pilot had to be 150 pounds. So when the man soloed me down there —I couldn't get an instructor up in Seattle —I flew my own airplane down to Centralia, Washington, twice a week for lessons. He got out of the helicopter, and I was supposed to solo it. During the flight, the helicopter kept trying to tip over. I set it down and tried it again and again, but with the same problem. Finally, I looked up, and the instructor was jumping up and down. He was yelling,

"Put it down! Put it down!" So I did, and he went and ran in the hangar. He had realized right away what was the matter, so he brought out a case of oil and put in the seat next to me. After that I had no troubles.

If you don't mind me asking, how much did you weigh then?

I weighed about 120 or 125 pounds. I weigh 95 now.

So you'd need a little bit more oil or sand if you flew now.

Oh yes, I've thinned down. But I was quite strong.

If you did condition yourself, what did you do?

Well, of course, I was busy with three boys, lifting them around. They figured that they were grown up and didn't have to mind me by the time they could pick me up.

Are any of your boys flying professionally?

My oldest son, Ted Potter, was the traffic pilot for KOMO-TV for 15 or 20 years. My middle son is a doctor. He quit flying because he said that one cannot be good at both. You have to focus on one or the other. The youngest one wouldn't study enough to do the written work. He just wanted to fly.

There's got to be some proud moment when a mother is up with one of her sons.

When I was flying for KIRO-TV, and my son was flying for KOMO-TV, he would be in the air and would call all the pilots

446

who flew traffic; they were always on the radio together. He would say, "Watch out, momma's on the air." So they would watch their language more when I was in the air. He would say, "Mother, you're a hundred feet high. If you don't stay at one altitude, I'm going to cut your tail-feather off." It was just a fun thing.

Where is the strangest place you landed? Someone said you landed on a house.

I had my own helipad at Hood Canal. Once I had an accident over there. I had been landing on the bulkhead of a neighbor's property for a long time. One day, I came in, and it was awfully windy. A gust caught me, and I tangled my tail rotor in a tree. So my husband took the tail rotor off and, of course, we had to have it replaced. He took it and put the bill in the tail rotor above my bed to remind me to be more careful. Then he had the helipad built over there, and later on, I had my own helipad there and on the carport roof at home.

That must have been pretty sturdy.

Oh yes, it was professionally done. There weren't too many women at that time who had their own helipad, much less a helicopter license. As far as I know, I was the first woman in the state of Washington and the fiftieth woman in the world. Jean Howard-Phelen of Whirly Girls kept track of all of that.

Are there any stories about you coming in on a helicopter and people thinking at first it was a man?

All the time I flew professionally, I had only one person who wouldn't fly with me. I used to fly for Jim Galvin. His operation was taking people out to Ocean Shores, Washington. That was quite popular at one time. Anyway, once I met his airplane out at Sea-Tac Airport and picked up his group to take them out to Ocean Shores, but when this man saw me, he said he wouldn't go. He had a framed picture with him and said, "Well you can't fit this in there." But, of course, we could have. That was his excuse.

What did you think about that?

It never bothered me. I was used to it. There was a man starting an operation out at Boeing Field. He asked me if I would go to work as chief pilot until I could get his man trained as chief pilot, and then he would want him, naturally. That was one of the times I thought I was discriminated against. It was kind of tough.

Could you describe that more?

He made it plain that I was only there to train his man who would take over and be chief pilot. So I was there about a year.

Tell me about your work as an FAA examiner.

I had a few men who tried to bluff me. I had this man, who was fairly wealthy, who was just overconfident. He had his own airplane and said he was leaving the next day after he got his instrument rating. He set the date for the instrument rating. Then he told me that he was leaving the next day and was going to take his wife and kids to California. I thought, "Boy, he better be good." When he came for the test, the first thing he did was take off and make a mistake. By the time we got through with the ride, I did not pass him, because I felt that his kids and his wife would not be safe with him to take that trip in case the weather was bad. Of course, you never know.

Also, I had an older man who had his own airplane. He was taking his instrument check and made a big boo-boo up at Everett, and I failed him, too. He got so mad at me that he went to my son, who was flying for KOMO-TV, and complained. He told him how he didn't like me and how unfair I was. Finally, he went to FAA and complained about me.

What did your son say?

He just passed it off as another old crank.

Who was the most memorable old-timer flier that you knew, male or female?

I had several. In helicopters, it was Bob Nokes. He was the chief pilot for Seattle Flight Helicopters, and we worked for Jerry Garbell. He was, I think, the closest friend I had in the group. I had even more respect for Jim Galvin. He was an older man. He's gone now.

Tell me something unusual about each of those men.

Jim Galvin always called me when he had a woman student that was difficult. He had this girl from Norway or Sweden, and she had an accent. She never could figure which was runway thirty-one and thirteen. She couldn't figure out which end of the runway she was supposed to be on. When they told her thirteen and thirty-one, which were two of the runways at Boeing Field, she would get awfully confused. So I finally made arrangements to go through an FAA inspector to give her rating and pass her, because nobody would give her an airplane alone. She never could get it. She had about 50 hours when Jim Galvin asked me if I could try and do something with her. She was a very likeable girl. When I took her over, she had never had to preflight an airplane herself and get her hands dirty. She was a little bashful thing.

So you broke that habit fast?

Yes. I said, "Well, I've got news for you. I'm not going to do it. So you better get busy." So we got started and got along fine.

How did she react when you told her she had to do it?

She didn't know what to do first. I told her she had to check the oil and the fuel and so on. Make sure the prop is secure and all that. We got along great. Then when she got her license, we rented a plane, and I went with her, and she took her son for a ride.

I had one man that I could never teach. He was nervous and uptight. He wanted to learn how to fly a helicopter. He finally gave up. I really got a little worried about his strength. He was stronger than I was. On one occasion my husband said to me, "Why don't you take a billy club in the airplane with you in case you have to hit him?"

He finally gave up. He couldn't relax enough to do it.

Do you have a philosophy of flying?

I think it's perfectly safe. I would rather be up there than on the ground in traffic. But I just think people have a bad habit of wanting too much to get home. I have lost, I know, people who had to get home but didn't make it because of the weather. They were qualified to fly in the bad weather and couldn't fly the airplane suitably.

What's the most wonderful experience you've had flying?

At sunup or sunset alone in an airplane, it's beautiful.

Where?

Anywhere you can see it. I've flown back and forth across the United States many times. It's always interesting that I think the most beautiful things I've been able to see are the sunrises and sunsets.

Did you ever fly over a nudist colony in a helicopter or anything like that?

No, but I did have somebody take a shot at me.

Take a shot at you?

Yes, I used to fly down in Maple Valley here. One time as I was coming back home, someone took a shot at the helicopter.

What did you do?

It kind of startled me, and it kept on coming. I had a student with me, and he said he saw the man aiming at us. I think it was someone in the Valley who objected to helicopters, because, you know, the helicopter's pretty noisy. Also, I've had one violation in all the years of my flying,

What was that?

A girlfriend and I were going to a Ninety-Nines meeting in Everett. I was to pick her up at about five o'clock in the afternoon from the schoolyard in the University District in Seattle. She had arrived a little early to make sure there were no kids around, and she did make sure of that. So I picked her up, and we flew on to our meeting. When I got home, it was a weekend and the FAA man was there telling me I was in violation for stopping in a schoolyard. The rules and regulations were few in 1960 regarding helicopters and where you could land, and where you couldn't. Back then I just did things and hoped they'd be right.

Give me another example of how fragile the rules were then.

There was no rule that I was aware of, or could find out about, in regard to building a helipad. When I had one built on my carport here in Seattle, someone said, "You can't do that. You've got to have all kinds of checks with different authorities," and so on. But it never turned out to amount to anything. I had my carburetor go bad on the helicopter while it was on the roof. I just took it off and took it down to the airport and had it rebuilt, then took it back home and put it back on. Then somebody said, "You can't do that." So it was just little things like that.

What sort of mistakes did some of those early helicopter pilots that you knew make?

There was a helicopter down in Oakland that took people to different places, and the pilot landed at a waterfront helipad. One time the pilot let his passengers off and forgot to move his battery. In those days, the Bell helicopter had a heavy battery that had to be moved on the boom in the back from one position to the other depending on the weight you had in the helicopter. The

452

pilot forgot to do it, and the helicopter tipped over backwards off the helipad. There was a lot of bad publicity about it.

You seem pretty confident about helicopters. Were you always confident about them?

I was. My kids didn't like it. They said it was an accident looking for a place to happen. Or better yet, the machine is looking for a place to disintegrate. No, I like it. I enjoyed it. My husband bought me a Hughes 269A when they first came out. I know that, every time I flew, somebody got a report at FAA. Don Frost, the inspector for that FAA department here, would call and ask me, "Where were you this morning? Where were you this afternoon?" He automatically blamed me every time they got a bad report. But he never did anything about it.

A bad report about a helicopter?

Yeah, that it was too low, or made too much noise or something. But that was only because there weren't that many around.

But those reports weren't about you. They were about somebody else, weren't they?

Usually they were, because I was pretty careful about not getting into trouble.

Describe being captain of the U.S. Helicopter team that went to England.

Yes, we were the first United States team to compete in the

world championships. The first helicopter championships were held in Germany, and there was not a United States team. It was held in England the next time. Anyway, Bell helicopter sponsored us and gave us support to have a women's team to go to England. We had three women pilots and three women co-pilots. it involved different maneuvers, so we practiced up here and got a team together and went to England and competed.

So, how did you do?

Terrible. We had never had a team, so nobody knew exactly what we'd do. When we got there, all the teams that we had to compete against were military. Of course, they were much better than we ever could hope to be. But we did not embarrass ourselves. We left no impressions other than that we behaved well and had a good time and did a good job. We didn't have any trouble. That was 1972.

How old were you at the time?

Fifty-four. Then the next competition was held in Russia. I went as a judge on the team to that. You had to be certified or know enough to recognize different maneuvers and what they should be. You had to be certified by this aeronautic organization in France. It was fun.

Did you suffer from any unusual communications or miscommunication over there in Russia?

The Russians used different maps. We were given maps when we were in England, but they used different maps. They were evidently what the military used. It took us a couple of days studying them to figure them out so that our computers would work with them. But that's really the only trouble we had.

Did you meet any interesting fliers over there?

Oh, yes. The Germans were good at helping us take care of our equipment, and so were the Russians. But they wouldn't talk directly to us very much. We met an English woman that was very nice and kept up correspondence for quite a few years.

They wouldn't talk directly to you?

The Russians weren't too friendly. They were hard to communicate with.

Do you think it had to do with your being a woman?

I don't know. It's hard to tell. But the Germans were a great help to us. We were housed in a nice hotel in the New Forest area, as they called it. We flew over to Southampton, England, for refueling.

What are you the most proud of in terms of your career?

Gosh, I don't know. I suppose if I have anything to be proud of, it would be of being the captain of that team. I got a big certificate of gratitude on the wall here. Oh, I know, I'm in the Smithsonian. Most people have to die to get there. My picture is in with Prince Philip and our team. It's in a section where they have helicopters. I've never seen it, but I had a girl take a picture of it and send it to me.

What does flight mean to you?

I guess freedom because you're on your own up there and it's peaceful and quiet and beautiful. If I got pressed with the kids or anything, I used to fly up toward the mountains and fly up the Green River Gorge and look around and just enjoy it. It was a really ideal way to get away from everything.

That's beautiful country over there. Is there any place you liked to land way out there with the wood nymphs and the faeries or something?

Oh, the little airports away from here are more inviting. It seems like I've had an awful busy life. There haven't been too many little trips like that. I know that I feel very deeply sorry that I lost one student in all the years of my instructing, and I feel very bad about him yet. That's been forty years ago.

Tell me about the student.

He was one that the FAA guy asked me to try to do something with because he was a little rebel. He had his own airplane, so he didn't think he had to learn how anything had to be done. Rules and regulations were foreign to him. He was smart, but he was just a kid. What I wanted to do, he did not want to do. Once I sent him on a cross-country, and he came back with oil all over his airplane. He'd forgotten to put the cap back on the oil. He finally got his license, and everything was legal. But he had to ask me every time he wanted to go any place across the country. This one time, he said he wanted to go to Everett to an air show up there. He was going to take his wife and his two kids. I said, "Well now, fine. You can go in daylight and good weather, but what are you going to do if the weather turns bad after you get there?" He laughed and said, "I'll call you; you'll come and get us." I said, "Just don't forget that."

When I came to work one morning, when I was in charge of that place, assigned to get a man trained, I found the kid had taken his airplane and left. It wasn't there. It was about five o'clock in the morning, and he had taken his plane and left. It didn't seem right. He was on a night shift — and his airplane was gone. He never came back.

You're still thinking about that after forty years?

They found his body a year afterwards. His wife talked to me and sent me all his subscriptions to magazines that involved flying, and she never held it against me. But I held it against me. I just wondered if I could have done something more.

Don't you think you were a little hard on yourself?

No. We looked for him. We knew where he had gone. His dad was sick down in Centralia, Washington, and he'd gone down to see his dad after working all night. He made the wrong turn in bad weather coming home and ended up in trees. It was a year before his airplane was found.

Were you kind of pins and needles during that year?

I went and took one of his relatives out searching for him for a long time afterwards. Then I just figured, like most of the accidents in the mountains here, it would take awhile to find the location of the crash. You just have to wait and see.

That must have been hard to get those subscriptions, too; wasn't that like a reminder when you all got all those?

Yes. I was glad when I ran out.

That's tough. Flying is an amazingly life-or-death occupation, isn't it? You say it isn't that risky, but it can be...

It is if you don't use your head. He thought he could do anything. There are sad things that happen, but there are a lot of good things.

It's been a great life of flying, hasn't it?

Oh, I loved it.

How many years did you fly?

I flew in 1940 until about 1943. Then I didn't fly because my children were young. Then in 1960, I went back to wide open and got all the ratings and had a lot of fun. My husband could afford to buy the airplanes, and he enjoyed it, too. It wasn't till after he died that I sold them. I had a Comanche 260 Turbo. It was a real nice plane, but I just couldn't fly it. When he died, I had to get busy with business and keep everything going.

When was the last time you flew?

I think it was 1980. It's been an awful long time. I couldn't pass the physical now. I can't even drive.

Was it hard for you to stop flying for those 17 years?

Yes. See, we had decided we couldn't afford to have a big enough airplane after our second son was born. So we decided we would take up boating. Everybody has to have a hobby, so we started boating for a number of years. Then when my husband had a heart attack, he said, "I don't care what anyone says, if I can't fly, you can fly, so we'll get another airplane." That's what we did.

Do you remember back in the late 1940s and early 1950s, sitting around frustrated or watching planes go overhead?

I look now sometimes and wish I were up there. No, when you have a husband and three kids and boats and cars and skiing and all that stuff the kids are involved in, you're too busy to think about entertaining yourself.

When were you most competitive in flying? When did you feel the most like you wanted to compete with someone?

I was still pretty serious the first time when I went to England. I also felt that way with the Powder Puff Derby. I flew in eight of those.

Tell me a Powder Puff Derby story.

There are a lot of things, good and bad. I had a good airplane, the first one, but one time in 1961, I got on top of the clouds, made a mistake, and had a hard time coming down.

Then when I came down, the radio station that served as the beacon was out of service and I got lost. That was my first experience with the Power Puffs.

When you got lost, where were you headed?

I was headed for Montgomery, Alabama. That was one of the stops we had to make. I ended up south of there by about a hundred miles.

That didn't help your time, did it?

No, but fortunately, I was not the last one to come in. But I was close to the tail end.

How did you feel about that?

Foolish. Very foolish.

Did you have any close races, involving any kind of personal rivalries?

I always thought that would be my goal if I could just beat Fran Bera once. When I got my helicopter rating, I knew she was taking lessons, too, and I didn't think she knew I was. She ended up being the 49th woman with a helicopter license, and I was the 50th. So I still haven't beaten her. But we're still good friends. You compete, but it's different than men, I think. They have to win. But you just don't want to embarrass yourself, and you want to do a good job. I've won money, and I've won prizes and been in the top ten in the Powder Puff Derby most of the time, but that's about it.

If you had not flown, what would you have done?

Oh gosh, I could not imagine not flying. Living in a

retirement home, I look at some of the old women here who are schoolteachers and accountants and all these other things, and there are a lot of them that have never done work. I think, gosh, what a life that must be, to never have worked and known the pleasures that I've known.

You've known a sky-full of pleasure, haven't you?

Oh, yes.

Louise Prugh

"Training with Trans World Airlines (TWA)"

Charles Lindbergh had made his historic flight when, several years later, a notice in the paper read: "Lindbergh coming to the Omaha Airport." Louise managed to talk her father into taking her to see her hero. As the two walked down the field, past the vendors and barnstormers, Louise suggested she'd like to take a ride in a plane. Her father scorned the idea, but did say that maybe they could move closer so Louise could shake Lindbergh's hand. Soon they were face to face with the famous flier. Louise recalls, "I was overcome, I was speechless. All I could think of was this person standing in front of me had flown solo across the ocean." Her father chatted with Lindbergh for a few minutes, and then they left. "This experience left such an impression on me that I knew some day I would learn to fly!"

Louise was born in 1916 in Omaha, Nebraska. Her father had a farm in Bennington, Nebraska, and he later got an appointment to the Federal Reserve in Washington, D.C. (Louise's mother had died in the flu epidemic of 1919.) During the years in Washington, D.C., she met Mrs. Herbert Hoover—among others—and, as a sixteen-year old, had a date with an Annapolis man.

Louise served as an instructor in the Training Department of TWA in Washington, D.C. and New York and Geneva in the years 1943 to 1947, during which time she learned to fly. Years later, in 1972, after raising a family and beginning her teaching career, she went to visit a friend at the airport and wondered if she could still fly. By August of 1972, she had her private pilot's license, and then later her commercial license and finally, the CFI (Certified Flight Instructor). This opened up a new epoch of flight for Louise, including the Powder Puff Derby and a trip to Mexico. In 1964, Louise began her career as an instructor in home economics at Eastern Washington University. She retired as a professor of fashion merchandising in 1985.

Do you remember your solo flight?

We had flown around the field, and all of a sudden, the instructor landed, got out, and he said, "It's all yours." And I wasn't really expecting it so soon. But anyway, he said, "Go around the field a couple of times and then land." And so I taxied down and as I took off, my goodness, all of a sudden I was airborne. It was a J-3 Cub—and without an instructor in the plane. It was quite a bit lighter when there is one person in the plane and, in those days, I weighed less than I do now. And that plane just soared. It was a wonderful feeling and I thought, I'm up here all by myself. It was just exhilarating. I flew around and made a couple of circles, and then I came in. I was able to get it down all right. I realized that getting it down was a little harder too because it didn't want to go down as quickly as with two people. That was in 1943 at a little airport in Annapolis, Maryland. I was actually out there practicing when they dropped the bomb ending WWII. We knew that something was happening, but we didn't know exactly, so when the good news came, we were excited. We celebrated and the only thing we had to drink was warm beer. There were a lot of fliers at the field that day.

The reason I was there was that TWA had put a little clip in their paper that the airline would be glad to teach any employees that wanted to learn to fly, so I went out to the field. The idea behind that was to teach employees as much as possible about flying, so they would be more informed as employees. As it turned out, I was the only girl and they weren't so sure they wanted to bother teaching a girl to fly. Still, the instructor was pretty nice and he said, "Wait and if I have time after I've taught all these others, I will give you a lesson." He didn't have time, but we set up an appointment for a week later, for April first—April Fool's Day, 1945. He turned out to be very nice and he taught me to fly. We flew out over Chesapeake Bay, and I was struck with the beauty of flying. Later, he took me up in a PT-19.

What sort of aeronautics did you like most?

The loop was kind of fun. Goodness it's been so long, I'm not sure. It was just, I mean, there were so many things you could do with a little airplane and have it come out all right. I will admit, when I later got my instructor's rating, I had to learn to do spins and show people how to get out of them, and I didn't enjoy that very much.

And why was that?

Well, I didn't like the responsibility of trying to teach some-body spins. I like to fly carefully. I am a cautious pilot. I've been told many times that I'm a very cautious pilot. "There are old pilots and bold pilots, but no old bold pilots."

How cautious were you? Give me an example. Was there any-thing where it was almost eccentric?

I didn't want to run out of gas. One time, much later, in the eighties, I was flying with my neighbor. He had been a pilot in

WWII. We were flying through North Dakota. It was pretty far between places where we could get gas. When we got down, we thought we had more gas than we did. We were very lucky to land without running out of gas. Always I liked to fly on the upper three-quarters of my tank. People would say, "That's ridiculous. You can fly down to another part of your tank." But I didn't trust the gauge that much. I especially liked to be sure I had enough gas to get where I had to go in case I had bad weather. Oftentimes I used to fly to Bozeman where I had a son. Sometimes the weather was not what the weather service had predicted, and I needed a little extra gas to go someplace else to land. I'll admit, I didn't tackle weather that I didn't think I could handle. I was instrument rated, so I felt prepared. But I didn't choose to do that purposely. If the weather seemed marginal, I would wait or go another route or something.

Did your husband ever tease you about it?

Well, no. Actually, I did a lot of the flying before I met him. This was my second husband. My second husband was a flier and flew B-26s—the Martin Marauder. He was shot down in Europe. We had an interesting experience. We went back to France and found where his plane had gone in.

Was that pretty emotional?

Very. Forty years later, my husband had wanted to go back. It was near Dijon, France, and he remembered very well the day he flew up into Germany. He had done the bomb run, and on the way home, he picked up enough flak that he lost one of the engines. He was on one engine, and he thought he could get back to the field, but he was losing altitude too fast. As a consequence, he gave the order to bail out, and all the crew bailed out. He was the last one to bail out and had 500 feet left. Fortunately, his parachute opened. The plane went into a mountain there and, of course, burned up.

The interesting thing was, we found a Frenchman who had been a little kid at the time and had seen the plane go down. He showed us where parts of the plane were. My husband had been stationed at a Château, and the Count, who owned the Château, was now there. He was in his 90s. When we came, he appreciated Americans so much that he went out and picked roses for me and opened a bottle of champagne. We had a toast to the Americans who had won the war.

Did you feel anything? Did you wish you had the opportunity to fly in the war?

No, because I felt I was in the midst of it. I was with the Intercontinental Division, which was the group that flew Roosevelt to Yalta. And, you know, we were flying all of the VIPs out of Washington D.C., I felt I was contributing. I didn't have a desire to join the WASPs because I was happy with my job.

Explain what your job was.

Generally speaking, I just oriented the employees to TWA about what their jobs would be. And, then they went on. If they were going to be in maintenance, then they would go on to maintenance. If they were going to be hostesses, which I was mostly interested in, then another hostess and I would teach them the rules—such as how you serve the people and what your duties would be while you were flying.

This was like helping flight attendants?

Yes.

Do you have any unusual stories that happened while you were at TWA?

Yes, I do. After the war was over, Dixie, the other hostess and I—plus the rest of the crew—were sent to Switzerland. We stayed over there a year and started a school to train Europeans about TWA. We, along with our crew, taught hostesses, ground crew, ticket agents, and all the people that would be stationed over there. Before that, TWA people had been flying for the military, but with our planes. Now, they were going to fly commercially. So we had to teach them all the rules of commercial flying and teach them what they did in an airplane.

We had a group of French, English, and Italian girls, all of whom were linguists. They had to be able to speak more than one language. That was why TWA hired girls in Europe. One time we took a group up to show them what it was like in the sky because they had never been in an airplane before. Included were three or four French girls, and at least that many others. Anyway, we got up in the airplane and, as luck would have it, we had a little rough weather so the girls were not feeling too well. And, of course, they were frightened. Then all of a sudden, the weather changed and it smoothed out. At that point, the French girls rushed to get out their perfume so that they would smell all right after this flight. They figured they had perspired and some of them had vomited. When the flight crew came to the back of the plane, one of them said, "We've never had a plane that smelled as good as this."

What was the most difficult thing to teach?

I think you had to explain to passengers what was happening so that, if they were in rough weather, they wouldn't be frightened. In those days, most people that didn't know about flying were frightened if the weather was bad or if they heard strange noises in the airplane that they didn't understand. You had to know enough about the airplane to try to explain what was happening, so they wouldn't be afraid. In essence, we had to sell flying, because we were going to fly commercially. Furthermore, we wanted to be sure that passengers were happy and taken care of. I think the thing we were taught to emphasize, over and over again, was that flying really was a safe means of transportation, comparatively speaking. And we were flying over the ocean. After WWII, the first over-ocean, commercial flying with land planes took place. Before the war, Pan American and BOAC with its Clipper were the only planes that flew overseas. The Boeing Stratoliners and Stratocruisers didn't carry enough people, so then, while I was there, we started flying the C54s or DC4s.

Did you meet any famous people?

An all-male crew flew the famous people. When the President—Roosevelt—flew, Otis Ryan, who was president of TWA at the time, and had been one of our best pilots, flew him. He was usually the Captain. And we got to know him pretty well. There was another one called "Swede," a Swedish man that had a good sense of humor, and he was on all the flights.

Do you have any stories about these people?

They didn't talk a lot about it. Because, of course, when

they were flying during the war we couldn't talk about what we did. Where we were going or when the plane was going, that was all very secret.

So did you fly on some secret missions?

No. I did not. Men stewards were on, because the crews were all men. Women didn't fly overseas as hostesses until after the war, when it gained commercial appeal.

What was the biggest insult you had as a woman?

This is hard to believe, I know. Maybe I don't want to remember bad things, but I had very few bad experiences. Because we were taught to take care of everybody, the planes were smaller, and there weren't so many people on board. When we had children, we'd help them take care of the babies and solve other problems. We didn't run into the problems that you run into today, because people were so happy to have someone there to hold their hand, so to speak, when they were frightened. I honestly can't remember any really bad experiences. But this was a long time ago and perhaps I've forgotten.

You also flew the airmail.

Well, Mark Conlin was the mail pilot. And, as a matter of fact, he still flies. Last summer, he flew the North Atlantic in a single-engine plane with a jet engine. But anyway, in the '70s, he was flying the mail between Spokane and Boise. Every night he'd take off and fly to Lewiston and then on to Boise. Mark would take another pilot with him because he was going to law school in the daytime. So he'd let the other pilot fly and he would take a nap. One time I was flying when we started picking up ice. I nudged him and said, "We're picking up ice." He said, "Now, don't worry Louise, we're flying the US mail." Another night we flew a load of little baby chicks, which were so noisy you could hardly hear the radios. Another time we flew orchids from Hawaii.

Even in the seventies there were not very many women flying?

That's true. Mark is a very small man and, at the time, I had hair that was starting to turn gray. We were a strange looking pair. Here I would be dressed in the warmest clothes I could find, because we flew in an old Aztec, which was not the best equipped as far as heating was concerned. I wore very warm clothing. I would help get the mail on and off because, of course, we wanted to get back as soon as we could. We'd leave Spokane around 10 p.m. and fly to Lewiston, load and unload, and then to Boise, so it would be three or four o'clock when we got home.

Did you have any close calls?

No, we did not. Mark is an excellent pilot, and I had the greatest confidence in him. While I was flying with him, nothing serious happened. I'm sure that if you talked with him, you'd find many more cases when he would run into bad weather because he did it all winter long—when weather can be a big factor in flying, especially in that area.

Tell me about the Powder Puff Derby.

I always wanted to fly the Powder Puff Derby and so the first thing I had to do was to find an airplane. I found out that I really needed to buy one. I bought a Cherokee 181 and then I had to lease it back in order to pay for it, so other people could fly it when I wasn't flying it. I got my instructor's rating and my commercial license and everything. So I did a little commercial flying in it, but I let other people fly it. It was instrument equipped because I don't like to fly a plane that doesn't have good instruments.

Then I had a friend, Marjorie Wood, from Lewiston that wanted to be my co-pilot. So we spent quite a few evenings. She'd fly up to Spokane and we would plan our course the best way. This was the last Powder Puff Derby, and it was a little different than most air races because they wanted to repeat what the original one had done 20 years before. We took off for Palm Springs and flew to Tampa, Florida, and had a certain route we had to fly. There were 150 little airplanes in a race. The most exciting thing about it was the start. That morning we got into our planes, and then all of a sudden a voice came on the earphone: "Ladies, start your engines." We started our engines. We each had a number, and so we taxied out. There were 150 little airplanes, and I was really concerned because I thought there might be some mid-air problems, but we didn't have any. Every so often, instead of the tower giving us instructions, we were flagged off. You'd taxi up and then someone would wave the flag. That meant it was time to take off. The pilot would wait until the other plane was far enough away, then take-off. Surprisingly enough, when all those little airplanes were in the sky, you could hardly see them from the air. I mean, everyone went her own way. We had designated places where we had to stop. We would have to fly by the tower. And the tower would take our time and then tell us to land. I remember the landing in Dallas. I thought, "Oh, what a great big airport!" After we had flown by the tower and the timers had gotten our time, the tower people would tell us to hold at such and such a place. That was a little frightening because some of the women had not had a lot of experience flying. Some pilots were not holding in the pattern the way you were supposed to. I was a little apprehensive about that because the one thing I didn't want was a mid-air collision. You really had to have your head on a swivel as they say, because there were so many planes. We landed safely, though. For the final portion, we went into Tampa. The weather was not cooperating too well. And as we were approaching Tampa, we must have been 20 or 30 miles out. We could see clouds building up, so I said to Marjorie, "I think we can get through between those two." We had to fly visual air rules; we weren't allowed to go by instrument. So we plowed through and we could barely see, but we were able to get through between these two immense thunderclouds on each side. And then the tower gave us our instructions to land, and was I really glad to get down! On the trip, we stayed overnight at two places, so it took us almost three days to do it.

Was that kind of a highlight of your career?

It was, because I'd heard about the Powder Puff Derby all my life. The Women's Transcontinental Air Race (AWTAR), dubbed the Powder Puff Derby, began in 1947. I had friends who had flown it, and it became a goal. The last Derby was scheduled in 1977. I had to do it. It marked the realization of that goal.

I realized this about myself—namely that I did not want to be a racing pilot. I am conservative when it comes to flying. Also, the beauty of flying is so wonderful that I never want to spoil it. I just love the world from the sky in a small plane because I find it so beautiful. I have seen sunsets and sunrises and the world is so beautiful.

What else has stunned you about the world as you see it from the air?

It isn't really as populated as we are led to believe. There are miles, especially in this part of the country, of places where there isn't any population. Also, I love the beauty of the mountains. I have wonderful pictures of flying from here to Seattle with the snow on the mountains. Those little airplanes fly very well when the weather is cool. I flew over to Seattle a number of times. I always flew when the weather was good. I have flown several times back to Nebraska and then on to Chicago. Actually we did not fly to Chicago; we flew to Rockford, Illinois, where I have friends that are pilots. I would meet them and then we would go on to New York. So I've flown across the United States several times in a little airplane, which gives you another view of what this lovely country we live in looks like from the sky. I've flown through South Dakota and I've seen Mount Rushmore. In spring of 1981, John and Martha King asked my husband, Wayne, and I to fly with them to Alaska, which was a wonderful experience.

Have you ever had a close call?

One time coming home from Bozeman, my hands got a little sweaty. I was concerned because the tower had cleared me; they said the weather was fine. When I got started, it wasn't good, and there were thunderstorms all over. When you have a little airplane, you don't want to try to fly through a thunderstorm, even if you have instruments because it can be too severe. So I was flying around these, and all of a sudden, I wasn't exactly sure where I was. When you are making quick turns, navigation needles have not had time to adjust exactly. So I climbed up high enough to call Salt Lake City and they vectored me into Missoula because I really wanted to avoid the weather. And after I got to Missoula, the weather cleared and I was able to fly on to Spokane. There was a period of time that I was worried. I wondered whether I should turn around and go back to Bozeman, hoping that the airport there would still be open.

How does it feel to be a woman pioneer in terms of flight?

I don't talk very much about it. I'm glad I did it, but at the time it was just something that I thought was exciting to do. I was young and adventuresome. After I graduated from college, I had experienced just one commercial flight from Omaha to Chicago. I told my father I did not want to go on a train, because I wanted to fly. I was going to Chicago, where I was going to look for a job. So I flew a United Airlines flight and the evening we flew, there was a rainbow. I have never seen a rainbow from the sky that looked so beautiful to me, even though this was almost 60 years ago. I can still see that rainbow in my mind, how beautiful it looked from the sky. I thought then, "This is something I want to do." But it didn't occur to me that I was doing something entirely different. I have had lots of people say, "Oh you were a pioneer," but I hadn't thought of it in that respect. I just wanted to do it because I liked the world from the sky. And I liked the feeling of flying a little airplane.

What did your dad say when you told him you wanted to fly?

He was very concerned, but he knew that I had somewhat of a spirit of adventure. He was quite an adventuresome soul himself. In fact, he had gone around the world himself in 1906. And so I felt like he couldn't talk. He understood this spirit of adventure, but I think he was mainly concerned about my livelihood. He didn't want anything bad to happen to me. My sister, who was just a little younger, thought it was a very foolhardy thing to do. It was something I just wanted to do so I did it.

I was old enough by the time I started flying. I was probably 22 or 23. I had graduated from the University of Nebraska. Before long, I had a job at Marshall Field and was on my own. So I wasn't hurting anyone else by doing it. It didn't occur to me that I was so much different from everybody else.

Your dad was a traveler, too. Tell me about that.

That was a wonderful thing. He had graduated from college and he had a degree in law. His father who was also a lawyer in Chicago said, "Well, maybe you should see a little of the world before you settle down." He went to Seattle and walked up and down the pier, and looked for a ship to go to the Orient. He got on a ship and he had a job. He stopped in the Philippines; they had just gotten cars in the Philippines. Because he knew how to drive a car, he stayed there a little while and taught them about cars. I always remember him talking about how the natives didn't want anything to happen to him because he knew more than they did and he was teaching them. The natives used to bring him bananas because they thought that would keep him healthy. Then he went on from there to the Orient. He played there—I think it was chess. Even though he couldn't speak the language, he got along all right because he showed them he knew how to make different chess moves. I have a record of his trip to China with pictures that he took. It is really quite remarkable because not many people were taking pictures and saving them like he did. He saw the Taj Mahal. This is one of the regrets of my life. I haven't walked the Great Wall or seen the Taj Mahal in the moonlight. But then he ended up in Europe. It took him two years to go around the world.

You don't have a lot of other regrets, do you?

No. I like Oriental art and I love textiles and I like the China silks, and so on. I used to teach textiles. I really had planned to go to China. I was all set to go about the time Nixon was president. A group planned to go over into China at that time. Since I was a woman, I was allowed to go, but then the trip didn't materialize. We could not get passports to get into the country.

Where would you be today without flight?

I'm glad I did it. I find now people are surprised if the subject of my flying happens to come up, but I really didn't know that I was doing something that a lot of people didn't do. I still think the greatest thing I ever did was raise two boys that turned out to be all right and who give something to the world, instead of taking from it. I loved my teaching. I really enjoyed teaching. I was at Eastern Washington University for over 25 years. I still am in touch with some of my students. In fact, this week I am having lunch with a number of my students. I met a lot of wonderful young people and they inspire me. I think the most rewarding thing I have done in my life is to teach and raise my children. Flying just added another little spark of interest. Also, I enjoyed travelling to other countries before they were overrun with American tourists.

You also flew to South America?

Yes, years ago I met a lady from Washington State University. She was also a member of the Ninety-Nines, which is the women's pilot group. She wanted to fly to Venezuela because she had a friend in Caracas. And she said, "I need a co-pilot." She had a beautiful Comanche. I said, "I'll go." So, I did. We started out and went to Mexico and on to Mazatlan. When we got to

476

Mazatlan, we were going south, and we could see this cloud that looked like it might be dangerous. All of a sudden, the controller came on and said, "Senorita, we advise you to turn around and land in Mazatlan." So we turned around and landed. We left the plane there. But then we flew—on a commercial carrier—to Caracas and stayed there with her friend for a few days. We went in to Angel Falls. In fact, we took a small plane that they had, and the pilot took us to this airstrip in the middle of Venezuela, which has now been developed into a tourist attraction because Angel Falls is the highest waterfall in the world. We were able to see the beautiful waterfalls and wild monkeys in the trees and parrots flying around. It was quite an experience.

Any unusual treatment you received down there, as flyers?

At the time, I always remember what Lois said when we went through customs. They waved us through without stopping us. She said, "You know we missed our golden opportunity. We could have brought in anything." But the custom officials did not believe we were flying that airplane. There were not many women pilots that flew to Mexico. This was in 1978, I believe.

Lois had said, when we go through, they are just not going to believe that we are flying this airplane. Of course, there was not room enough for anybody else to get in the plane. When we came back to Mazatlan after we had been to South America, the little boys took hold of our luggage, and we started to tell them where our plane was. They said, "Oh no, senorita. We know where the plane is. Everybody knew where the plane was that the women were flying." Lois was a tall blonde, and here I was with practically white hair. We were a strange looking pair.

Terry Rinehart
"Following a Great Tradition"

Terry Rinehart came from a flying family. Her mother is Barbara Erickson London, who flew in WWII; her father, Jack London. Rinehart received her bachelor of science degree from San Jose State in 1974. Then she went to work for United Airlines in its maintenance bay in San Francisco, doing power plant and airframe scheduling. At that point in her career, she had about 2,000 hours of flight time and was working on her airline transport rating. The fuel crisis struck about this time, and that, coupled with an overabundance of pilots and a downturn of the economy, caused Terry to seek work with United Airlines in engine and airframe maintenance. Finally, in February 1976, the moment she had waited for came. Terry became the first woman pilot for Western Airlines, flying Boeing 737s. In 1987, Delta Airlines bought out Western Airlines. She retired after 29 years and then flew as a corporate pilot. The tradition of family flight has carried on with her twin daughters, Lauren and Kelly, and son Justin, following husband Bob and Terry and Barbara's path, or "flight pattern."

What are your earliest memories of flying with your mother?

From the earliest time I can remember, my sister and I were always thrown in the back of an airplane going somewhere and doing something. It always seemed we were being transported to Grandma's house or to Palm Springs for the weekend. From as far back as I can recall, my sister and I would get in the back seat with dolls and crayons and sit there. When my mother was running the Powder Puff Derby—which she did for 20 years—my father did all the time trials on every make and model of airplane being flown in the races. As a consequence, we spent every weekend with him. My dad would go and fly each make and model airplane around the course and over the breakwater in Long Beach, and we kids would just sit in the back of the airplane and go along for the ride. Really, we were in an airplane more than we were in a car. Having my mother fly was not any different than climbing in the car and seeing my mother drive. I figured every mother flew like that.

Was there any particular or unusual flight that you remember?

No, not really. I can remember my mom turning around and saying, "Don't you want to look outside? It's a beautiful day." To that, I would reply, "No, I see it all the time." Mom would then say, "Yes, but other kids would kill to see this." I would say, "Yes, but I see it all the time." I do remember how very cavalier I was about the whole thing. The perspective from above to the earth from a couple thousand feet, which children usually do not have, seemed like the normal way to look at things to me.

Do you remember any old-time fliers from your youth?

It is funny but basically, all my mother's friends were pilots like Fran Bera and Claire Walters. In fact, my first job was at the airport working for Claire Walters at her flight school.

All these women were history makers—even at the time—but they had to make a living and because they could not fly in the military or for the airlines, they did other things. In a way, they were all very quiet and subdued about their history. I did not know for years and years and years that my mother had such a colorful history in the military because that was just something they did in the past. The women really didn't wear it on their cuff—it was just something they had done. They didn't walk around saying things like, " Well, I flew a P-51 a couple years ago." "I have a lot of time in a B-24 and a B-17." Now, it amazes me when I think of some of the airplanes my mother flew. Sometimes she flew with very little flying time in that airplane—the P-51. It was virtually just a couple hours. It was like, "Oh, this is good enough. You go out and fly the P-51 for your first time by yourself." Things like that seem phenomenal to me now.

When did you realize that you wanted to fly, and when did taking everything for granted about flying wear off?

I started flying when I was sixteen when I got home from working on the Powder Puff Derby with my mom. Claire Walters had offered me a job. She was going to start a new flight school at Long Beach and said she would give me flying lessons if I would work in the office and answer the phones, wash the airplanes, and so on. I was interested, but not ecstatic about the job. It seemed like one more thing to do. At the time I was more interested in learning how to drive a car than I was in learning how to fly an airplane. But I went to work for her and got to fly on the weekends. I got my private license, and then at nineteen, when I had my private and my commercial licenses and was still flying and didn't really know what I wanted to do career-wise, I read an article about a girl who had been hired by Scandinavian Airlines as a pilot. She was flying a 707 or a 720. I was so impressed. I was like, "Okay, well, I think I will go do that."

I didn't see anything in general aviation that really inspired me for the long term and did not want to be a flight instructor or corporate pilot for the rest of my life. Still, when I saw her get a job with the airlines, I thought, "This is something I really could do. I want to fly a big jet." In 1969, there were no female pilots at all in the United States, and there would not be for another four years. Still, nobody discouraged me; nobody said, "You cannot do it"; nobody said, "It is going to be a tough road" or anything else like that. They just said, "Okay, you have got to go to school to get your ratings and a college degree. And you will have to work really hard to do it." But nobody, including my mother or my father, said, "There are no woman airline pilots, and this is going to be an uphill battle." So that is basically how it started for me just seeing that article in the paper about this girl getting hired by Scandinavian Airlines in 1969.

Nobody disparaged you anywhere along the line?

No, nobody. I think it was subtler than that. A few of the male flight instructors along the line never thought that most women students would amount to anything, so they did not put a lot of time or effort into teaching you. It was hard to get a good instructor that thought you were going to do something with flying other than just go out and fly on Sunday afternoons. It was hard to convince some of the male instructors to take you seriously and to appreciate that you did want a career in aviation.

How did you communicate that you needed to be taken seriously?

I think I just basically was following in the footsteps of a lot of the males I was working with, because I would see these guys coming back from Vietnam and talking about airline interviews and things like that. I kept thinking that flying was something I wanted to do, but never really confided in anyone that much. I did not say to them that this was what I wanted. I was striving for the goal and was not yet qualified. I was not saying, "This is what I am going to do some day." Basically, I kept that to myself and held it in the back of my mind and just kept working towards the goal of becoming qualified and having the requirements I needed to get an interview for a job.

Was there ever a time in the preliminary that you almost gave up?

No, I don't think so. I put 100 percent into it. Though I was a normal teenager, I did a lot of other things. One time, when I was 21, I took a year off and went to Europe and Africa and traveled around. At that time, I was focused on getting the job, but I was not so unidirectional that I didn't do other things. I was not really ever discouraged. There was a time when I didn't have 20/20 vision, and I thought, "Oh my gosh! Maybe I won't make it." Then I just put that to the back of my mind and said, "I think my eyesight is good enough. I am going to keep striving on the premise that, by the time I get to the airlines, the requirements for flight will not have to be exactly 20/20." That is exactly the way it worked out.

In the mid-1970s, when I got hired, that was when the airlines had recently lowered the requirements from 20/20 to correctable 20/20. But I never really allowed myself to think that I wasn't really going to make it. When I started going through job interviews, I heard some people flat out say, "We don't interview women." In addition, I heard some people say, "We will probably never hire women." In fact, some people wouldn't even give me the interview.

Terry Rinehart

Tell me the weirdest interview that you have had?

Back in the 1970s, I basically was able to walk my application in, because my name was spelled like a man's. I was named after Terry and the Pirates. I think my parents wanted a pilot from the beginning. The name "Terry" could have been for a male or female, and most of the applications did not ask for your gender at that time, because they never considered that you might be a female. They did not think a female would even apply. In fact, if you just looked at my application, you would probably think I was a guy. I remember when I walked it in a couple of places, and they said, "We don't take applications from women." A couple of others said, "We will keep it," but I knew it was destined for the round file by the end of the day. Nonetheless, I actually got the interview with Western Airlines and the way I got it was, initially, I had walked in and said, "I want to turn in an application as a pilot." The lady at the desk thought it was so humorous that she called the secretary of the chief pilot and said, "I've got someone here that wants to turn in a pilot's application. Can I send them up?" She said, "Sure, send them up." And I showed up, and the chief pilot thought it was humorous, so he called the assistant vice-president of flight operations. Basically, these women sent me from secretary to secretary to secretary until I got right up to the top. But when I finally did get in the chief pilot's door, he said, "I'll take your application. Call me." He explained that the airline did not have any women pilots at the time—but he knew this was the wave of the future. He figured that eventually he would be hiring pilots and hiring women. Remember, this was 1973 to1974— about the time of the fuel crisis—and nobody was hiring, but I put applications in anyway. I was hired in 1976.

I stayed in close contact with the two pilots from Western Airlines for years after that. During that time, I finished up my

483

college degree, went to work for United Airlines, and got my ratings. I called them probably once a month and said, "This is what I am doing, these are the hours I have, and these are my additional ratings." When I got my job offer from United, I called my friends and said, "If I take this job with United Airlines, will Western still hire me as a pilot?" They said, "Sure! Just keep us posted on what you are doing." So there were people who were very encouraging to me throughout the process.

PSA had a training program where one could apply and they would pay for part of your training. I tried to apply and hoped they would include me in their new-hire classes. They accepted me until they found out I was a female, and then said, "We don't train female pilots to become pilots at PSA," and they turned me down. But most of the time, people were quietly accepting—and who knows what they said when they closed the door. But Western and American Airlines were both very encouraging. Both of them said, "We are going to hire women, and you are on top of the list once things start on the uphill swing." Later in the decade, I got hired in the first class that Western Airlines hired. It worked, but it was something where you had to be tenacious. As for someone applying today, the hardest part of getting the job is just convincing kids nowadays that if you put in an application, and the airlines don't hire you the first week, it doesn't mean that your career is over.

Once you were hired, you had to go through the regimen. What was the toughest thing about that?

The toughest thing was just learning what airlines were all about, since I had never been in a real crew concept before. I had been through flight engineer school, but that was different from really having the airline job. It was just overwhelming to be part of the group and to sit there in the backseat as a flight engineer. Actually, I was the G. I. B., the person in back. There were three people in the plane: the captain, the copilot, and the second officer. I thought, "I can't believe I am really in the cockpit of a big jet. I can't believe that I am really here." Even though I wasn't even flying it, I was ecstatic.

Did the guys try to test you?

Yes! They were interested in whether you were qualified or whether you were just there for show because they had to hire women. I think once the male pilots talked to us and found out our backgrounds and that we had college degrees and ratings, they gave us the respect we deserved. Obviously, none of us were from the military because there weren't any military pilots back in the early 1970s, but once they found out that we had flown equipment as big as we could get our hands on, I think they reacted positively. Most of the guys on the 737s were very young too so they were very accepting of females coming up through the ranks. Maybe had we started off on the big equipment where the older guys were—we may have found them less open.

So you are saying that you really didn't have a problem? I think your mom painted a little more difficult picture of things.

I think that every time you go to work, you have to prove yourself. That's true even now because you are flying with people who want to make sure that they are not flying with people that are not there just because of affirmative action or the fact that the company had to hire you. I think that as soon as a basic white male walks into the cockpit, it is assumed he is qualified—that he doesn't have to prove himself. As a female, I think every time you go to work, you have to prove yourself; every time you go in the simulator, you have to do a little bit better. You have to be a little sharper, and you feel like you have to try harder because people look at you more closely.

Does that get tiresome?

Yes, I think it does, from the standpoint that you know you are always being watched a little more carefully than everyone else is, but I don't think it is that unusual. It is so in other careers also. I think when people think of doctors, they automatically call it a "he." If the female is there, maybe she worked harder or people are watching her more. I think it is still unusual enough to see a female in the cockpit that people do give you a second look—even the people with whom you work.

Describe your first flight. Was that quite an experience? It must have been exciting?

Oh yes! It was thrilling. It was from Los Angeles to Las Vegas and back. It was fantastic. I can remember taxiing out to the end of the runway and looking out at other airliners going. I was thinking, "Wow, I can't imagine what it would be like to be in the cockpit of one of those big jets," and I looked down and around and looked where I was. I said, "I can't believe I am in the cockpit of a big jet. I am there, you know, and I still can't believe I am there." The guys were really great. In fact, I have the cards from the guy who flew my first flight with me, and he wrote that it was great and that we had a lot of fun. It really was a good airplane to be on as a female for the first few years of experience because Western Airlines was pro-female. There were two of us—and in the same class that got hired together.

Were you the first two for Western?

Yes, so we each had someone to go through the whole process with. We are both six-foot-tall females, so we look pretty intimidating as we walked down the hallway. We looked the part. We kidded around about the fact that we had to get into pilot class because we were too big to be flight attendants. Humor—and not taking yourself too seriously—played a big part back in that era. Back then, you did not have to be too worried about being too politically correct and laughing at the jokes and things like that; whereas nowadays, I might not be quite that easy going. I think back then—when you two were the only females out of 1,500 guys— you were basically trying to figure out how to fit in, how to be one of the boys without being a boy. You had to play it by ear in each particular case and each particular situation, but you didn't go in with a chip on your shoulders. You did not say, "I deserve to be here." I think Valerie and I both went in with the feeling that we were happy to be there, and that we were thrilled to be given the chance. We were going to try to prove that we could do the job, and yet not try to throw it up in their face. "See, I am a female, and I am here," and I think we both pulled it off pretty well, and we had a good time. A lot of that was credit to the guys that we were flying with and that they were very open to us. They were very accepting of us. These guys had never flown with females before, for the most part, unless they were civilians. They had never been with a female before because, in the military, there were not any females. On the other hand, I think they were pretty good sports, considering. I had always worked with males, so for me it was no big deal. But for them it was a huge transition.

Do you remember any unusual passenger responses to you?

Yes, I think originally it was quite a shock for the passengers. They would look in the cockpit and see me at the engineer's panel and say, "Boy, if I knew there was a woman on this flight, I would have had another drink." Or "Is it safe if she is up there?" I would say, "Yes, because they don't let me touch anything. All I do is go get coffee and answer the phone." I think a lot of it was in their nervousness and in their desire to say something to you and have some sort of interaction, but they would come up with these off-the-wall comments which sometimes would be funny and sometimes wouldn't. I think a lot of it is the idea that I can't believe that a woman knows how to do this because I couldn't do this.

I had a boy, who was probably eight years old, come up to the cockpit one time and say, "Now how did a girl learn how to do all these buttons and dials and things?" I was thinking here is a boy at eight years old, who already doesn't think women could handle this. But I think times have changed. A lot of people kid around about the fact that a woman is up there flying. They will say things like, "Well, that was a good landing. I might have known it was a woman flying." You get a lot more positive responses than you do negative responses.

Tell me about Valerie.

She was Clint Walker's, the actor's, daughter. She was very used to being in the spotlight. She is very beautiful, very articulate and very funny. She was raised originally in Los Angeles, and luckily for me got to do all the publicity and do all of the things for the company, as far as the public relations go, regarding having the first females hired. So she was great with that. She did all the pictures and all of the publicity and things for Western, and she was great at it.

488

Was there any time when you two really had to put your heads together to solve a problem?

No, because we didn't ever fly together. In fact in 25 years with the airlines I have only had another female in the cockpit in the last year. So even now as a female captain in Salt Lake City, I have probably two or three other female copilots that I would ever have the opportunity to fly with. The last year is the first time I have ever had an all-female crew. Or even had one other woman in the cockpit with me.

Tell me an unusual thing that happened while flying.

In 25 years of flying, I have had very few problems, very few incidents. The maintenance is fantastic, and I have had only one engine failure. That was when I was a copilot on a 737 with Western, and we had an engine failure on take-off out of Vancouver. The captain stopped the airplane on the runway. Fortunately, we only had 35 people on the airplane. We evacuated on the runway, and there was no problem. But in 25 years, that is the only real emergency I have had.

What is the best flying that you have ever done?

The best flying is Jackson Hole, Wyoming, flying through the mountains and flying in uncontrolled airports. That is where you have to use a lot of your skills that you learned as a basic pilot to fly—without radar or a control tower to land on a snowy runway. Flying in a snowstorm at night in Jackson Hole is probably some of the most challenging flying I have had to do with the airlines.

Just flying into Jackson Hole with the 13,000 foot Grand Teton Mountains on one side and flying down a valley to land on a runway at 6,000 feet elevation in a snowstorm is not easy. Basically, when you do things like that everything has to be right.

What do your mom and you talk about? Obviously, you have been close all along right, but you must be even closer through your flying.

Yes, I think in a lot of ways, she lives vicariously through me because this is the kind of flying she would enjoy doing that she will never have a chance to do. She cannot totally relate to it, but she knows that she would be good at it and is fascinated with the process and is happy for me that I made it. She is always thrilled about my experiences and what I am doing and where I am going. She is also thrilled to hear that I am flying with a female copilot and wants to hear how much fun we have together. In the same vein, I love to hear about her flying and airplanes. I will never even be able to sit in the cockpit, much less be able to fly the airplanes she did. I think of the experiences that she had and the opportunities that she had and the abilities that she had—with very little training—to climb into a multi-engine aircraft and fly across the country by herself. She was able to fly fighter airplanes, so in a sense, I think we are both envious of each other. And we are both proud of what we did in life, but we are envious of each other.

That is an interesting dynamic isn't it?

Yes, it is because we sort of have a reversal of roles in some ways, and we can live a little bit vicariously through each other. I think that she is extremely proud of me and lives a little bit through my joy of my job, and as I look at her and realize how proud she is of what she did, I am more than a little bit proud to be her daughter.

When did you first realize that she was as proud as she is?

I think that she has always been really proud of me. In fact, I think she has probably been my biggest supporter. She never once said, "Terry, this is going to be hard. You may have some people out there who think that you are not able to do this or that you are not qualified." She never once gave me any words or discouragement or even said anything that might be construed as "This may not work for you." It was always encouraging words and confidence that I can do this. She always said, "Don't give up; don't get hung up on little discouraging things. Just keep the goal in mind and keep focused, and eventually all will work out." She has always been a very steady, confident force behind me, pushing me and supporting me. I can remember calling her a lot and saying, "I don't know if I can do this," "I don't know if this is gonna work," or "I don't know if anybody is ever gonna give me a job," and she would say, "Don't worry. It will all work out." I think I have always known that she is really proud of me. It is probably part of the reason I kept flying and started flying at such a young age because I did get the ego boost that a lot of teenagers don't get because I was doing some things that were different such as flying airplanes. Certainly, nobody else in my high school was flying airplanes.

Did you get unusual responses from your classmates?

Yes, I did from a lot of the kids who knew, when I was a senior in high school, that I was flying airplanes. A lot of them knew that, on the days I did not show up for school, I was probably out flying and playing hooky. In my senior year I think I did that a lot because I was ready to move on to college and to other things. I was excited about getting out there and being

491

with an older, more adventurous age group than the kids I was with in school.

When you're flying around, do you ever get a little emotional and start thinking, "Boy, maybe I wouldn't be here without the work of my mom and others like her"?

Oh, yes, I do. I look at the airplanes, and I think if I was just a kid growing up in Kansas, would I have looked up at an airplane and said, "Gee! This is really something I want to do." I think I am fascinated with airplanes. I can look up at a rocket and say, "I am fascinated with this," but I don't know if I would have had the same tenacity or the same interest or the same beliefs if I had not had the leadership of my parents. I think I owe all of that to my parents and my parents' encouragement and my parents' belief.

So then they're optimists, basically?

Yeah, I think that is exactly right.

And you're an optimist?

Yes, I am. I think that I am because I think that you can do anything that you want to do, and it's a crime to limit a kid's enthusiasm or say, "You can't do this." Don't spoil their dreams, because who knows? If someone had told me when I first wanted to be an airline pilot, that there aren't any women airline pilots, or if they had said that my vision was not 20/20 so that I'd never make it, I would have said, "Oh, okay, I guess I will do something else like be a dentist." I never did say that, and it all worked out. So lucky for me, the timing was perfect. It all came together.

Describe the beauty of flying, the great thing about the beauty.

Actually, the most beautiful thing for me is flying at dawn when the sun comes up and it is calm and it is clear and there is no turbulence and it is just smooth when I start off my early-morning flying, I think it is the most beautiful and serene time for me. I would much rather fly early in the morning with the airlines in my own airplane anytime and watch the sun come up and just start the day like that. It is a good way to start the day.

Maybelle Fletcher
"Entrepreneur, Educator, Pioneer"

Maybelle at Eastern Shore Air Service, Paisley, Virginia

When Maybelle Fletcher graduated from high school at sixteen, she convinced her mother and dad to stop at an airfield and let her take a short flight. An elderly barnstormer took her up and once she got above the clouds, she found the experience had hooked her. "It was so beautiful. I felt like opening the door and walking out into the snow." The year was 1941. From there she worked at Richland Air Field in exchange for treasured flying lessons.

Since then, Maybelle Fletcher has distinguished herself in many ways—as a female flight pioneer, a business entrepreneur, an air racer, and flight educator. She has flown an amazing number of airplanes, over 170 and amassed more than 30,000 hours of flying. She was one of the earliest female flight examiners for the FAA.

Maybelle helped start the Southwest Flying Club in 1962, one of the nation's oldest such organizations. And in 1962, she began Fletcher Aviation, Inc. in Sugarland, later moving it to Hobby Airport. She had begun a flight school as early as 1945. Maybelle received the Lloyd P. Nolan Lifetime Achievement Award.

This wonder of the air and land passed on October 16, 2016.

At the time of the interview, I was curious about that first wide-eyed flight she had described before the recorder was set and was curious about the barnstormer who took her up.

Where was the barnstormer from?

He was in Waco, Texas. They had a little grass strip just right outside of Waco, and he would fly and land at different fields— not even an airport—and take people up for a ride. That's where he was raised, in Waco. He took me up in a little old two-seater. When we came back down, I wanted to learn to fly. I couldn't get anyone to teach me. Nobody wanted to teach a 16-year-old girl to fly. Finally, I got an instructor to fly with me.

How long did that take?

I had five brothers and one sister, and they thought I was crazy. They said, "You shouldn't fly; you'll kill yourself." But, I guess I could talk my way into anything. I wanted to buy an airplane, so my dad helped me with the purchase.

I saw an ad in the paper for a plane, and the guy brought it down from Ohio to me and I paid him. The instructor and I got in it and we took off. At least we tried to take off. We got just above the ground and could hardly make it around the pattern to land. It needed a new engine. I had offered to fly the guy that I purchased the plane from back, but he said that he'd just catch an airline back.

So, anyway, during the war it was hard to get parts to fix the engine. There was an Air Force base there in Waco, and I had friends there. I had one guy who was a mechanic who was working on my plane part time, but it took about a couple of years to get it repaired and everything.

So, in the meantime, I went to New York, with a friend of mine, whose husband was there. At the time we were working at the Southwestern Bell Telephone Company. So my mother and dad had let me transfer up with this older lady. Otherwise they wouldn't have let me. We decided we didn't like Southwestern Bell, so we went to work for U.S. Hoffman and Steel Company making parts for airplanes. I became a supervisor there, and I repaired machines—lathes, and things like that, and kept everything going.

Did any unusual things happen in that defense job?

It was mostly women in these shops. Some of the 4Fs (people who couldn't qualify physically) were in there. They had a few of those there.

Were there any unusual happenings? How did the 4Fs and the women get along?

Fine. I was 18 and I was supervisor of one whole shift. I had men and women under me. They were really girls. I was supervisor in the afternoon and evening shift.

That's a lot of responsibility for an 18-year-old girl, isn't it?

Yes, it was. We had the studs that we were making for airplanes that had to be run on these lathes. When the lathes would start cutting them wrong so they wouldn't pass inspection, I would fix the machine and get it started again. I had to x-ray all of them.

I stayed there for a year. Then I decided at Christmas that I was going back home. I had known this instructor before I moved to New York. The instructor and I rented an airplane on the way home and he soloed me. That's when I really started flying.

When I started home, they had the biggest snowstorm they'd had in years. It took me some time. We couldn't go anywhere on the highway so we stayed at a farmhouse. There were about 20 of us. After that, I finally got to Texas. That's when I started flying. I got a job in this flight office. I talked two guys on this flight crew into letting me work in the office and learn to fly. So I worked in the office and learned to fly. In the meantime, I sold my airplane.

Did you make any money on it?

No, I just wanted to get rid of it.

What kind was it?

It was a little Aeronica C-3—Aeronica Champ. Anyway, I worked and got my pilot's license. That was in 1944. I was still working for that school. I was the only girl that was flying. I built up my time there, got my license.

I met my husband at the Air Force base there. He came out to the airport when he had time off, and he and I would get in the airplane and go fly. I guess it was in about two weeks that he asked me to marry him. He said he had enough money to buy me a real big ring or a little airplane. I told him I'd take the airplane and that he could tie a string around my finger. So we got married. He didn't buy me a ring but on our honeymoon we bought a little J-3 Cub. I think we bought it in Ohio on the way to Niagara Falls in 1945. We got to Virginia and started our first flight school.

Where?

It's on the peninsula—Akamack County and Singatig. They have a big naval base at Singatig. They use to have wild horses on Estig Island, and the horses would swim across to Singatig. I use to fly these photographers that would come down from Baltimore, Philadelphia, or New York to take pictures of the horses. I'd fly in, land in a little field, and they'd go over and take pictures. Then I'd pick them up.

Any strange things happen when you were doing that—anything unusual?

Yes. We were flying along and had just taken off from a little field and one of the photographers lit up a cigarette. We were in a Taylorcraft—a fabric airplane. He's smoking and all of a sudden he looks down. I asked him what he was looking for, and he said he'd dropped his cigarette. It didn't take me long to get that plane on the ground. He couldn't find that lighted cigarette, and I could just see us up in flames, because that plane would burn. I landed in a field and told him we are going to sit here and wait until we knew that cigarette is out. We never could find it. So finally, after a long time, we took off. That was the last time anybody ever smoked in an airplane with me. A scary deal.

Were the horses beautiful down there? Tell me about it—
how close did you fly and was there anything unusual that
you saw?

We flew within about 200 feet of them. We'd fly around
and watch them come over.

You mentioned, before we got started, a book called Misty.

Yes, there was a pony named that over there. She was kept
in a pen, and someone wrote a book on her. One time I got a
piece of her mane for my little girl. When it was show-and-tell
at school, my little girl brought a piece of her hair. Everybody
was excited about that because Misty was a very famous pony.

How did you get the hair?

She was there in the pen, and the little pony wasn't real wild.
I got my instructor rating in 1947. Sometimes when I didn't have
a babysitter, I made my daughter a little bed in the plane. Later,
after she was 28 days old, she started flying with me every day
in the baggage compartment.

Finally, when she was not quite two, she went on all the
instructional flights, because I didn't have anybody to leave her
with. After awhile, she had listened to me instructing for about
200 hours. One day I was going to solo a student I had trained,
and she noticed that I wasn't saying anything to this student. We
were about 15 feet off the ground, and she said, in her little baby
voice, "Get your nose up, get your nose up!" She said it at exactly
the right time—she'd heard me say that so many times. Later we
landed and we both came unglued. The student came unglued
and he looked over and said, "I quit. When I have a two-year-old

telling me how to land this airplane, it's time for me to quit." I explained to my little girl, Sandy, that she had to stop telling us what to do. I told her when we went up again not to say anything when we started to land. We went up again and he landed. Then we got out, stood over at the side of the runway, and watched him land again, and she said, "That's good!"

I probably would have soloed her in an Air Coupe when she was eight years old. The air coupes don't have rudders. All you have is a steering wheel. She would sit in my lap. Before that, she could sit in the back seat, and she'd taxi. She'd taxi about the same rate that she should. After I ran it up and turned it onto the runway, she'd put that throttle all the way through. That's when she was two years old—sitting in the back with real high cushions. So when I put her in my lap in the Air Coupe—there are no rudders at all—I told her that if she wanted to go to the beach and land, we'd go. I'd put the throttle in and she'd steer it right straight down the runway. She'd get to a spot and she'd come back on that wheel and we'd go. She'd take off, and I'd say, "Let's go to the beach," and she'd turn that airplane and go straight to that beach.

Does your daughter fly now?

No, what happened is that she got mad at me one day. I was getting in the airplane, and she threw a fit. She wanted in the front seat because that is where all the pilots flew. She knew. I told her, no, that she had to stay in the back seat. She just threw a temper tantrum. I gave in and told her okay. She got in the front seat and I got in the back seat. We went out—she was taxiing out and I gave it full power, started off, climbed up—and she came unglued. She could not see her mom and felt as though she were by herself. She started jumping over the seat and into my lap.

We were six feet off the ground. I let her come on back in my lap and we went on around and landed. It scared her. Something happened there. She's soloed and everything but since then she's gotten involved in other things such as music. I didn't push her, but she didn't care about flying anymore.

So, you didn't worry about taking her up—was that kind of daring—were you ever afraid the plane might crash?

Oh no. No. No. I've had props come off before. I flew the Powder Puff Derby for years.

Tell me one of your favorite Powder Puff Derby stories.

I forgot what year it was, but we were racing from California to Michigan. I was in a Z10. My co-pilot's husband owned the Z10, and she had a brand-new private license. She was doing the time aspect. Finally, I knew the airplane needed a paint job and a lot of work on it to make it go faster. So that year they painted the airplane, and I would have been in the top 10, I know, but something happened.

We had crossed the mountains and were about four minutes out of Oklahoma City. I had told my co-pilot that we should take a ground-speed check. She took it, and we were doing fine. I commented, "That's great." About that time, it was like a shotgun going off in the front cockpit. All of a sudden, there was oil all over the windshield and the engine quit. In Oklahoma, there are a lot of wheat fields, so I wasn't worried about a flat place for landing. I didn't know whether I'd hit something or not because I couldn't see out the front. I traded air space for altitude. We were going about 200 miles an hour, so you can climb it up until you get to approach speed and level off. I did that.

After putting the gear down, I turned back to look for a field underneath me to put it down. The split second that it happened, I got the gear down. My co-pilot had a little space on the right- hand side where she could look out, and she said, "Maybelle, we don't have a prop!" I said, "Okay, we can't start it, can we?!" That's when I planned what to do next. So when I banked, I saw about three miles on my side. It was then I knew where I was going to land. So, I landed. I didn't have enough altitude to go around and land in the wind, so I had to land downwind. Yet, I wasn't as low as I wanted to be. So I was making these big wingovers and such, getting it down.

I was looking out the side and my co-pilot could look far enough out, too. I asked her how much room I had left, and she told me she saw the end coming up. About that time, I could feel the wheels touch. There was a sigh of relief. I went down and turned it off the runway and faced back into the wind. So we got out and I told her to punch that clock because this was going to be a bigger problem than what we could fix, before we could continue. We were both almost in tears because of this. We got out and went around the front of the airplane and we were standing there looking. What happened was that one blade left, and the instant it left, the crankshaft broke and the hub and the other blade left. It just took a second. I didn't have any vibration at all. It was just like a shotgun. I was standing there and two men came racing down the runway. I knew I was going to have to explain why I landed downwind. They came up behind me and they said, "What in the world is wrong?" I said, "Well, I lost my rubber band out here." One guy didn't say anything and he came around the front and said, "She doesn't have a prop on this airplane." And I said, "Yes, I lost it just south of here. That's why I landed downwind, and if you all wanted to know why I landed downwind, I didn't have enough altitude to go around and land into the wind."

The men got a tow truck and pulled it up to the hanger. Then they opened the cowling and said, "Hey, come here, I want to show you something." There was not even one motor mount attached to that engine. The second it came off — you have four motor mounts attached to hold the engine on the airplane—all that was attached to the engine was the electrical wires. It was just lying on the nose gear. To think that I was up there trying to do wingovers. If the wingovers weren't coordinated real easy, the motor would have dropped off and I wouldn't be here. Anyway, there wasn't anything hurt, except where the blade had dented the nose and popped some rivets in the cowling underneath the engine. Then the accident had resulted in a big oil streak over the left wing, but it didn't touch my wing. The next year the guys asked me if I was going to fly that plane and I said, "Yes, you only lose a prop once in a lifetime." So I wasn't worried about it in the least.

So, you're not superstitious?

No, but the second time, the next year we flew it, I was coming back from the race and my co-pilot that was with me (it was the same airplane—it took a year to get it ready, overhauled, etc) was sitting in the back seat. We were going west and the temperature outside was hot. I looked over at my manifold pressure and it wasn't up very much. Of course, I had it pulled back. I eased the throttle forward and my manifold pressure didn't do anything. It didn't go up. It should have gone up. You have a high manifold pressure when you have full power. I started looking for a place to land. I don't care if you're flying instrument or VFR. I didn't have that one section there. I knew where I was going through. I had just called for the weather in Mississippi. The state had thunderstorms all around, and I knew I was going around the thunderstorms and that they were moving east. It was raining like mad over McComb Airport. I didn't have a sectional and I didn't have any other way of trying to find these little airports. I told my co-pilot that I thought we were going to have a little problem. She jumped up in the front seat and started looking. I said, "Don't look—I've been looking for a place to land and there's nothing but trees and I think something's wrong. We may have to land in the top of the trees, I don't know." I started easing over in the rain and finally I made out McComb Airport.

I was going on the downward leg, and I smelled gas. I thought maybe it was my imagination. About that time, my co-pilot looked over and said, "Maybelle, do you smell gas?" I said, "No, we don't!" I didn't have a lot of power and, by that time I'd gone down and landed, I thought I heard a swishing sound, like shhshhhshhh. I looked and saw gas was pouring out underneath the engine. We got out of the plane fast. Two mechanics that were working there started shaking their heads.

What happened is the brace to the alternator, which is right in front of the pilot, broke and the alternator fell down and severed my main gas line. It was like a hose had broken and sprayed over that hot engine. They said they'd known one other Z10 to do that, and the pilots weren't as lucky. It might have ignited. So that was the last time I flew that airplane.

So, did that kind of make you superstitious of that airplane?

As for that airplane—I said good-bye!

Did you junk it—or what did you do?

No. They got the brace to the alternator fixed and the hose

(I've got the little hose that came off in my scrapbook), but I said I really had had enough. Finally, they said it was safe to fly to Houston. I got in it, flew it back, and said, "You can have it, here are the keys!"

You taught Army cadets.

I was teaching the cadets how to fly in Waco in 1950. It was real hard for them to get a girl to teach them to fly. You know—macho!

Give me an example of that—give me a story.

Even when we started flying school in 1945 and I had my instructor rating there, it was hard to get somebody to fly with me because they hadn't seen any girls fly. They'd come out on Sunday afternoon just to see if I was going to fly. I could get anybody to go with Larry, of course. One guy said, "Maybelle, I'm going to fly with you." I realized I had to really prove myself a better instructor or make him think I'm a better instructor than Larry. I really put out all effort to teach this guy. Andy, this guy, told people that if they wanted to learn to fly that I was a great teacher. That's what started it.

Explain that further.

This lieutenant came and said he was going to fly with me. I said, "Good, what's your problem?" He said, "I can't land the darn thing!" I told him, "Well, that's easy." He said, if I could show him how to land the airplane, that I would have a lot of students. I went out there and told him to do exactly what I said. At the time, the planes were all taildraggers. I had a talk with him before and told him what to do in landing the airplane and the configuration, etc. I said, "Just do it!" He went in, landed that thing, and said, "I'll be damned." I told him to go on around and do the same thing, and he went around and did it again and again and again. Finally, he landed and said, "Gosh, if you want to pass your 21 check, you better get with her." At that time the instructors were teaching them to get the stick all the way back. Unfortunately, every time they did that, they'd have to go around—they couldn't do it. After that, it broke the ice, and I stayed in the airplane eight hours a day. I never got out of it—someone would bring me a sandwich. At the end of the day, I was exhausted. Still, every one of them passed their 21-hour check with flying colors.

Did you ever have one come back to you and thank you and say that they couldn't have done it without you?

The lieutenant I thought left, and then came back later, was curator of the Army museum in Ft. Rucker, Alabama. I got a letter from him one day and about forty years later. When I instructed him, he was about 20. He saw my picture in the Trade-A-Plane publication. He said, "Well I'll be." He never did know where I was, so I got this letter from him and a picture of us together. He said, "Maybelle, I don't think you remember me but here are some pictures. You taught me to fly back in 1950 and I just found out where you were by the picture in one publication." I have letters from all over the country from students.

Did you also hear from commercial pilots?

Yes, from all the people that I taught to fly years ago. That was great. I've enjoyed that so much. Sometimes I would go apply for a job and the company would take my resume. Back then the students that I'd taught would get the job over me. Here I had many hours of instruction and he's just a brand-new pilot—commercial instrument, etcetera —and he got the job. So that's the way it went for years.

So your students were getting the job over you, even though you taught them to fly?

Oh yes, yes.

Can you give me a specific example or any particular job you applied for?

I went into one office and applied for a corporate flying job. I had a nice interview, and the person I interviewed said he'd keep it and call me back if he can use me. I said, "Okay thanks." I went out the door and I stood for a little while. Then I went back in. He said, "Oh hi." I said, "I just wanted to see you throw that application in the trash can!" He said, "Oh, no—no!" I knew what he was going to do with it. This went on for a long time. Right now it's wide open for women, and it's good to be a women now.

From Waco, I moved to Houston in 1956. When I came back to Houston, I started a flying club, which I just got a notice it is the oldest flying club in the state of Texas and is still active. We were just a small operation then. Right now I'm in three large hangars, which are about 150,000 square feet. I have hangars for storage and for jets. Now I have a large flight school, which is approved for VA. I have a new college contract. Also, I have Japanese and Korean students coming over to learn to fly.

Explain the different air spaces.

In the sky, there are designated air spaces. You've got A, B, C, D and E. So you have different air spaces for different kinds of airports. Your busiest airports are the ones where all the airlines are going in and out. Then you have another little airport that's out of the air space. It's a C air space. It just has a tower and that's all. The B airspace you have to get clearance to get into that air space, and you don't violate it. If you do violate it, you could be fined or something like that. Of course, with radar, they can tell you where you are.

Habey Airport was in a C air space and they were going to make it a B air space but everybody didn't like it. One day my tower chief said, "Maybelle, why don't you do something about it?" I said, "What can I do?" He said, "Well, just quit bitchin' and forget it then, if you don't want to try to change it." I said, "Well, how can I change it?" He said, "Write up the air space and present the proposal to the folks in Washington."

I decided to start drawing an airspace plan up for Habey Airport, which took me about three months. I'd get up in the middle of the night and think of what I wanted to include. Then I got an ad hoc committee together to meet with the FAA. I called the FAA together—the local and Oklahoma—and presented my plan. I told them that there were nine flight schools on Habey at that time. I also told them that the city wanted their rent every month. I said that, if we have to fly 50 miles out from the airport, we won't get business, because people won't come here, because they are going to spend a lot more money to go to outlying airports. I said I think this plan I am proposing would work for everybody. So they took it and sent it to Washington and everything.

In the meantime, the guy that works for Boeing down at

Nassau wrote his senator and said that he didn't think Habey Airport needed the air space. The senator wrote to Washington about it and told them that people here didn't want this air space. The senator got a letter back and said we have an air space drawn up by Maybelle Fletcher from Houston that we are looking at. Low and behold, they took my air space plan and it's on the charts now. Later, I told the tower chief, "Thank you. If it wasn't for you, I wouldn't have done it." So I wanted to give him the credit. Sometimes you say something and people listen—in the government.

What's the greatest compliment you've ever received, in terms of flying?

People that come back and say really how much I taught them and how they appreciate me. That's what I get a joy out of. They come up and say, "You remember me? You gave me a check ride in 1979 or something like that. I'll always remember something you told me." I'll say, "Oh what did I tell you?" That's really a good feeling to know that they have remembered things I've taught them for years and years and years.

Did you have a saying for anything you really hit on harder than most people do?

I always tell students that they have to know their limitations, know the airplane's limitations, and use common sense and good judgment. Flying is two things—it's using common sense and using good judgment. If you follow these two things you'll live to be an old pilot.

You've lived to be a medium-old pilot!

An old pilot!

Well, late middle-aged!

Middle-aged, are you kidding?

I'm just teasing—late middle-aged. I'm being nice!

Yes, you are. Thanks! I made my first sky-dive a year and a half ago. It was wonderful. My daughter and my granddaughter decided to give me that for a birthday present.

Tell me about skydiving.

My granddaughter went skydiving first. No one knew she did it, so she came back and said, "Let's give Nanna a birthday present. Let's give her a skydive." My daughter said, "I think you better ask Mother first!" So they had to ask me first and I said, "Sure, I don't turn down any birthday presents!" So we got in the King Air and we were going up to 15,000 feet and at about 8,000, I said to my instructor, "You know, this is kind of stupid." At about 12,000 I said, "You know, this is getting stupider!" We got up to 15,000 and I said, "This is downright stupid—stupid— let's go!" We jumped at 15,000 and it was great. I don't like to free-fall. We free-fell for 10,000 feet and then opened the chute at 5,000. Of course, it was beautiful. I didn't even want to land. The photographer went out first and came up right to my face and said, "Put your hands out." I was afraid they'd break off if I put them out. He took pictures all the way down and we went on down and landed and he took a picture of me coming in. You come in so slowly and you land softly. It's not anything like I thought it would be. I thought it would be kind of a hard landing like jumping off a 10-foot building. I didn't even feel it.

How old were you at the time?

It was on my 75th birthday. George Bush and I are about the same age.

Yes, I recall he did a jump.

He says he's going to jump on his 80th birthday. I'll think I'll call him and see if he's going to jump on his 80th birthday and if he is, I'll tell him I'd like to jump with him. Usually pilots don't jump.

What insights did you gain about the air? Did you have a little different insight from having jumped?

It's very different. Flying has been my life—my goal and love. It's been almost 24 hours a day, since I was 16 years of age. I'm more involved as I get older. Jumping out is such a free feeling. Someone asked me, "What if your chute doesn't open?" I said, "Look at it this way, I enjoyed everything and I've done just about everything I want to do." I haven't done everything—there are still things I'd like to do or accomplish, but I was born too early. Parachuting is a sensation you'll always remember. It's like, when your chute opens, you feel like a bird. You can control your chute—whereever you want to go. It's just great. I can understand why a lot of people parachute.

You said you were born too early. What would you do if you were born 25 years ago?

I've got friends who are retired airline pilots I had years ago. They're not working and they're enjoying life and making good money and everything like that. After not seeing them for years, I've had them come in and say they've been retired for so many years. They've been with that airline and they're traveling and doing their thing. I say, "I taught you how to fly and I could be doing that now."

As the years went by, more women started flying and more women started getting their instructor ratings. Things are different for women now. I've got about 10 instructors that fly and a lot of them get about 100 hours a month. If an instructor gets about 1,000 hours or less and they get 200 hours of multi-engine, they're hired with the airlines.

I should say I am the worst airline passenger. As I was flying the last few weeks, I went to St. Paul and Minneapolis. I said, Oh Lord—he was making a very bad approach. I could tell what kind of landing he was going to make from the way the airplane was being handled. He had the most unstable approach I've ever ridden through. When we landed and stopped, I relaxed and said, "Good Lord, let me out of here." The pilot was standing at the door when we were getting off and I looked at him and I said, "You had quite a bit of wind there, didn't you?" He said, "Yes."

Kimberly Olson
"From Refueling to Iraq"

Colonel Kimberly (Kim) Olson served as Commander of the KC-135R, 96th Air Refueling Squadron of the 92nd Air Refueling Wing, Fairchild Air Force Base near Spokane, Washington. She was, at the time, one of but eight female flying squadron commanders in the United States Air Force. Now, years later, this illustrious and talented woman has expanded her resume.

Colonel. Olson entered the Air Force as a second lieutenant through Officer Training School, Lackland AFB, in November 1979. Her degrees include a B.S. in Physical Education and Health from Ohio State University an M.A. in Business Administration and Management from Webster University and an M.A. in National Security and Strategic Studies from the Naval War College.

Assigned as a KC-135 pilot to March AFB, she saw her crew receive "Crew of the Year, Strategic Air" in *Command Safety Magazine,* 1982. She has served as assistant flight commander,

T-38 instructor pilot at Williams and Randolph Air Force Bases. She was selected to Air Force Headquarters, Pentagon in Operations and Plans as an Air Staff Training Officer, then returned to the KC-135 as standardization/evaluation pilot and flight commander at Dyess AFB. She was handpicked as an initial cadre instructor pilot flying the T-1A trainer aircraft and served as flight examiner, flight commander, and supervisor of flying at Reese AFB.

Colonel Olson has served on the Board of Directors for the Women Military Aviators. She is also a member of the Airlift/Tanker Association, the Air Force Association, Order of Dandelions and the Women in Military Service for the American Memorial Foundation. Married to Kent Olson, a pilot for Northwest Airlines, they have two children, Keegan and Katelynn.

Colonel Olson is tall and somewhat imposing, but I found her easy, open manner and humor disarming. Throughout the interview, she broke her staccato speech patterns for a good laugh. She seems not at all reticent to relate her philosophy and ideas, and as she speaks, a clear intelligence and a precise direction stand out. Now retired, she lectures on educational issues, political strategy, and leadership. In her book, *Iraq & Back: War to Win the Peace*, Colonel Olson lends insight into the Middle East conflicts.

Colonel Olson founded Grace After Fire, a Fort Worth organization offering assistance to female veterans, and it has helped countless women gain self knowledge and self renewal.

What were you earliest thoughts of flight?

I tell this story and people look at me weird, but when I was a young child in Iowa, I was on my grandparents' farm. I remember lying on the grass, looking skyward. And as I did, I saw the contrails and told my mother that I'd like to be a pilot someday. I said the contrails looked like ribbons. It's funny how things come back. Some thirty years later, my daughter, Katelynn, was in the backyard looking skyward. The sun was setting and there were pink contrails. Katelynn said to my husband, "Look, there's Mommy!" And my husband said, "How do you know it's Mommy?" "Because she told me she'd leave ribbons in the sky for me."

Speaking of ribbons, how would you like to be remembered?

You give this a lot of thought when younger. At that time, you have grandiose ideas of records, but I'd like to be remembered not by the things that I have accomplished, but I'd like to be remembered by people. It's nice that I'm the first female in a lot of things, but that's not how I want to be remembered. I want to be remembered because someone thought I was a good boss, or someone who helped at the time they needed it, that I cared for their families. Maybe I said something that inspired them to go on and do good things in life. Maybe it's egotistical, but I would want to be remembered because I made a difference in someone's life. You want to make a difference that you were here in this squadron, at this time, in the service of the United States Air Force. You want to feel that in these turbulent times for the service that people like me have made a difference and have made it easier for the troops—and for my boss, because obviously I serve someone higher.

What do you think guys can learn from you, a woman?

That's tricky. Obviously growing up in a male-dominated area, I have found that a lot of woman made the mistake—as I did in my youth—of trying to be a guy. I'm doing a guy's job at the time, sitting in guy's clothes, so I tried to become a guy. Not that I tried to become a man, but I was trying to act like a guy to fit in. A lot of woman did that that were first, like myself. When you get a little older, you get a little more secure and you get a little more reputable in your flying skills. At that point, you begin to see that you don't have to act like a guy, that you can be a female and still fit in. Finally, you understand that there are things that you bring to the table that are unequally ingrained in women. I think that's why men and women are such great teams, because they have complementary skills.

What I bring to the table, I think, is that women are great communicators—some men would say too much, but that's okay because people usually know where they stand with you. A lot of people will hold knowledge because it's power in some people's eyes. "These are the cards." I lay them right on the table, and we'll deal with it as we see fit. I think women tend to do it anyway. When we are growing up, we are always working for something bigger than ourselves. Men are more focused on the individual. Again, these are just leadership styles. I have no trouble telling people what to do—you can ask my troops.

Another thing is that woman tend to be good cheerleaders. I don't mean in the sense of the football team cheerleader. What I mean is that, we are quick to praise and slow to criticize—I have found. These qualities work very well for me. I am my squadron's cheerleader. I am the person who says, "Go team; things are great; you're doing a great job." That is what women do.

How important is it to show competence out there flying?

I have and in years past, I have worried about it. I could never have a bad landing. I could never not make the approach.

There was tremendous pressure to not just be good at flying an airplane, but to be very good. I mean, you had to be outstanding, because if you weren't, the rumor would be that she's weak. You couldn't be average. I found that out. You were in one of two categories: you were good or you were bad. There's no mediocrity with women aviators because the guys wouldn't let us.

Ever embarrass yourself?

Oh heavens, yes. The first time I was back here for my first night landing—I'd been out of the airframe for five years, I just blew a landing. I didn't scare anyone, but I was the Operations Officer and I had this bad landing. I thought, "Oh, great! I'll never live this down." But I think as you accumulate rank and have more flying time, you don't worry about that sort of thing. I'm a senior pilot, a command pilot, so I don't worry about proving myself as a pilot anymore. The Air Force didn't hire me to be a pilot; they hired me to be a commander. So I take my energies and focus them on that. I'm a very competent pilot and a very good instructor, I think, and I've had experience in four separate airframes (aircraft). I began in a KC-135 as a copilot. Then I went on to T-38 as an instructor pilot—one of the first women to come back and fly the T-38. From there I went to Randolph and taught on the T-38 as an instructor of the instructors. Then from there I came back to the KC-130, upgraded all the way to evaluator pilot in the A model, then to an initial cadre instructor pilot in the AF's newest trainer aircraft the T-1A, Jayhawk.

Talk about the hardest teaching.

Probably it was the T-38. Here I had the most difficult students. Most of the students are six-month lieutenants who have just entered the flying world, and the program is pretty tight. You have to accomplish a lot of things in a short period of time.

Tell me how that female intuition has manifested itself in your flight teaching.

That's a good question. I think what happens in UPT (Undergraduate Pilot Training) is that if they find out that you're a good instructor, you get very challenging students, the students really struggling to get through UPT, trying to earn their wings. For about two years I had only the students who were having trouble. My focus was, "What student was the worst of the bunch?" You always worked hard, but you were always ready because they were going to do something stupid.

For example, one day we were flying the T-38. We were practicing an approach where the procedure involved a heavyweight single-engine. As you got to the overrun, you were supposed to drop your flaps full to help you stop. As we come in over the overrun, the student takes the flaps and puts them to zero, which puts us 20 knots below stall speed. Of course, the T-38 was not a very forgiving jet when it came to those type of things. She began to fall out of the sky. Of course, I was just yelling at this guy, "You idiot." So I put the one engine in burner and reached back to the other one and slammed it into burner. I came back to get the flaps to drop them, so as to get some lift on the wings, because we were literally falling out of the sky.

If I'd have helped on the stick, we'd probably fallen and would have had to eject, because we were stalling. She was coming down. "Please make the overrun. Please make the overrun," I was thinking. I was worried we were going to catch the fence. The whole time I'm doing this, I'm yelling at this guy because your adrenaline is pumping. We make the overrun, but the dust and dirt are flying all over the place. The guys in the airfield control tower are screaming, "Go around. Go around." And I'm thinking, "What do they think I'm doing?" So we hit and it's just one big dust ball and out of the dust ball, we come. The burners light just about the time we hit and the plane just comes out like a bat out of hell. I've got the plane standing on its tail, so I request and pull close. And I'm just cussing at this guy; my mouth didn't stop the whole time.

We pulled close, the landing gear came down and we landed full stop. I chopped the jet, and then filled out the forms. Then I just threw the forms into the cockpit. This kid is just sitting there in the cockpit, and he won't get out. "Get out of the jet," I say. So he kind of gingerly gets out of the jet. He still has his helmet on, and his G-suit, and he's all hooked up. Normally, we don't do that. We take our helmets and G-suits off. We'd carry them because it was so hot. So he promptly gets on the bus and is sitting there with his helmet on still. Finally, I got calmed down. Later that night, this same kid is telling the boys at the bar whom my husband knows, that he kept the helmet on because he thought I was going to beat the hell out of him. This student actually thought I was going to pound him into the dirt, which of course I never did. You didn't hit students, even if you did yell at them.

What year was that?

That was about 1984. That was in the years when you were tough on students.

Are you and this guy still friends?

Oh, yeah. We still laugh about that.

519

Ever have a circumstance where you felt you were too tough?

I think I was the kind of instructor where you have a hard shell, but a soft underside. I was given these students, who were very difficult, but I never washed out one; I never lost a student. I used to have a little clipping in my office. It was a picture of a squirrel skiing. Printed underneath it said, "If they can teach a squirrel to ski, I can teach you to fly." It was sort of an ego thing. Once you were assigned to me, you graduated. That's the deal.

One time I was training in the T-1A, I barked at this female and made her cry. I was with two students at the time, so I kicked the guy out of my office. Then I turned to the female and I said, "You want to fly in that man's Air Force? If so, you had better learn when to cry and where not to cry. I know how you are as gals. Sometimes it is a release because you're so angry. It's not that you're sad or a wimp, but it's a release. But here's your trick of the trade: you go to the bathroom and you clear away those tears. Don't ever cry in front of me again." She never did. I was kind of hard on her because she was so young and it was a lesson she needed to learn early and survive.

Anybody that came back to thank you for what you did?

The guy's name was Carl K. It's almost a Top Gun type of thing. Carl mentioned to me at a bar that he was going from the T-37 and that he was going to move up to the T-38. My husband was sitting there, but Carl doesn't know who I am. I said, "Tell me, Carl, do you think it's hard to fly that plane?" He answered, "Only the best five get to the T-38 supersonic jet." I said, "Oh, how exciting for you." A month later, he reported in to me and became my student. As he saluted in a military manner, he looked at me and I see his mind spinning: "Oh God, I know her from somewhere. I know her from somewhere." Then the light goes on and he says "Oh, my god." I said, "Hi, Carl, I'm Kim Olson. I'm going to teach you how to fly that T-38 supersonic jet." So we leave the room and he turns to the other guys and says, "I think she's gonna teach us how to fly a broom!" Carl called me some fourteen years after that happened. Your students do remember you, though. A lot of times, you don't remember them, but they remember you.

There must be a step where sometimes you are too open with someone, and ironically, it gets you in trouble.

When I was 21, I was in UPT. There were some not very nice people there at the time. I was the only woman there, and there were 500 guys. It was the last class at the Air Force Academy before they admitted females. I remember a squadron commander who came to me and said, "Don't trust anyone you wouldn't show your butt to." I said, "I wonder what he meant by that." But women will say, I trust you therefore I will tell you everything about me, and that becomes the way I show my trust to you, while guys will not do that. But that approach is one thing I don't do now that I did as a youth.

There were funny times. When I had my first child, I went right back into the KC-135 and re-qualified. I was breast-feeding my son. We were on a training sortie and it got delayed and delayed. The pain became excruciating. At the time, we were doing touch and goes. I remember telling Dave, my instructor that we just had to full stop. I was on the radio trying to think what to say, to justify coming back. After I had my second child, a friend of mine and I were both breast-feeding. This time we were accompanied by a guy who was disgusted with us nursing. We had these battery-powered breast pumps, and we carried them with us. He'd say. "Where is the copilot?" I'd say, "Oh she's gone off in the back to pump." He'd say, "Oh, that's disgusting." Colleen, my co-pilot, said, "Oh, you've got to check out this pump too." So I go back, put regular milk in the bottle, and then say, "Want some for your coffee?"

You were in Saudi Arabia.

When we deployed in Saudi, we took maintenance and they became deployed to us. I was commander when we went over to Saudi, but I didn't know a lot about maintenance. I decided to go down at midnight with the guys and work. We changed a tire, a field bladder, and fueled jets. I emptied urinals—I did all the things they were doing. After several hours, the crew was done with their work, so we ended up playing ping-pong. There was an old guy there. He and I had been teased about our ages and our gray hair, so we teamed up together and won seven of nine games. "Just one more game," they'd say. "Just one more game."

We flew Christmas Day and New Year's Day. On Christmas, a bunch of us made stockings for all 200 personnel. The guys stuffed them, and we delivered them to all the tents. We took the extra stockings and delivered those to the guard posts at midnight shift. When we drove up to the posts, all these women jumped out with Santa Claus hats on. That night I think I learned the true meaning of giving without getting anything back. On New Year's Day as I went to my jet and climbed in, I found streamers, horns, hats, everything to do with New Year's inside the jet. Every jet that flew that day was decorated. But that gesture really touched my heart.

In Saudi, we flew our brains out without having any problems with the jets. That was very fortunate for the amount of time put in on them. Still, I had this one kid, who said of his boss who was my peer, "These guys can't run a popsicle stand." When I heard that, I just went through the ceiling. I thought, "You have no clue of what it's like to sit in the command chair, and yet you get to throw darts." I think I learned that sometimes no matter what you do and how hard you try, it's not enough. You have to not take the criticism personally. I think you will kill yourself as a commander if you do. I learned that, which was hard for me—a tough lesson to learn.

Did you fly in Saudi?

Yes, I had sixteen crews over in Saudi and my goal was to fly with every single one. That did several things. It got me out of the office, and I got to see what went on, which gave me credibility. Flying with my crew also gave them my undivided attention for four or five hours that the flight lasted. I could tell how their morale was, and they could complain to me if they wanted. There are four members on the KC-135, and I found out how each of them and their families were doing. So I flew quite a bit.

How many missions?

I flew eighteen missions over there.

Any scary missions?

I didn't have any scary mission, but the other troops did. We had several near mid-air collisions. Once an F-15 came right by one of our KC-135s. That I got upset about it, so I went and visited the F-15 CO. I said, "You back off my track or next time I'm going to find the biggest guy in my deployment, and I'm going to beat the tar out of you." There were so many airplanes over there and you had to be right on altitude and on the right corridor. We had several instances where we had a refueling track and a rival corridor cut it at a thirty-five degree angle. In fact, I had one incident that almost made me sick. I wondered if they had collided, how my day would have been so very different: I'd be writing family condolence letters. But by the grace of God, both planes broke out of the weather and saw each other. The copilot told me, "I had bad feelings about that flight." You know how we pilots are—we have bad feelings. Anyway, she said, "I looked up and here was an AWAC." Both ships broke hard right and threw everyone off in the back of the plane. The planes went through each other's wake and turbulence, which tells you how close a call it was. It makes you realize that even with all the radar and technical stuff, the eyes of the pilot are still the greatest thing we have for midair collision prevention.

Tell me how you got your Grace Under Fire organization going and what the goals are?

I was asked to help the founder bring the budding organization up to par. It needed lots of work in getting up to a level which could really make a difference for women vets.

The goal is simple, get women equitable access to care.

Proudest achievement of that organization?

Our team was part of a bigger movement to bring awareness, funding, outreach, medical help, and hiring out for women veterans. We made that happen.

I read your book, Iraq and Back, *and it's a terrific read. Was it hard for you to be so direct and, I feel, honest in the book?*

Writing the book was cathartic. It moved the experiences of war from my mind into something tangible and seems to help those who read it to understand the human heartbreak that is war. Many tell me you can hear my voice in the book. I do speak directly, so it makes sense I would write that way, too.

Worse communication screw-up in Iraq?

Probably what the real objective was from the political point of view. We won the war in 30 days, then proceed to lose the peace for over a decade.

When you turned more toward command from flight, did you want to go back and forth?

Not really; my job of being the best pilot was over, and now I wanted to be the best commander. I found commanding

young men and women the highlight of 25 years. To this day, I still visit with many who worked for me and am so proud of their accomplishments.

You called your daughter from Iraq. That was powerful emotion. Can you explain?

My daughter has become an incredible woman, I sure had a lot of guilt about leaving her so much. Luckily children are really very resilient. Both my children are wonderful young adults and contribute to the society. It is interesting, they tend to remember all our adventures as a military family, where I tend to remember how I left them so much.

Do you have any nightmares from the plane hitting the Pentagon?

No, watch the movie *Sully* and you will gain great insight into a pilot's conscience.

You were at the Pentagon on 9/11.

Yes, I was, but in life it is really the 9/12 that matters more. It's what you do the next day.

What did you learn from General Garner?

What makes a great general. He is an enlightened man and respected and admired by many.

At the Women's Memorial, you spoke and thanked your fellow women. That was something. Many would want to thank you.

Kimberly Olson

What do you think about that?

Well, I believe each generation contributes to the next. The WASPs made it possible for women to fly in the military, my generation made it possible for the gals to fly fighters and go into combat; eventually we will have equity in the ranks, lots of women generals, and then fewer wars.

How would you like to be remembered?

As a champion for women, funny and an inspirational woman.

Catherine Cook
"From Desert Storm to Commercial Flight"

Catherine Cook is a new generation of flier. She broke barriers as a military pilot for ten years—seven-and-one-half active and two-and-one-half reserves and flew during the Gulf War. Later, she became a pilot for Delta Airlines, where she flew Boeing 767-400. Catherine's story is infused with a little bit of lucky timing, but also of keen intelligence and personal perseverance. In the interview, Catherine also speaks to the down-to-earth qualities she feels have helped her bridge the gender gap in flying.

Born in Redlands, California, in 1957, she moved with her family to Berkeley so her father, Edward B. Cook, could study architecture at the University of California. After he completed his degree, the family moved to Sacramento. Catherine attended California State University at Sacramento where she graduated with a degree in economics, and a minor in political science. By grand accident, an aunt's visit to the recruiting station resulted in Catherine's joining the military—she had to overcome a chauvinistic instructor, who seemed intent on making her fail. Since that, it's been easier going.

Catherine is lively and positive and full of enthusiasm for life, which is clear, as the interview proceeds.

How did you get interested in flight?

Originally, I think it all goes way back to my childhood.

My dad liked to build model airplanes. We didn't have any spare rooms, so he put up a card table in my bedroom and we started building "fly by wire" airplanes together. I was the oldest and kind of a "daddy's girl," so I would be interested in everything he did. Together we would build model airplanes—those kits made with balsa wood, real engines, and working flight controls controlled by wires. You'd get a dry-cell battery to start the planes, fill up the fuel tank, and crank up the propeller. I still have scars on my knuckles where I'd have to turn the prop with my fingers and try to get them out of the way before the engine caught. The planes were connected by wires, and I'd stand in the middle of a field and my dad would stretch out the wire and hold the little airplane. I'd say, "Okay, let it go." Then it would take off and fly around in a circle and you'd just move the wires up and down to make the plane fly. We probably built four or five of those planes in my lifetime. I have very happy memories of those times. My dad had the interest in it, and so that gave me the interest in it.

Later on, my dad, who is an architect, worked for a guy who had his own private airplane. As a special treat, his boss took me flying with them. We flew all over Sacramento, circled over our house and the Nut Tree, a little airport over on Highway 80. I don't even remember what kind of airplane it was. When we were up in the air, they let me take the controls, and I actually flew. It was just so much fun, I just loved it. That's when I got bit by the flying bug and thought, "This is great—this is what I would love to do." I must've been about 13 or 14 years old, you know—not very old at all—but I never really thought it was possible for me to be a pilot. I just knew I loved it. Growing up, I always liked sports, and I always liked to drive things, to fly things, and to sail things, you know—mini-bikes, motorcycles, boats, roller coaster. It was fun. I liked the thrill of that kind of stuff.

*Do you remember any favorite planes that you built in
those days?*

I do. There was one called the Blue Streak. I did most of
the work on it myself. This one I was building, though my dad
helped me with it. We painstakingly painted it. It was beautiful.
The wings were blue with a silver trim edge on it. We put a lot
of time into it and it turned out beautiful. When it was finally
ready to fly, we took it out to the high school, to the big field on
a bright sunshiny day. I was going to get to fly it first. We got the
engine started and were all ready to go. I got to the end of the
controls and said, "Okay," and my dad let it go. There was a little
bit of slack in the wires, and it went straight up out of control. I
tried to gain control but it started coming at me and stalled in the
air. It came straight down, and it smashed into about a thousand
pieces. It probably had taken us a month to build, and it took me
about ten seconds to destroy!

Your dad—it sounds like he's kind of a would-be flier.

He is. He loved to fly. When I was a junior in college, I had
wanted to take flying lessons. My dad had a friend who had his
own airplane, was an instructor, and gave lessons. I said, "Come
on, Dad, let's take ground school class." So my dad and I took a
ground-school class together over at Sacramento Junior College.
We both really enjoyed it, and it was a really fun thing for us to
do together. When we finished the class, we both started taking
lessons from his friend, Rulon Blackburn.

My dad always made me pay for my own thing. I didn't
mind that because it makes you a stronger, independent person,
and you appreciated what you earn. Anyway, he started taking
lessons and actually got his private pilot license first. I was going

to Sacramento State working on my degree. I was also working part-time at the Potted Cedar Room, a 1970s-style restaurant where you'd go for raw vegetables, omelets, crepes, and sandwiches with cucumbers and alfalfa sprouts. I was making $2.00 an hour, and a flying lesson cost $35.00 hour, so it was taking seventeen and-a-half hours to have enough money for one hour of flying time. I was taking one lesson a month and just fighting it and not getting anywhere, so I kind of gave up at that time. When my dad got his license, he would take me up. We would go flying, and he would give me the controls and let me fly. That kept the desire in me to want to fly.

So then you got your license?

Actually, I never did get my private pilot's license. I took lessons with Rulon for a while, but because it was so expensive for me back then, I never really could afford to get my license. Still, I took enough lessons to know that I loved it and knew that that's what I wanted to do. My senior year of college. I was finishing my degree in economics and planning on going to law school. That seemed a sensible thing to do. At that time, flying wasn't even open to women, at least as far as I knew. None of the military forces were taking women. One of my roommates in college said, "What are you really gonna do with your life? It's weird that, about that time, I saw this plane taking off from Sacramento Metro Airport. I said, "If I could just do what I really wanted to do, I'd be an airplane pilot." She said, "Well, okay, you know you can't ever be an airline pilot, so what are you really going to do?" I always thought that was funny. She's the first who asked what I really wanted to do, and that was the first time I really verbalized my dream. Unfortunately, I lost touch with her, so I don't even know if she knows that I became an airline pilot.

How would you like to run into her on one of your flights?

That would be great. What a surprise that would be! I'll be greeting passengers as they get off the airplane, and out of the blue, I'll see her. She'll recognize me, and I'll say, "Look, I've become an airplane pilot." We could have a lot of fun reminiscing.

How did you get into the military?

In my senior year of college, right before I was graduating in 1979, things were starting to change in the military. The Air Force opened pilot training to a select group of women. They all had prior military service, exemplary records, and had been hand picked to go through the flying program. I remember reading about it because I was interested in flight training myself. At the time, I had an ear for any news articles or TV reports on the subject. My aunt, who was my roommate that year at college, was going to be graduating also. For some reason, she went and talked to an Air Force recruiter. She was interested in going into the medical field. (She ended up not going into the Air Force.) Anyway, the recruiter said to her, "Well, do you know anybody else who would be interested?" I guess he was trying to get his quotas of women. She said, "Well, my niece, Cathy, my roommate, is. She's always wanted to be a pilot." And the recruiter said, "We're not taking women to be pilots, but have her come for an interview."

So I went just on a whim. I mean, it wasn't even my idea. If she hadn't done it, who knows what course my life would have taken? But because she said, "This guy wants to meet you and talk to you," I said, "Okay, I have the time." I went and talked to him and told him that I wanted to be a pilot in the Air Force. He told me that pilot training wasn't an open field for women. I said that I knew that there had been some women who had gone through, but he explained that it was this real special program. He said, "What these women did was, they went into the Air Force in some different capacity, and then they were hand-selected to become pilots." And he added, "That's the way you have to do it, if you're interested." He said the military was taking women to become navigators. He said, "A lot of time, if you become a navigator, navigators can cross train and become pilots." That sounded good to me, and I said, "Okay." He explained that navigators were practically the same as pilots, and that they were right up there in the airplanes and flying and doing all this stuff anyway. So it's almost the same thing.

I didn't know any better, so I pursued it and took all the tests. First, you have to take a standard officer qualifying test and then, in addition to that, if you're going into either the pilot field or navigation field, the military will give you an extra test to see what your aptitude is toward that. I scored very well on the pilot/navigator aptitude test. I attribute that to the ground school class I'd taken and from building model airplanes. For example, I knew what ailerons were and flaps and rudders from my little bit of flying. I remember they'd show us pictures of airplanes and different altitudes, and they'd ask, "Is the plane climbing or descending? Is it in a right turn or a left turn?" Things like that. The test also featured mechanical questions, which I knew about from hanging around my dad. In college, I had this old '61 MGA. On weekends, I would work on the car with my dad, and so I knew a lot about nuts and bolts. I think that really helped me on the test also. But anyway, I scored really high on both of those tests, and the recruiter called me in, and he was all excited, and he said, "You really did well. They'll accept you into navigation school if you pass the physical." I passed the physical with flying colors.

The last thing I had to do was to be interviewed by some lieutenant colonel in the Air Force, based at Mather Air Force Base. I had to get a recommendation from this officer to get accepted into navigation school. I was talking with this man and, over the course of the conversation, he said, "Well, why do you want to be a navigator?" I said, "I really don't want to be a navigator, I want to be a pilot, but I understand that for me to become a pilot, the best way for me is to become a navigator. That way, I can cross-train and become a pilot after I become a navigator." This guy just got this big smile on his face and said, "That recruiter is full of BS. That is not how you become a pilot. Once you become a navigator it's really hard to cross train. I mean, one out of maybe a thousand will get a chance to cross-train. That's not the way to become a pilot. If you really want to be a pilot, don't go in and become a navigator or chances are you'll never be a pilot."

So he saved me with that information because I didn't know any better. I believed everything this recruiter was telling me was true. I went back to the recruiter and, in the meantime, all the paper work had been done and I was accepted for navigation school. I told him, "You know what, I don't want to be a navigator, I want to be a pilot." He said, "Well, I explained to you that pilot training is not available. It's not an option for women." I said, "Well you know what? I think I'm just going to continue what I'm doing, and I'm going to go to law school. I've changed my mind and I don't want to go into the Air Force and become a navigator." This guy was crushed. He acted like, "You've got to be kidding me. I've done all this work." It had been a lengthy process, probably two months to take all the tests and to take the physical and the jump through all the hoops you had to jump through. He liked me also. We had a good rapport with each other. He said, "Well, I'll tell you what, I'll just keep all your records on file. Everything is good for at least a year, and if something changes, I'll give you a call." I said, "Okay, that sounds good."

I was working at the time for the California Energy Commission back in the days of Governor Jerry Brown, on solar energy and wind power. One day, I was at my desk, and totally out of the blue, the telephone rings, and this voice said, "Cathy, this is Sergeant Pearson. I just got this message, and pilot training is available. They're starting this experimental program, taking women with no prior experience, and you don't have to already be in the Air Force. They're going to take a group of women and see how they do in pilot training. Are you interested?" I remember saying, "I have my bags packed. When do I go?" He said, "Wait a minute, just a minute here." Since I had already done all the prerequisites, my package was ready to go to the selection board. Because of that, I'm sure mine had to be one of the first packages to get to the board. The timing was just right. I was ready, willing, and qualified right when the flight training policy changed and opened up to women.

In September, Sgt. Pearson called me up all excited on the phone, and said, "You've been accepted to pilot training. I can't believe it. You're the first woman I've recruited for pilot training." He was just as excited as I was. So that was the start of it. I took my oath and joined the Air Force on October 31, Halloween of 1979. It's turned out to be a treat. It wasn't a trick; it was the best treat of my life!

Any tough aspects of training when you first went in?

It has been tough the whole way through. Even though I had taken some flying lessons, the military program is totally different, very regimented and fast-paced. You have to make it through each training section at their pace—not your own pace.

When I got to flight school, some of the other pilot candidates not only had their private license, but they were already commercial pilots. They already had hundreds of hours of flying. Here I was, when I found out I was being accepted to pilot training, I thought I'd better take some more lessons real quick from my old instructor. I got to the point where I soloed in a Cessna 150, right before I went in to the Air Force. I had maybe a total of 20 hours of flying time in my entire life, plus the little hour here and hour there of flying straight and level with my dad and with his boss. I had done my flying up in Cameron Air Park, which is this little tiny airport with about a thousand-foot runway in the hills of Sacramento. There was no control tower, so I didn't even know how to use the radio. I mean, I was so green it was unbelievable. When I look back now, I realize the incredible amount I had to learn both academically and for practical ability.

Were there times when you were almost ready to give up?

That first year of pilot training is the toughest thing I've ever done. No, I never gave up. I always persevered. There were lots of times when there was lots pressure put on me, and I thought I wasn't going to make it through. But I studied and worked as hard as I could, and the hard work paid off. I had some tough instructor pilots, but that's just the military's way of doing business.

Was there ever a dramatic confrontation?

When I first went in to the Air Force, I had to pass a flight screening program. If you didn't pass that, then you didn't even make it to pilot training, and you didn't have a commitment to the Air Force. The flight-screening program involved soloing a Cessna 172 and taking a flight check ride. I had been flying a Cessna 150, so I made it through that program pretty easily. Then, to become an Air Force Officer, I had to go through Officer Training School (OTS), which is like a boot camp for officers. That was actually fun. Then I got assigned to Vance Air Force Base in Oklahoma for pilot training. There were two women in my class, but we were in different sections. Really, you don't even know the students in other sections because you're on opposite schedules. If we were flying in the morning and doing academics in the afternoon, they were doing academics in the morning and flying in the afternoon. We started flying T-37s. The T-37 is a twin-engine military jet trainer. I had a great instructor. I mean, he got me off to a really great start. He was fair and understanding. He had good teaching techniques. I learned really well from him and learned to fly the T-37 really well. I think I had over a hundred hours in T-37s. We learned navigation, acrobatic formation flying, and instrumental flying. Then we upgraded to the T-38. The T-38 is an advanced supersonic jet trainer that is designed to separate the fighter pilot from the cargo pilot. I had done well in a T-37, and I had done well in the flight-screening program, and so I thought, okay, the T-38 is just kind of upgrading and learning a little different airplane and learning some advanced maneuvers.

With the T-38, I finally ran into a really hardcore, old-fashioned, chauvinistic instructor. He gave me a very hard time, and his teaching techniques were extremely negative. He would yell and scream at me in the jet while I was trying to fly. He would take the controls away from me. He would berate me while we were flying. I was not learning from this guy. I'm the kind of person who is fine if I'm concentrating and trying to do something, but if somebody is yelling and screaming at me, it throws off my concentration, and I was getting more and more frustrated. I think he was particularly tough on me and wanted to see if he could get me to break. He was a hard-line, traditional male chauvinist and believed that women didn't belong flying airplanes. It seemed as though he was on a quest to see if he could wash me out of the program. At least that's what it felt like to me.

My best friend, my tablemate, a guy named Bob, and I had to fly with this guy. Bob would tell totally different stories of when he would fly with this guy. The instructor just let him fly. He would let him make mistakes. And I'd say, "Well, I did the exact same thing, and he'd yell and scream at me and take the airplane away from me and say, 'Well, that's the end of the ride for you today. You've busted this ride.'" And if you'd busted two rides in a row, you'd have to go fly with a different instructor. If you busted that ride with the second instructor, then you'd get tossed right out of the program. I would say, about a third of our class did end up busting out of the program somewhere along the way. It's not a given when you get to flying school that you're going to make it through. It was pretty serious.

The instructor busted me two flights in a row, and I had to go fly with the flight commander. When I flew with the flight commander, he said, "Lieutenant Cook, what's the problem? You fly a fine airplane." I said, "It's just the instructor. We just don't get along. And I think I need an instructor change." For some reason, he would not give me an instructor change, but he let me continue to fly.

Was that tough going back to the same guy?

That was really tough because now my instructor knew that I was trying to get another instructor. Now I'm being put back into the cockpit with this guy. So, I mean, he probably thought that he was within a week of having me totally knocked out of the program. I remember that I had nobody to really talk to. I did have my tablemate, my buddy Bob. He gave me some welcome support when things were bleak. I remember calling my dad at home and just crying on the phone. I was strong in class, and I was strong around everybody else. I could keep the emotions in, but I'd get back to my room, and I could just remember breaking down and just sobbing in tears and calling home and talking for probably an hour or two. I can remember calling my dad and him just saying he was proud of me and, if it was too tough, he understood. My dad gave me encouragement. That's a time when I really needed my dad, and he really came through for me. He gave me the encouragement I needed. It gave me the power and strength I needed to resist the tactics of that tough instructor. He said he was proud of me no matter what, whether I made it through the pilot training or not. He was still proud of me and loved me. I can remember him saying, "Don't let that bastard get you!" It just gave me enough strength, enough spirit inside that I was able to get through. Luckily, I only had to fly with that instructor one more time, and finally, the flight commander realized there was a conflict with this guy and I got an instructor change.

It just seemed as if my initial T-38 instructor didn't want women to be flying. It was his domain, and he was going to do everything he could to protect the domain of flying for men only, and women were not going to be allowed into this special fraternity. He didn't want to instruct a woman, and he didn't want to be responsible for allowing a woman to enter his exclusive club. After that, I was assigned to an instructor who had a completely opposite attitude towards me. He encouraged me as his student, and for the rest of the time in T-38s, he was my instructor. With a fair instructor, I started flying the T-38 with confidence. I aced the T-38 program and got an "Outstanding Performance" grade in navigation. I didn't have another problem through the whole training program once I got this new instructor. I actually started to relax. I did have some catching up to do because I had fallen behind in my training as a result of the first instructor that I had. But I have to say, I'm a real book-smart person, and I'm a hard worker. I'm also pretty well coordinated—good hand-eye coordination. I played sports when I was in high school. When I was a senior in high school, I was voted the best female athlete in my senior class. I lettered in volleyball and basketball. I knew I always had the abilities. Still, you need the support of the instructors that teach you. Once I got that support, and once I recovered from the jerk instructor, I did fine and graduated with flying colors.

Once you graduate from pilot training, you are assigned to a specific aircraft, and you go to specialized school to train for the plane you're going to fly for the rest of your career in the Air Force. I was assigned to the KC-135, an air refueling aircraft belonging to the Strategic Air Command. My first real assignment was to a KC-135 squadron at Travis AFB, California.

You flew in Desert Storm, is that right? Any unusual things happen over there?

Yes, that was one of the most exhilarating times in my life. I was an aircraft commander of a KC-135, flying actual combat missions and logging hundreds of hours of combat flying. I was so proud to be serving my country. It was a challenge and a thrill to take all my experience accumulated during peaceful times and then apply it in wartime conditions. We refueled every kind of aircraft in both the Air Force and Navy inventory: B-52s loaded with bombs heading for Iraq; fighters with live missiles flying air combat patrols. Every moment was action packed and the missions were vital. I've never flown so much in such a concentrated period. We also flew re-supply missions between a staging base in Spain and Barksdale Air Force Base in Louisiana. I was in a couple of those missions in a row to the point that I didn't know what day it was, or whether it was even day or night, because I'd be over the Atlantic Ocean. Even though KC-135s are tankers and do mainly air refueling—and we did do air refueling missions over there. We also got to fly long-range logistical support missions. The route I flew the most was going back and forth from Barksdale Air Force Base. We would pick up spare parts, including brakes for B-52s, and get them back over to Spain to keep the B-52s flying and operational so that they could bomb in Iraq. I think that, in one month, I got 150 hours, or close to it. By regulation, 120 hours is the maximum a pilot can get in a month. Usually, it's around 60 to 70. Because it was wartime conditions, the military gave us a special waiver for up to 150 hours. At this point, there were still probably four or five days left in the month. The Air Force wanted us to fly beyond that, but they couldn't get a waiver for more hours, which is a good thing because, by that time, we were zombies.

Did you have any tough landings?

The interesting thing about being a woman, when we were first tasked to Saudi Arabia, there was a big question over the powers that would be sending women over as flight crew members. There was some high-level diplomacy that was taking place because the Saudis don't even let their women drive cars, let alone fly airplanes. At first, our military planners were trying to put crews together without women, but then they realized that they wouldn't be able to send as many crews over as they needed to send. So women flight crew members ended up getting to go over there and into combat flying for the first time in U.S. history. At first, if I would be talking on the radios, the Saudi controllers wouldn't answer the women. They would just totally ignore us, but finally they got over that. We had a couple of pretty close calls where they didn't inform us that other airplanes were flying through our air space.

I remember one time we were refueling a plane on its way to deliver cargo to Riyadh. In the middle of refueling a cargo plane, I was operating the radios. It had been silent for a long time. The controllers didn't tell us that there were any other planes in the vicinity. Maybe they didn't know, but I'm sure that they had radar and could see our track. We were hooked up with a C-5 flying and offloading huge amounts of fuel, and all of a sudden, here comes this U.P.S. airplane straight across our path. It was a near miss. I made a little evasive maneuver, but with a big C-5 behind you, you can't be making any dramatic maneuvers or you'll knock him off of you. If that happens, his wake is so great that he could cause you to go out of control and have a midair collision with him. I'd say we came within 200 feet of this U.P.S. DC-8. That was probably my closest call during the Gulf War. It had nothing to do with the Iraqis. They were never a threat. It turns out that near misses were fairly common over Saudi airspace because there were so many airplanes flying in such a concentrated area, and in the beginning, there wasn't a lot of good communication between the Saudi controllers and the aircrews. I think it was even worse because I happened to be a woman. As the war went on, after that first week, safety reports started piling up, and very quickly, we started getting American controllers, or at least Americans sitting right next to the Saudi controllers. So after that, things kind of smoothed out, and there were a lot fewer near misses.

Did you get any more unusual treatment over there?

First they tried to separate us and put all the women in one area and all the men in another area. It was the first time that women had ever been in a combat situation like this. Nobody really knew how it all was going to work out. We were adjusting day by day, but the catch was that we were all on different crews and we all had different schedules making gender an inefficient way to pair people up. The effective way is to put a crew together so that a crew can get crew rest. An integral flight crew needs to be on the same schedule. They eat together, and then they go fly the mission together, and then they can rest at the same time.

The way they were doing it was to have four women sharing a one-room apartment, even though we were all on different schedules. That worked for about two or three days, and none of us were getting any rest. We were not coordinating with the rest of our crews and the other guys were staying together, so they were basically doing all of the work for us. At that point, we said this isn't working out. Finally, logic prevailed, and we ended up bunking as a crew. The commanders were really having a tough time figuring out what to do with the female flight crew members. In their mind, a woman should not be staying in a one-bedroom apartment with three other guys. They thought the wives at home were going to be worrying about their married husbands and possible fooling around going on. Eventually, they realized that we were there as professionals, flying missions and supporting the war. We were not interested in fooling around with a fellow crew member. That was the furthest thing from our minds. We also realized that we were very high profile and were under scrutiny. Our conduct would influence the way future female flight crewmembers would be utilized in following conflicts.

That controversy re-occurred throughout my career because I was always one of the first women in a flying squadron. When I got to Travis Air Force Base, I pulled hard alert and I'd live in this cinder-block building for a week at a time. Alert was a third of Strategic Air Command's nuclear force, and if there was ever a war with Russia where the U.S.S.R. would launch their missiles, then we were on standby within seconds of our airplanes. The airplanes were cocked and fully loaded. We had predesignated missions that we would go on and refuel B-52s that would carry out nuclear strikes against Russia. That's what Alert was, and that was basically the mission of the KC-135s. There were three flights, and we would take turns being on Alert. You'd be on hard alert for a week at a time, and you'd live in the alert facility. It was completely self contained, had its own cafeteria, sleeping areas, bathrooms, training rooms, and entertainment rooms, so you just lived there on standby for a week at a time. You lived in your flight suit. The only time you took off your flight suit was if you were going to do some exercise, which consisted of jogging around the Alert airplanes. At night you'd sleep in your underwear, but you'd keep your boots right next to your bed. We were like firemen. When the alarm went off, we'd jump up, throw the flight suit on, and sprint out to the airplanes. We had to be launched within minutes or, theoretically, the incoming missiles would destroy us.

I was the first woman pilot assigned to Travis Air Force Base in the KC-135 squadron. They didn't know what to do with me or where to put me on Alert, because usually the junior officers would have to bunk up together and then the most senior person, the aircraft commander, would get his own bedroom. They weren't about to put me in a room with another guy, so in a way, that was kind of nice. I always got my own bedroom. They didn't have separate bathrooms either. They only had a male bathroom, so they devised a scheme to give me 20 minutes a day, from 7:10 a.m. until 7:30 a.m. to use the bathroom. They hung this little sign out on the bathrooms. It said, "Do not enter, women only." That was the only time in the morning I had to get ready for the 8 a.m. briefing. That arrangement led to some funny situations. Old habits are hard to break, and a lot of guys had been pulling Alert forever. I remember one time, I was in there taking my shower, and this guy, half awake, just came walking right in. There I was, standing naked in the shower, minding my own business. All of a sudden, he realizes what's happening and is totally embarrassed. He's like, "Oh, Lieutenant Cook, oh I'm so sorry," and he's trying to cover his eyes and he's trying to back out and he's falling all over himself. Little embarrassing moments like that happened a couple of times, but I just tried to roll with the punches and keep my sense of humor. The same kind of thing happened over in Saudi Arabia, too. We were just learning to adapt to the circumstances as we went along. Nowadays, in Alert facilities, women are more commonplace and most of those little details have all been worked out.

How many hours did you fly in Desert Storm?

I think approximately 300 hours.

How did you get with the commercial airlines?

I served seven and a half years of active duty, my required commitment to the Air Force. I used the military as a stepping-stone toward my airline career. When my original commitment was up, I sent out my resume to Delta and United, the two best airlines at that time—best in terms of taking care of their pilots, for pay and benefits as well as management rapport and career opportunities. Delta Airlines sent me a letter within a week to come for an interview. I got out of the Air Force on March 17, and I had a class date with Delta starting April 10.

What about transitioning from miltary flying?

It was a very easy transition for me. The KC-135 is a Boeing 707. When I started flying commercial, I was a flight engineer on the Boeing 727. The systems were very similar since they were both Boeings. There were differences, though, and I did study hard. Nonetheless, the flying was second nature for me by that time. I'm modest, but also I want to say that I am a good pilot. I couldn't have made it this far otherwise. Flying isn't like some other kinds of jobs. You have to perform at very high standards every single flight. You have to know your stuff or it will be blatantly obvious that you are weak. With flying, you have to go out there and prove your abilities. Every day, when you take off, fly the leg, do all the maneuvers required and then land in all kinds of different conditions. You're constantly being tested, and your flying skills evaluated by fellow pilots and passengers. You have to be skilled and you have to be good. No way to fake it. You just can't be in this profession unless you have lots of ability.

What is the reaction of flight attendants to you?

Most flight attendants are really happy to see women finally make it to the cockpit. A lot of flight attendants have come up to me over the years, and they always make me feel really good. They say, "You know what? When we were coming up, we never had the opportunity to ever become pilots." They love the flying profession themselves and they probably would've been great pilots themselves, but the opportunity wasn't available to them. So they've always been supportive and friendly towards me—proud of me. They'll say, "Oh, you know, I'm so glad to see a woman in the cockpit. It's just so great."

Tell me your greatest moment flying commercially.

We were taking off out of Dallas. I was still a co-pilot, but it was my leg of the trip, so I was flying the airplane. We took off, and I'd say just seconds after liftoff, we heard this big explosion and got a fire warning in the cockpit. It turned out one of our engines had caught fire. The tower called and said, "Delta, you guys look like a Roman candle. You've got a torch coming out of the right side of the airplane." The captain was handling the radios because I was flying. He says, "Roger, we're declaring an emergency. It looks like we have a fire in number-three. We'll be coming back around for a landing." I had that airplane completely under control. We go through so much training in simulators. We practice losing an engine on take-off, which is probably one of the most serious things that can happen to the airplane when you're flying, and it is one of the most difficult things to control. The passengers in the back hardly felt anything. They heard the big explosion; they heard the bang. The flight attendants were ringing the cockpit, saying, "Pilots, we had a big explosion in the back of the airplane and we can see some flames off of the right side!" Anyway, we flew the airplane, controlled it, and climbed up to about a thousand feet. We did everything right by the book. We went through the checklist procedures and made one big square pattern. We had everything under control and came in, and everything was going so well that the captain let me keep the airplane and he let me bring it in.

I made one of the best landings I've ever made in my life. It was smooth. It was done with total concentration. Usually, the captain will take control of the airplane during an emergency. So that made me very proud that he trusted me in a serious situation, and he let me land the airplane. We came to a stop and were completely surrounded immediately by all the crash and rescue equipment. They inspected everything and it's amazing. What had happened was that one of the compressor blades in the number-three engine had just totally disintegrated. When it disintegrated, it kind of acted like a drill and completely shelled out the whole engine. So by the time we landed the airplane, there was nothing left in the number-three engine but the cowling. There was no engine left in the airplane anymore.

The next day it was all in the newspapers in Dallas that this Delta airplane had started this huge grass fire. I guess we caused this big grass fire in Dallas, off the end of the runway because of the burning engine, which was about the best thing that could've happened for it to just fall, disintegrate, and get out of the airplane instead of staying in there. But anyway, they towed us back to the gate. All the passengers got off, and, of course, I stood at the door and the captain stood at the door, and as people got off, we were trying to say goodbye to the folks and make sure that they weren't panicky and that they were relieved. Passengers were shaking our hands and telling us what an outstanding job we did, and saying that we were the best pilots in the whole world, so that was a really proud moment.

When the last passenger got off, all of a sudden, that's when it hits you and you get the shakes and go, "Dang, that was a close call." Then the fire captain comes up and you go down and we look in the engine, and it's all this black streaking smoke and there's nothing left and you realize how you averted a catastrophe. Next, we went down to pilot operations to fill out an accident/incident report. That took about a half-hour. The chief pilot from Dallas came over and talked to us and then, out of the blue, he goes, "You know, we still need to get those people to Denver. Do you guys still think you could fly? We have a spare airplane, or do you want us to call out a reserve crew?" We all just kind of looked at each other and said, "Hey, we've had our accident for the night, so we're probably pretty good." So we said, "Yeah, we'll keep on flying." Probably about an hour after landing the emergency airplane, we were out preflighting a new airplane. I'd say all the passengers but about five got back on our airplane and stuck with us. They were all so complimentary, saying, "Hey, if you guys can handle that, then you're the crew that we want to fly with." We were probably about three or four hours late, but all of them wanted to go, so we ended up getting to Denver that night.

Are there any other anecdotes or other stories that you can think of in any venue?

I've lost hydraulics a couple of times, but that's just normal stuff. In the Air Force one time, we lost an engine, but it was while we were airborne so it wasn't as dramatic as this one. What made this one so serious was that we were so heavy, just taking off and it's that real critical time of flight. Overnight, I've been thinking about my career and what has helped me the most in getting through the whole thing. I think what it's been is that I have a good sense of humor and I'm easy going and I like to get along. I've made friends with these guys who fly, and I fit in with these characters. That's why I don't think I've ever had many problems. Just with that one instructor in the very beginning. Luckily, he turned out to be the exception rather than the rule.

I was a prankster when I was in the Air Force. When we'd be on Alert for seven days at a time, we'd play tricks on each other—I was just one of the guys. I'd go along with it. We'd sometimes do silly things to make the time pass.

Here's a good example from Desert Storm. It was the middle of the night, out over the Pacific. We were all punchy, trying to stay alert. It was around Easter and my mom had sent me a care package to Saudi Arabia or Spain. We spent half the time we were over there in Saudi Arabia and half the time in Spain. We would rotate, because when you're in Saudi Arabia for a long time, it gets pretty oppressive. You never could get away from it. You couldn't drink over there. They were real strict. It was more restrictive. We had to stay in these really small compounds in uncomfortable quarters, and there wasn't anything to do there. We couldn't go off base because there were terrorists and constant threats. We'd have to take an unmarked bus from the compound where we were living to get to the airport to fly our missions. The military would close all the windows, which had drapes on them. We were even carrying pistols at the time because there was a terrorist threat. One day, after we had flown our mission and been on the bus, that same bus was attacked and shot up with machine gun fire. Luckily, nobody was killed, but I think the driver was hit in the leg with a bullet, and that was just an ongoing worry.

I remember being on Alert. All the telephones were the black military telephones, and we would put black shoe polish around the receiver of the telephone. Then we would page one of the colonels or one of the majors that they had a telephone call. They'd come and answer the telephone, and then we'd hang up on them. They'd be walking around and their ear would be black. Or, one time, we sewed someone's pants. He'd already gone to bed, and we snuck in to his room and sewed his pant legs shut and then we called him like there was going to be an alert. We made it sound like, "Major J, Major J, Major J! Klaxon! Klaxon!"

He woke up out of his sound sleep and fell all over himself trying to get his pants on. He couldn't figure out why he couldn't get his pants on. Boy, did he cuss us out for that! We liked to tease the guys who took themselves a little too seriously. They were the ones that we would go after. Then they would say, "What if that had really been the real thing? What if the Russians had attacked right then?" So anyway, having a good sense of humor and being one of the guys, I think that's been the key to my success and to a good career.

I've always been able to get along with everybody. I've seen some women that are too uptight, and they make everybody in the cockpit feel uncomfortable. I go out of my way if there's somebody I haven't flown with, to tell them right off the bat to just be themselves. I love dirty jokes, if you've got them. I can tell them just as good as anybody. Just do what you would do anyway. Speak normally. Be comfortable around me. I just want you to think of me as a pilot. I'm not a woman in the cockpit. I'm just another pilot. The greatest compliment that you can pay to me is to just treat me like one of the guys and to say that you didn't have to be on your best behavior, that you have to change the way that you were. At times, I've been around some really gross guys, but, in a way, I feel privileged that I've been able to be on the inside and see what the man's world is really like. And now, as more women get in, it's kind of evolving and changing. I thought from the very beginning, when it was really a man's domain, that I had a good perspective on things. I get along well with men and I think I understand them. Now I have a great time.

We were over in Mildenhall, a Royal Air Force Base north of London, England, at the Officer's Club. They had a great Officer's Club back then. This was back before everyone was so worried about drunk driving and DUIs and there was a little bit more open policy. Back then, when you'd go TDY, it was kind of almost expected that you'd go out and you'd have a good time. The saying was, "What goes TDY, stays TDY." Anyway, we got over TDY and were working. You work hard, you play hard. In our times off, we would be at the Officer's Club. Being the only woman in the Officer's Club—which means it was ninety-nine-percent men and one-percent women—I could dance the whole night long. Furthermore, I never had to buy a drink because the guys would just buy me as many drinks as I wanted.

I'm not a hard drinker; I just drink beer. But there were times after dancing and dancing and dancing all night long and just having a grand old time, I'd have an abundance of beers. I'd come back to the table, and there'd probably be three or four beers that guys had bought sitting on the table. I was just having a grand old time, so I'd drink a beer and I'd go back out and dance some more, come back and guzzle one down, and then go back out and dance some more. We were just having fun. It's not like boyfriend and girlfriend or anything like that. Shoot, the guys would practically dance with each other. Sometimes, they would actually bring in some civilian women, but the ratio was always still more men than women. The women always had great times when they went to the O-Club.

I was TDY one time on New Year's Eve and we were in Scotland. One of the neatest times I had was when my crew was standing on the main road that led to King's Palace. At the time, it was like Time's Square. There were that many people, and we were singing songs, all those people with Scottish accents, passing the booze. We were drinking and, like everybody else, just singing and swaying. This bottle would just be floating around and passing around. We never got in any trouble, and we were always ready to go fly the next time when we were scheduled to. That's how it used to be. We would take care of each other.

Clearly, you made the right decision to fly.

It has been wonderful flying. I am living a charmed life. I couldn't be doing anything else that could make me happier. I love it. Also, I never really thought I would have kids because I concentrated so much on the career. All through my 20s and 30s, I was flying for the Air Force, and then I was getting started with my career for Delta. I didn't get pregnant, and I didn't have my first little boy until I was 39 years old. He's only six years old right now. So now I'm blessed in that way. In October of 2000, I had my second little boy at age 43. Two perfect, wonderful sons make a happy family. It's been a blessed life. I've stuffed a lot into it. Do you know what? If I could go and start all over, I would love to do it again. I've had so much fun. I'd even take that rotten instructor. I'd love to go back and run into that guy.

How would you handle him now?

I'd love to get him on a flight some time. "Hey, Don, remember me?" He probably wouldn't even remember me. It's my memory; it's not his memory. I would love to run into him and for him to be the captain on the flight. I'd say, "Oh, you're going to fly with me. I thought you didn't think I had the stuff to become a pilot." But I think he was testing me to see how much I really wanted it. Was I just going to give up? That's part of being a pilot, too. You can't give up. You have to have a pretty strong personality, and you have to be able to handle a lot of adversity. I've been able to do it.

Dr. Dora Dougherty Strother McKeon

"Aviation Psychology Pioneer, Flew B-29"

As a young girl in Garden City, Long Island in New York, Dora was introduced to flying early. Her family lived near Roosevelt Field, and every Sunday afternoon her parents, Dora and her two brothers would travel over to the airport to watch the airplanes. Five years of watching many of the pioneers of aviation—from age five to age ten—made an impact.

At age ten, the family moved to Chicago, settling in Winnetka. Nearby was the legendary Curtiss Field, and the family tradition of Sunday afternoon drives to the airport continued.

Dora graduated from high school in 1939 and attended a girl's school in Missouri, Cotter College. While home for the summer after a year, she learned to fly. Dora joined the Civilian Pilot Training Program at Northwestern University and she and two others became WASPs.

In the interview, Dora talks about being one of two women in the WASP program who flew the B-29. She was taught by Colonel Paul Tibbetts, Jr., who flew the Enola Gay that dropped the bomb on Hiroshima. Later, she worked for Bell Helicopters and was number twenty seven in the Free World to gain a helicopter rating. She got her Ph.D. and worked in aviation psychology in the Aviation Psychology Laboratory at the University of Illinois.

Was that a leisurely Sunday thing to do or was your family interested in flying?

No, that was a family activity. Dad had been in World War I and he did not have an assignment with aviation, although he had been up in some airplanes on casual observation—but not at any great length. He was not particularly interested in aviation. Aviation caught my interest, I'm sure, because I wanted to learn more and more about it.

I joined a radio club in high school. We learned Morse Code and related techniques of amateur radio. Also, I joined the Mariners of the Girl Scouts, where we learned basic navigation. I had no idea that I'd ever be a pilot. These were things that were building blocks. Of course, my brothers and I built model airplanes.

How were you looked upon? Did any of your friends think it was unusual for you to be interested in navigation?

I don't think so. I was fortunate in that my parents were believers in continuing to learn. My mother was a very strong advocate of education. She had a double bachelor's degree in chemistry and physics and taught chemistry. So she was very unusual in a day when there were barriers about the idea of what women could and couldn't do. Both she and my father always wanted us to keep learning. We always had to go to summer school. They didn't care what we took as long as we took something of interest.

Did your brothers ever fly?

No. My brothers were younger than I. They wanted to fly during the war, but one became what's now called a SEAL. They called them underwater demolition, in those days, with the Navy. My other brother was too young to get into the war. He did sign up at the very end, as he had just gotten old enough. He was called back in Korea and served in the Navy on a destroyer. My older brother eventually got a pilot's license and flew light planes.

What did your brothers think when big sister goes out and becomes a flyer? They must have been proud of you.

My whole family was happy I was doing this. My whole family was very supportive.

Tell me about your solo flight.

My training was done under the auspices of Northwestern University. It was in a Civilian Pilot Training Program. The university had a contract with an airport operator at a place called Palwaukee Airport. That's where we got our flight training. It was at the intersection of Palatine Road and Milwaukee Avenue. Milwaukee was north of where we lived. At Northwestern, they were allowed to take 10 percent women in the CPT program. In my class, we had four women. Three of us went on to become WASPs. This was in 1940 before the WASPs or WAFS ever started.

On the solo flight, one is so busy trying to be aware of everything. I think I was very proud because as a girl I was allowed to fly, and because I could measure up to it. The plane I flew was a little side-by-side, high-wing plane called an Aeronca Chief. I remember how it felt so empty, when the instructor was there and suddenly wasn't there. I don't remember too many specific things about my solo flight.

What is next in the chronology?

I graduated from high school in 1939 and I attended a girl's school in Missouri called Cotter College. It was a small town on the southwest corner of Missouri—south of Kansas City. When I went back home for the summer between the two years—it was a two-year school—that was the time I learned to fly. I learned in the summer of 1940, when I went back to college that fall. I found they did not have an airport in town. But the local mail carrier bought an airplane and kept it out in the field on the east side of town. I saved my allowance because I wanted to go check out the airplane, which I did. That was something my college wasn't prepared for. The college was a rather strict little school. They weren't sure they wanted their students going out to the airport. They got my parents' permission, so I was allowed to do that. After graduating from the junior college, I went back to Northwestern University, which was near my home, and enrolled for my junior year. Of course, the Japanese bombed us that December.

Do you remember where you were when the bomb-
ing occurred?

Yes, I remember distinctly. My high school had a college career day in the gymnasium. That's where I was when I heard it. When President Roosevelt made his talk the next day, declaring war, the radio was amplified at the Northwestern University auditorium. The tension there, I remembered, was extreme. In 1942, I heard rumors at the airport that the government was thinking of using women to fly for the Army. Shortly thereafter, a recruiting person came to Chicago to recruit for the WASPs, which wasn't called the WASPs then—they really didn't have a name for it. The recruiter would interview candidates at the Palmer House in Chicago. I took the train down and talked to her and was accepted. I had to go take an Army physical to make sure that I was physically fit. I just barely had enough teeth, because

557

I had knocked three of my teeth out as a kid when I had fallen off a bicycle. I don't know why you have to have your teeth in the Army. I just barely had enough.

Maybe you had to have enough to be able to chew k-rations.

I guess so! When I went to take my physical, my pulse was so fast that they said, "Unless you can get your pulse down, we will have to reject you. You come back tomorrow." So I went home and tried to be calm. I went back the next day and passed. That was the only unusual thing that happened to me. Then, I was accepted to enter the third class, which started in January 1943. The training program had started in the latter part of 1942. The Women's Auxiliary Flying Service (WAFS) had started just about the same time. My letter of acceptance told me to report to Houston—it came from Ft. Worth. The head of the training command was in Ft. Worth, Texas, and Jacqueline Cochran's office was in Ft. Worth in the Texas and Pacific Railroad Building.

Today, the Federal Housing Authority has taken over the building. There is talk of turning it into a hotel.

What did you feel when you heard about Pearl Harbor? Were you pretty impassioned?

I think everyone was outraged. War talk had been in the papers for years: the Battle of Britain, Hitler and aggression. War was on everybody's mind. People who had been at war like my father—war was still too close. He never talked about WWI at home. I don't think any of the men did. People of my generation are only now beginning to talk about it. I think the horror of it has eased from their minds and they start remembering good things.

Your dad and mom didn't have misgivings about you going into the military?

If they did, I didn't know of them. Whatever I wanted to do, they were for me and supported me.

Did you go down to Texas for training? Where did you go first?

The first few classes started in Houston, at the municipal airport. It was realized quickly that it was a bad place to try to run a flight school. As for living quarters, the military didn't have any buildings. We were housed in motels. On the flight line, there were "ready rooms" and classrooms. Some were in one building and some were in another. It was realized quickly that the school needed to move out of Houston. Many places were considered but Sweetwater, Texas, was the final selection.

When the fourth class entered training—in February of 1942, half of the class entered in Houston and half entered at Sweetwater. As quickly as possible, the school started moving the Houston girls and airplanes up to Sweetwater. By the time the second class graduated—which would have been in May 1942—they graduated in Sweetwater and everyone had been moved. The first class to graduate, graduated at Ellington Field in Houston, but all the rest of the training was done at Sweetwater.

Was that hectic when they were moving from Houston to Sweetwater?

Yes, it was. When half of the fourth class went, they took the primary training aircraft for their mode of transportation. When my class went, we took the Basic Trainers. When the

559

second class flew up to Sweetwater, they brought the Advanced Trainers. So by the time the girls in Sweetwater were ready for those planes, the planes were there.

How did the male commanders treat you?

The only males we saw were instructors. We were forbidden to have any social contact with them. We were treated well.

As instructors, did they treat you respectfully or was there any condescension?

They treated us well.

Did you ever have a forced landing or anything up there?

No. We were in constant panic of check rides—everybody was! It was wrenching to see friends who didn't pass them and had to leave.

Do you remember a friend specifically who washed out?

No, generally it went so fast. I know a friend who did not wash out, but she was fearful that she might. She had a railroad ticket home, in her locker, the entire time we were in training.

How long were you in training in Sweetwater?

My class graduated the first part of July and we had reported in January. So we were in training about five months. Reading the histories of Sweetwater, the Army really didn't know what to do with us. They didn't know whether we would learn as fast as the men. So essentially, they gave us the same curriculum as the men. When I went in, I had about 200 hours of flight time. They had to start us all over again to be sure we knew what we were doing. Like the WAFS, when they went in, they had to have flight checks to make sure they were qualified. It was the same with us. As more women went into the WASPs program, the amount of time they came in with lessened, until at the end they had a private pilot license. Everybody, at least in the first year, had to have a pilot's license to get into the program. Soon girls with less flight time were accepted. The curriculum for flight and ground school changed frequently. The type of airplanes also changed. Some classes had twin-engine experience. My class was fortunate that we did. The primary trainers initially were a single-wing airplane. Later, they switched to the bi-plane open airplane. The curriculum changed almost constantly as the program got older and the Army knew more and more what they wanted to do with us.

From there, where did you go?

When I graduated, there were only four places we could go. These were ferrying bases. There was Love Field in Dallas, Texas; there was a base in Romulus, Michigan, one in Newcastle, Delaware, and March Field in California. We were told to put down what our preference was. My preference was to go to Romulus. That was near Chicago and I would not be too far from home. My second choice was California. I think Texas was my last choice. I should have listened to my father who said, "Never tell them what you want to do because they'll give you the opposite." They sent me to Dallas, which was my last choice. Anyway, I went to Dallas and was here maybe a day or two when a telegram came to the commanding officer at Dallas, saying that certain WASPs, who were named, were to report to Washington to Jacqueline Cochran. I assume that the Army was satisfied that women could ferry planes. It was decided we could tow targets for the anti-aircraft practice. Twenty-five of my class were selected and sent to Washington. Miss Cochran and General Hap Arnold, commanding general of the Army Air Corps, told of this decision at Bolling Field, and we were given lecture about high-altitude flying. We were put in a pressure chamber to show us the effects of high-altitude flying. Then, we were sent down to North Carolina to Camp Davis, which is outside of Wilmington, North Carolina, on the shore of the Atlantic Ocean.

Did any unusual things happen there?

Yes. Everything was unusual and new. The aircraft we flew were Navy dive-bombers, the Douglas SBD and later the Curtiss SB2C. The airspeed indicators were calibrated in knots, not miles per hour. This was a little strange to us. The SBD aircraft were "war-weary" and were restricted to certain maneuvers. For example, you could not extend the dive-flaps. The missions were either tracking or touring at different altitudes, depending on the kinds of guns. Tow-target squadron probably had a very low level of priority for spare parts. As you can imagine, during wartime, combat units had priority. We had a lot of trouble with tire blowouts. Rubber was at a premium. We had two fatalities at that base. One fatality was from my class. One fatality was from the next group to be assigned to Camp Davis.

Do you remember the young lady who died?

I remember the one from my class. She was from Kalamazoo. Her name was Mabel Rawlinson.

Dr. Dora Dougherty Strother McKeon

Was she the one you took a collection to get her body home—when the government wouldn't?

That's the story that goes around a lot.

Tell me about Mabel—what do you remember about her?

Mable was a good pilot—pretty and blonde. She was friendly and quiet. She and I were among the first five WASPs scheduled for night orientation flights at Camp Davis. We were all flying with an instructor to show us the locations for night missions. Walking to my assigned plane, I saw a plane fly over the field. It was obviously in trouble. They tried to land on the only lighted runway and crashed at the far end of the runway. In that part of the country you find swamp and forest. The crash set the trees on fire. The instructor, who was in the backseat of the aircraft, was thrown clear. In fact, his safety belt was still on when they found him. The connection of the seat to the aircraft had broken and thrown the whole seat out of the aircraft. He survived with minimal injuries, but Mable was in the front seat. A big gunsight sits on the top of the instrument panel. If you were in a crash, I'm sure your head would hit that. We didn't wear crash helmets in those days. Our helmets were canvas. We didn't have shoulder harnesses, only a lap belt.

That must have been pretty devastating.

It was not the first fatality we had experienced. There were fatalities at Sweetwater, but it was the first one close to me. was on August 23, 1948. Yes, it was painful for us all.

Another new experience at Camp Davis involved drone aircraft. This was a highly classified program. Some of the girls were sent to another anti-aircraft base in Georgia to learn to fly drones, or pilotless aircraft. I was one of a second group to be sent there. We learned how to control the drone by radio signals. We would fly the drone in front of the guns and the guns could fire at the "real" airplane.

We were at this school maybe three months. When we qualified, we were sent out to other air bases to do the same thing. I went to Cape Cod. It was lovely duty but it was the middle of the winter. The Navy was to take over the base, Otis Air Force Base at Hyannis. I flew only a couple of utility missions and then we were shipped out. Five of us went to Eglin Field, Florida.

When they trained us in this activity, of flying the drone, they trained us in groups of five and we never flew with anybody except our group of five. We always flew with each other, and the idea was that we would have such an awareness of each other that you could almost communicate with a single word.

Did you feel that was the case?

Yes. As for the group I was with, we became very good friends. I would say if that was their objective, it worked very well. My group of five was sent to Eglin Field. When we got down there, they didn't want five of us, they just wanted two of us. Two of the gals who got there first were selected to be in the main field and the other three were sent out to an auxiliary field. The auxiliary fields, at Eglin, were training fields for air-to-air combat. When the men went through their pilot training and got their wings, they were sent down to one of these fields to learn to fly combat. The three of us were sent to the maintenance field. It was our duty to pick up airplanes needing maintenance from several training fields and when they were done—take them back.

Dr. Dora Dougherty Strother McKeon

Did you have a favorite airplane?

Yes, I did. I had a love affair with the A-2 Havoc. It is an attack bomber, a single seat, twin-engine plane that was used extensively in Europe and Africa. I always wanted to fly the A-20. At an auxiliary field, at Eglin, there was an A-20. One of the instructors asked, "Would you girls like to check out in the A-20?" They didn't have to twist my arm. I got to check out in the A-20. It was a marvel to fly—I loved it.

Right about that time, an airplane came into Eglin Field to the main base. There was a guard put around it. Nobody could get near it. It was a B-29 Superfortress, the Army's newest bomber. WASP Dorothea Moorman, who worked on the main base at Eglin, met a lieutenant colonel who was looking for two women to check out in the B-29. He asked her about the experience all of us had. He said to Dorothea that he would take her and the girl that had flown the A-20. His objective was to demonstrate that the B-29 was so safe and easy to fly that even women could fly it. At the time, the B-29 had a lot of engine fires and was getting a bad name. The two of us were taken up to Birmingham, Alabama, and in three days, checked out in the B-29. We learned to do engine-out procedures, stall, landings, and everything necessary to fly. At the end of three days, we were to fly with the FAA, which was then called the CAA, the Civil Aeronautics Administration. The purpose of having the CAA fly with us was to further show that there was no bias from the Army, and that we were not privileged. So, again, we drew straws to see who would go first. I went first.

Was this the luck of the Irish?

I'm Irish. Yes, it may be that. The CAA inspector got into

the co-pilot's seat and I was in the pilot's seat. We went up and did all the air work: stalls, engine-out procedures etc. That was such an easy airplane and a beautiful airplane to fly. You would have thought it would be heavy, and I thought I wasn't strong enough for a four-engine aircraft. I was wrong—it was a dream airplane, as far as I was concerned. As we returned to the field, he said, "Okay, we'll do two landings and then we'll trade places. You can trade places with the other girl."

On the final approach to my first landing, I had a fire in one of the engines. The tower had seen it before I could call and tell them I had an emergency. I was on a long final and was "committed" to my landing, so I went ahead and landed. The fire truck met us. As we touched down, the truck was running alongside of us. By the time we stopped, they were putting foam all over the place. We didn't get to finish, but it was an exciting experience to me.

That must have been pretty scary.

No! You might think so, but in any phase of aviation, you are trained in emergency procedures. That's one of the things you have to learn in practice and know what to do. I think I was too busy! It wasn't a big fire, and it didn't worry me because we had fire extinguishers on the engine. I had turned to my flight engineer and told him to pull the fire extinguisher on that engine and feather it. I knew how to fly on two or three engines so it was really not a problem.

You're sort of spoiled at this point—isn't it like, where do you go from here?

After three days, and after our check-out, we were assigned

an aircraft and were to take it to one of the B-29 crew training bases. Incidentally, the man who taught us was Colonel Paul Tibbets, who flew the Enola Gay, the man who would drop the first atomic bomb. The component of the crew on a B-29 is six or seven. By the time, you get the tail gunner, the navigator, radio operator, a flight engineer, and co-pilot—you've got a crowd of people. During our training flights, Tibbetts had almost doubled the number of men who flew with us. Before going on the demonstration mission, he asked every one of the men, unannounced to us (we didn't know this until after the war) if they would like to go with us. He wasn't going to assign them—it was a volunteer thing. Every one of the men who flew with us volunteered, except one, whose wife was about to have a baby. When we heard that afterwards, it made our hearts warm. They were a marvelous and supportive crew. I can't say enough about the help and encouragement they gave us. They were like big brothers.

Describe Paul Tibbitts—any particular thing that he said or compliment he gave.

He was a man of few words. One of the crew said to me, "If you have anything to say to the colonel, go talk to him when he's smoking his pipe, but don't talk to him while he's smoking his cigarette." He was a person who knew the aircraft. If something was wrong with his aircraft, he could fix it. Once the colonel came up, rolled up his sleeves and started working with him. The two of them fixed it. You don't find too many officers who are that type of a person. He was detailed in everything. His crew and everyone who worked with him honored and admired him. In addition, he was a superb pilot.

Our first flight took us to Clovis, New Mexico. There we flew several sample missions with flight crews who were in training.

We were demonstrating what the aircraft could do. The idea that two women were doing this spread like wildfire across the face of the country. We had maybe a week, out of Clovis, taking people on demonstration flights. Finally, the Pentagon heard about it, and we were told to stop. Unfortunately, we never got to go to the other places because women were never supposed to fly the B-29 after that.

It was heartbreaking, I bet.

It was a disappointment, but not too bad, because we felt we had done what we had been trained to do. We knew it wasn't going to last.

On our way back to Eglin, we stopped at Grand Island, Nebraska, and met the base commander, General Frank Armstrong, a one-star general. He didn't know that any women were flying Army aircraft. He pondered that, and then he asked us if we could type. We were insulted because we were pilots. We shouldn't have been. What he had in mind was this: as a general he had to travel with a general's aide, a co-pilot and a secretary, at least. He thought if he could have a co-pilot who could type then he could get rid of several extra people. We agreed to work for him. He had Dorothea "DiDi" Moorman transferred to Grand Island, Nebraska. His wife found out about it. She insisted that only the married women could fly with her husband. DiDi was married; I was not. I was transferred to the transport section. Actually, that was fine with me. "DiDi" was gregarious and could preside well at the luncheon tables. She met people beautifully. I was happy transporting cargo.

Soon I was transferred to Wendover, Army Air Base, a small base; it seemed to be in the middle of nowhere. Unknown to everyone and me, it was where they were exploring and developing delivery techniques for the atomic bomb.

The base was small but well-guarded. In addition to the pass to get in the base, you had to have a pass to get onto the flight line. Once I was on the flight line, I could not go beyond the ramp unless I had yet another pass. I didn't know what in the world was going on.

It really didn't bother me. I didn't have to know it. I was a utility-transport pilot. While there at Wendover, we got word that the WASPs program was being cancelled, and on December 20, 1944, the WASP program was disbanded. Never again were we allowed to fly military aircraft.

That was a heartbreak again.

Of course, we were all disappointed. We expected to stay until the end of the war and the war wasn't over. We were unaware of all the problems involved with getting a bill through Congress, which would put us women in the Army. The effort failed. As with a lot of the soldiers, I wanted to get home and get on with my life. I was in the middle of my schooling when I volunteered. I wanted to finish college. Still, I would have been happy to stay flying because I felt I was contributing to the war effort and because I enjoyed my assignments.

So you went home.

Yes, I did some ferrying of used military aircraft and earned my flight instructor's rating. Then I found I had to go to work. I didn't have the finances to go back to school. WASPs weren't entitled to the G.I. Bill. The only thing I knew to do at that point was to fly.

I got a job as a flight instructor. I went to night school and finally graduated with my bachelor's in 1949.

I found a better job at the University of Illinois as a flight instructor. They decided they'd try a woman flight instructor. I instructed in the primary and secondary and taught the instrument course there. I became interested in a program run by Aviation Psychology Laboratory. Their research studied flight trainers and flight simulators to identify what had to be faithfully simulated to optimize the transfer of training from the simulator to the aircraft. In order to obtain flight data, they had to have a flight instructor.

Did you like that?

Yes, but I didn't quite understand what statistical and experimental design was needed. I took some more courses and got my master's degree. The Lab was studying not only simulators and trainers, but also the design of aircraft instruments.

Of course, the whole idea of aviation psychology started in World War II, when psychologists told the Army that pilots could see better at night, if they had red lighting in the aircraft. It grew from there. The University of Illinois Aviation Psychology Lab was one of the pioneers in the new field called Human Engineering. It became apparent to me that, if I was to stay in this field, I had better get my Ph.D. I sold my car, and my widowed mother rented her home. I went to New York University for the year 1952-53. I was getting my Ph.D. I had a great advisor who was an old aviation enthusiast and pilot himself.

You really must have had a unique skill at that point.

You were one of the few.It was a new field. I didn't want to be a flight instructor for the rest of my career. I had been there, done that. I saw this new academic and technical field and it looked great to me. When I got my degree, I returned to Illinois to the Aviation Psychology Lab. Now I was employed as research associate. I soon left academia and went to work for the Martin Company in Baltimore as a Human Factors Engineer in the Advanced Design section of the Engineering Department. But soon the company decided to go out of the airplane business and build space rockets. I decided to move again. Bell Helicopter in Fort Worth was doing exciting work with helicopters, so I called to see if they needed some new people, and they did. I moved to Texas. At Bell I learned to fly helicopters and had an opportunity to break some world records. I broke two female records in distance and altitude. Our work centered on research that developed means by which a helicopter could fly on instruments. It can fly on instruments that use fixed-wing instruments, so it can only go like a fixed wing. The helicopter has no instruments that allow it to go backwards or straight down, because these instruments had never been developed at that time. If they were, how would they be? These were the questions being asked by an experimental program the Navy sponsored, and for which Bell had a contract. This work was very exciting. It continued to be exciting. When my boss quit I was offered his job, in charge of the Human Engineering group with the engineering department. I stayed there and retired in 1986.Right now, this continues to be a very exciting time because the computer allows designers to make displays we never could have thought of before. Now the information for visual and audio displays is so available and easily put together that it is just a fantastic time. I'm almost sorry I retired.

You are not saying that you'd prefer to be coming up in this day and time as opposed to the years that you flew, are you?

Oh no. I was in the "Golden Age" of aviation.

Tell me about breaking the world records.

One was altitude. The year was 1961; I flew a Bell Helicopter Model 47-G3B. The altitude I reached was over 19,000 feet. To break an official world record that would be authenticated by the Federation Aeronautique Internationale, you have all kinds of verification. For example, you have to take a picture of the altimeter every thousand feet while climbing. I was circling over the heliport and wore a parachute and oxygen mask. There was a strong westwind that day. When I started down, I was going at a ground speed of about 40 miles an hour. It took me a long time to get back to the heliport. When I did, the president and several vice presidents of my company were out on the helipad waiting for me and hoping I would get their equipment down in good shape. I did.

Selfie of Irv Broughton and Violet Cowden

About the Author

Author of 18 books of non-fiction, fiction, poetry, and anthology, Irv Broughton holds B.A. and M.A. degrees from Florida State University, as well as an M.A from the distinguished Writing Program at Hollins College (now University), where he received an Academy of American Poets award. In the early seventies, he traveled across the country to capture stories of American life. Writer George Garrett once referred to Irv as a "budding Studs Terkel," referencing the well-known interviewer, best-selling author/historian and Chicago radio host. Today, years later, Irv continues working to chronicle American life in both book and film forms—whether everyday old-time Floridians, writers, pilots, or producers. A top-notch interviewer, his specialized skill illuminates a life's work of documentary and informs his various publications. Broughton was born in Orlando, Florida, and spent his earliest years in Wellfleet, Cape Cod, Massachusetts, and in Winter Park, Florida. Irv is an avid basketball player and also enjoys book-collecting and gardening..

Made in the USA
Middletown, DE
02 September 2019